HOT LINKS &
COUNTRY FLAVORS

HOT LINKS & COUNTRY FLAVORS

sausages in American regional cooking

BRUCE AIDELLS

& DENIS KELLY

Illustrations by John King

· Alfred A. Knopf · New York · 1990 ·

Grateful acknowledgment is made to the
following for permission to reprint previously
published material:

Addison-Wesley Publishing Co.: *Recipe from*
Grain Gastronomy *by Janet Fletcher.*
Copyright © 1988 by Janet Fletcher. Reprinted
by permission of Addison-Wesley Publishing Co.
Bon Appétit Publishing Corp.: *Two recipes,*
"Flank Steak Stuffed with Sausage, Basil and
Cheese" and "Ya Ca Mein," by Bruce Aidells
(Bon Appétit, *November 1989, pp. 168, 172).*
Copyright © 1989 by Bon Appétit Publishing
Corp. Reprinted with permission.
Chevron Chemical Company: *The recipe*
"Creole Skewers with Mustard Butter" from
Barbecuing, Grilling & Smoking *by Bruce*
Aidells. Copyright © 1988 by Chevron Chemical
Company. The recipe "Creole Baked Eggs with
Andouille, Ham and Asparagus" from Regional
American Classics *by Bruce Aidells. Copyright*
© 1987 by Chevron Chemical Company.
Reprinted with permission.

Library of Congress Cataloging-in-Publication
Data

Aidells, Bruce.
    Hot links & country flavors : sausages in
American regional cooking / by Bruce Aidells
and Denis Kelly. — 1st ed.
        p.   cm. — (The Knopf cooks American
series ; 1)
    ISBN 0-394-57430-3
    1. Cookery (Sausages)   2. Sausages.
3. Cookery, American.   I. Kelly, Denis,
[date].   II. Title.   III. Title: Hot links and
country flavors.
TX749.5.S28A37   1990
641.6'6—dc20   89-19781   CIP

Manufactured in the United States of America
First Edition

Acknowledgments
The authors would like to thank the following
friends and colleagues for their help: our agent,
Martha Casselman, and our editor, Judith
Jones, for their encouragement, enthusiasm,
and common sense; all those who contributed
recipes, especially Loni Kuhn, Janet Fletcher,
Lonnie Gandara, Tom Blower, and Brian Stack;
Robin Cherin, for testing all the recipes; Sandy
Rosenzweig, for the use of her fine library;
Evan Jones, for his book *American Food: The
Gastronomic Story;* and John King, for his
illustrations.

· contents ·

· introduction ·

Sausage — as soon as you say the word, the memories begin:
Sunday morning, thick patties sizzling in the pan, filling the house with
smells of sage, pepper, and succulent pork. Or a late spring Saturday afternoon at the ball game, eating hot juicy franks with mustard and sauerkraut.

Just about everyone in America from any background and region has
fond and satisfying memories of sausages. Wherever you grew up, from Bayonne to the Bayou Teche, it's likely that sausage of one kind or another was
found on your table or in the streets of your neighborhood. Whether it's a hot
dog or kielbasa, boudin or bratwurst, there's something about a sausage
that excites the taste buds and stays in the memory.

Both of the authors grew up eating sausages of every type, taste, and
description. Although we're from different regions and ethnic backgrounds,
we both pursued a passion for sausages across America, eating them at
festivals and greasy spoons, fancy restaurants and waterfront dives, sampling Sheboygan brats, Cajun boudin, Italian cotechino, Oakland hot links,
Chicago franks whenever and wherever we had the chance. And one day,
putting away a prodigious platter of Cajun cassoulet at a favorite restaurant, we decided to write a book about sausage in America — its history and
traditions, how to make it, how to use it, how it flavors so much of the best of
our cooking.

By this time we had both been involved with food and wine profes
sionally for many years — Denis Kelly as a writer and teacher and Bruce
Aidells as cookbook author, cooking teacher, and expert sausage maker.
Bruce had become so enthusiastic about the savory subject, in fact, that he is
now one of the country's premier sausage makers, producing delicious,
hand-crafted sausages at his Bay Area–based Aidells Sausage Company.

"I first started making sausages when I was living in London, working
as a cancer researcher, and trying to convince myself that the traditional
British banger was made from anything other than sawdust, salt, and grease.
I'd been eating sausage all my life from traditional, garlicky Jewish salami
and frankfurters to more exotic types found in my neighborhood in Los Angeles, like chorizo and linguiça. After a few months in cold, gray London sub-
sisting on a diet of pub food and bangers, I was suffering from sausage
deprivation and figured I could do better making them myself.

"So I got hold of a cookbook and a small electric grinder and made
up tasty batches of chorizo, American pork sausage with sage and pepper,
Italian sausage with fennel, and Provençal sausage with garlic and herbs. It
took me most of the night to stuff all I'd made, but the next day when I fried
them up and sat down to a hearty and delicious meal for the first time in months,
I was hooked. From then on I never looked back, making (and eating) sausage at every opportunity.

"When I returned to Berkeley, the Gourmet Ghetto near Chez Panisse was in full swing, and I ended up becoming a chef at Poulet, a popular restaurant and charcuterie. I just naturally kept on making sausage and learned what a wonderful flavoring ingredient it can be in soups, stews, pâtés, salads, and other hearty dishes. I found what European peasants and regional American cooks had known for years: that sausage is a great flavoring for almost anything you cook and that you don't have to use a lot to create exciting flavors and taste in a variety of dishes.

"From then on the sausage phenomenon grew and grew, and finally I found myself making and selling a whole range of sausages—andouille and chaurice, duck sausage, Italian sausage, chorizo, and kielbasa—to restaurants and chefs. The response from them and from butchers, retailers, and home cooks all over the country testifies to the interest in authentic handmade sausages in America today."

· ethnic and regional roots ·

Sausage is found in virtually every region and ethnic tradition in America. From the simple and satisfying pork and sage sausage of the Midwest, Cajun chaurice and New Bedford linguiça to Sheboygan brats, Italian sweet fennel sausage, and Coney Island franks, sausage in one shape or another has long been an important part of American cooking. Sausages can serve as main dishes or as accompaniments and flavorings with vegetables, pasta, or beans. Whether you make them yourself or buy them ready-made, you can use sausages in dishes that range from traditional specialties like red beans and rice or cotechino with white beans to creative new combinations with vegetables, poultry, pasta, and seafood. Try Salmon Sausage in Champagne Sauce, for example, or Zucchini and Rice "Sausage" or Duck Sausage with Pasta and Wild Mushrooms for a surprising new taste in sausage.

In this book we take a close look at the regional and ethnic traditions that are at the heart of American cooking, and see how sausages are used to flavor and lend individual accents to these varied cuisines. We'll show you exactly how to make the authentic sausages indigenous to each region: andouille and boudin from the Cajun country, hot and mild sausages from the Italian neighborhoods of northeastern cities, the ubiquitous American breakfast sausage, smoked and fresh kielbasa as Polish-Americans make it in Chicago, Sheboygan's famous bratwurst, Chicago hot dogs, chorizo, linguiça, Oakland hot links, and many more.

But this is more than just a "How To" book about sausage making. It is an overview of American cooking, using the sausage to link all the themes together. We'll describe America's regions and neighborhoods, their history, culinary traditions, and festivals. And we'll give you plenty of recipes that use sausage to flavor everything from a traditional gumbo to fashionable composed salads.

You don't have to make your own sausage to use and enjoy the book. Fine, high-quality sausages are increasingly available in American markets, and many can be purchased by mail order. These and similar commercial sausages can be used in almost all of the recipes. Our addendum on Mail Order Sources (see page 357) will give you a guide to ordering sausages as well as sausage-making ingredients and equipment, and other products.

One characteristic of American cooking today is an emphasis on lightness and flavor. Sausages have long been used as an accent in dishes, and, contrary to popular myth, can provide protein and spiciness without adding excessive amounts of calories or cholesterol. As you'll see in our section on making sausage, the fat content of homemade or small-production sausages is much lower than that of the commercial products—most often on a par with lean hamburger. When used as a flavoring, sausage can provide excitement to a great range of foods. One of the reasons sausage has been such a popular part of cooking throughout history is its ability, at little extra cost, to enhance even the most humble ingredients.

· a succulent history ·

"A cook turns a sausage, big with blood and fat, at a scorching blaze, without a pause to broil it quick." A modern Californian grilling a tasty sausage over mesquite charcoal? Well, it was probably a blood sausage much like our boudin noir and it might even have been grilled over charcoal, but the time and place were Greece in about 700 B.C. This quote from Homer's *Odyssey* is just one of many ancient references to one of mankind's oldest and most succulent delicacies, the sausage. Homer, who like many writers owned to a particular affection for sausages, refers to them again and again in his descriptions of food and feasting. References to sausage abound in early Greek and Roman sources, from Athenaeus' marathon banquet described in *Deipnosophistae* (The Learned Drinkers) to one of the earliest cookbooks extant, Apicius' *De Re Coquinaria*.

The origin of sausages dates back even further in culinary history. The art of salting, curing, and smoking meat goes back to the beginnings of domestication and agriculture in the Near East, and perhaps even earlier. As soon as mankind was able to achieve a regular surplus of meat, we began to look for ways to preserve it. Cutting up scraps of meat, salting them, and sealing them in casings made from the intestines and other organs of animals was one of the first discoveries of early pastoralists. The pig, which was as it is now the main source of most sausages, was domesticated quite early, in about 5000 B.C. in Egypt and China, and pig-raising spread quickly throughout the Near East, Europe, and Asia.

Since then, virtually every society has developed its own version of sausage. The name derives from the Latin word for salted, *salsus,* and salt for preserving meat, fish, and cheese has been an important commodity from Roman times to the present. Sausages are found in virtually every region in Europe, and give flavor and substance to dishes that define the style and flavor of its varied cuisines. Try to think of German, Italian, Polish, and Portuguese cooking, to name a few, without traditional sausages like knockwurst, salami, kielbasa, and linguiça.

In America, the original population of Native Americans found ways to preserve the land's bounty and they passed their methods on to early settlers. Pemmican, a mixture of buffalo or venison, fat, berries, and herbs, was packed into hide containers and helped many an Indian (and settler) village through winter and hard times.

Settlers from England brought with them a long tradition of sausage making. Colonial cookbooks recorded English recipes published by Hannah Glasse and other early writers, and gave the basic ingredients of American breakfast sausage as it is made even today: ground pork, black pepper, and sage. As settlers arrived from other areas in Europe, Asia, and Africa, they brought with them their culinary traditions, and these almost always included sausages. The French in the South and Louisiana; Italians, Jews, Greeks, Portuguese in the teeming cities of the Northeast; Germans, Poles, Hungarians, and Swedes in the Midwest; Spanish in the Southwest; and Chinese on the West Coast—all brought with them the sausages that gave character to their cooking.

The history of American food and its sausages is, like America, a history of immigrants. In this book, we'll present this rich array of flavors, and see how sausages are used to define many of America's favorite dishes. And we'll show some of the ways that today's creative chefs are inventing new sausages, which are expanding the frontiers of American cooking.

· types of sausage ·

There are as many types of sausage as there are cooks and cultures, offering a tremendous variety of flavors, textures, and uses. The most basic definition of sausage is: a combination of chopped meat, fat, salt, and spices. Over the years sausages have been made from an ever-widening array of ingredients—beef, poultry, game, seafood, even vegetables—but pork has been the constantly recurring favorite. Pigs are easy and economical to raise, and their bland and succulent meat combines well with spices and flavorings. Pork also has a mild-tasting fat that binds well, and gives a rich and juicy flavor to the sausage.

The most common and easiest-to-make sausage is our standard breakfast patty consisting of freshly ground pork seasoned with salt, sage, and black pepper. Virtually every culture has some kind of similar, easy fresh sausage. Many Italian sausages are simply made of freshly ground pork that is flavored and then stuffed into casings of hog or sheep intestines. In fact, as we'll see below, Cajun boudin, spicy southern country sausage, fresh bratwurst, kielbasa, and chorizo are all popular and easily made fresh sausages. Fresh sausage is perishable, however, and will keep in the refrigerator only for a few days. But it freezes well for 2–3 months, and fresh sausage, in bulk or in casings, can be one of the most versatile and helpful ingredients in your freezer.

Edna Lewis, that fine interpreter of regional American food, says that having some country ham in your refrigerator is like owning one good black dress. You are always prepared, no matter what the occasion. The same could be said of sausage, fresh or smoked. With a stash of sausage in the freezer, you can always turn the most meager leftovers, dried beans, or pasta into a feast, whatever the circumstances or no matter how many guests drop in unexpectedly.

Many sausages are dried and/or smoked to aid preservation and enhance flavor. In the days before refrigeration, householders discovered that hanging pieces of salted meat, poultry, or fish above the hearth preserved them for future use. Smoked sausages, where the meat is mixed with salt and spices and then hung for a time in smoke, have long been a source of protein through the cold winter months. Air-drying sausages, such as salami or Lebanon bologna, dehydrates the meats, discourages bacterial activity, and helps to preserve them even more. Drying and smoking also concentrate flavors and add a special tang to these sausages that makes them very popular as seasonings in dishes. Care must be taken when using these techniques, however, to prevent spoilage, and in our section on smoking (see page 337), we describe how to air-dry and smoke sausages safely.

There is another major type of sausage in which the meat is emulsified with the fat and spices to provide a smooth texture and subtle flavors. America's most popular sausage, the hot dog, is the most common emulsified sausage, but knockwurst, bologna, and other smooth sausages are also widely appreciated in the United States. Emulsified sausages are generally tricky to make in the home kitchen. But we have worked out a recipe for a Chicago-Style Hot Dog that produces very good results (see page 154).

· how to use this book ·

As we said earlier, you don't have to make your own sausage to cook most of the recipes in this book. Although at the beginning of each chapter you'll find recipes for making each of the major regional sausages, if you prefer you can simply buy them or similar types that will work well in our dishes. Most of our recipes are about how to *use* sausage. Thus you can enjoy our Smoky Black-Eyed Peas or Hoppin' John using good, store-bought smoked sausage, or serve up to hungry friends a big pot of spicy gumbo using some of the fine commercial andouille in the market these days. Making your own sausage is a lot of fun and not very difficult as we describe it in our chapter "Making Sausage in the Home Kitchen." We hope you'll try it, but if you prefer to skip the sausage-making recipes, simply turn to the sections of each chapter entitled "Appetizers and Soups," "Main Dishes," or "Side Dishes."

Although all the recipes have been carefully tested, and the amounts are exact, no recipe is written in stone and we hope you'll feel free to experiment and improvise. We often list alternate ingredients or suggestions for changes in the recipes, which should serve as guidelines. Cooking is fun, and cooking with spicy and flavorful sausages can be even more so. Let your taste buds be your guide, try new ingredients when the spirit moves, and enjoy yourself.

Our portion sizes tend to be on the generous side. We don't like to run out of food, and would rather err on the side of too much than too little. Many of the dishes are even better rewarmed, and we'll usually tell you about how to heat them up again or use them as delicious leftovers. Some dishes can be served either as hors d'oeuvres or as a main course, and we try to indicate probable servings for each.

· a note on ingredients ·

Meat for making sausage should be impeccably fresh and full of flavor. Vegetables, herbs, and seasonings should be as fresh as possible, and used soon after purchasing.

In our recipes we suggest you use the following:

· **butter** · unsalted unless otherwise specified. It tastes better, is generally fresher, and lets you control the amount of salt in the recipes more exactly.

· **salt** · kosher salt. It has fewer impurities than table salt, and a less salty taste. If you only have ordinary table salt, then use about 20 percent less than we call for in the recipe.

· **stock** · homemade stock from beef, chicken, or other poultry or meats. It has more taste than most canned or frozen stock, and doesn't contain high levels of salt and MSG. You can substitute canned stock, but you should cut back on the salt in the recipe to compensate.

· **tomatoes** · We suggest using fresh tomatoes, peeled, seeded, and chopped in many dishes. But if you can't get good, fresh, vine-ripened tomatoes, you are better off using Italian-style canned tomatoes.

· **herbs** · Use fresh herbs whenever they are available. We'll often give proportions of fresh to dried herbs (in general use half as much dried herbs as fresh), but if we just specify marjoram or oregano, for example, we mean dried herbs.

THE **S**OUTH
· pigmeat and pone ·

Savory crab turnovers

Tomatoes stuffed
with sausage and oysters

Smoked sausage, potato, and
roasted pepper salad

Shrimp and eggplant bisque

Georgia peanut soup with
smoked sausage

Red bean and sausage soup

Quick and easy soups

BREAKFAST
DISHES

Alabama country breakfast
(buttermilk biscuits)

Country sausage with sweet
and tangy red-eye gravy

MAIN
DISHES

Crab and sausage cakes
with Tidewater tartar sauce

Pork chops stuffed with
country sausage and baked in a
bourbon mustard glaze

Crown roast of pork with
sweet potato, sausage, and
apple dressing

Pork loin stuffed with spring
greens and smoked sausage

Braised chicken with
sausage stuffing in country
ham and port wine sauce

Rabbit or chicken stew
with sausage, hominy, and
crispy onions

Smoked chicken with
sausage and savoy cabbage

Miami black beans

SIDE DISHES

Smoky black-eyed peas or
Hoppin' John

Baked hominy and country
sausage

Grits, sausage, and cheese
casserole

Grits soufflé

Spoonbread with sausage

Smoked sausage and
smothered greens

Stewed okra and country
sausage

Swiss chard with smoked
country sausage, garlic,
and cheese

The South's first pigs wandered off from de Soto's expedition along the Gulf Coast in the 1540s. They thrived in the palmetto groves, rooting in the lush and muddy undergrowth of southern swamps, pig paradise. Others escaped from Jamestown's Hog Island and roamed the tangled forests of the Tidewater. From the beginning, hogs were raised in settlements and plantations up and down Virginia and the Carolinas. These half-wild razor-backs fed on acorns and hickory nuts, wild persimmons and chestnuts, the rich mast of the forest floor. Fattened on table scraps or what it could find in the back streets of frontier towns, fed on corncobs and hot mash, the pig became the South's main source of protein. Fatback, salt back, white bacon, sowbelly or middlin', Virginia ham or country sausage, chitterlings or hog jowl, ham hocks or cracklin' — pork was the meat most often found on southern tables, of rich or poor, of Tidewater planters or leaner folk from up-country.

The pig offers real benefits to frontier settlers. No other animal, domestic or otherwise, gets fat so fast, increasing its body weight 150 times in the first eight months. Hogs are remarkably self-sufficient, able to feed on the lowliest of foods from farmhouse leavings to whatever they root out from forest or swamp. And the pig thrives on local southern products such as peanuts, peaches, and, especially, corn, the South's other staple.

Pork has another advantage over other meats. Because of the subtle unctuousness of its fat and the sweet blandness of its flesh, it usually tastes better preserved (pickled or salted, smoked or seasoned) than fresh. Put up in myriad ways, a constant source of nourishment throughout the year, pork became the South's main meat. It was cooked fresh at butchering time in the fall, but pork was most prominent in southern cooking in its preserved forms — cured and smoked as bacon or ham, laid down in the pork barrel as side-meat or fatback, seasoned with herbs and spices as sausage. Its importance is evident from the records of an early plantation on the James River. In just one year, the planter's family, servants, slaves, and guests consumed over 27,000 pounds of different kinds of pork.

Just as pork quickly became the region's most popular meat, from the beginning corn was the main starch for most of the South. During the first years at Jamestown in the 1600s, settlers learned from Indians how to grow, store, and prepare it. We find the names of some of these culinary adventurers in Evan Jones's *American Food: The Gastronomic Story* — Joane Pierce, Elizabeth Joones, Temperance Flowerdieu. Women lived in Indian villages, where they learned to cook and serve corn in a startling variety of ways, plucked fresh from the stalk and roasted green in the ashes of a campfire, dried and ground into meal and baked as ashcake or hoecake, leached with ashes for hominy, dried and ground for grits. Popped corn, ground corn, fresh corn, dried corn, corn pone or hush puppies—maize or Indian corn soon became the staple of southern cooking.

Beans were another indigenous American food that early colonists learned about from Indians. In all their forms, from tender young green beans to the multicolored variety of shell and dried types, beans became one of the mainstays of southern cooking. Especially popular in Spanish Florida and the Southwest, beans, dried or fresh, are found in many traditional southern dishes. The black-eyed pea (variously called cowpea, cornfield pea, crowder pea or whippoorwill) is actually a form of bean, one of the many southern staples brought from Africa by slaves. Southern cooks soon learned how well beans marry with pork, especially when it's cured, salted, smoked, or pickled.

Rice was brought to southern plantations early on, most likely from Italy, and was soon widely cultivated near Charleston and throughout the Carolinas. It forms the base for one of the South's most popular casseroles or "covered dishes," pilau (or perloo, perlow, purlow, depending on the local accent), and is combined with beans in many traditional favorites like red beans and rice or Moors and Christians (black beans and rice).

Corn and pork, beans and rice commingle in many of the South's most popular foods such as sausage and hominy and Hoppin' John. Ham and bacon, salt pork and sausage are universally used to season and enrich southern staples, adding flavor and interest to otherwise bland starches and greens.

Game, fish, and seafood have been an important part of the southern diet since settlers first discovered the incredible bounty of the forests, Chesapeake Bay, and the Gulf Coast. Deer, wild turkey, mallard and canvasbacks, quail, raccoon, possum, squirrel, and other game animals have always been an important part of traditional southern cooking. Blue crab and oysters from the Eastern Shore of Chesapeake Bay, shrimp and redfish from Gulf waters, and crawfish or mudbugs from the bayous are among the finest seafood in the world, and are found in some of the South's best dishes. Often smoked meats and sausages are mixed with fish and seafood in savory combinations like crab and sausage cakes, oyster and sausage fritters, gumbo, and jambalaya.

Southern sausage has its origins in the English culinary traditions that were maintained in plantation kitchens. The basic mix of ground fresh pork, sage, and black pepper can be found in Hannah Glasse's *Art of Cookery*, published in the late eighteenth century in Dublin and widely circulated throughout England and America. Mary Randolph, whose *The Virginia*

Housewife (1824) was perhaps the most influential cookbook in nineteenth-century America, reproduces Glasse's sausage recipe virtually intact (an early example of "creative borrowing" of recipes by cookbook authors).

· **to make sausages** · *Take the tender pieces of fresh pork, chop them exceedingly fine, chop some of the leaf fat, and put them together in the proportion of three pounds of pork to one of fat, season it very high with pepper and salt, add a small quantity of dried sage rubbed to a powder, have the skins nicely prepared, fill them and hang them in a dry place. Sausages are excellent made into cakes and fried, but will not keep so well as in skins.* (The Virginia Housewife, *page 67*)

Later cooks added cayenne and other spices that reflected the fiery flavors of African, Spanish, and Creole cooking to create the many lively variations on this basic country sausage found today throughout the South.

Barbecue, like so much of American cooking, is an amalgam of European, Indian, and black culinary traditions. Native Americans were experts at grilling meat and fish on greenwood racks over hot coals. Spanish, French, English, and black cooks brought their own ingredients and traditions together to create a uniquely American cooking technique. Based on the pig and sausage in the South, beef in Texas and the Southwest, *cabrito* and baby lamb in the Chicano tradition, grilled steak and seafood in California, barbecue is one of the most popular forms of cooking today. Throughout the South, sausages—smoky, spicy, and sometimes incandescent—are often barbecued with pork and chicken or beef. Barbecue with its tangy sauces swabbed on grilled and slow-cooked meats is an integral part of southern life. The rich smells and flavors bring to mind long afternoons filled with good talk, friendship, and that special quality of the South—the warm fellowship of folks sharing hearty and satisfying food.

· southern-style barbecue ·

It's easy enough to host your own southern-style barbecue, and you don't have to grill a shoat or two to do it. We suggest using a Weber or other covered barbecue, but just about anything from a built-in brick behemoth to a hibachi will do. It's traditional to serve a mix of meats and side dishes. Here are our recommendations, but feel free to improvise. Just remember, the food at a barbecue should be hearty, fun to eat, and above all, plentiful. We've added a couple of sauces given to us by that fine southern barbecue chef and author of *Grilling, Barbecuing and Smoking,* Ron Clark. You can use either or both, or your favorite homemade or commercial barbecue sauce.

Serve the barbecue with full-bodied, high-hopped beers such as Anchor Steam or Sierra Nevada, or with a cool, crisp Italian Pinot Grigio.

· Mixed grill, southern style ·
2–3-lb. frying chicken, cut into 8
　pieces
3–4 lbs. country-style spareribs
2–3 lbs. Smoked Country
　Sausage, Barbecue Style
　(see page 14)

· North Carolina basting sauce ·
1 c. cider vinegar
2 tbsp. red pepper flakes
1 tsp. Tabasco or other hot pepper
　sauce

· Georgia barbecue sauce ·
1½ c. tomato puree
1 c. cider vinegar
½ c. vegetable oil
⅓ c. Worcestershire
　sauce
½ c. packed dark brown
　sugar
¼ c. molasses
3 tbsp. yellow mustard
2 tsp. minced garlic
Juice of 1 lemon
Tabasco or hot pepper
　sauce to taste

Grill the meats on a Weber or other covered barbecue, using the indirect method. Put the chicken and ribs on first. Mix together the ingredients for the basting sauce and swab it on liberally as the meats cook. When they are about half cooked, add the sausage, coiled in one piece with two metal skewers through the center crosswise to hold it together. Continue to swab liberally with the basting sauce as the meats grill. Mix together the ingredients for the barbecue sauce and glaze the meats with that sauce for the last ½ hour of cooking. Depending on your grill size and distance from the coals, the meats should take 1½–2 hours. The pork should reach an internal temperature of 160° F.

Serve with our Smoky Black-Eyed Peas (see page 36), cornbread, and Stewed Okra and Country Sausage (see page 41), or Smoked Sausage and Smothered Greens (see page 40).
Makes 8–10 servings

· spicy fresh country sausage ·

When Southerners reminisce about thick patties of sausage frying in black skillets, filling the kitchen with smells of spice and pork, it's country sausage they're dreaming of. Just about every farm family had its own variation for sausage made fresh at the fall hog-killing time. Most recipes share the basic mixture of fresh pork and pork fat with seasonings that usually include salt and sage, red and black pepper. After this, variations abound. Spices like allspice, nutmeg, cloves, and ginger are often added along with aromatics like lemon peel or garlic. Fresh or dried herbs that range from mild hints of parsley to the more powerful flavors of thyme, rosemary, marjoram, or savory add color and complexity. Amounts of pepper, red and black, vary considerably, depending on the heat tolerance of local palates.

The recipe that follows gives the basics and is open to whatever variations you'd like to add. You might want to follow it exactly the first time, taste the results with family and friends, and then start experimenting. Another possibility is to purchase good-quality bulk sausage meat, and add your own spices, peppers, and herbs. You can mix in one or more herbs like marjoram, summer savory, or dried rosemary along with a spice like nutmeg, cloves, allspice, or ginger. Amounts will depend on your preferences, but a good rule of thumb is to start by adding ½ teaspoon of a dried herb and/or a pinch of spice to the basic recipe given below or to about 4 pounds of store-bought bulk sausage. Two teaspoons of minced garlic can also be added. Fry up a small patty to test and taste, and mix in more flavor as you go. Asking friends to help with the testing and stuffing makes sausage making fun. Tasting can get out of hand, though. Be sure to save enough sausage meat to fill a respectable amount of casings.

3 lbs. pork butt	2 tsp. sugar
¾ –1 lb. pork back fat	1 tbsp. red pepper flakes
4 tsp. kosher salt	1 tsp. cayenne
2 tsp. coarsely ground black pepper	½ c. water
2 tsp. dried sage	Medium hog casings (optional)
1 tsp. dried thyme	

For details on making sausage, see page 332.

Put the pork meat and fat through the meat grinder, using the ¼-inch plate. In a large bowl, mix the ground pork, fat, spices, and water, kneading and squeezing the meat until everything is nicely blended. If you are making the sausage for patties, simply wrap it in bulk and refrigerate until use. Or stuff the seasoned meat into medium hog casings and tie into 4-inch links. Fresh sausage will keep for 3 days in the refrigerator, frozen for up to 2 months. Makes 4–5 pounds

Southern farm wives used to stuff bulk sausage into small muslin bags or pokes, or fry patties and layer them in their own fat for preservation over the winter. The modern alternative is, of course, freezing.

· herbed fresh sausage, plantation style ·

This recipe has obvious English roots, and was adapted from Hannah Glasse's *Art of Cookery*. It is typical of the mild and aromatic style of sausage that was often found in plantation kitchens. The flavors are more delicate and complex than in the Spicy Fresh Country Sausage, without its bite of cayenne and red pepper, but with a lovely perfume from the herbs and spices. The bread crumbs give this sausage a softer texture.

1 lb. pork butt
1 lb. veal shoulder
¾ lb. pork back fat
1 c. bread crumbs from day-old loaf
2 tbsp. grated lemon zest
1 tbsp. kosher salt
1½ tsp. freshly ground black pepper
1 tsp. ground sage

¾ tsp. dried marjoram
¾ tsp. dried thyme
¼ tsp. dried summer savory
½ tsp. ground mace
½ c. cold water
Sheep or medium hog casings
 (optional)

For details on making sausage, see page 332.

Put the pork butt, veal shoulder, and pork fat through the meat grinder, using the ¼-inch plate. Mix with the bread crumbs and spices and grind again. It makes things easier if you chill the mixture for about ½ hour before the second grinding. Add the water, and knead and squeeze until all is well mixed. Stuff into sheep or medium hog casings and tie into 4-inch links. Or, if you prefer, leave the sausage in bulk, wrapped in plastic wrap, and fry patties when needed. It keeps 3 days in the refrigerator, up to 2 months frozen. Makes 3–4 pounds

This sausage makes a quick and delicious meat loaf when half of the following recipe is combined with a chopped onion, an additional cup of bread crumbs, and an egg for binding.

· Kentucky-style pork sausage ·

Here is a variation of Spicy Fresh Country Sausage that you might find in
Kentucky. This sausage is usually used in bulk, although you can stuff the
meat into hog casings if you prefer links.

2 lbs. pork butt	1 tsp. cayenne
1 lb. pork back fat	1 tsp. ground coriander
1 tbsp. kosher salt	½ tsp. freshly grated nutmeg
2 tsp. freshly ground black pepper	½ c. cold water
2 tsp. ground sage	Medium hog casings (optional)

For details on making sausage, see page 332.

Grind the pork and fat through a ¼-inch plate. Mix the meat, fat, spices,
and water together, kneading and squeezing until all the ingredients are well
blended. For links, stuff the sausage into medium hog casings and tie at 5-inch
intervals. Like most fresh sausage, if wrapped tightly, this
will keep in the refrigerator for 3 days, in the freezer 2
months. Makes 3½ pounds

*Shape the meat into one large roll, 2
inches in diameter, wrap in wax
paper, and refrigerate overnight. The
next morning, slice the sausage into
½-inch-thick patties and fry them in a
skillet until brown.*

· country ham and pork sausage ·

Country ham is one of the delights of southern cooking. The hams from
Smithfield County in Virginia have the greatest reputation and are widely
available. With their smoky and pungent aroma and a special flavor that is
reputed to come from the peanuts the hogs feed on, Smithfield hams are on a
par with the great hams of Westphalia, York, Parma, Bayonne, the Dalma-
tian coast, and the mountains of Auvergne, all with their own regional styles
and special flavors. Country hams from other regions in the South have special characteristics derived from the feed of the pigs (peaches, corn mash,
peanuts, etc.), the type of cure (dry salt, brine, honey, sugar), and the smoking medium (hickory, oak, corn cobs). The hams from Georgia, Kentucky,
and Tennessee are especially prized, but just about any area in the rural
South will have its own country ham, and its ardent advocates. Country hams
are usually quite salty, and require soaking and long simmering before
eating.

Most commercial hams pale in comparison to country hams. Some of
the more heavily smoked versions, like Black Forest ham, can be substituted

if you can't find the real thing. In the South, and in specialty meat shops elsewhere, you can often find good-quality country ham vacuum-wrapped by the slice. Another good source for ham is a Chinese pork butcher. Smoked ham is an integral part of many Hunan dishes, and Chinese cooks value the flavor and quality of the Smithfield variety. We had no trouble finding excellent Smithfield ham in San Francisco's Chinatown. An added advantage is that you can buy the ham in Chinatown by the piece, so you don't have to get a whole ham just to make this sausage.

If you're lucky enough to have a whole country ham, however, this recipe gives you a good way to use the trimmed fat and any leftover meat. The sausage can be substituted in any recipe that calls for country ham, and we've used it in place of ham in some traditional southern dishes. It works particularly well in recipes that depend on long, slow braising and where you want a smoky ham flavor, as in Smoky Black-Eyed Peas, our version of Hoppin' John (see page 36).

2 lbs. pork butt
½–¾ lb. leftover boiled or baked country ham or ¾ lb. raw country ham
½ lb. fat trimmed from ham
½ lb. fresh pork back fat
2 oz. skin from ham (optional)
1 tsp. freshly ground black pepper

¼ tsp. ground cloves
½ tsp. ground sage
1 tsp. red pepper flakes
½ tsp. ground ginger
1 tsp. sugar
¾–1 c. water
Medium hog casings

For details on making sausage, see page 332.

Grind the pork butt through a ⅜-inch plate, the ham, ham fat, pork fat, and skin through a ⅛-inch plate. If you are starting out with raw country ham, simmer a ¾-pound piece for about 2 hours, and then cool before grinding. The ham stock can be used for pea or bean soup (see page 68). Taste to make sure it's not too salty, though. Mix together thoroughly the ground meats, fat, and skin with the spices, sugar, and water. Stuff into medium hog casings and tie into 5-inch links. Refrigerate for up to 5 days or freeze for 2 months. Use fried as a patty or poached in links as a less salty but very tasty addition to any dish that calls for ham as a seasoning. Makes 4 pounds

Be sure not to add salt to this recipe because country ham is usually quite salty and should season the mixture very nicely just by itself. Start with ½ pound of ham, then fry and taste a small patty of the sausage. You can add more ham if you want a saltier and more intense ham flavor.

·smoked country sausage·

In the South smoked sausage is usually seasoned with the same spices used to make fresh sausage. As always, there are regional variations, but most smoked country sausage contains the basic mix of pork and sage, with red and black pepper for emphasis. Often, smoked sausage is not tied into individual links. Instead, a continuous rope of sausage is coiled around a stick in large, one-foot loops. Customers simply say to the butcher, "I'll take a foot or two of that smoked sausage there," and it is sliced off and wrapped.

2¼ lbs. pork butt
¾ lb. pork back fat
1 tbsp. brown sugar
2 tsp. red pepper flakes
1 tsp. ground sage
1 tsp. dried thyme

1 tbsp. paprika
Pinch ground allspice
1 tbsp. kosher salt
¾ tsp. curing salts (optional)
½ c. water
Medium hog casings

For details on making sausage, see page 332.

Grind the pork butt through a ⅜-inch plate, the fat through a ¼-inch. Mix together with the sugar and spices. If you are going to cold smoke the sausage for later use, you must add curing salts (see "Note on Nitrites," page 343). Dissolve the optional curing salts in the water and add to the mixture. If you are going to smoke-cook (hot smoke) and eat the sausage directly after making it, you won't need any curing salts. Just add the water to the meat and spices, and knead everything together thoroughly. Stuff into medium hog casings, coiling the sausage as you go. To cold smoke (see "Smoking," page 338), loop 1-foot lengths of sausage over a smoke stick of ½-inch doweling 3–4 feet long, and air-dry in a cool place in front of a fan overnight until the surface is dry to the touch. Cold smoke for 8–10 hours, following the techniques described on page 340. You can keep cold-smoked sausage for 10–12 days in the refrigerator or up to 2 months in the freezer. If you are going to smoke-cook the sausage, it will keep fresh for a week in the refrigerator or 2 months in the freezer. Makes 3 pounds

Hickory is the most common wood for smoking sausage, bacon, and ham in the South, but depending on the area, maple, apple, cherry, oak, or pecan can also be used.

· southern landscape, with barbecue ·

We slow down for the sign saying "Narrow Bridge" about an hour down from the hills toward the coast. There's a little town clustered around a black iron bridge cantilevered across a stream: one store, a white clapboard church, four or five houses huddled under sycamores, with cottonwoods and pines down by the creek bed. Just another small southern town to pass through this hot afternoon, I think, when suddenly there it is —the sweet and unmistakable smell of pig meat cooking.

Hot fat vaporized on the coals mixes smoke with tomatoes and spices, garlic and cayenne. Talk and good laughter rise up from the creek bed, people singing, happy and loud. I say to my friend, "I think we've found barbecue here."

So we pull off to the shoulder of the road and walk down by the side of the bridge. We follow our noses to the party. The path is well worn.

The creekbank is crowded with people, black and white, young and old. It seems the whole town's gathered here at the long tables, passing ambrosia and opinions. Children, raucous under a huge oak, swing on a spare tire out over the stream. Young folk flirt across the fried catfish, while two lawyers in white short-sleeved shirts discuss, with intensity, the nature and techniques of barbecuing sausage. A line of courtly old women edges the bank; they dip their bare feet in the passing stream, decorously conversing. Five black Baptist ladies create God's true and only harmony right there under the cottonwood, while two spiritual masters of barbecue lay chopped pig meat and sausages down on the platters as they go by.

On a huge grill propped over the hot coals, a good-sized shoat, splayed and transfixed with iron rods, drips succulent fat. The

skin is
swabbed
from time to
time with a big
bunch of mint dipped into saltwater and vinegar. A washtubful of sauce and chopped
meat simmers to the side, deep mahogany,
redolent of tomatoes, vinegar, peppers, sweet
and secret smells. Fat links of smoked sausage sputter between the pig and the sauce,
swollen with juice, red with cayenne, and
flecked with black pepper. Two other washtubs hold hot water and fresh-picked corn.
Pans of cracklin' bread keep warm by the
fire's edge, along with pots of melted butter,
casseroles of Hoppin' John, red beans and
rice, hominy, boiled greens, and other covered dishes brought by folks from home.

We're made welcome. Plates are filled
and friendly questions asked, like
where we're going and where we're
from. Southern hospitality surrounds
us, warm and rich and satisfying to
the soul. It's like we've come home
after many years away to this gathering by the river, sharing food
and laughter at the end of a long,
hot summer day.

· smoked country sausage, barbecue style ·

Serve this herb-flavored pork and beef sausage with grilled ribs and chicken, with a tangy potato salad on the side, and you'll think you died and went to Barbecue Heaven, where the hot fat drips on the fire all day long, and the angels fan the smoke away with their wings.

2 lbs. pork butt	1 tsp. paprika
¾ lb. beef chuck	1 tbsp. dry red wine
¾ lb. pork back fat	1 tbsp. sugar
4 tsp. kosher salt	1 tsp. curing salts (optional) (see page
2 tsp. freshly ground black pepper	343)
½ tsp. ground sage	½ c. cold water
½ tsp. dried thyme	¼ c. chopped fresh flat-leaf parsley
¼ tsp. dried marjoram	Medium hog casings

For details on making sausage, see page 332.

Cut the meat and fat into ¾-inch-wide strips and mix with the salt, spices, herbs, wine, and sugar. If you intend to cold smoke the sausage, dissolve the curing salts in the water and add to the meat mixture (see "Note on Nitrites," page 343). If you are going to smoke-cook them, you can leave out the curing salts. Cover and marinate the meat and fat overnight in the refrigerator. Grind the mixture through a ⅜-inch plate, adding any liquids, herbs, and spices remaining from the marinade. Mix thoroughly with the chopped parsley and stuff the sausage meat into medium hog casings. For cold smoking (see "Smoking," page 338): loop the sausage over a smoke stick and dry overnight with a fan in a cool place. Cold smoke the sausage for at least 12, or up to 36 hours. Cool to room temperature and refrigerate for 10–12 days, or freeze up to 2 months. If you are going to smoke-cook the sausages, you can refrigerate them for up to a week before use, or freeze them for up to 2 months.

Makes 3½ pounds

You're likely to find this smoked sausage grilled over hickory and doused with a fiery sauce at a country barbecue.

· phyllo triangles with spicy country sausage ·

The combination of the flaky, buttery phyllo dough and the spicy sausage filling makes these savory little pastries well-nigh irresistible.

1 lb. Spicy Fresh Country Sausage
  (see page 7) or other spicy bulk
  sausage meat
1 c. finely chopped onion
1 c. whipping cream
1 tbsp. Dijon mustard

Pinch freshly grated nutmeg
¼ c. finely chopped green onions or
  scallions
10 phyllo pastry sheets
½ lb. (2 sticks) unsalted butter,
  melted

Cook the sausage and onion in a heavy skillet over medium heat until the meat is no longer pink inside and the fat is rendered, about 10 minutes. Break the meat apart with a fork as it cooks. When cooked, strain the meat through a fine sieve, pressing to extract as much moisture as possible. Drain on paper towels. Wipe out the skillet and return the sausage to the pan. Stir in the cream, mustard, and nutmeg. Simmer, stirring frequently, until the sausage absorbs most of the cream, and the mixture can form a mound on the spoon, about 15 minutes. Stir in the green onions and cool while you prepare the phyllo.

Butter 2 baking sheets. Place 1 phyllo sheet on a work surface, keeping the rest covered with a damp towel to prevent drying. Brush the sheet with melted butter. Place another sheet on top of the first, and brush it with butter also. Cut the sheets crosswise into five 3–4-inch-wide strips. Put a heaping teaspoon of the sausage mixture about an inch from the bottom of one of the phyllo strips. Fold the right-hand corner over the filling to form a triangle. Brush lightly with butter. Continue folding the triangle up the entire length of the strip, brushing lightly with butter after each fold. (This sounds a little complicated, but once you start folding, the technique becomes clearer. If you were ever in the Scouts and folded up the flag, you'll get it down pat.) Repeat with the remaining phyllo and filling. Arrange the triangles as you finish them on the buttered baking sheets about an inch apart. At this point, they can be frozen and baked later. Preheat the oven to 350° F. Bake the pastries until they are golden brown and crisp, 20–25 minutes (fresh take 20, frozen 25 minutes). You can serve them hot from the oven, or let them cool a bit to keep your guests from burning their tongues in a feeding frenzy. Makes 25

Serve as an hors d'oeuvre with a full-bodied Sauvignon Blanc from California's Livermore Valley or a dry white Graves from Bordeaux.

· cheese and sausage biscuits ·

These zesty biscuits make great appetizers, and are also delicious to nibble on throughout a long and leisurely breakfast. Match with a malty, highly hopped beer like Sierra Nevada, Anchor Steam, or Samuel Adams for hors d'oeuvres or half-time snacks. You can use our recipe for Buttermilk Biscuits or your own favorite recipe.

½ c. fried and crumbled Spicy Fresh Country Sausage (see page 7) or other spicy bulk sausage

½ c. grated sharp Cheddar cheese
1 batch Buttermilk Biscuits (see page 26) or equivalent

Fry any good spicy bulk sausage, breaking the meat up with a fork as it cooks. Drain through a sieve and cool on paper towels. Mix the meat and the grated cheese into the biscuit dough just before you add the liquid to it. Roll out and cut into 1½-inch rounds before baking. You can vary this formula as you wish by using smoked or fresh sausage, different types of cheese like Asiago, Parmesan and smoked Gouda, or by adding a teaspoon or two of herbs such as thyme or oregano, a couple of teaspoons of chopped garlic, green onions, and/or chopped red bell pepper. Bake at 450° F for 10–15 minutes. Makes 2 dozen

Be creative and use herbs and cheese that suit your fancy or whatever you happen to have lurking in the back of the refrigerator, but don't forget to add the sausage!

· oyster and sausage fritters ·

Serve these spicy fritters with Tidewater Tartar Sauce or Lee Coleman's Rémoulade Dressing (see recipes on pages 27 and 353).

· Fritter batter ·
½ c. all-purpose flour
¼ tsp. kosher salt
1 tbsp. salad oil or melted butter
1 egg, lightly beaten
½ tsp. black pepper
½ c. beer
1 egg white
....
Flour for dredging

Vegetable oil or fat for deep-frying
24 medium oysters, shucked, or
    1½ 12-oz. jars
48 ¼-inch rounds (about 1 lb.)
    Smoked Country Sausage (see page
    11) or other good-quality smoked
    sausage like andouille or kielbasa
Lemon wedges
Tabasco or other hot pepper sauce

Blend the flour and salt together and beat in the oil, egg, pepper, and beer. Stir until the batter is fairly smooth, but do not overmix. Let it rest at room temperature for at least 1 hour. When you are ready to begin frying, beat an egg white until it forms stiff, but not dry, peaks, then gently fold into the batter until no streaks of egg white remain.

Heat 3 inches of oil to 375° F. On a toothpick or short wooden skewer, sandwich each oyster between 2 rounds of sausage. Dredge in flour, then dip into the batter and let any excess drain off. Carefully drop the fritter into the hot fat. Deep-fry 5 or 6 at a time for 3–4 minutes, until they are puffy and golden brown. Drain on paper towels and serve at once. Garnish with lemon, and serve with Tabasco and one of the spicy, mayonnaise-based sauces listed above. Makes 10–15 servings as an appetizer
....

Perfect for stand-up hors d'oeuvres paired with a crisp dry sparkling Blanc de Blancs from California or northern Spain.

· savory crab turnovers ·

This recipe is best made with fresh crabmeat from the Atlantic blue crab, the "beautiful swimmers" (*Callinectes sapidus*) of Chesapeake Bay and the Gulf Coast. If you can't find blue crab, you can use Dungeness or any other *fresh* lump crabmeat. Don't bother with canned or frozen crab, which often has the flavor and texture of wet, shredded cardboard.

· **Pastry** ·
1½ lbs. cream cheese
¾ lb. (3 sticks) unsalted butter
1¼ tsp. kosher salt
6 c. all-purpose flour
· **Crab and sausage filling** ·
4 tbsp. unsalted butter
½ lb. Smoked Country Sausage
  (see page 11) or other smoked
  sausage, finely diced
1 c. finely chopped onions

¼ c. thinly sliced green onions or
  scallions
1½ c. heavy cream
¼ c. freshly grated Parmesan cheese
½ tsp. Tabasco
1½ tsp. Worcestershire sauce
2 egg yolks
1 lb. cleaned fresh lump crabmeat
....

1 egg beaten with 1 tsp. water for egg
  wash

The pastry here is almost foolproof: simple to make, but wonderfully rich and buttery. Use any high-quality smoked sausage such as andouille or smoked country sausage.

Make the pastry using an electric mixer. Cream the cheese and butter together, add the salt and flour, and blend thoroughly. Gather the dough into a ball, cover, and chill for at least an hour. (At this point, the dough can be frozen for later use.) Roll it out onto a well-floured surface to about ⅛-inch thickness. For hors d'oeuvre–sized turnovers, cut into 3-inch circles. For larger turnovers, make 5-inch circles. Overlap the pastry circles on a sheet pan and refrigerate them until they are ready to be filled.

To make the filling, melt the butter in a heavy skillet over medium heat. Fry the sausage for 5 minutes, and then drain off all but about 1 tablespoon of the fat. Add the chopped onions, and cover the pan. Cook over moderate heat for about 10 minutes or until the onions are quite soft. Add the green onions, along with the cream, cheese, Tabasco, and Worcestershire sauce. Bring to a boil and cook, uncovered, stirring until the cream begins to thicken, about 10 minutes. Beat the egg yolks in a bowl. Gradually stir in 1 cup of the hot cream and cheese mixture, being careful not to curdle the eggs. Add this back to the frying pan while off the heat, and stir until all is blended together. Fold in the crabmeat, taste for seasoning, and cool for at least an hour or overnight in the refrigerator.

To assemble the turnovers, place 1–2 tablespoons of the filling on the small pastry circles or ¼ cup on the large. Flip one half of the circle over onto the other to make a half-moon shape. Crimp and seal the edges. At this point the turnovers can be frozen for baking later. When ready to bake, preheat the oven to 375° F, brush the turnovers with the egg wash, and bake 20–25 minutes (25–30 minutes if frozen), until lightly browned. Makes 30 small or 14 large turnovers

tomatoes stuffed with sausage and oysters ·

Combining oysters and other seafood with sausage has long been popular in southern coastal cities, especially those where French and Spanish influences prevail. For other toothsome minglings of sausage and oysters, see our recipes for Oyster and Sausage Fritters (see page 17) and Oyster and Pork Sausage (see page 113).

8 firm ripe tomatoes, about 3 inches in diameter
Salt and pepper to taste
1 tbsp. unsalted butter
¼ c. finely chopped onion
¼ c. finely chopped green onions or scallions
¼ c. finely chopped mushrooms
1 tsp. minced garlic
¼ c. dry vermouth
¼ tsp. cayenne
¾ lb. Smoked Country Sausage (see page 11) or other smoked sausage, finely chopped

12-oz. jar small oysters, or 18 shucked; if large, chop coarsely
¼ c. heavy cream
1 egg
1 tbsp. chopped fresh basil or 1 tsp. dried
½ tsp. Tabasco
¾ c. fresh bread crumbs

· Topping ·
¼ c. dry bread crumbs
¼ c. freshly grated Parmesan cheese
2 tbsp. olive oil

Slice off the tops of the tomatoes. Using a melon baller, teaspoon, or tomato scoop, carefully hollow out the tomatoes, leaving a ¼-inch-thick shell. Lightly sprinkle the inside of each tomato with salt and pepper, and set aside.

In a heavy skillet, melt the butter over medium heat. Add the chopped onion and cook for 5 minutes. Put in the green onions, mushrooms, garlic, vermouth, and cayenne along with a pinch of salt. Cook over high heat, stirring frequently, until most of the liquid has evaporated. Remove to a bowl and mix in the sausage, oysters, cream, egg, basil, and Tabasco. Gently stir in enough fresh bread crumbs to bind the stuffing. The mixture should be moist enough to hold together when molded on a spoon.

Preheat the oven to 350° F. Divide the stuffing evenly among the 8 tomato shells, mounding it above the top of the tomatoes, and arrange in a shallow baking dish. Mix together the dry bread crumbs, grated Parmesan, and oil, and sprinkle the topping generously on each. Bake for 30–40 minutes, until the sausage is cooked at 150° F on an instant-read thermometer, and the tomatoes heated through.

Makes 4–6 servings for lunch or 6–8 as a first course

Serve as a first course or luncheon entree with a lighter style California Chardonnay like Fetzer's Sundial Ranch.

· 19 ·

· smoked sausage, potato and roasted pepper salad ·

The robust flavors of peppers and onions along with smoky sausage and a tart vinaigrette make this tangy salad great for a picnic or barbecue or as a first course for a hearty meal.

½ lb. Smoked Country Sausage
   (see page 11) or other smoked
   sausage, diced
1 lb. red boiling potatoes
1 red bell pepper
1 green Anaheim or poblano chile or
   green bell pepper
1 c. chopped red onion
3 green onions or scallions, chopped,
   white and green together
½ c. chopped fresh parsley

· Vinaigrette dressing ·

2 tbsp. red wine vinegar
1 tbsp. Dijon mustard
1 tsp. minced garlic (optional)
6 tbsp. olive oil
Salt and pepper to taste
Tabasco to taste

Brown the sausage in a heavy skillet over medium heat for about 5 minutes. Remove from the pan and set aside. Cook the potatoes in salted boiling water, in a partially covered pot, for about 20 minutes. Don't overcook. You'll know they are done when a knife point can be easily inserted. Rinse them under cold water to cool, then cut in half lengthwise, and slice into ¼-inch-thick pieces. Roast the peppers over an open flame or under the broiler until the skin chars lightly. Put in a plastic bag to steam for about 15 minutes, then slip the charred skin off with your fingers, using a knife to remove any tough pieces of skin. Wash under cold water, and cut into narrow strips.

Make the Vinaigrette Dressing by whisking the ingredients together. In a clear glass salad bowl or on a white platter mix the peppers, sausage, potatoes, red and green onions, parsley, and dressing. Toss gently until the potato slices are well coated. Do not overmix or the potatoes will break up. Chill slightly before serving or serve at room temperature.

Makes 4–6 servings

Try this with a rich dark beer like San Francisco's Anchor Porter or Prior's Double Dark from Philadelphia. You can use any high-quality store-bought linguiça or andouille or one of our smoked sausages.

· shrimp stock ·

Clam juice, chicken stock, or a combination of both also works well.
Shells from ¾ lb. or more shrimp
6 c. water
2 cloves garlic, chopped
1 onion, chopped
Tops from 4 ribs celery, chopped
½ bunch parsley, chopped
2 bay leaves
Pinch dried thyme
1 tsp. pickling spice
   Boil shells in water; skim. Reduce heat, add vegetables, herbs, and spices. Simmer for about 45 minutes, uncovered. Strain.
Makes 4 cups

· shrimp and eggplant bisque ·

This recipe comes from Steve Armbruster, a fine southern chef. Besides having cooked in several restaurants, he writes a popular food column for *Wave Length*, a New Orleans newspaper.

¼ c. olive oil
1 large eggplant, cut in half
1 lb. ripe tomatoes
½ lb. Smoked Country Sausage
  (see page 11) or other smoked
  sausage, diced
1 c. chopped onion
2 ribs celery, chopped
½ yellow or red bell pepper, chopped
3 cloves garlic, minced
2 tbsp. flour
2 tsp. dried basil

½ tsp. black pepper
¼ tsp. dried thyme
½ tsp. cayenne
3–5 c. shrimp stock or equivalent
  (see opposite page)
½ c. dry white wine
¾ lb. shrimp (shelled—save shells for
  above stock)
¼ c. chopped fresh parsley
2 c. half-and-half
Salt and pepper to taste
Tabasco to taste

Preheat the oven to 350° F. Reserve 2 tablespoons of the olive oil and rub the rest on the eggplant. Roast the eggplant in a baking dish, cut side down, for 15 minutes. Add the tomatoes, whole and unpeeled, and bake for 30 minutes more, or until the eggplant is completely soft. Once the eggplant is cool enough to handle, remove the skin from the flesh. Peel, seed, and chop the tomatoes. Puree the eggplant and the tomatoes in a food processor and push the mixture through a strainer to remove any seeds and skin.

If you leave the ingredients a bit chunky, this becomes a hearty one-course meal. As a finer puree, it makes an excellent first course.

Meanwhile, in a heavy 6–8-quart pot, fry the sausage in the reserved olive oil over medium heat for 5 minutes. Add the onion and celery, and cook until they soften, about 10 minutes. Add the chopped bell pepper, and cook 5 minutes more. Add the garlic (reserving 1 clove), flour, basil, black pepper, thyme, and cayenne and cook 3–4 minutes, stirring so that the vegetables are well coated with the flour. Pour in 3 cups of the stock, the white wine, and the tomato and eggplant mixture, stirring well. Bring to a boil, reduce to a simmer, and cook the bisque, uncovered, for 15 minutes. The soup should have the consistency of heavy cream. Add the shrimp, more stock if necessary, the reserved clove of garlic, minced, and the chopped parsley. Cook 3–5 minutes until the shrimp are just cooked through. Stir in the half-and-half. Adjust the seasoning with salt, pepper, and Tabasco. Makes 8–10 servings

· Georgia peanut soup with smoked sausage ·

Peanuts (also called groundnuts or goobers) originated in Peru, traveled from Brazil to the Slave Coast, then back to America. This versatile legume is used in a great variety of dishes from Africa to America's South. Peanuts often flavor vegetables as a sauce or dressing, and are used whole or ground with chicken or pork.

1 tbsp. butter
½ lb. Smoked Country Sausage (see page 11) or other smoked sausage, chopped
½ onion, chopped
1 leek, split, cleaned, and chopped
1 carrot, chopped
4–5 c. chicken stock
1 tsp. cayenne
½ c. peanut butter

2 tbsp. lemon juice (or more, to taste)
2 tsp. low-sulfur molasses or Steen's Syrup *
Salt and pepper to taste
¼ c. finely chopped green onions or scallions
¼ c. chopped roasted peanuts
Tabasco

* Steen's Syrup is a high-quality molasses available in the South.

Melt the butter over medium heat in a 2–3-quart heavy pot or Dutch oven. Add the sausage, cook 5 minutes, then add the onion, leek, and carrot. Cook, covered, for 5 minutes more. Stir occasionally, scraping the bottom of the pan to incorporate any browned bits. Add the stock and the cayenne, and cook the soup, covered, for another 20 minutes over medium heat, until the vegetables are soft. Strain the liquid, and put the solids in a food processor with the peanut butter.

Peanuts add richness and texture in this tangy, African-influenced puree. Use a spicy smoked sausage such as andouille if you want a little extra kick.

Puree the vegetables, sausage, and peanut butter, pouring in the liquid as you go, until the soup is smooth and creamy. Return the pureed soup to the original pot. If it is too thick you may add more stock; if too thin, cook down until it reaches a creamy consistency. Add the lemon juice and molasses and simmer for 5 minutes to marry the flavors. Taste for salt and pepper, and add more lemon juice if desired. Ladle into individual bowls and garnish with green onions and chopped peanuts. Your guests can add Tabasco to taste. Makes 4–6 servings

· red bean and sausage soup ·

Serve these beans up with Cheese and Sausage Biscuits (see page 16) and some steamed turnip or mustard greens for a stick-to-the-ribs country dinner. A big, full-bodied Zinfandel from California's Amador County or a high-hopped ale like Anchor Liberty or Canada's Black Horse would wash everything down right nicely.

1 lb. red beans
4 qts. beef or chicken stock
2 ham hocks (about 1½ lbs.)
½ lb. Country Ham and Pork Sausage (see page 9) or smoked sausage, chopped
2 c. chopped onions
1 c. chopped celery
½ tsp. black pepper
1 bay leaf
1 tsp. dried thyme

½ lb. Smoked Country Sausage (see page 11) or other smoked sausage, sliced into ¼-inch rounds
¼ c. red wine vinegar
Salt and pepper to taste
Tabasco
3 hard-boiled eggs, chopped (optional)
½ c. finely chopped green onions or scallions

Place the beans in enough water to cover by 2–3 inches and soak overnight. In a 6–8-quart pot, bring the stock to a boil. Drain and rinse the beans and add them to the pot along with the ham hocks, chopped Country Ham and Pork Sausage, the onions, celery, pepper, bay leaf, and thyme. Reduce the heat to a low boil and simmer, stirring occasionally, for 2 hours, or until beans are tender. Remove the ham hock bones, and discard. Chop the meat and skin coarsely and return them to the pot. Add more stock if the soup is too thick. Put the rounds of Smoked Country Sausage into the pot, and cook 10 minutes more. Add enough wine vinegar to give everything a slightly tangy flavor. Adjust the salt and pepper, and add a couple of healthy jolts of Tabasco. To serve, ladle the soup into bowls and garnish with chopped egg and green onions. Your guests can add more Tabasco to taste. An alternative is to puree the soup in a food processor after removing the ham hocks. Add the sausage rounds to the smooth soup, and cook until they are heated through, about 10 minutes. Season and serve as above. Makes 8 servings

If you haven't the time to make our Country Ham and Pork Sausage, you can use any good-quality smoked sausage with these tangy beans.

· quick and easy soups ·

Soups are hearty, nourishing, and, with a little sausage on hand, astonishingly easy to make. With ½ to ¾ pound of sausage and 6 cups of good beef or chicken stock you have the basis for many fine soups. The sausage may be smoked or raw. If you wish, it can be precooked and drained to get rid of some of the fat.

For a delicious vegetable soup: to the stock and sausage, add 3 cups of a mixture of chopped potatoes, carrots, leeks, and celery, and cook gently until the vegetables are done. Another delicious soup: to the stock and sausage, add 3 cups of chopped broccoli, a chopped onion, and a few garlic cloves chopped and sautéed briefly in olive oil, along with some freshly cooked macaroni. Cook gently until broccoli is just done.

To make a satisfying cream soup, add to the sausage/stock mixture ¼ pound chopped smoked sausage, 2 cups diced zucchini, and 1 cup of cooked rice. Cook gently until the zucchini is just tender and puree everything in a food processor. Add a little lemon juice and taste for salt and pepper.

The possibilities are endless. Put together whatever combinations of vegetables, stock, and sausages appeal to you—you'll soon find that a flavorful soup, served with good crusty bread and a glass of wine, makes an easy and satisfying meal for family or guests.

· Alabama country breakfast ·

This hearty breakfast is typical of how the day begins all over the South. Breakfast is an important meal, a time to plan the day and socialize with family and friends. Such a breakfast approaches the sublime when accompanied with flaky buttermilk biscuits spread with sweet butter and sage honey, along with strong chicory coffee mixed with hot milk, all taken on a veranda on a cool spring morning with mockingbirds making melody among the wisteria.

· Country sausage with grits and cream gravy ·

1½ lbs. Spicy Fresh Country Sausage (see page 7) or other spicy fresh sausage, formed into 6–8 patties

2 tbsp. flour

1½ c. half-and-half or milk

¼ tsp. Worcestershire sauce

Pinch freshly grated nutmeg

Salt, pepper, and Tabasco to taste

1 c. instant grits

Heat a heavy 12-inch skillet over medium heat. Fry the sausage patties until they are brown and crispy, about 5 minutes a side. Transfer them to a platter and keep warm. Pour the fat and juices into a clear Pyrex measuring cup or bowl. Put 3 tablespoons of the fat back into the pan and return to medium heat. Pour off the remaining top layer of fat and discard, but save the lower layer of meat juices in the measuring cup. Add the flour to the pan and stir until well mixed with the fat. Be sure to scrape up the brown bits of sausage stuck to the bottom of the pan. Pour in the half-and-half and the remaining meat juices. Continue to stir until smooth. You can add more or less half-and-half, depending on how thick you like the gravy. Raise the heat and bring the gravy to a boil, stirring constantly. Lower the heat, and add Worcestershire sauce, nutmeg, salt and pepper, and Tabasco if desired. Prepare the instant grits, following the directions on the package. Spoon the cream gravy over the grits and sausage patties. Serve with poached eggs and hot Buttermilk Biscuits (see page 26).

Makes 4 servings with 1½ cups gravy

With a food processor you can whip up a small batch of Spicy Fresh Country Sausage in no time flat. Use any of our recipes for fresh country sausage here, or a good-quality store-bought variety. Figure on 2–3 sausage patties per person.

· country sausage with sweet and tangy red-eye gravy ·

Fried country ham or sausage served with red-eye gravy and grits or biscuits is a traditional southern breakfast. Red-eye gravy is usually made by deglazing the skillet the ham or sausage was fried in with black coffee. We've embellished the idea by adding molasses, mustard, Worcestershire sauce, and vinegar to produce a sweet and tangy sauce. This sauce can also be boiled and used as a marinade for beef, pork, or chicken, or thickened with a little cornstarch and served over baked ham.

1½ lbs. Spicy Fresh Country Sausage (see page 7) or other fresh sausage, formed into 3 x ½-inch patties
½ c. black coffee

¼ c. low-sulfur molasses
2 tbsp. Dijon or Creole mustard
1 tsp. Worcestershire sauce
2 tbsp. red wine or cider vinegar

In a heavy 12-inch skillet, fry the sausage patties over medium heat until brown and crusty on both sides, about 7–10 minutes. Transfer them to a serving platter and keep warm. Pour off the grease, leaving about 1 tablespoon in the pan. Return to medium heat and add the coffee, scraping and deglazing the brown bits as it boils up. Turn the heat up, and add the remaining ingredients, stirring vigorously. Reduce the sauce slightly over high heat, and pour the gravy over the sausage patties. Serve with grits and/or biscuits. Makes 4 servings with ½ cup gravy

Not only great for breakfast, this makes a hearty lunch or supper with boiled greens and pot likker (the savory liquid from the greens) on the side.

· buttermilk biscuits ·

2 c. flour
1 tbsp. baking powder
¾ tsp. salt
¾ tsp. sugar
4 tbsp. (½ stick) cold unsalted butter
¼ c. vegetable shortening
½ tsp. baking soda
¾ c. plus 2 tablespoons buttermilk

Mix flour, baking powder, salt, and sugar. Cut in butter and shortening. Combine baking soda and buttermilk, pour into dry ingredients, stir until soft dough forms. Turn out onto lightly floured surface and knead gently for about 10–20 seconds to form ball. Roll or pat to ½ inch thick. Cut 2½-inch circles, place on lightly greased cookie sheet, and bake 10–15 minutes in preheated 450° F oven until lightly browned. Makes about a dozen

· crab and sausage cakes with Tidewater tartar sauce ·

The sausage's spicy, smoky flavors complement the sweetness of crabmeat. Frying in clarified butter will give them a rich, buttery quality.

1 lb. fresh lump crabmeat, picked over and cleaned

¼ lb. Smoked Country Sausage (see page 11) or other smoked sausage, finely chopped

2½ c. fresh bread crumbs

1 egg, lightly beaten

1 tbsp. chopped green onions or scallions

1 tsp. Worcestershire sauce

1 tbsp. chopped fresh parsley

3 tbsp. Tidewater Tartar Sauce

Salt and pepper to taste

Tabasco (optional)

4 oz. (1 stick) butter, clarified, or ¼ c. vegetable oil plus 4 tbsp. butter

Lemon wedges

Mix together the crab, sausage, and ¾ cup of the bread crumbs with the egg, green onion, Worcestershire sauce, and parsley. When all is well blended, stir in the Tartar Sauce. Taste for salt and pepper and add Tabasco if desired.

Form the mixture into cakes about 3 inches in diameter and about ¾ inch thick or make hors d'oeuvre–sized cakes 2 inches in diameter and ½ inch thick. Coat the cakes with the remaining breadcrumbs, place on a platter between sheets of wax paper, and chill them for at least an hour. When ready to cook, heat the clarified butter or the equivalent vegetable oil and butter in a frying pan over medium-high heat. When the butter is hot, carefully add the cakes to the pan. Do not overcrowd. Fry the cakes for 2–3 minutes a side until they are golden brown. Serve immediately with lemon wedges and plenty of Tidewater Tartar Sauce (below) or Lee Coleman's Rémoulade Dressing (see page 353).

Makes 20 large cakes or about 30 small

· Tidewater tartar sauce ·

3 tbsp. lemon juice

2 tbsp. Creole or other spicy mustard

½ tsp. cayenne

1 tsp. salt

½ tsp. black pepper

3 eggs, lightly beaten

1½ c. oil

½ c. finely chopped green onion or scallion

¼ c. finely chopped fresh parsley

½ tsp. soy sauce

1 tsp. Worcestershire sauce

2 tbsp. finely chopped dill pickle

1 tbsp. capers

2 tbsp. chopped fresh dill (optional)

1 tsp. or more Tabasco

In food processor make mayonnaise with first 7 ingredients. Add other ingredients and pulse once or twice. Taste for seasonings. Will keep 1 week in refrigerator. Tastes even better made up a day ahead to allow all the flavors to mellow.

Makes 3–4 cups

pork chops stuffed with country sausage and baked in a bourbon mustard glaze ·

The sweetness and luscious flavors of pork merge with the spicy sausage and a tangy, bourbon-flavored glaze to make this a great centerpiece for a dinner party or special gathering of friends. You might want to start off with some mint juleps and Cheese and Sausage Biscuits (see page 16). Then cook up some hearty side dishes like Hoppin' John or Smoky Black-Eyed Peas (see page 36), and Stewed Okra (see page 41). Our Kentucky-Style Pork Sausage works well here (see page 9), but any good sage-flavored fresh sausage will do.

· Pork chops ·
6 1½–2-inch-thick pork chops
(3–4 lbs. total)
Salt and pepper to taste

· Stuffing ·
1 tbsp. butter
1 rib celery, finely chopped
1 medium onion, finely chopped

1 c. coarse fresh bread crumbs in about ¼-inch pieces
¾ lb. Kentucky-Style Pork Sausage (see page 9) or other fresh bulk sausage
2 tbsp. dry white wine
1 egg
2 tbsp. olive oil

Cut a large pocket into each chop and season the meat with salt and pepper. Set the chops aside while you make the glaze and stuffing. To make the stuffing, melt the butter over medium heat in a heavy skillet, and cook the celery and onion, covered, until soft, about 10 minutes. Transfer the onion and celery to a bowl and mix in the bread crumbs, sausage, white wine, and egg. Knead and squeeze the stuffing until all the ingredients are thoroughly blended. Divide it into 6 equal amounts, and stuff each chop, molding the dressing with your hands against the side.

Serve with a cool, dry Alsatian or Oregon Riesling.

Preheat the oven to 375° F. Heat the olive oil in a heavy 12-inch skillet until the oil begins to haze. Brown the chops, 3 at a time, 4–5 minutes on each side. Transfer them to a 9 x 12 x 2-inch pan, brush with the Bourbon Mustard Glaze (see box), and bake the chops, uncovered, for 30–45 minutes, or until an instant-read thermometer registers 155–160° F when inserted into the middle of the stuffing. Baste the chops generously every 10 minutes with fresh glaze. Makes 6 servings

· bourbon mustard glaze ·
Also a superb marinade for roast or grilled beef, pork, or lamb, and a tasty glaze for baked ham.
¼ c. brown sugar
2 tbsp. low-sulfur molasses
¼ c. bourbon
¼ c. Dijon or Creole mustard
¼ c. soy sauce
2 tsp. Worcestershire sauce
½ tsp. black pepper
Whisk all the ingredients together until smooth.
Makes about 1 cup

· crown roast of pork with sweet potato, sausage, and apple dressing ·

Crown roast is an elegant centerpiece for a holiday banquet, but pork butt or loin will serve equally well. Use any of the recipes for fresh sausage, or a good-quality commercial brand here.

· Pork roast ·
1 tsp. salt
1 tsp. black pepper
¼ tsp. ground sage
½ tsp. dried rosemary
¼ tsp. dried thyme
5–6-lb. crown roast or other pork roast

· Dressing ·
2 lbs. sweet potatoes or yams
1 lb. Spicy Fresh Country Sausage (see page 7) or other fresh bulk sausage

2 c. chopped onions
½ c. chopped celery
2 green apples, cored, cut into ½-inch dice
½ c. apple cider
⅛ tsp. *each* cinnamon and ground ginger
3 c. ½-inch dried bread cubes, preferably homemade
½ c. rich chicken stock
Salt and pepper to taste
3 tbsp. butter (if baked separately in a casserole)

Preheat the oven to 350° F. Mix together the salt, pepper, and herbs, and rub over the roast.

Boil the sweet potatoes in their skins until a knife can just be inserted. It's better if they are slightly undercooked. When the sweet potatoes are cool enough to handle, remove the skin and mash them roughly.

Fry the sausage in a heavy skillet over medium heat until just cooked through, using a fork to crumble the meat into small pieces. This should take 5–7 minutes. Add the onions and celery to the pan, cover, and cook 10 minutes more until they are soft. Add the apples, cider, and spices, and cook, covered, for 5 more minutes—the apples should remain firm. Mix the contents of the skillet with the sweet potatoes and bread cubes. Moisten with stock, using just enough to make the mixture hold together. Season dressing with salt and pepper. Mound the dressing into the crown roast, place the roast on a rack in a roasting pan, and bake until the internal temperature of the roast reaches 160° F, about 1½–2 hours, depending on which cut you use. Or you can put the dressing into a casserole buttered with 1 tablespoon of the butter, dot with the remaining 2 tablespoons of butter, cover, and bake next to the roast for 45 minutes. Remove the cover, and cook 10 minutes more until the top is bubbly and lightly browned. This dressing can be made up a day ahead, refrigerated, and baked just before you are ready to eat. Makes 6–8 servings

The dressing can also be baked separately from the roast, and is delicious with baked ham or turkey too.

· pork loin stuffed with spring greens and smoked sausage ·

The time to make this dish is in the spring or summertime when the greens are fresh and tender. It is just as good cold or hot, which makes for a tasty picnic or cold supper. Greens are easy to grow, and increasingly available at specialty and ethnic markets. Use whatever mix you can find or suits your fancy. We've listed some of our favorites below, but you'll discover your own special mixture of bitter, hot, and sweet greens after you've tried this and other recipes a few times.

4 c. spring greens, loosely packed (you should include both bitter and sweet greens, e.g., collard, mustard, turnip greens, and/or arugula, mixed with spinach, escarole, and/or chard)
1 onion, finely chopped
2 tbsp. butter
1 tsp. chopped garlic
Salt and pepper to taste
4–5-lb. center cut pork loin, boned

½–¾ lb. Smoked Country Sausage (see page 11) or other smoked sausage (in one piece the length of the roast)
3 tbsp. bacon fat or butter
¼ c. Creole or other coarse-grained mustard
½ tsp. cayenne
1 tsp. fresh sage or ½ tsp. dried ground sage
1 tsp. black pepper

Carefully wash the greens, remove the stems and discard, and coarsely chop the leaves. In a Dutch oven over medium heat sauté the onion in the butter until soft, about 5 minutes. Add the greens, garlic, and a pinch each of salt and pepper, and cook, covered, until the greens are wilted, about 10 minutes, stirring occasionally. Butterfly the boned pork loin, and spread a layer of wilted greens over the cut surface. Lay the piece of smoked sausage lengthwise down the center of the roast, and trim the sausage to fit. Reassemble the roast by rolling the loin around the sausage and greens, and tie it in several places with kitchen string.

If you're not up to butterflying the pork loin, ask your butcher to do it for you. Most will be happy to oblige.

Preheat the oven to 350° F. Melt the bacon fat or butter, and whisk it into a small bowl containing the mustard, cayenne, sage, and pepper. Brush the loin generously with this mixture. Place it in a roasting pan and bake until the interior of the roast reaches 155–160° F, about 1½ hours. Let the roast rest for about 10 minutes and then slice and serve, or cool it in the refrigerator to be eaten cold. Makes 6–8 servings

· braised chicken with sausage stuffing in country ham and port wine sauce ·

Tangy ham and sweet wine make a delicious sauce for this casserole-roasted chicken. Use leftover cooked country ham or some good smoked ham here; raw country ham would be too salty. Any fresh country-style sausage will work fine, but our Country Ham and Pork Sausage (see page 9) is especially good in this recipe.

· Stuffing ·

½ lb. Country Ham and Pork Sausage (see page 9), removed from casings, or other fresh country sausage
1 c. chopped onion
½ c. chopped celery
½ tsp. *each* dried thyme, sage, and marjoram
½ tsp. pepper
2–3 c. dry bread cubes
½ green apple, peeled, cored, and cubed
½ c. or more chicken stock

· Chicken and sauce ·

1 whole 3½–4-lb. chicken
¼ c. finely chopped fat trimmed from a country ham or other smoked ham or bacon
½ tsp. *each* dried thyme and sage
½ tsp. *each* salt and pepper
¾ c. chopped onion
¼ c. chopped shallots
2 cloves garlic, minced
1 c. port wine
½ c. chicken stock
½ tsp. dried thyme
1 bay leaf
½ tsp. dried marjoram
½ c. diced cooked country ham or other smoked ham
1 c. sour cream
Salt and pepper to taste

To make the stuffing, cook the sausage in a heavy skillet for 5 minutes over medium heat, using a fork to break up the meat. Add the onion and celery, and cook, covered, for 10 minutes until the vegetables are soft and translucent. Stir occasionally. Put in the thyme, sage, marjoram, and pepper, and cook 1 minute more. In a large bowl, mix together the sausage and vegetables, bread cubes, and apple. Add just enough stock to moisten the bread; too much will make it soggy. Do not overmix or the dressing will become pasty. Stuff the bird loosely and truss the opening with thread or skewers. Bake any leftover stuffing in a covered buttered casserole or loaf pan.

To cook the chicken and sauce, render the ham fat or bacon in a heavy skillet over medium heat. Preheat the oven to 375° F. Combine the herbs and spices and rub them all over the chicken. Brown the chicken in the skillet, turning the bird so that all sides are nicely colored. Drain off all but 1 tablespoon of fat. Remove the chicken and add the onion, shallots, and garlic. Cook for 2–3 minutes in the remaining fat. Deglaze the pan with the port and chicken stock. Put the vegetables and deglazing liquid into a casserole large enough to hold the chicken. Add the

The stuffing is also excellent in roast poultry or stuffed pork chops.

· 31 ·

thyme, bay leaf, marjoram, and diced ham. Place the chicken on top of this mixture. Cover the casserole and bake for 45 minutes, or until the chicken reaches an internal temperature of 160° F. Transfer the chicken to a warm platter and cover it with foil while you finish the sauce. Skim the fat from the cooking liquid and place the casserole over high heat. Reduce the liquid until it just coats a spoon. Remove the sauce from the heat and stir in the sour cream. Taste for salt and pepper. Cut the chicken into serving pieces and arrange over a mound of stuffing. Pour a little of the sauce over the chicken and dressing, and put the remaining sauce in a gravy boat to pass at the table. Makes 4 servings

· rabbit or chicken stew with sausage, hominy, and crispy onions ·

Game has always been an important element in southern cooking. Rabbit, squirrel, possum, and raccoon form the base of many traditional recipes, and are still often found on southern tables. The spice rub is also delicious on pork or turkey.

· **Spice rub** ·
½ tsp. salt
1 tsp. black pepper
1 tsp. dried marjoram
Pinch ground cloves
1 tsp. cayenne
2 tsp. paprika
1 tsp. dry mustard

2-lb. frying rabbit, cut into 6 pieces,
   or 2–3-lb. chicken, cut into
   8 pieces
1 tbsp. bacon fat or olive oil
1 lb. Smoked Country Sausage (see
   page 11) or other smoked sausage,
   cut into ⅜-inch rounds

4 c. thinly sliced onions
1 carrot, diced
2 mild fresh chilies (Anaheim or
   similar), seeded and sliced, or
   1 green bell pepper, chopped
1 tbsp. chopped garlic
1 c. rich chicken or beef stock
2 c. canned Italian plum tomatoes or
   equivalent fresh, peeled, seeded,
   and chopped
1-lb. can hominy with liquid
½ lb. green beans, cut into 2-inch
   pieces
Salt and pepper to taste
Tabasco

Mix the spices and herbs together, and rub them over the rabbit or chicken. Set it aside to season while you prepare the remaining ingredients. In a large heavy pot or Dutch oven, heat the bacon fat or olive oil over medium heat. Add the sausage and cook until it is lightly browned, about 5 minutes. Remove from the pot and reserve. Brown the rabbit or chicken pieces in the remaining fat, turning them often to achieve a nice gold color overall. Transfer the pieces to a platter as they brown. Pour off any excess fat into a heavy skillet, and reserve, leaving about 2 tablespoons in the Dutch oven.

Add half the onions and the diced carrot to the fat remaining in the Dutch oven. Cover. Fry the vegetables for about 10 minutes over moderate heat, scraping up any brown bits. Add the chilies or green pepper and garlic, and cook for 2 minutes more. Add the stock, tomatoes, and hominy with its liquid, along with any leftovers from the spice rub. Bring everything to a boil in the Dutch oven, and add the rabbit or chicken along with the browned sausage. Reduce the heat, cover, and simmer the stew for about 40 minutes while you prepare the crispy onions.

We use domestic rabbit here, but squirrel or a young possum would also be mighty tasty. And this dish is awfully good with chicken, too.

Heat the skillet with the reserved fat over medium-high heat. If you haven't saved the fat, use 2 tablespoons of bacon fat or olive oil. Add the remaining 2 cups of sliced onions and ¼ teaspoon of salt to the hot fat. Cover the pan, and reduce the heat to medium. Cook for 15 minutes, stirring occasionally. The onions should begin to brown evenly, but not burn. Increase the heat to medium-high, and remove the lid. Brown the onions, stirring and shaking the pan frequently. Continue for another 10 or 15 minutes until the onions are crisp and a rich mahogany brown. Drain on a paper towel.

To complete the dish, cut a small piece from the rabbit's front leg or the chicken wing and taste to see if it is tender. If not, continue to cook until done. Add the green beans to the stew. Cook 7–10 minutes more until the beans are just cooked. They should be tender but crisp. If the sauce is watery, remove most of the meat and vegetables with a slotted spoon to a serving bowl, and reduce the liquid until it just coats a spoon. Degrease the sauce, if necessary. Taste for salt and pepper, and add Tabasco if desired. Serve the stew over rice in a shallow bowl, and garnish the top with the crispy onions. Makes 4–6 servings

· smoked chicken with
sausage and savoy cabbage ·

This is a wonderful and simple way to use smoked chicken, but a fresh roaster will do just about as well. If you are cooking a fresh, unsmoked bird, cut it in 8 pieces, salt and pepper generously, and brown in hot fat before adding it to the cabbage.

¼ lb. slab bacon, with rind removed, diced

3–4-lb. smoked or fresh chicken, cut into 8 pieces

1 large onion, thinly sliced

3 medium leeks, split, washed, and sliced

2 medium carrots, chopped

1 2-lb. head savoy cabbage, quartered, cored, and coarsely chopped

1 c. beef or chicken stock

1 c. dry white wine

1 tsp. dried thyme

2 bay leaves

½ tsp. cayenne

1 tsp. black pepper

1 lb. Smoked Country Sausage (see page 11) or other smoked sausage, sliced into ¾-inch rounds

You could also use 1 or 2 partridges, 2 pheasants, or 2 wild ducks in place of the chicken.

In a 4–5-quart heavy pot or Dutch oven, fry the bacon over medium heat until browned, about 10 minutes. If using a fresh bird, brown in the hot fat, remove, and reserve. Add the onion, leeks, and carrots, and cook, covered, for 10 minutes. Add the cabbage, cover, and cook 10 minutes more, stirring occasionally, until the cabbage is wilted. Add the chicken, stock, wine, thyme, bay leaves, cayenne, and black pepper. Bring to a boil, reduce the heat, and simmer, covered, for 40 minutes. Add the sliced sausage, and cook, uncovered, 10 more minutes. If the sauce is too soupy, remove the chicken and vegetables with a slotted spoon, and reduce the liquid over high heat for 5 minutes or more. Don't cook it down too much, though, as you want to end up with plenty of sauce. Serve with yams baked in their skins or boiled new potatoes.

Makes 6–8 servings

· Miami black beans ·

A lively addition to southern cooking comes from the large Cuban population of southern Florida. Black beans are a Cuban staple, and they are found
in soups, main courses, and side dishes. A typical Cuban dinner just doesn't
seem complete without black beans and rice. Black bean soup, Cuban style,
is one of the most popular dishes in Miami's homes and restaurants.

1 lb. black beans
4–6 c. chicken or beef stock
1 ham hock, sawed into 3 or 4 pieces
2 pig's feet, about 2 lbs., sawed into
  3 or 4 pieces (optional)
2 lb. Chorizo (see page 209) or other
  garlicky sausage such as andouille,
  kielbasa, Portuguese chouriço, or
  linguiça
2 bay leaves
2 tsp. ground cumin
2 large onions, chopped
1 tbsp. chopped garlic
1 tbsp. annatto oil, if available, or a
  pinch of saffron and 1 tbsp. olive oil

1 small head cabbage, quartered,
  cored, and shredded, about 4 c.
¼ c. dark rum
1 c. tomatoes, peeled, seeded, and
  chopped, fresh or canned
Freshly ground pepper
Salt to taste
Malt vinegar to taste

· Garnishes ·
Lime wedges
Chopped red onion
Chopped cilantro
Tabasco

Soak the beans overnight in cold water to cover by about 4 inches. Drain
and wash well. Put them in a heavy 4–5-quart pot or Dutch oven with enough
stock to cover by 2 inches. Bring to a boil. Add the ham hock, optional pig's feet,
a ½-pound piece of the sausage, the bay leaves and cumin, and half the chopped
onions and garlic. Reduce the beans to a simmer and cook, partially covered, for
2–3 hours or until the beans are soft enough to mash against the side of the pot
with a spoon. Add more stock if needed while cooking.

Heat the annatto oil or the olive oil and saffron in a heavy skillet over
medium heat. Slice the remaining sausage into ½-inch rounds, and fry them until
lightly browned. Remove the sausage with a slotted spoon and add to the beans.
In the same fat, cook the remaining onions until they are soft but not brown, about
5 minutes. Add the rest of the garlic, and the cabbage. Sauté, stirring frequently,
until the cabbage has wilted. Add the rum and tomatoes, along with a few grindings
of pepper. Bring to a boil, and cook, stirring often, for about 3–5 minutes. Stir
this tomato/vegetable mixture into the bean pot. Cook the beans over moderate
heat for 5–10 more minutes. Taste for salt and pepper, and add malt vinegar to
taste. Remove the whole piece of sausage, the ham hocks, and pig's feet. Slice
the sausage into ½-inch pieces, bone the hocks and pig's feet, chop the meat
coarsely, and add to the soup. Pass garnishes of lime wedges, chopped red onion,
cilantro, and Tabasco. This dish is even better reheated. Makes 6–8 servings as
a main dish, 10–12 as a soup course

· smoky black-eyed peas or Hoppin' John ·

At New Year's celebrations in the South just about everybody eats black-eyed peas in one form or another. The little peas are thought to represent coins, and are supposed to bring you luck and prosperity for the whole year to come. Also called field peas or crowder peas, black-eyes are actually a member of the bean family.

This dish is usually made with a chunk of salt pork, bacon, or ham for seasoning, and is most often served as a side dish. With sausage added, it can become a substantial main dish. The sausage cut into thick rounds resembling coins adds to the wealth and "good luck" of the dish, and also provides more nutrition and flavor than the traditional salt pork or ham bone.

1 lb. dried black-eyed peas
1½ lbs. Smoked Country Sausage
  (see page 11), Smoked Country
  Sausage, Barbecue Style (see page
  14), Cajun-Style Andouille (see
  page 521), or other good-quality
  smoked sausage
¼-lb. chunk country or smoked ham,
  or a ham bone
6 c. chicken or beef stock, or water
1 tbsp. bacon fat or olive oil
1 medium onion, finely chopped
1 rib celery, finely chopped
1 tbsp. minced garlic

1–2 dried hot chile peppers or 1 tsp.
  red pepper flakes
2 bay leaves
2 sprigs fresh thyme or 1 tsp. dried
1 tbsp. chopped fresh basil or 1 tsp.
  dried
½ tsp. pickling spice
1 tsp. black pepper
Salt to taste
4 c. cooked rice
Chopped sweet red onion
Tabasco or Pickapeppa sauce
Cider or malt vinegar

Soak the dried peas overnight in water to cover by 2–3 inches. Drain and add them to a 6–8-quart pot together with a ½-pound piece of the smoked sausage, the chunk of ham or the ham bone, and the stock. Bring to a boil, then reduce to a simmer.

Heat the bacon fat or oil in a large heavy skillet, and add the onion and celery. Cover, and cook 10 minutes over medium heat until soft. Add these vegetables to the simmering peas, along with the garlic, chile peppers, herbs, and spices. Continue to cook slowly for 2–2½ hours, or until the peas are tender and the liquid begins to thicken. Slice the remaining pound of sausage into ½-inch rounds, and fry briefly before adding to the peas. Remove the whole piece of sausage and the chunk of ham, chop the meat roughly, then return to the pot. Cook another 15 minutes. Prepare rice by your favorite method so that you'll end up with 4 cups of cooked rice. Serve the black-eyes and sausage ladled over the rice in a deep bowl or dinner plate. Diners can add chopped red onion, hot sauce, or vinegar to taste. Makes 8–10 servings

This savory mix of black-eyes and rice is often served on New Year's Day with a silver coin buried deep in the pot. The lucky finder is assured of good fortune in the New Year.

· baked hominy and country sausage ·

In addition to being a substantial side dish, this casserole is excellent for breakfast, brunch, or lunch.

½ lb. country sausage, bulk or links
½ c. chopped onion
1 mild green chile (Anaheim or poblano), seeded and chopped
1-lb. can hominy, drained
1¼ c. milk
2 eggs, beaten
½ tsp. salt

½ tsp. sugar
½ tsp. black pepper
1 c. fresh bread crumbs
¼ c. chopped fresh parsley
2 c. shredded sharp Cheddar cheese
2 tbsp. chopped green onions or scallions

Brown the sausage in a large heavy skillet over medium heat. If you are using bulk sausage, break the meat up into small pieces with a fork as it cooks. Leave links whole. When browned, remove the sausage and discard all but 2 tablespoons of the fat. Add the onion and chopped chile to the pan, and cook for 7 minutes until soft.

Preheat the oven to 350° F. Mix together the hominy, milk, cooked bulk sausage (if using links, reserve them), onion, chile, eggs, and the remaining ingredients except half of the grated cheese and the green onions. Spoon the mixture into a buttered 2-quart casserole. Sprinkle the remaining cheese and green onions on top. Place the casserole in a larger pan half-filled with hot water. Bake for 1 hour. If using link sausages, bake the casserole for 30 minutes, then arrange browned links on top in a spoke pattern, and continue baking for another 30 minutes. The casserole is done when it is just firm. Serve immediately.

Makes 6–8 servings

· grits, sausage, and cheese casserole ·

The smell of this cheesy, smoky casserole baking in the oven is almost too much to bear. It's a great breakfast dish with poached or fried eggs, and guaranteed to get those hungry slugabeds up and to the table. It is also just fine for lunch with a fresh garden salad of young greens and marinated onions, or as a side dish to liven up the dinner table.

2 tbsp. unsalted butter
½ lb. Smoked Country Sausage
  (see page 11) or other smoked
  sausage, cut into ¼-inch dice
½ c. chopped onion
½ c. chopped red bell pepper
2 tsp. minced garlic
3 c. milk
½ tsp. salt

1 c. quick-cooking grits
2 tsp. Tabasco
2 eggs, beaten
½ c. half-and-half or heavy cream
1 c. finely sliced chives or green
  onions or scallions
¼ c. chopped fresh parsley
1½ c. shredded medium or sharp
  Cheddar cheese

Form any leftovers into thick patties and fry them up in a little butter — delicious for breakfast, or just about anytime.

In a medium-sized skillet, melt 1 tablespoon of the butter over medium heat. Add the sausage and brown for 3 minutes. Pour off all but 2 tablespoons of the fat. Add the onion, red bell pepper, and garlic and cook them for 5 minutes more, until the onion is translucent. Meanwhile, gradually bring the milk to a boil over medium heat in a 2–3-quart saucepan. Add the salt. Pour the grits slowly into the milk, stirring it constantly and keeping it boiling. Boil the milk and grits for another minute, stirring well, and then reduce the heat and simmer for 2–3 more minutes until the grits have thickened and are soft. Taste to make sure. Remove the cooked grits from the heat and stir in the vegetable/sausage mixture, the Tabasco, eggs, half-and-half, chives, and parsley, along with all but ¼ cup of the cheese. Preheat the oven to 350° F. Butter a 2-quart casserole with the remaining tablespoon of butter. Spoon the grits/sausage mixture into the casserole, and sprinkle with the remaining cheese. Bake in the middle of the oven for 35–45 minutes until set. When done the top will be beautifully puffed up and a light golden brown. Makes 6–8 servings for lunch, 10–12 as a side dish at breakfast or dinner

· grits soufflé variation ·

For a lighter variation of the Grits, Sausage, and Cheese Casserole, use exactly the same ingredients, but separate the eggs. After adding the vegetable/sausage mixture, egg yolks, and other ingredients to the grits, fold in the egg whites beaten to stiff peaks. Bake in a 375° F oven for about 30 minutes until puffed and browned. The texture and appearance of this dish will be more like a soufflé, more "company" than "down home."

· spoonbread with sausage ·

This moist and custardy "bread" is really more like a pudding. It makes a super side dish with roast or grilled meat, poultry, or fish.

½ lb. Country Ham and Pork Sausage
  (see page 9), crumbled or finely
  chopped
2 c. milk
1 c. half-and-half
½ tsp. salt

2 tsp. sugar
1 c. white or yellow cornmeal
2 tbsp. butter
4 eggs, separated
1 c. fresh or frozen corn kernels

Use any of our fresh or smoked southern sausage recipes here or a good commercial product, but be sure to fry the sausage meat first to get rid of some of the fat.

Fry the crumbled or chopped sausage in a heavy skillet until the fat is rendered and the meat is thoroughly cooked, about 5–7 minutes. Remove the meat and set aside. Save a tablespoon of the grease. Preheat the oven to 350° F. Heat the milk, half-and-half, salt, and sugar in a heavy 3–4-quart saucepan over medium heat. When small bubbles form around the edge, slowly pour in the cornmeal, stirring constantly. Continue to stir as the mixture cooks and thickens. After about 5 minutes, when the cornmeal is smooth and creamy in texture, remove the pot from the heat and stir in the butter and the reserved tablespoon of sausage grease until they are completely absorbed. Beat the egg yolks briefly, until they are a light lemon color. Gradually add them to the cornmeal mixture, beating vigorously until they are completely incorporated. Stir in the corn and the browned sausage meat.

Beat the egg whites until they form stiff but not dry peaks. Mix a large spoonful of the whites with the cornmeal mixture to loosen it. Then, using a rubber or wooden spatula, gently and thoroughly fold in the remaining egg whites.

Butter a 2-quart casserole or soufflé dish thoroughly. Add the spoonbread mixture, smoothing the top with a spatula. Bake for 1 hour in the middle of the oven until puffy and golden brown. Serve directly from the baking dish.
Makes 6–8 servings

· smoked sausage and smothered greens ·

Southern cooks really know how to cook greens, and everybody loves to eat them, along with the pot likker, the savory juices in the pot. The secret is cooking the greens with smoked meat such as country bacon, ham, or tasso. Or, as we do here, with smoked sausage.

4 bunches of greens in whatever mix
   you fancy (about 3–4 lbs. total)
1 onion, finely chopped
2 cloves garlic, minced
2 tbsp. bacon fat or olive oil
½ lb. Smoked Country Sausage
   (see page 11) or other smoked
   sausage, cut into ½-inch dice

2 c. water
1 tbsp. sugar
¼ c. red wine or cider vinegar
1 dried red pepper or ½ tsp. red
   pepper flakes
½ tsp. salt
Tabasco
Salt and pepper to taste

    Wash the greens thoroughly, removing and discarding any tough stems. Chop the greens coarsely, dry, and set aside. In a large pot or Dutch oven, sauté the onion and garlic in the bacon fat or olive oil over medium heat until the onion is transparent, about 5 minutes. Add the smoked sausage, and cook it for 3–5 minutes, stirring while lightly browning the meat. Add the water, sugar, vinegar, and dried red pepper. Turn the heat to high and boil for 3 minutes. Add the chopped greens and salt, cover, and reduce to a simmer. Cook until the greens are just tender, 40–45 minutes. Uncover and boil off some of the liquid if the greens are too soupy. Don't reduce the liquid in the pot too much since you want plenty of tasty pot likker for you and your guests to dip cornbread into. Taste for Tabasco, salt, and pepper. Makes 4–6 servings

We like to use a mixture of bitter greens like turnip, collard, or mustard, and milder ones like chard, spinach, or Chinese bok choy. Experiment with what's available in your garden or local markets.

· stewed okra and country sausage ·

Okra, another contribution of black cooks to southern cuisine, was brought over from Africa by slaves and quickly incorporated into plantation cooking. Used as a thickener and seasoning in gumbos and stews, okra is also delicious as a vegetable or side dish, especially when coupled with Spicy Fresh Country Sausage.

½ lb. Spicy Fresh Country Sausage (see page 7), Kentucky-Style Country Sausage (see page 9), or other spicy fresh bulk sausage
2 c. chopped onions
1 lb. okra, stems removed, sliced in ½-inch rounds
1 tsp. chopped garlic
4 ripe tomatoes, peeled, seeded, and chopped
1 c. chopped red and/or green bell pepper
½ tsp. black pepper
Pinch each sugar and dried thyme
½ c. chicken stock or water
Salt to taste
Tabasco (optional)

Fry the sausage over medium heat in a heavy 12-inch skillet or Dutch oven until browned, about 10 minutes, breaking the meat up with a fork as it cooks. Remove and reserve the sausage meat. Pour off all but about ¼ cup of the fat, and add the onions. Stirring and shaking the pan, cook for about 10 minutes over medium heat until the onions are soft. Add the okra and cook it for 10 minutes, stirring occasionally. Add the garlic, tomatoes, chopped pepper, black pepper, sugar, thyme, and stock. Cover and continue to cook for 10 minutes more, stirring once or twice. Add the reserved sausage, cover, and cook for 5 more minutes to heat the sausage through. Season to taste with salt and Tabasco.
Makes 4–6 servings as a side dish

Use either fresh or smoked country-style sausage in this dish.

· swiss chard with smoked country sausage, garlic, and cheese ·

Swiss chard is a mainstay in southern kitchen gardens, and is one of the many delicious and nourishing greens so often found on southern dinner tables.

· **Buttermilk cheese sauce** ·
2 tbsp. butter
3 tbsp. flour
1 c. half-and-half
1 c. buttermilk
Pinch freshly grated nutmeg
1½ c. grated Swiss cheese
Few drops Tabasco
Salt and pepper to taste

2 bunches Swiss chard (2–3 lbs.),
   stems and leaves separated
¼ lb. Smoked Country Sausage
   (see page 11) or other smoked
   sausage, diced
4 tbsp. minced garlic
½ c. grated Swiss cheese

To make the Buttermilk Cheese Sauce, melt the butter over medium heat in a heavy 1½-quart saucepan. Whisk in the flour, reduce the heat to low, cook slowly, stirring continuously, for 2–3 minutes. Remove the pot from the heat, and stir in the half-and-half. Continue to stir until you form a thick sauce. Whisk in the buttermilk. Set the pot back over medium heat, and continue to whisk until the sauce comes to a boil. Reduce to a simmer, and cook for 2–3 minutes more. Add the nutmeg, 1½ cups cheese, and Tabasco.

This recipe combines the fresh, slightly bitter taste of chard with a rich buttermilk cheese sauce and tangy smoked sausage.

Stir until the cheese has completely melted, and the sauce is smooth. Season with salt, pepper, and more Tabasco, if desired. You will have 2–3 cups of sauce.

Slice the chard stems into ¼-inch pieces and roughly chop the leaves. Blanch the chard stems in a large pot of boiling salted water for 4 minutes. Add the leaves and continue cooking for 5 more minutes, or until the leaves and stems are tender. Drain and cool under cold running water. Preheat the oven to 400° F. Fry the sausage in a small heavy skillet over medium heat until it is crisp. Add the garlic and cook for 1 minute more.

In a 2-quart casserole mix the cheese sauce with the sausage and chard. Sprinkle ½ cup cheese over the top and bake the casserole in the middle of the oven for 20 minutes, or until the cheese is melted and the sauce is bubbly.
Makes 4–6 servings

LOUISIANA
· Cajun & Creole ·

Skewered andouille and shrimp with Creole mustard butter

Cajun meat pies

Crawfish and smoked sausage beignets

Andouille and liver pâté

Lentil and andouille salad

Cajun-style pea soup

Too-easy-to-believe spicy lentil soup

BREAKFAST DISHES

Baked eggs, Creole style

Hot boudin patties with poached eggs and tasso béarnaise

Andouille hash

Quick and easy breakfasts

MAIN DISHES

Shrimp, sausage, and potato Creole

Artichoke stuffed with shrimp and andouille

Red bell pepper stuffed with seafood and hot boudin

Chicken and andouille gumbo

Chicken Pontalba

Tasso béarnaise sauce

Chicken stuffed under the skin with andouille, ricotta, and spinach

Turkey, smoked sausage, and tasso jambalaya

Stuffed ponce

Pork chops stuffed with hot boudin

Veal chop and andouille étouffée

Hot sausage po' boy

Cajun carbonara

Chaurice baked with mashed potatoes

White beans with pickled pork and pickled-pork sausages

Ya ca mein

Gumbo z'herbes

SIDE DISHES

Smothered cabbage with andouille and tomato

Oyster and andouille stuffed eggplant

Mushroom, tasso, and chaurice dirty rice

When Pierre Le Moyne, Sieur d'Iberville, nosed his small boat into the bank of the Mississippi a few miles in from the Gulf of Mexico on a muggy afternoon in 1699, he didn't know he was about to make culinary history. It was March 3, Shrove Tuesday, and Iberville decided it was time for a little celebration before the rigors of Lent set in. He named the bayou Mardi Gras, in honor of the day, and told the cooks to make a special meal.

Unfortunately, history hasn't given us the menu of this first Mardi Gras celebration in Louisiana. But we can be pretty sure that the banquet included some local game or fish, seasoned most likely with wild greens and local herbs, along with some carefully hoarded spices brought over from France. We also expect, this being a French expedition after all, that the dinner was prepared with care and discrimination, eaten with gusto, and thoroughly discussed afterwards by the diners. Wines were drunk, and the toasts and songs and laughter went on long into the night.

Thus begins the long adventure of Louisiana cooking. In 1718 New Orleans was founded by Iberville's brother, Jean-Baptiste Le Moyne, Sieur de Bienville, in a bend of the river about 100 miles up from the gulf. As the years passed and the province of Louisiana grew in importance and prosperity, the city became the center of a great cuisine, and the feasting and revelry of Mardi Gras, or Fat Tuesday, its favorite celebration.

Louisiana cooking is rooted in French techniques, enriched by native ingredients and cooking methods, and nurtured by cooks from various lands and cultures. Much of the excitement of the cuisine comes from this energetic amalgam of French cuisine with native Indian, African, Spanish, and other European traditions and ingredients.

The French influence is primal, and persists through all the vicissitudes of colonial rule in New Orleans. Louisiana was French for more than forty years from its founding in 1718, then a Spanish colony for forty more, then briefly French again just before being sold, along with the "lands drained by the Mississippi and its tributaries" to the United States in 1803. France gave New Orleans its language and culture, its love of food, a fervor for culinary experiment, and a respect for tradition.

The French passion for food has permeated New Orleans from the beginning. In fact, just four years after the city was founded, Governor Bienville faced a rebellion of young wives who marched on his headquarters, beating on their black iron skillets with spoons to protest their dreary diet of cornmeal mush, day after day. They demanded some culinary action, a way to break the monotony and add spice to their cuisine and to their lives. The story has it that Madame Langlois,

the governor's housekeeper, instructed the women in tricks she'd learned from the Indians, using fish and game from the surrounding canebrakes and swamps, hominy and peppers, the ground leaves of the sassafras tree, and other native herbs.

As elsewhere in our burgeoning country, the colonists here borrowed heavily from the local tribes—the Houmas and Opelousas, Choctaw and Natchez—using plants grown in their gardens like corn, squash, and beans, along with native game, fish, and herbs. Choctaw women were long a colorful part of the French Market, selling filé powder (ground sassafras), bundles of bay leaves, and other herbs. The abundant game and seafood that is still featured in so many Louisiana gumbos and stews along with filé, bay leaves, and other local ingredients tie these dishes to the native Indian tradition.

Black cooks have been a strong influence in Louisiana cookery ever since the introduction of African slaves. Black women cooks prepared the food in plantations along the river and in the great houses of Le Vieux Carré and along the Esplanade, adapting traditional European recipes and often using ingredients brought over from Africa like eggplants, yams, peanuts, sesame, and okra. In fact, the word for the ubiquitous stew of the region, gumbo, derives from the West African word for okra, "ngombo." Later, with the rise of the great restaurants of New Orleans and the sumptuous floating dining rooms of the riverboats, much of the actual cooking was done by black men. The black tradition continues in some of New Orleans' finest restaurants—Dooky Chase and the Hotel Ponchartrain are prime examples—and black cooks are found "on the line" in professional kitchens throughout Louisiana.

With the coming of the Spanish in the 1760s, Creole food acquired even more heat and liveliness. The Spaniards brought the pepper from Mexico in its varied forms from mildly spicy to incandescent, and made the tomato a key part of the repertoire of Louisiana cooks. Some traditional dishes (jambalaya is a good example) are Spanish in origin, with grace notes added by local cooks. Jambalaya is called "a Spanish Creole dish" by Celestine Eustis in her book, *Cooking in Old Creole Days* (1903), and the spicy mix of ham (French *jambon,* Spanish *jamón*), seafood, tomatoes, peppers, and rice most likely has its roots in *arroz con pollo* and *paella.* Other popular vegetables introduced from Mexico by Spanish cooks include the mirliton or chayote squash and the avocado.

During this same period, exiles began to drift into Louisiana as a result of the wars and revolutions that were transforming Europe and the New World. In the 1750s and in the years following, French-speaking farmers and fishermen displaced from Acadia (later Nova Scotia) by the English conquest of Quebec drifted up the bayous and rivers west of New Orleans and created a rich and vibrant culture in the swamps and on the prairies. These Acadians, or Cajuns, as they came to be called, incorporated local ingredients into their own Norman and Breton traditions and came up with an earthy, vibrant style of cooking that makes the heart—and the taste buds—sing. Using hot peppers and local spices, the Cajuns cooked just about anything that walked, flew, swam, or crawled in the region, and added energy and a peasant richness to the elegant Creole cuisine of New Orleans. Paul Prudhomme, the foremost proponent of the Cajun style, sums it up nicely in Betty Fussell's fine book *I Hear America Cooking* (Viking Press, 1986): "Cajun and Creole are dialects of the same swamp language, one in country style and the other in city style." Later, French-speaking émigrés from the French Revolution and Toussaint L'Ouverture's slave revolt in Haiti added even more elegance and Gallic spice to Louisiana life and food.

Immigrants from other European countries found their way to New Orleans in the nineteenth century, by now a thriving port for midwestern America and its products. The Irish settled along Irish Channel, Germans occupied the Côte des Allemands upriver from the city, and Italians, Chinese, Greeks, and East European Jews all added to Louisiana's ethnic and culinary richness. Some of New Orleans' most popular dishes, such as muffaletta, po' boys and ya ca mein, have their origins in the bars and restaurants of neighborhoods like the Third District and the Irish Channel.

Sausages and preserved meats are an integral part of Louisiana cookery, and contribute character and flavor to many traditional dishes from gumbo and jambalaya to chicken étouffée and red beans and rice. Sausage is used as a main ingredient, as a flavoring, and as a spice to add background and color. Cajun and Creole cooks, perhaps more than any others in America, use local sausages to define their style of cooking and to add an extra dimension of flavor. From the beginning the spice and tang of sausages have provided an excitement and liveliness to Louisiana cuisine that helped to make this one of the greatest regions in American cooking.

The Picayune's *Creole Cook Book* (1901) speaks of the importance of sausages in Creole cuisine: "From the old Creole negresses who go about the streets in the early morning crying out, 'Belles Saucisses!' 'Belle Chaurice!' to the

'Boudins' and 'Saucissons' so temptingly prepared by the Creole butchers in the French market, the Creole sausage enters largely into domestic cookery."

Many of the region's most popular sausages bear names of traditional French sausages, such as boudin noir and boudin blanc, andouille, and saucisse; others have Spanish roots, such as chaurice, or plain English names like hot or smoked sausage. But all have a distinctly Louisiana flavor, and many have little resemblance to the originals. Andouille in France, and in earlier times in New Orleans, contained chopped-up chitterlings, or intestines, stuffed into casings. The modern version is a spicy, chunky pork sausage, and is heavily smoked. Chaurice is hot and spicy, and in this way similar to Mexican or Spanish chorizo, but the Louisiana sausage is a unique and fiery mix of onions, herbs, and ground pork. Cajun boudin has some vague relation to the delicate French boudin blanc, but its heat level would make the average Parisian's eyes bulge out with astonishment and send him into terminal hot pepper shock.

Sausages are made all over Louisiana, but the Cajuns around Lafayette and New Iberia are the acknowledged masters of andouille and boudin. Signs advertising "Hot Boudin, Cold Beer, and Fais Do-Do This Sunday" testify to the Cajun love of hot food, cold brew, and letting the good times roll with dancing and zydeco music. Spicy smoked pork shoulder, tasso, is another Cajun specialty and is used to "hot up" many favorite dishes like jambalaya and red beans and rice.

The German community has been a strong influence in sausage making throughout the region, and some of the finest producers of all types of sausage are of German origin. Immigrant German butchers and sausage makers taught many Cajun cooks their techniques and recipes, and influenced the development of today's most popular sausages. In fact, Laplace, at the center of the Côte des Allemands, calls itself the andouille capital of the world and holds an andouille festival each fall. Restaurants like Kolb's in New Orleans offer a great variety of traditional Creole sausages, along with the typical German varieties.

Sausages and smoked meats are an integral part of Cajun and Creole cuisine. Whether you make them yourself or purchase Louisiana-style sausages from specialty shops or by mail order, you'll find that they add the extra tang that makes a gumbo or étouffée not just a meal, but a memorable gustatory experience.

·Fais Do-Do: let the good times roll with a Cajun feast and "Ma Jolie Blonde"·

Down in Cajun country, folks get together for food, music, and good times at the Fais Do-Do on the weekends. Fais Do-Do means something like "Rock-a-bye Baby," and the hope is that the little ones are sound asleep in their cradles while the parents whoop it up with the neighbors. A Fais Do-Do can vary from a few friends playing fiddles and eating boudin on the back porch, to a full-scale, county-wide brouhaha that makes the bayous rock for miles. They all have a few things in common, though: plenty of good food, music, and dancing, and a sufficiency of beverages, starting with Dixie beer, and including wine, soda pop, and what you will.

You can throw your own Fais Do-Do, and you don't especially need a bayou to do it. You can come pretty close with plenty of good Cajun food, some cold beer and wine, and a tape of Michel Doucet and his band Beausoleil singing "Donnez-moi Pauline" or Ambrose Thibodeaux belting out "Ma Jolie Blonde" on the Cajun accordion.

Here's a sample menu, but you can use your own imagination. Just make sure the food is hearty and hot, the beer is cold, and the music loud enough to wake the alligators three bayous down.

FAIS DO-DO
Hot Boudin

Skewered Andouille and Shrimp with Creole Mustard Butter

Cajun Meat Pies

Chicken and Andouille Gumbo

Cabbage Braised with Tasso and Tomatoes

Dixie Beer or Anchor Steam Beer

Sauvignon Blanc and Zinfandel

Barq's Root Beer or Dr Pepper

Music by Michel Doucet dit Beausoleil, Ambrose Thibodeaux, Clifton Chenier, Dewey Balfa, Queen Ida's Bon Temps Roulé Zydeco Band, etc. etc.

· hot boudin and Dixie beer ·

The roads outside of Breaux Bridge, Louisiana, run along levees high above the flat countryside, skirting the bayous and swamps of Cajun country. Each little town has its own Mom-and-Pop grocery store, and just about every one has a handlettered sign announcing "Hot Boudin" in the front window. That's what we're here for.

The smell's the first thing you notice when you walk into one of these country stores: pork and onions and pepper from the quintessential Cajun snack—boudin. The sausage is usually right on the counter by the cash register, keeping hot in a Crockpot or baby-bottle warmer. Boudin is not twisted into links in Cajun country. You just show the man how much sausage you want, and he cuts a length from the coil and wraps it in wax paper. The rest is up to you.

When you walk out into the parking lot, the smell of the boudin becomes well-nigh irresistible. Most people can't wait to get home, or even into the car, before they start in eating. Standing in the hot sun with your Dixie beer or Barq's Root Beer in your left hand, you grab one end of the hot boudin in

HOT LINKS & COUNTRY FLAVORS

your right hand, put the other end in your mouth and squeeze. Suddenly you know why it's called *hot* boudin. For a second you're not sure of survival as the incandescent mixture gushes into your mouth. Then as the sweat pops out on your forehead and the flavors begin to sing, you experience the bliss that only Cajun boudin can give.

A long draft of ice-cold Dixie beer prepares the palate for another onslaught, and you squeeze and squeeze again until the casing's limp and empty. Then you toss the beer can, wax paper, and boudin casing in an old oil drum full of beer cans, wax paper, and boudin casings, and head for the next town. And the next boudin.

On and on through a long, hot, and spicy day until at sunset we're standing in yet another parking lot, waiting for the roadhouse that serves great alligator gumbo to open up, snacking on one more boudin, just for comparison of course, hearing the accordions and fiddles tuning up inside, licking hot grease from tired lips.

· Cajun-style andouille ·

This spicy, heavily smoked sausage is a Louisiana favorite, and one of the most versatile and full-flavored sausages in this book. There are so many uses for andouille that we could have written a whole cookbook based on this wonderful sausage alone. In France, andouille, and its close relative andouillette, are made from intestines wrapped in a casing. The sausage was originally made this way in Louisiana (it was called chitterling sausage in The Picayune's Creole Cook Book, published in New Orleans in 1901), but these days andouille is made from large chunks of highly seasoned lean pork, stuffed into sausage casings and then cold smoked. It is traditionally used to flavor gumbo and jambalaya, but inventive cooks have found many other uses for its tangy, smoky flavors.

2 tbsp. minced garlic

2 tbsp. kosher salt

1 tbsp. freshly ground black pepper

1 tsp. red pepper flakes

2 tsp. cayenne

3 tbsp. paprika

¼ tsp. ground mace

½ tsp. dried thyme

2 tbsp. sugar

1 tsp. curing salts (see page 343) (optional)

5 lbs. pork butt, fat and lean separated, cut into 2-inch chunks

½ c. cold water

Wide hog casings

For details on making sausage, see page 332.

Mix the garlic, salt, spices, and thyme along with the sugar and optional curing salts in a small bowl. Separate the meat and fat into 2 bowls, and rub each thoroughly with the spice mixture. Cover and refrigerate overnight. Grind the fat in a meat grinder fitted with a ¼-inch plate. Grind the lean meat using a ⅜-inch plate. Mix the meat and fat together in a large bowl, add the cold water, and knead until the water is absorbed and the spices well blended. Stuff the mixture into wide hog casings. If you are hot smoking the sausages, dry for 2 hours in a cool place and smoke-cook in a covered barbecue. If you prefer cold smoking, dry the andouille in front of a fan in a cool place overnight, and cold smoke for at least 12 hours, following the directions in "Smoking Sausages" on page 337. Cold-smoked andouille should be cooked before eating. Hot-smoked sausage is ready to eat. Makes 5 pounds

Andouille is best cold smoked for at least 12 hours to give it a rich smoky flavor; you'll need to add curing salts if you cold smoke it. If you prefer to leave curing salts out, hot smoking will still give enough of the smoky taste that makes andouille so popular.

· hot boudin ·

Every culture has a favorite snack food, whether it's peanut butter and jelly or satay, tacos or a bowl of noodles. In the Cajun country of southwest Louisiana the universal snack seems to be hot boudin. Everywhere you go, on country back roads or the main streets of towns like Lafayette, Opelousas, or Breaux Bridge, you see signs advertising this spicy sausage.

Although this spicy mixture of rice, cooked pork, and onions is stuffed into a casing, the casing itself is rarely eaten. The boudin's casing gets a bit tough from steaming, and its stuffing is so soft and juicy that everything seems to gush out when you bite down. The best thing to do is to abandon any hope of elegant dining, and hold the boudin in one hand, put one end into your mouth, and squeeze the savory mixture out of the casing into your mouth as you go along.

The smell of boudin steaming evokes the sounds of Cajun fiddlers and accordion players warming up for their Saturday morning jams in small towns such as Eunice or Opelousas. There is always a greasy sack or two of boudin ripped open and spread on newspaper to munch on during the festivities. Boudin is quite perishable and should be refrigerated immediately after being made. If not used in 2–3 days, it can be frozen for up to 2 months.

4–5 c. water
3½ tsp. kosher salt
3 lbs. pork butt, cut into 2-inch
   chunks (make sure there is some fat
   attached to the meat)
4 bay leaves
2 whole chile peppers
2 tsp. freshly ground black pepper
Pinch dried thyme
1 medium onion, peeled and
   quartered
1 c. long-grain rice
2 tsp. minced garlic

1 tsp. ground sage
1 tsp. dried thyme
2 tsp. red pepper flakes
2 tsp. cayenne
⅛ tsp. allspice
Pinch ground mace
½ c. finely chopped fresh parsley
   (flat-leaf variety preferred)
2½ tsp. salt
¾ c. finely chopped green onions or
   scallions
Medium hog casings (optional)

For details on making sausage, see page 332.

Put the water and 1 teaspoon of salt in a saucepan large enough to hold the pork along with any bones or scraps. Bring the liquid to a boil and add the pork, bay leaves, chile peppers, 1 teaspoon of black pepper, and pinch of thyme. Bring the pot back to the boil, reduce the heat, and simmer, covered, over low heat for 45 minutes to an hour, or until the pork is tender. Add the onion and cook for 5–7 additional minutes, until tender. Remove the meat and onions to a platter to cool. Add the rice to 1½ cups of the pork stock in the pot, cover, and cook it over low heat until tender, about 20 minutes.

In a meat grinder fitted with a ¼-inch plate, grind the cooked pork and onions into a large mixing bowl. Add the garlic, sage, thyme, red pepper flakes, cayenne, allspice, mace, parsley, the remaining teaspoon of black pepper, and the remaining 2½ teaspoons of salt, along with the chopped green onions and the cooked rice. Using a wooden spoon, stir the mixture until it is well blended. Taste and correct the salt or other seasonings. Cool the mixture in the refrigerator for 30 minutes, and then stuff it into medium hog casings or leave it in bulk for further use. It's not necessary to tie boudin into links — just coil it up as you go along.

Boudin is best heated by steaming. Coil the boudin in a colander or on a plate and place it in a large pot above an inch or so of water. Cover the pot and steam over moderate heat for 15 minutes. Makes about 4 pounds

Steaming boudin in the casing is the traditional way to heat up the sausage, but we like to form the meat into thin patties and fry it for breakfast or a quick and spicy lunch. It helps to add an egg or two to the mixture to bind it before frying (see Hot Boudin Patties with Poached Eggs and Tasso Bérnaise, page 71). This is as good as any corned-beef or roast-beef hash you've ever tasted.

· Cajun boudin noir (spicy blood sausage) ·

When you live close to the land, killing a pig is an excuse for neighbors to gather and have a good time—with lots of hearty food, music, and talk. The *boucherie* or pig-killing is one of the big events in the late fall all through the Cajun country of southwest Louisiana. As you'd expect, pig meat and sausage of every kind provide lots of good eating at these lively gatherings.

These days in Louisiana, if you want to taste boudin noir you have to try it at a *boucherie* or find a Cajun home cook to make some for you. It's illegal to make commercial blood sausage in the state, most probably because it's difficult to collect pig's blood under sanitary conditions. But a lot gets made and eaten at festivals and family gatherings, and it sure tastes good. If you know a friendly farmer or pork butcher, getting the blood isn't too difficult. We used beef blood, a good substitute, available in most states from ethnic butchers. You can make the sausage with just blood, or add a little ground pork for the meatier texture that we prefer.

1½ lbs. pork butt
½ lb. pork back fat
2 onions, finely chopped
2 tbsp. lard, vegetable oil, or
   rendered pork fat
1½ c. cooked rice
2½ c. hog or beef blood
1 c. chopped fresh parsley
5 tsp. salt
1 tsp. ground allspice

1 tsp. ground mace
3 tbsp. freshly ground black pepper
½ tsp. ground bay leaves (use
   blender or spice mill)
1 tbsp. fresh marjoram or 1 tsp. dried
1 tsp. dried thyme
2 tsp. cayenne
1 tsp. red pepper flakes
3 cloves garlic, minced
Medium hog casings

For details on making sausage, see page 332.

Grind the meat and fat through a ¼-inch plate. Sauté the onions in the lard, oil or fat in a heavy skillet over medium heat until they are transparent. Mix together the ground pork and cooked rice with the blood, parsley, salt, spices, herbs, and garlic. Add the cooked onions and stir to combine the mixture evenly. Tie off the end of a 10–12-foot length of medium hog casing and stuff with the mixture. It's best to work over a large pan or plastic dishwashing tub, as things can get a bit messy. Tie into 4–5-inch links.

Bring a large pot of water to just below a simmer. Add the sausages. Keep the heat very low, with the water at about 180° F, so the sausages don't burst. Poach the sausages for 30–40 minutes, until you can prick the sausages and no blood comes out, and the internal temperature reads 150° F. You can store the sausages in the refrigerator for 2 or 3 days, loosely wrapped, or freeze them for up to 2 months. To serve, sauté them in butter or oil over a low heat.

Makes about 4 pounds

· chaurice ·

The name most likely derives from *chorizo*, a Spanish and Mexican pork sausage, and chaurice is part of Louisiana's Latin heritage. It is also one of the hottest sausages in a cuisine known for its fiery flavors. Our recipe is a traditional Louisiana version, but just about every local butcher shop has its own variations. Most chaurice is pure pork, but sometimes beef is included. It is usually fresh, but some sausage makers give it a light smoke.

Most recipes contain onions and parsley, along with chile powder, cayenne, garlic, and aromatic herbs and spices. We like to blanch the onions in boiling water for a minute or so to take away their raw, sometimes metallic taste. Use only fresh parsley, preferably the flat-leaf Italian variety. Forget about dried parsley—it's like using dried grass clippings.

In Louisiana, chaurice is sometimes fried for breakfast, but it takes an iron stomach to eat such hot food first thing in the morning. It's great used to make a Hot Sausage Po' Boy (see recipe page 85). Because the onions give chaurice such a savory flavor, it goes well with lentils, cabbage, and potatoes. At Aidells Sausage we make a smoked chaurice, which is our favorite sausage with sauerkraut.

Chaurice is often just called "Hot Sausage" in Louisiana, but don't get it confused with the "Louisiana Hot Sausage" found in other parts of the country that is generally a poor-quality emulsified German-style pork sausage with a predominant flavor of cayenne. It's not very good, never found in New Orleans, and a poor substitute for chaurice.

1 medium onion, coarsely chopped	2 tsp. red pepper flakes
2¼ lbs. pork butt	1 tsp. freshly ground black pepper
¾ lb. pork back fat	½ tsp. ground bay leaf (use blender or
4 tsp. kosher salt	spice mill)
1 tsp. sugar	½ tsp. ground allspice
2 tsp. minced garlic	1½ tsp. whole thyme
3 tbsp. pure New Mexico chile	½ c. finely chopped fresh parsley
powder	(flat-leaf variety preferred)
2 tsp. cayenne	Medium hog casings

For details on making sausage, see page 332.

Bring 2 quarts of water to a boil and blanch the chopped onion for 2 minutes. Strain and cool under running water. Combine the meat, fat, salt, sugar, garlic, spices, thyme, and onions in a large bowl. Marinate the mixture in the refrigerator for at least 30 minutes or up to 4 hours. Grind everything through a ¼-inch plate. Add the parsley and knead well to mix the meat and flavorings thoroughly. Stuff into medium hog casings and tie into 5-inch links. If you wish, you can hot smoke the Chaurice using the method discussed under "Smoking Sausages" (page 338). Makes a scant 4 pounds

· Louisiana-style smoked sausage ·

This spicy smoked sausage is a real favorite all over Louisiana, from the bars, cafés, and restaurants of New Orleans to the home kitchens, roadhouses, and diners of Cajun country.

1½ lbs. pork butt
1 lb. beef chuck
½ lb. pork back fat
1 tbsp. kosher salt
2 tsp. finely chopped garlic
2 tsp. red pepper flakes
1 tbsp. coarsely ground black pepper
¼ tsp. ground sage
¼ tsp. dried thyme

¼ tsp. dried savory
1 tsp. cayenne
Pinch ground allspice and cloves
2 tsp. sugar
1½ tsp. curing salts (optional) (see page 343)
½ c. ice water
Medium hog casings

For details on making sausage, see page 332.

In a food processor or a meat grinder fitted with a ⅜-inch plate, grind the meats and fat. Mix with the salt, garlic, spices, herbs, sugar, curing salts, and ice water. Blend well with your hands, kneading and squeezing as you mix. Stuff the mixture into the casings and twist into 6-inch links. Dry overnight at room temperature. Cold smoke the sausages (see smoking instructions, page 338). These sausages must be cooked before eating. They will keep 3–4 days in the refrigerator or up to 2 months frozen. If you wish to leave out the curing salts, omit air-drying overnight and hot smoke the sausages. Makes 3 pounds

Use this sausage in any recipe that calls for andouille or country-style smoked sausage or in any dish you want to liven up with the smoky tang and hearty flavors of the sausage.

· tasso and pickled pork ·

Both of these versions of preserved pork involve curing chunks of pork shoulder in brine. Pickled pork is ready for use after it is fully cured. It is similar to the French *petit salé*, and, like the French product, pickled pork is usually boiled as a flavoring with legumes or other vegetables.

Tasso takes pickled pork a step further and is heavily seasoned and smoked. It is used as a flavoring agent in many Cajun dishes, and adds zest and spice to jambalaya and gumbo. Along with these Louisiana favorites, it also is delicious in any dish where you might use bacon, ham, prosciutto, pancetta, or salt pork for flavor.

While neither tasso nor pickled pork is, strictly speaking, sausage, pickled pork meat is often made into a tasty sausage in New Orleans and the surrounding countryside (see recipe for Pickled-Pork Sausage, opposite page). Tasso is paired with sausages for flavoring in many gumbos and stews. Both preserved meats are an integral part of the spicy cuisines of southern Louisiana, and provide much of the flavor in its traditional dishes.

· Pickled pork ·

2 boneless pork butts (10–12 lbs. total)
18 oz. kosher salt (2 cups)
8 oz. sugar (1 cup)
4 qts. water
4 oz. (½ cup) curing salts (see page 343)
1 tsp. red pepper flakes (optional)

Cut each pork butt into 5 or 6 large chunks of approximately equal size. In a 2-gallon or larger stainless steel, plastic, crockery, or glass container, dissolve the salt and sugar in water, stirring continuously until completely dissolved. Add the curing salts (see page 343), and stir until dissolved. Submerge the meat completely in this brine by placing a heavy plate or weight on top. Refrigerate the meat in the brine for 2 days. To see if the pork is completely cured, cut a chunk in half. The pork should be uniformly pink throughout. If it is not, leave the meat in the refrigerator another day. Repeat the test. Once the pork is completely pickled, it can be used directly, or serve as a base for Pickled-Pork Sausage or tasso.

Pickled pork is most often found in the famous Louisiana Monday night dinner, Red Beans and Rice.

To store pickled pork, wash the cured meat under cold running water, drain, and store it in a covered container for up to 1 week. For longer storage, pickled pork can also be frozen for up to 2 months. Makes 10–12 pounds

· Tasso ·

To season 10–12 lbs. of drained pickled pork:
½ c. Hungarian paprika
½ c. pure ground New Mexico chiles
¼ c. freshly ground black pepper
¼ c. cayenne
¼ c. red pepper flakes
1 tsp. ground sage
1 tsp. dried thyme
¼ c. minced garlic

While the pickled pork is draining, mix all the herbs and spices together in a large bowl. Roll each chunk of pickled pork in the spice mixture. Shake off the excess. Using meat hooks or string, suspend the meat in a cool place, and dry it overnight with a fan. The surface should be dry to the touch. Set up a smoker for cold smoking (see page 340). Smoke the tasso at no greater than 120° F for 12 to 24 hours, stirring and adding sawdust if needed. Remove the meat from the smoke when it's done, and cool it to room temperature. Loosely wrapped and refrigerated, tasso will keep 2 weeks. It can also be frozen for up to 2 months. Remember, the tasso has not been cooked, so do not eat it as is. It must be cooked thoroughly before eating. Makes 9–11 pounds

Tasso is made by rubbing brine-cured pickled pork with a blend of herbs and spices, and then air-drying and cold smoking it (see page 340) using an aromatic wood such as hickory, pecan, or apple.

· pickled-pork sausage ·

This spicy sausage uses pickled pork in place of fresh pork, and is great in bean dishes like our White Beans with Pickled Pork and Pickled-Pork Sausages (see page 59), or anywhere you want a tangy flavor.

2½–3 lbs. Pickled Pork (see recipe page 58)
1 tbsp. coarsely ground black pepper
¼ tsp. cayenne
1 tsp. red pepper flakes
¼ tsp. ground sage

¼ tsp. dried thyme
Pinch ground allspice
2 tsp. minced garlic
¾ lb. fresh pork back fat
¼ c. cold water
Large hog casings

For details on making sausage, see page 332.

Wash the pickled pork under cold running water and drain well. In a small bowl, mix together all the spices, herbs, and garlic. Cut the pickled pork and fat into strips small enough to go through the meat grinder. Toss the strips with the spice mixture. Grind the meat through a ⅜-inch plate. Add the water and knead the meat mixture thoroughly. Stuff it into large hog casings and tie into 8–10-inch links. Suspend the sausages on a rack over a bowl in a cool place, and dry overnight in front of a fan. The sausages should be dry to the touch.

Set up a smoker for cold smoking (see instructions page 340). Smoke the sausages overnight at no greater than 120° F, stirring and adding sawdust as needed. Remove from the smoke and cool to room temperature. They will keep, loosely wrapped, in the refrigerator for 2 weeks, up to 2 months in the freezer. The sausages must be thoroughly cooked before eating. Makes 3 pounds

· crawfish boudin ·

Louisiana is crawfish country, and the name of the succulent freshwater crustacean is pronounced just like that in the bayous, not crayfish or crawdad. You might also hear it called yabbie, mudbug, or creekcrab, but whatever you call it, crawfish is big business around Lafayette or Breaux Bridge. As you drive through the countryside you can see the ponds and small processing plants that supply this thriving trade. Most crawfish are farmed these days, but the creeks and bayous still supply many a crawfish boil or étouffée.

Breaux Bridge, 120 miles southwest of New Orleans, proclaims itself the Crawfish Capital of the Universe. The town hosts a raucous Crawfish Festival each spring where thousands of hungry Cajuns get together to eat boiled mudbugs, drink lots of Dixie beer, and sample the delicious crawfish boudin made by local producers.

Crawfish boudin is a relatively recent invention of creative Cajun cooks, and is one of the most convenient and delicious ways to sample this wonderful shellfish. In Louisiana, peeled crawfish tails can be purchased in 1-pound bags along with the orange crawfish fat. This fat is important to Cajun cooks, as it adds flavor and richness. A dedicated Cajun chef will do just about anything to procure this unctuous delight.

½ red or yellow bell pepper, fire-roasted, peeled, and chopped
4 tbsp. butter
1 c. chopped onion
1 tsp. chopped shallot
1 clove garlic, minced
1 lb. cooked and peeled crawfish tails with fat, or 2 lbs. uncooked shrimp in shells and 1 stick unsalted butter
1½ c. cooked rice
¼ c. heavy cream
2 tbsp. sweet sherry
1 tbsp. tomato paste

2 tsp. fresh tarragon or ½ tsp. dried
2 tsp. sweet Hungarian paprika
1 tsp. fresh thyme or ½ tsp. dried
½ tsp. cayenne
½ tsp. freshly grated nutmeg
1 tsp. red pepper flakes
½ c. finely chopped green onions or scallions
¼ c. chopped fresh parsley
1 egg
1 tbsp. lemon juice
1 tsp. grated lemon zest
Salt and pepper to taste
Medium hog casings

Roast and peel the bell pepper following the directions on page 20, seed, and chop. Heat the 4 tablespoons butter in a medium frying pan, and add the onion, shallot, and garlic. Cover and cook 10 minutes, until the vegetables are soft. Set aside.

In a food processor or by hand, coarsely chop the crawfish tails and fat. Be sure not to overprocess. Put the chopped pepper, cooked vegetables, crawfish, rice, and cream in a large bowl. Add the remaining ingredients and mix well. Chill for ½ hour. Stuff the crawfish mixture into medium hog casings. To cook, coil the boudin in a colander in a stockpot or Dutch oven. Add boiling water to just below the colander, cover, and steam for 20 minutes.

If crawfish are unavailable, shrimp makes a tasty alternative. Boil unpeeled shrimp in a large quantity of salted water until just done (3–5 minutes, just after they turn pink; do not overcook). Peel and cool. Add the shells to a food processor and chop coarsely. Melt the stick of butter over low heat. Add the shells and sauté for 5 minutes to extract the shrimp flavor. This shrimp butter will substitute for the crawfish fat. Strain the butter and proceed with the recipe as described above, using the shrimp and butter mixture in place of the crawfish and its fat.

After steaming the boudin, you should eat it immediately, or refrigerate it. These seafood sausages are quite perishable, but will keep for a day or two in the refrigerator. Crawfish boudin, like traditional Cajun boudin, can be eaten out of hand, stripping the stuffing out of the casing as you go. Or you can sauté it, as in the following recipe. Makes 2–3 pounds

Crawfish tails and fat are easily frozen and can often be found in specialty stores in large metropolitan areas. They can also be purchased by mail order (see page 357).

· crawfish boudin with Scotch whisky and crawfish sauce ·

This is an elegant dish and quite rich.

1 lb. cooked Crawfish Boudin (see
  preceding recipe)
2 tbsp. butter
½ c. finely sliced green onions or
  scallions
¼ c. Scotch whisky
½ c. stock (use seafood, fish, or
  chicken stock, or bottled clam juice)

1 tsp. tomato paste
½ tsp. paprika
½ c. heavy cream
Salt and pepper to taste
¼ lb. crawfish tails with their fat
  (optional garnish)

*A beautiful first course for a special
dinner.*

In a large heavy skillet, lightly brown previously steamed
Crawfish Boudin in the butter over low heat for about 5
minutes. Gently turn and fry until lightly golden on all
sides. Some stuffing might spill out the ends and the casing might burst during
cooking. Not to worry, it all can be tidied up before serving.

With a large spatula and slotted spoon, transfer the boudin to a warm
platter. To the same pan add the green onions, and stir and cook for about 1
minute. Add the whisky and ignite. Shake the pan continuously until all the alcohol
burns off. Add the stock with the tomato paste, paprika, and cream. Boil to reduce
and thicken the sauce for about 5 minutes, or until it coats a spoon. Taste for salt
and pepper. Add the optional crawfish
tails and cook 1 minute more. To
serve, divide the boudin into 4 servings. Ladle the sauce and crawfish tails
over and around the boudin. If the casing bursts during cooking, cover any
breaks with extra sauce.
Makes 4 servings

· Creole mustard butter ·

This mustard butter is also excellent
on grilled fish, chicken, or meat. It
freezes well, so you can keep some
on hand for last-minute inspirations
or drop-in guests.

½ lb. (2 sticks) unsalted butter
4 tbsp. minced garlic
6–7 tbsp. Creole or other spicy
  mustard
3 tsp. Worcestershire sauce
2 tsp. Tabasco
⅓ c. lemon juice
Salt and pepper to taste

Melt butter over low heat, add
garlic and cook 1 minute. Whisk in
other ingredients, taste for seasonings. Can be used hot or chilled.
Keeps 1 week in the refrigerator.
Makes 1 cup

· grilled shrimp wrapped in tasso ·

This recipe is very simple and delicious and can be served as an appetizer or entree. Serve 6 shrimp per person for a main course, 2 for hors d'oeuvres. You can also use the same technique for large sea scallops.

1 lb. large shrimp (20–25 count)
¼ lb. tasso, cut into very thin slices

1 recipe Creole Mustard Butter (see opposite page)

Peel and devein the shrimp, leaving the tails attached. Cut thinly sliced tasso into strips ½ to ¾ inch wide. Wrap the tasso around each shrimp in a spiral pattern. Secure the tasso with a wooden toothpick or skewer. Brush with Creole mustard butter and grill 2–3 minutes per side over hot coals. Remove the shrimp from the grill and brush generously with more Creole mustard butter before serving. Makes 10–12 servings as an appetizer, 4 as a main course

If you don't have tasso, use Westphalian or country ham cut into paper-thin slices.

· skewered andouille and shrimp with Creole mustard butter ·

This simple skewer can be used as an hors d'oeuvre or a main course. The delicate flavors of shrimp with the spicy, smoky sausage and the piquant mustard-flavored butter always bring cheers from grateful diners.

25 6-inch bamboo skewers, soaked in water
1 red bell pepper, cut into 1-inch chunks
1 red onion, cut into 1-inch chunks
1 lb. andouille, cut into ½-inch rounds
1 green bell pepper, cut into 1-inch chunks

1 lb. large (20–25 count) shrimp, peeled and deveined, with tails left on
Creole Mustard Butter (see opposite page)

For each 6-inch skewer, begin with a piece of red bell pepper and red onion, and a chunk of andouille (with the skewer through the casing so the cut edge is parallel to the skewer). Then put on another piece of red onion, followed by a piece of the green bell pepper, a shrimp skewered lengthwise, another piece each of red bell pepper and onion, and another chunk of andouille. Finish the skewer off with one more piece each of onion and red bell pepper.

Brush each skewer generously with Creole mustard butter and grill over a hot charcoal fire or in a broiler for 2–3 minutes on each side until the shrimp is just done and the sausage is lightly browned. Serve with a small ramekin of the mustard butter on the side. Makes 4 servings as a main course, 8 as an appetizer

· Cajun meat pies ·

These spicy morsels are a specialty of the northwestern Louisiana town of Natchitoches, and make wonderful hors d'oeuvres.

1 lb. chaurice or other spicy fresh
    sausage, removed from casing
½ c. finely diced celery
¼ c. finely diced carrot
¼ c. each finely diced green and red
    bell pepper
½ c. thinly sliced green onions

¼ c. tomato puree
½ c. beef or chicken stock
Salt and black pepper
1 recipe Edy's Foolproof Pie Dough
1 egg
1 tbsp. cream or milk

In a large heavy skillet, fry the sausage meat over medium heat for 5 minutes, stirring occasionally with a fork to break it up. Add the celery and carrot. Cover and cook for 3 minutes. Put in the bell peppers and cook 3 minutes more, stirring occasionally. Add green onions, tomato puree, and stock. Cook, uncovered, over medium heat until all the liquid is absorbed and the carrots are soft, about 7–10 minutes. Stir the pan from time to time. Taste for salt and pepper. Transfer the filling to a bowl, strain off and discard any fat, and cool for 30 minutes in freezer or refrigerate 2 or more hours.

To make large pies, roll out the dough to ⅛-inch thickness. Cut 6-inch circles and place ⅓ cup of filling on each. Fold them in half and crimp the edge with a fork. Refrigerate until ready to bake. To make cocktail-sized pies, cut the dough into 3-inch circles, and fill with 1–2 tablespoons of the filling. Proceed as for larger pies. Preheat oven to 400° F. Combine the egg with the milk or cream and brush onto each turnover. Bake for 25–30 minutes, until golden. Cool for a few minutes and serve. Makes 16 large or 32 small pies

These pies freeze well unbaked. Brush with the egg wash just before baking and bake them, frozen, until golden, 30–35 minutes at 400° F.

· Edy's foolproof pie dough ·

Edy Young's simple-to-prepare dough always makes tender and flaky crusts.

½ lb. (2 sticks) salted butter, cut
    into ½-inch pieces
3 c. all-purpose flour
1 large egg yolk
Enough milk to make a total volume
    of ½ c. when combined with the
    egg yolk

In a food processor fitted with the metal blade, process the butter and flour until the mixture looks like coarse meal. Add the combined egg yolk and milk through the feed tube and process in short bursts until the dough just begins to ball up.

Remove the dough, divide it in half, and form each piece into a ball. You can use the dough immediately, or wrap in plastic wrap and refrigerate until ready to use (up to 2 days), or freeze for up to 2 months.

Makes enough dough for a 10-inch two-crust pie or two 9-inch single-crust pies

· crawfish and smoked sausage beignets ·

Beignets are the light and delicate fried pastries that are a tradition in the French Quarter. Revelers wind up the evening (or the morning, depending on the revel) at one of the many cafés of the Vieux Carré, reorienting the universe with strong chicory coffee and hot, crisp beignets dusted with powdered sugar.

Lately Creole chefs are widening the range of the beignet by blending savory ingredients like sausage and seafood into the batter. The Tour Eiffel in New Orleans serves cocktail-sized beignets like these, and they are mighty tasty.

1 c. all-purpose flour
½ tsp. salt
1 tsp. baking powder
1 c. water
½ c. finely chopped red bell pepper
1 tsp. chopped garlic
3 green onions or scallions, finely chopped
¼ tsp. dried tarragon

¼ tsp. black pepper
¼ tsp. Tabasco
½ c. coarsely chopped Smoked Country Sausage (see page 11)
1 c. coarsely chopped crawfish tails or chopped cooked shrimp
Oil for deep-frying
Lemon wedges to garnish

Sift the flour, salt, and baking powder together into a medium bowl. Add the water, and stir until the ingredients are well blended. Do not overmix. Fold in the remaining ingredients except the oil and lemon wedges. Cover and let the batter rest for 30 minutes. Pour 4 inches of oil into a heavy pot or deep-fryer, and heat to 350° F. Using a teaspoon, carefully drop the batter into the hot oil, and fry the beignets for 2 minutes until golden brown. Taste one to be sure they are cooked all the way through. If not, cook a little longer in the oil. Drain on paper towels and serve with lemon wedges, tartar sauce or rémoulade dressing.
Makes about 2 dozen

You can use Louisiana-Style Smoked Sausage, Pickled-Pork Sausage, andouille, or any high-quality smoked sausage for this spicy appetizer. Serve with Tidewater Tartar Sauce (see page 27) or Lee Coleman's Rémoulade Dressing (see page 353).

· andouille and liver pâté ·

This simple country pâté goes well in summer for picnics or as part of a holiday buffet or special party.

1 lb. pork butt, cut into 1 x 5-inch strips
1 lb. andouille or other high-quality smoked sausage
1 lb. pork or chicken liver
¾ lb. pork back fat, cut into 1 x 5-inch strips
1 c. coarsely chopped onions
2 shallots, coarsely chopped
2 cloves garlic, coarsely chopped
¼ c. brandy
½ c. water or stock
⅓ c. uncooked rice
2 tbsp. butter
2 eggs
1 tsp. Quatre Épices
1 tsp. thyme
2–3 tsp. kosher salt
1 tbsp. freshly ground black pepper
1 lb. caul fat or bacon
2 whole bay leaves

Grind the pork butt, andouille, and liver through a coarse (⅜- to ½-inch) plate. Grind the fat through a ⅛- to ¼-inch plate. Melt 3 tablespoons of the pork fat in a 12-inch skillet over medium-low heat. Add the onions and cook, covered, for 15 minutes. Add the shallots and garlic, and cook 1 additional minute. Transfer to a bowl and cool. Deglaze the pan with the brandy.

In a small saucepan bring the water or stock to a boil and add the rice and butter. Lower the heat to a simmer. Cover the pot and cook over a low flame for 20 minutes, or until rice is tender. Set aside.

To assemble the pâté, grind the onions, shallots, garlic, and rice through a ¼-inch plate. Combine with the ground meats, fat, and liver in the bowl of an electric mixer. Add the eggs and mix at a slow speed while you add the remaining ingredients except the caul fat and the bay leaves, including the deglazed juices from the frying pan. Continue to mix at a moderate speed for 2 to 3 minutes. Make a small patty, fry it, taste, and adjust the seasonings as necessary.

This dish is equally good when eaten cold, at room temperature, or still warm from the oven.

Preheat the oven to 300° F. Line a 2-quart baking pan or terrine with caul fat or bacon and fill with the pâté mixture to ½ inch from the top. Cover with caul fat or bacon and place bay leaves on top. Seal the pan with foil and bake for 2 to 3 hours, or more important, until the internal temperature of the pâté reaches 160° F. Cool, then refrigerate overnight. Serve the next day. Tightly covered, the pâté should keep for up to 10 days in the refrigerator. Do not freeze. Makes 8–10 servings as lunch, 12–14 as part of buffet

· quatre épices ·

7 tbsp. freshly ground black pepper
1 tbsp. ground ginger
1 tbsp. freshly grated nutmeg
1 tbsp. ground cloves

Mix the spices and store in a sealed jar. Keeps 6 months. Makes ½ cup

· lentil and andouille salad ·

This makes a substantial picnic dish in summertime, but would also serve well on a buffet table any time of year.

2 c. dried lentils
2 qts. chicken stock
1 lb. andouille sausage or other high-quality smoked sausage
2 carrots, cut into ¼-inch dice
1 red bell pepper, fire-roasted and peeled
1¼ c. Tangy Vinaigrette Dressing (see page 354)

1 red onion, finely diced
6 green onions or scallions, thinly sliced
1 c. finely chopped fresh parsley
½ c. celery, cut into ¼-inch dice
Salt and pepper to taste

In a large pot or Dutch oven, simmer the lentils in the stock for 30 minutes. Add the andouille in 1 piece, and poach it for an additional 10 minutes. Remove and reserve the sausage. Taste the lentils to see if they are tender. If not, continue to cook until they are. Drain the lentils. You may want to save the liquid to use later for making soup.

Any good-quality smoked country-style sausage can substitute for andouille if it's not available.

While the lentils are cooking, blanch the carrots in 2 cups of boiling water for 3 minutes. Strain and cool under running water. Drain and reserve. Roast and peel the bell pepper following the directions on page 20, and cut into strips. Cut the cooled andouille into ¼-inch rounds. Prepare the vinaigrette dressing.

To assemble the salad, mix the sausage and lentils in a large bowl with the red and green onions, carrot, parsley, celery, and half the red pepper. Toss with the dressing. Taste for salt and pepper. Arrange on a platter or in a shallow bowl and garnish with the remaining red bell pepper. Makes 6–8 servings

· Cajun-style pea soup ·

On cold, gray winter days nothing satisfies more than a bowl of hearty pea soup.

2 qts. beef or chicken stock
2 large ham hocks (about 1½ lbs.)
1 lb. green split peas
2 c. chopped onions
2 carrots, chopped
4 ribs celery, chopped
½ green bell peppper, chopped
1 leek, thinly sliced (optional)
2 cloves garlic, minced
1 tsp. ground sage
1 tsp. dried thyme
2 bay leaves

1 tsp. cayenne
1 lb. Cajun-Style Andouille (see page 521), Pickled-Pork Sausage (see page 59), or other good-quality smoked sausage, sliced into ½-inch rounds
2 tsp. filé powder (optional)
1 c. chopped fresh parsley
½ c. finely chopped green onions or scallions
Salt and pepper to taste

In a heavy 4-quart pot, bring the stock to a boil and add the ham hocks. Reduce the heat to a simmer and cook for 1 hour. Then put in the split peas, onions, carrots, celery, green bell pepper, leek, garlic, herbs, and spices. Simmer, covered, for another 45 minutes, until the peas are falling apart. Add the sausage to the soup, and simmer for 10 minutes more. Stir in the optional filé powder, parsley, and green onions, and season with salt and pepper to taste. Serve in large bowls. Makes 6–8 servings

This Cajun pea soup is simple to prepare, but substantial enough to serve as a one-course meal with biscuits or cornbread.

· too-easy-to-believe spicy lentil soup ·

Because chaurice has all the flavor you need to make a wonderful soup, you only have to add lentils and a few other ingredients for this spicy and satisfying dish.

5 links chaurice or other spicy fresh
   sausage (about 1¼ lbs.)
1 c. chopped onion
½ c. chopped celery
1 c. chopped carrot
1 lb. lentils

6–8 c. chicken or beef stock
½ tsp. dried thyme
½ tsp. ground sage
Salt and pepper to taste
¼ c. chopped fresh parsley

Remove the meat from 2 links and fry it in a heavy 3–4-quart pot or Dutch oven over medium heat. Break up the sausage meat with a wooden spoon while it browns, for about 5 minutes. Add the onion, celery, and carrots. Cover and cook over medium heat, stirring occasionally, until the vegetables are soft, about 10 minutes. Put in the lentils, stock, thyme, and sage. Bring to a boil, then reduce to a simmer. Cook, uncovered, for 45 minutes, until the lentils are soft. If too dry, add more stock, water, or a little dry sherry.

Poach the remaining 3 links in the soup for 15 minutes. Remove, and when they are cool enough to handle, slice them into ½-inch rounds. Put the sausage rounds back into the soup. Correct the salt and pepper. Ladle the soup into bowls and garnish with chopped parsley. Makes 6 servings

· baked eggs, Creole style ·

This spicy egg dish is not only good for breakfast, but makes an excellent lunch or light supper. It is a good example of the Spanish influence on Creole cooking.

16 3–4-inch green beans (about ½ lb.)

1 tbsp. olive oil

1 lb. Cajun-Style Andouille, Smoked Country Sausage, Pickled-Pork Sausage (see pages 52, 11, 59), or other smoked sausage, cut into ½-inch rounds

¼ c. finely chopped onion

6 green onions or scallions, white part finely chopped, green tops thinly sliced

2 tsp. minced garlic

½ c. diced green bell pepper

¼ c. dry sherry

6 plum tomatoes, fresh or canned, peeled and quartered

½ tsp. cayenne

Salt and pepper to taste

6 large shrimp (20–25 count), peeled and cooked (optional)

1 pimiento or red bell pepper, cut into ¼-inch strips

6 eggs

Bring 4 quarts of salted water to a boil. Add the green beans and blanch for 5 minutes, until they are tender but still crunchy. Cool under running water. Drain and set aside.

In a large heavy skillet, heat the olive oil over medium heat. Put in the sliced sausage and fry until browned on both sides. about 10 minutes. Add the onion, the green onion, and the garlic, and sauté slowly for about 10 minutes, until soft. Add the green bell pepper, and cook for an additional 2–3 minutes. Add the sherry, tomato, and cayenne and cook for 10 minutes more. Season this sauce with salt and pepper to taste.

Preheat the oven to 450° F. Spread the tomato sauce and sausages evenly over the bottom of a 14 × 8-inch gratin or baking dish. Arrange the green beans, optional shrimp, and the pimiento strips on top. Break the 6 eggs one at a time onto the sauce and arrange them evenly over the dish, taking care not to break the yolks. Garnish with the green onion tops, and bake until the egg whites are set, about 10–12 minutes. Makes 6 servings

Best served warm and not hot directly from oven, this is ideal for a party buffet or brunch.

· hot boudin patties with
poached eggs and tasso béarnaise ·

Egg is added to bind the Hot Boudin mixture to make patties that won't fall apart when you fry them. If you don't have the time or the inclination to make the poached eggs and the Tasso Béarnaise, these boudin patties are delicious with any style of eggs for breakfast.

1 recipe Tasso Béarnaise Sauce (see
   page 79) (optional)
1 lb. Hot Boudin mixture (see
   page 53)

9 eggs
2 tbsp. butter
2 tsp. white vinegar

Make the Tasso Béarnaise sauce, and keep warm in a bowl in tepid (85° F) water until needed. This is optional, but adds flavor and a touch of elegance to the dish.

Preheat the oven to 200° F. Combine the Hot Boudin mixture with 1 beaten egg. Form into 8 equal-sized patties, about ⅜ inch thick. Heat the butter over medium heat in a heavy 12-inch skillet. Fry the patties until they are brown, about 5–7 minutes a side. Transfer to an ovenproof platter, and keep them warm in the oven while you prepare the eggs.

Poach the remaining eggs in 1½–2 inches of water with 2 teaspoons of white vinegar in a heavy, deep-sided skillet for 2–3 minutes, until whites are firm and yolks still soft. Remove them with a slotted spoon. To serve, trim off any ragged egg whites, and place 2 eggs on a warm plate with 2 boudin patties. Spoon about ¼ cup of the sauce over each egg. Serve with Buttermilk Biscuits (see page 26).
Makes 4 servings

If you're making up a batch of Hot Boudin, set some aside for a great weekend breakfast. You can also wrap and freeze Hot Boudin for later use, either as links or in bulk for patties.

· andouille hash ·

This simple but delicious hash is featured at Regina's, a popular Creole restaurant in San Francisco.

2 lbs. red potatoes, cut into ½-inch
dice
1 large onion, chopped into ¼-inch
pieces
4 tbsp. (½ stick) unsalted butter
1 lb. andouille or smoked ham, cut
into ½-inch dice
½ c. red bell pepper, chopped into
¼-inch pieces

½ c. green bell pepper, chopped into
¼-inch pieces
¼ tsp. salt
½ tsp. black pepper
¼ tsp. cayenne
¼ c. finely chopped green onions or
scallions

Flaky biscuits, poached or fried eggs, and this savory hash make a marvelous combination for breakfast or lunch.

In a large heavy frying pan, fry the potatoes and onions in the butter for 15 minutes over medium heat. They should be light brown on the outside and soft in the center. Add the diced sausage, bell peppers, salt, black pepper, and cayenne, and continue frying until potatoes and sausage are nicely browned, about 5 minutes. Taste for salt and pepper, sprinkle with the green onions, and serve. Makes 6–8 servings

· quick and easy breakfasts ·

Sausages and eggs are an obvious combination, but you might want to vary the usual black pepper and sage sausage with other types of sausages. Try dicing smoked sausage and mixing it with scrambled eggs or use a precooked sausage as part of an omelette filling with sautéed mushrooms or cooked spinach. Make a French toast sandwich with 2 slices of French toast and a mild sausage such as bockwurst or Turkey Sausage with Drambuie in between. Serve this with sautéed apples or fruit syrup. Dice up bits of smoked sausage and add to pancake or waffle batter. Roll sausages in brioche, biscuit, or bread dough and eat hot out of the oven with some home fried potatoes.

Here are some other sausage breakfast possibilities:
Shirred Eggs and Sausage (see page 176
Sausage and Cornbread Bites (see page 173
Sheepherder's Omelette of Wild Greens, Potatoes, and Chorizo (see page 262)
Baked Eggs, Creole Style (see page 70)
Hot Boudin Patties with Poached Eggs and Tasso Béarnaise (see page 71)
Andouille Hash (see page 72)
Alabama Country Breakfast (see page 25)
Country Sausage with Sweet and Tangy Red-Eye Gravy (see page 26)

· shrimp, sausage, and potato Creole ·

This recipe works best if you can find fresh Roma or other Italian-style plum tomatoes. If not, you can use canned Italian plum tomatoes, available in most Italian delicatessens and quality markets. These often come packed in tomato sauce that can substitute for the tomato puree.

The first time I had a dish like this was for "brunch" at Dooky Chase's, the wonderful New Orleans Creole restaurant. "Brunch" got started about 2 p.m. (hence the quotes), and this was just one of 7 or 8 dishes at a gargantuan fast-breaker. I'm not sure just when this particular "brunch" ended, but I think the sun was going down as we staggered out into the street to head on to dinner.

⅓ c. peanut oil
⅓ c. all-purpose flour
2 c. chopped onions
2 ribs celery, chopped
1 green and 1 red bell pepper, cut into
  ¼-inch dice (about 3 c.)
1½ c. thinly sliced green onions or
  scallions
3 tbsp. minced garlic
1 tsp. dried thyme
½ tsp. dried basil
4 bay leaves
½ tsp. black pepper
Pinch ground allspice
½ tsp. cayenne
2 c. shrimp stock made from the
  shells (see page 20) or chicken
  stock or clam juice

1 c. dry white wine
1 c. tomato puree or juice from
  canned Italian plum tomatoes
2 lbs. fresh plum tomatoes, skinned,
  seeded, and roughly chopped, or
  1 large (28-oz.) can Italian plum
  tomatoes
1½ lbs. red or white boiling potatoes,
  unpeeled, cut into ½-inch dice
¾ lb. andouille or other smoked
  sausage, sliced into ½-inch rounds
2 lbs. medium shrimp (30–35 count),
  peeled
¼ c. chopped fresh parsley
Salt and pepper to taste
1 tbsp. or more fresh lemon juice
Tabasco to taste

In a heavy 3–4-quart pot or Dutch oven, make a roux the color of peanut butter with the oil and flour (see page 77). Add the onions and celery, stirring frequently over medium heat for 2–3 minutes. Put in 1 cup of the chopped bell peppers, 1 cup of the green onions, and the garlic. Cook 5 minutes more, stirring continuously. Stir in the herbs and spices, and cook for 1 minute. Add the shrimp stock, wine, and tomato puree. Bring to a boil while you stir well. Reduce to a simmer, cover, and cook 10 minutes. Add the tomatoes and potatoes, and cook, uncovered, 15 minutes more. Add the sausage and the remaining bell peppers, and cook an additional 10 minutes, or until the potatoes are tender. Put in the shrimp and cook until firm and pink, 3–5 minutes. Add the chopped parsley and remaining green onions. Taste for salt and pepper, and add lemon juice and Tabasco as desired. Serve with plain boiled rice, or as is. Makes 6–8 servings

· artichoke stuffed with shrimp and andouille ·

This elegant yet hearty dish, which reflects the Italian influence in Louisiana cooking, is a complete meal in itself and only needs a salad and some crusty French bread to accompany it.

4 medium artichokes, stems cut so they can sit straight up on a flat surface
4 c. water
¼ c. fresh lemon juice
¼ c. olive oil
5 cloves unpeeled garlic
1 tsp. dried marjoram
1 tsp. dried basil
2 tsp. salt
½ tsp. coarsely ground black pepper

· **Stuffing** ·

1 lb. andouille or other smoked sausage such as kielbasa, finely chopped
2 tbsp. butter

1 c. finely chopped green onions or scallions
1 onion, chopped
3 ribs celery, chopped
½ green bell pepper, finely chopped
½ red bell pepper, finely chopped
2 cloves garlic, minced
½ lb. raw shrimp, coarsely chopped
1 tbsp. fresh lemon juice
1 tsp. dried thyme
½ tsp. cayenne
1 tsp. Worcestershire sauce
2 c. homemade dry bread crumbs
1 c. freshly grated Parmesan cheese
1 egg

If andouille is unavailable, you can use any high-quality country-style smoked sausage.

Break off the tough outer leaves of the artichokes and discard. Using a scissors, cut off the leaf tips. In a pot large enough to hold the artichokes, bring the water to a boil. Put in the ¼ cup lemon juice and the olive oil, garlic, herbs, salt, and pepper, along with the artichokes, stem side down. Set a plate on top of the artichokes to keep them submerged. Boil about 10 minutes, or until the leaves are pliable. The artichokes will only be partially cooked. Drain and cool them upside down, reserving ¼ cup of the cooking liquid for the stuffing.

To prepare the stuffing, brown the sausage in the butter in a heavy 12-inch skillet over medium heat for 5 minutes. Add the green onions, chopped onion, celery, and bell peppers. Cook until the vegetables are soft, stirring frequently, about 10 minutes. Add the garlic and the shrimp and sauté for 3 minutes more. Stir in the tablespoon of lemon juice, thyme, cayenne, and Worcestershire. Transfer to a bowl and mix in the bread crumbs, cheese, and egg. Add enough of the reserved artichoke cooking liquid to moisten the mixture so it binds together. It should not be too soggy, however.

Gently open the center of each artichoke. Pull out the cone of light green leaves and discard. Using a teaspoon or melon baller, scrape out each choke. Fill the center of each artichoke with some of the stuffing, then gently spread each leaf apart and place about 1–2 teaspoons of stuffing between each leaf. The artichokes will spread out to become quite large and impressive. Arrange the artichokes in a baking pan large enough to hold them comfortably. At this point the artichokes can be refrigerated for use the next day.

Preheat the oven to 350° F. Pour enough boiling water into the pan with the artichokes to come 1 inch up the sides. Cover with foil and bake until the base of each artichoke is tender, about 45 minutes. Remove the foil and continue to bake until the stuffing on top begins to brown lightly, about 5 minutes.
Makes 4 servings

· red bell pepper stuffed with seafood and hot boudin ·

Louisiana cooks, both Cajun and Creole, just love to stuff peppers with meat, seafood, or a combination of the two. Hot Boudin sausage meat makes a natural stuffing, either by itself or with seafood. It tastes great with lump crabmeat, but shrimp or crawfish tails work just about as well. It's best to use uncooked shrimp in any of our recipes, fresh preferably, but frozen will do. Precooked shrimp is usually tasteless and dry.

1 tbsp. butter
½ c. finely chopped onion
¼ c. finely chopped celery
½ lb. raw shrimp, shelled and coarsely chopped into ¼-inch chunks, or ½ lb. lump crabmeat, or ½ lb. peeled crawfish tails and fat, coarsely chopped

1 lb. Hot Boudin mixture (see page 53)
¼ c. finely chopped green onions or scallions
2 eggs, beaten
1 tsp. Worcestershire sauce
Salt and pepper to taste
4 large red bell peppers

In a medium-sized skillet, heat the butter over medium heat. Add the onion and celery and cook for 10 minutes, until they are soft and transparent. If you are using shrimp, add them to the pan and sauté, stirring continuously, for 1 or 2 minutes, until they are lightly pink. No extra cooking is necessary if you are using crab or crawfish tails. In a bowl, combine the onions and celery with the seafood, Hot Boudin, green onions, beaten eggs, and Worcestershire sauce. Taste for salt and pepper. Cut each pepper in half lengthwise from stem to blossom end. Seed, and stuff generously with the boudin and seafood mixture. Preheat the oven to 350° F. Place the peppers in a shallow baking dish or roasting pan with 2 cups of boiling water on the bottom. Cover with foil and cook for 20 minutes, 10 minutes longer if you like your peppers on the soft side. Remove foil and bake 10 more minutes at 400° F, until the top is lightly browned. Makes 8 servings as an appetizer, 4 as a main course

Great as a main course or as an appetizer. Serve half a bell pepper per person for appetizers.

· chicken and andouille gumbo ·

**Gumbo, redolent with the smoky flavors of sausage and dark roux, thick-
ened with okra or filé, is the best-known dish to come out of Cajun and
Creole cooking. This spicy soup or stew is best made up one or two days
ahead so the flavors can mellow.**

3½ -lb. chicken

2 qts. water

1 bay leaf

1 rib celery

1 onion, unpeeled and split in half

1 carrot, cut into 2 pieces

1 c. peanut oil

1 c. all-purpose flour

3 c. chopped onions

1 c. chopped celery

1 green bell pepper, chopped into
   ¼-inch pieces

1 red bell pepper, chopped into
   ¼-inch pieces

¼ lb. andouille, chopped into ¼-inch
   pieces

1 tsp. dried thyme

½ tsp. dried sage

1 tsp. cayenne

1 tsp. black pepper

2 tbsp. minced garlic

6 c. stock from the poached chicken

1 lb. okra, cut into ½-inch slices

1 lb. andouille, or other spicy smoked
   sausage, sliced into ¼-inch rounds

1 c. thinly sliced green onions or
   scallions

Salt to taste

Tabasco to taste

3 c. cooked rice

½ c. chopped fresh parsley for
   garnish

Put the chicken whole into the water and bring to a boil. Skim any froth
from the surface, then reduce the heat to a simmer, and add the bay leaf, celery,
onion, and carrot. Simmer for 40 minutes, or until tender. Remove the chicken to
cool, and continue to simmer the stock while you prepare the rest of the recipe.

In a heavy 3–4-quart pot or Dutch oven prepare a deep-brown roux (see
opposite page for instructions) using the peanut oil and flour. Remove the pot
from the heat, and add the chopped onions and celery. The vegetables will cool
the roux so that it does not burn. Return the pan to me-
dium heat, stirring the vegetables until they are soft, about
5 minutes. The roux will continue to darken. Add the
green and red bell peppers along with the ¼ pound of
chopped andouille, and cook for 5 more minutes. Add the
thyme, sage, cayenne, black pepper, and garlic and stir in the chicken stock,
mixing well. Bring to a boil and reduce to a simmer. Simmer for 15 minutes,
uncovered. Add the okra and continue to cook for an additional 30 minutes. While
the gumbo simmers, remove the chicken meat from the bones. Discard the skin
and bones, and cut the meat into ¾-inch pieces. At this point you can refrigerate
the gumbo and the chicken meat separately overnight.

If you have refrigerated the gumbo overnight, gradually bring it to a simmer. Otherwise, add the sliced andouille to the gumbo and cook for 10 minutes.

*Making the roux is an essential step
and will demand your attention,
so make sure all the ingredients are
chopped and ready before you start.*

Put in the chicken meat and green onions, and simmer for 5 minutes more. Taste for salt and Tabasco.

To serve, spoon about ½ cup of warm cooked rice in the bottom of a large soup bowl. Ladle the gumbo over the rice, and garnish with chopped parsley. Provide extra Tabasco sauce for those brave souls who really like things hot. Makes 6–8 servings

· roux ·

Roux, a mixture of flour and oil, is an essential ingredient in Louisiana cooking, where it not only adds body, but also functions as an important flavoring ingredient, giving soups, stews, and sauces a nutty, smoky taste and aroma.

Making roux is a fairly time-consuming process, so you may want to make extra. Cool it and store it in an airtight jar in the refrigerator, where it will keep for 4–6 months. Then, when you need some, spoon out the amount called for, gradually heat it, and proceed with your recipe.

To make roux, use equal amounts of flour and oil. Heat the oil in a cast-iron or other heavy pan over medium heat for 5 minutes. Remove from the heat and gradually stir in the flour. Return the pan to medium heat and continue to stir.

As you cook the roux it will go through several stages of coloring. The first stage is tan, followed by light brown (the color of peanut butter), brown, and then deep red-brown. Finally the roux will turn black. Some cooks like to use black roux in gumbo; I think that it is too bitter and recommend stopping at the red-brown stage. If the roux begins to darken too quickly during cooking, remove it from the heat and continue to stir. Lower the heat and then continue to cook until the roux reaches the desired color.

To stop the cooking process, remove from the heat and stir in the chopped vegetables called for in your recipe. The roux will continue to cook and darken for 2–3 minutes. Return pan to low heat and cook for 5 minutes more. Make sure that your vegetables and seasoning mixtures are chopped and prepared ahead of time and are ready nearby. Depending on the color and the quantity of roux you are making, the process will take between 30 minutes and an hour to complete.

· chicken Pontalba ·

In the traditional version of this New Orleans classic, named after the historic Pontalba buildings in the heart of the French Quarter, the chicken is battered and deep-fried, which makes this a very rich dish indeed. In this version we've lightened the dish by grilling the chicken and we've oven-browned the potatoes instead of deep-frying them. Although this recipe has several steps, it produces a complete and elegant meal. The only addition needed might be a simple steamed vegetable like spinach or zucchini. Make the Tasso Béarnaise first and keep it warm in tepid (85° F) water placed on the back of the stove. This way everything will come out hot and fresh.

1 tsp. dried thyme
¼ tsp. ground fennel seed
¼ tsp. ground sage
½ tsp. dried tarragon
½ tsp. cayenne
Salt and pepper to taste
2 1-lb. chicken breasts, boned, skinned, and halved
3 tbsp. unsalted butter
1 tbsp. olive oil
1 lb. red or white boiling potatoes, cut into ½-inch dice
¾ lb. andouille or other spicy smoked sausage, diced

¼ lb. tasso or smoked ham, diced
1 medium yellow onion, finely chopped
¼ lb. mushrooms, thinly sliced
1 tbsp. minced garlic
½ c. dry white wine
½ c. thinly sliced green onions or scallions
¼ c. chopped fresh parsley
1 recipe Tasso Béarnaise Sauce (see opposite page)

Cornish game hen, squab, quail, young pheasant, or rabbit are also delicious in this dish.

In a small bowl, mix ¼ teaspoon of the thyme, the ground fennel seed, sage, tarragon, and ¼ teaspoon of the cayenne with ½ teaspoon each of salt and pepper. Rub this mixture all over the chicken breasts. Let the chicken marinate in the spices for 30–60 minutes at cool room temperature.

Preheat the oven to 400° F. Melt 2 tablespoons of the butter and all the olive oil in a roasting pan in the oven for 5 minutes. Toss the potatoes in the butter and oil and lightly sprinkle them with salt and pepper. Roast the potatoes in the oven for about 20 minutes, turning them occasionally so they are evenly browned and beginning to crisp. Set them aside.

In a heavy 10-inch skillet, melt the remaining tablespoon of butter over medium-high heat. Add the andouille and sauté, stirring occasionally, for 3 minutes, to render some of its fat. Add the tasso and cook for 1 minute more. Drop the onion into the skillet. Cover the pan and cook over medium heat, stirring occasionally, about 10 minutes, or until the onion is lightly browned. Add the mushrooms, garlic, and white wine, along with the remaining thyme and cayenne, to the mixture. Season to taste with salt and pepper. Sauté, uncovered, over high heat, stirring, for 3–4 minutes, until the juices have reduced and begun to thicken.

Stir in the green onions or scallions, and sprinkle with the parsley. Set the pan aside while you grill the chicken.

Preheat a broiler or prepare a hot charcoal fire in your barbecue. Place the chicken on a broiler pan or grill and cook about 5–7 minutes on one side, until the chicken breasts begin to brown lightly. Turn and grill another 3–5 minutes until the breasts are firm and lightly browned. They should still be juicy and not over-cooked.

To finish the dish, heat the andouille-onion mixture briefly and add the roasted potatoes to heat them through. Spoon this mixture onto a large warmed serving platter. Top it with the chicken breasts and cover each with a generous spoonful of the Tasso Béarnaise Sauce. Serve at once. Makes 4 servings

· tasso béarnaise sauce ·

A smoky, tangy version of the classic sauce. Great over chicken or fish, steak, or veal chops. Always use fresh lemon juice for best results.

½ lb. (2 sticks) butter
¼ c. dry white wine
2 large shallots, finely chopped
1 tbsp. chopped fresh parsley or fresh chervil
1 tbsp. fresh lemon juice
1 tsp. dried tarragon
¼ lb. tasso or good smoked ham, minced
¼ tsp. black pepper
Salt and Tabasco to taste
3 large egg yolks

Melt butter and reserve. Reduce wine over high heat with other ingredients except egg yolks to 2 tablespoons of liquid; remove from heat. Place yolks in double boiler over simmering water. Whisk for a minute until yolks thicken, add reduced wine and other ingredients, and whisk until blended. Add melted butter in a steady stream, whisking vigorously until blended in and sauce thickens. Remove pan from heat, taste for seasonings. Can be kept warm in tepid water bath (85° F) for up to an hour. Makes 1½ cups

· chicken stuffed under the skin with andouille, ricotta, and spinach ·

Served cold with a salad of mixed fresh greens in a tangy, garlicky dressing, and a bottle of cold Italian Verdicchio, this dish makes a great lunch for a summer afternoon.

1 3½–4 lb. chicken
¼ lb. andouille, finely chopped
1 tbsp. butter
1 tbsp. minced garlic
1 bunch spinach (1 lb.), blanched in
   boiling water, drained, and chopped

½ lb. ricotta cheese
½ c. stale bread crumbs
1 egg, lightly beaten
Salt and pepper to taste
2 tbsp. melted butter

Split the chicken along the back. Gently loosen the skin and flatten the chicken, pushing down on the breastbone firmly with the heel of your hand or the flat side of a cleaver. Sauté the andouille over medium heat in butter for 2–3 minutes, and then add the garlic. Cook for an additional minute, and put into a bowl. Squeeze the chopped spinach to make sure you've gotten most of the water out, and add it to the bowl, along with the ricotta, bread crumbs, and egg. Mix the dressing well, and adjust for salt and pepper. Cool in the refrigerator for about 30 minutes; it should be fairly stiff in texture.

Perfect for a picnic since it is equally good eaten hot or cold.

Preheat the oven to 350° F. Stuff the dressing under the chicken skin with your fingers, forcing in as much as you can. Make sure the thighs and drumsticks are fully covered with dressing before stuffing the breast. The layer of dressing overall should be about ½ inch thick. Use your hands to mold the outside of the skin, shaping the stuffing into a plump version of the chicken's natural shape. Brush the bird with melted butter and roast on a rack, skin side up, for about 1 hour or until the thigh reaches an internal temperature of 170° F. Serve hot from the oven or cold for a picnic or buffet. Makes 4 servings

· turkey, smoked sausage, and tasso jambalaya ·

Jambalaya is a dish with distinct Spanish origins and has as its ancestor the classic combination of seafood, smoked meat, sausage, and rice called paella. The name derives from the Spanish *jamón* or French *jambon* — ham. Like paella, jambalaya can be made with any combination of smoked meat, sausage, poultry, and seafood. In Louisiana, two basic types of jambalaya can be found, the usual tomato-based version and the brown style. We prefer the brown type in which the rice absorbs all of its wonderful flavor from the smoked meats, spices, and stock without the overpowering taste of tomato. The brown color comes from cooking the onions slowly until they are caramelized. Just to get a bit more brown color we cheat a little by adding a very un-Louisiana condiment, soy sauce.

2 fresh turkey thighs (about 3–4 lbs.), or about 4–6 c. leftover turkey meat, diced

2 qts. homemade chicken or turkey stock

2 lbs. Louisiana-Style Smoked Sausage, andouille, or other good-quality smoked sausage, sliced into ½-inch rounds

½ lb. tasso or smoked ham, cut into ½-inch dice

2 c. chopped onion

½ c. chopped celery

2 tbsp. soy sauce

2 c. chopped green onions or scallions

1 tbsp. minced garlic

1 green bell pepper, chopped

1 red bell pepper, chopped

1 tsp. cayenne

2 bay leaves, crumbled

1 tsp. dried thyme

½ tsp. sage

½ tsp. dried marjoram

3 c. long-grain or converted rice

Salt and black pepper

Poach the turkey thighs in the stock for 45–60 minutes, until the meat is tender. Remove and allow them to cool. Discard the skin, remove the meat from the bones, and cut into ½-inch pieces. Reserve the stock. If you are using leftover turkey, you won't need this step. In a large, high-sided skillet or Dutch oven, gently fry the sausage rounds and diced tasso over medium heat for 10 minutes, until lightly browned. Remove them from the pan, reserving the rendered fat.

Chicken works just as well as turkey. Another favorite combination is rabbit, andouille, and shrimp.

In this fat, sauté the onion and celery over medium heat until deep brown in color, about 30 minutes, stirring occasionally. Add the soy sauce and cook for another minute. Put in the green onions or scallions, garlic, and bell peppers and fry for 5 minutes. Add the cayenne, bay leaves, thyme, sage, and marjoram to the mixture along with 4 cups of the stock, bring to a boil, and stir in the rice. Reduce the heat to a simmer. Cover and cook about 20–30 minutes, until the rice is almost done. Stir in the turkey meat, sausage, and tasso. Cover and cook another 10 minutes, until all the liquid is absorbed and the rice is cooked but firm. Taste for salt and pepper. Makes 8–10 servings

· stuffed ponce ·

In Cajun country, Stuffed Ponce is a pig's stomach filled with a spicy meat mixture, and braised for a long time, a sort of Cajun haggis. It's most often served at *boucheries*, and is delicious both hot and cold. Here we provide the traditional recipe, and an easier method using aluminum foil.

· The stuffing ·

3 slices day-old homemade or other good-quality bread (whole wheat seems to work best, but any chewy bread will do)

½ c. milk

1 tbsp. butter

¼ lb. andouille, Louisiana-Style Smoked Sausage, or country-style smoked sausage, finely chopped

¼ c. *each* finely chopped green and red bell pepper

¼ c. finely chopped celery

½ c. thinly sliced green onions or scallions

1½ lbs. Chaurice, removed from casings

1½ lbs. red yams, cut into ½-inch dice

2 eggs, lightly beaten

Salt and pepper to taste

· Baking foil method ·

12 x 18-inch sheet of heavy-duty foil

Oil or butter

3–4 c. chicken stock or water

· Using a pig's stomach ·

1 pig's stomach

2 tbsp. oil

1–3 c. water or stock

If you don't happen to have a pig's stomach lying around the kitchen, you can make this delicious dish using aluminum foil. It tastes just as good as the traditional recipe and is a lot easier to make.

Soak the bread in the milk until it is all absorbed. Press out any excess milk, and reserve the bread. Melt the butter over medium heat in a heavy skillet. Sauté the chopped smoked sausage to release some of its flavor. Add the bell pepper and celery, and cook for 5 minutes until the peppers soften. In a large bowl, mix together the bread, the sausage, vegetables, green onions, chaurice, diced yams, and eggs. Knead and beat the mixture vigorously with a wooden spoon. Fry a small sample and correct the seasoning for salt and pepper.

· **Baking Foil Method** · Allow the stuffing to cool in a freezer for 15–20 minutes, until it is stiff enough to work with. Grease one side of the foil with oil or butter. Add the stuffing and form it into a roll about 3 inches in diameter. Seal the foil and twist the ends to make a large sausage shape. Puncture the foil in several places with a sharp fork. In a heavy metal casserole large enough to hold the roll, bring 2 cups of stock to a boil. Add the ponce, and return the stock to a boil. Reduce to a simmer, cover, and cook gently for 2½–3 hours. Add stock as necessary to maintain a level of about ½ inch of liquid in the pot.

Remove and let the ponce rest for 5 minutes. Reduce the sauce over high heat, degrease, and pour it into a gravy boat. Slice the meat through the foil into ½-inch slices. Remove each slice, and serve the spicy meat with the gravy.

· **Using a Pig's Stomach** · Remove any bits of fat clinging to the lining or surface of the stomach. Soak the stomach in cold water to cover for at least 2 hours or overnight in the refrigerator. Rinse it thoroughly, drain, and pat dry. With kitchen thread, sew up one of the stomach openings. Fill the cavity with the stuffing, and sew up the other opening. Heat the oil over moderate heat in a heavy casserole large enough to hold the ponce. Brown it lightly on all sides, turning the stuffed stomach carefully with wooden spoons. Pour in 1–2 cups of water or stock to a depth of about ½ inch. Bring the liquid to a boil, cover the casserole, and steam over low heat for about 3 hours. Regulate the heat to keep the liquid at a simmer, and add more liquid as needed to maintain the ½-inch depth. Check this about every half hour.

Transfer the stuffed ponce to a heated platter. Cover it with foil while you finish the sauce. Reduce the liquid in the casserole until it is slightly syrupy, and has enough intensity to suit your taste. Degrease the sauce. Cut the stuffed ponce into ¼–½-inch slices and serve with the sauce on the side. Makes 6 servings

This is also delicious cold with Lee Coleman's Rémoulade Dressing (see page 353), and makes a wonderful and unusual appetizer, or perhaps the greatest meat loaf sandwich ever.

pork chops stuffed with hot boudin ·

Hot Boudin is the perfect stuffing for pork, chicken, or vegetables like tomatoes or bell peppers. If you've made some and saved it in the freezer, putting this dish together is quick and easy.

6 1½–2-inch-thick pork chops	½ tsp. ground sage
1 lb. Hot Boudin mixture (see page 53), removed from casing	1 tsp. dried thyme
	1 tsp. dried rosemary
¼ c. finely chopped smoked ham or tasso	1 tsp. black pepper
	½ tsp. cayenne
½ red bell pepper, chopped	1 c. dry bread crumbs
1 c. chopped onion	2 tbsp. oil
1 egg, lightly beaten	¼ c. Creole or Dijon mustard

Lay the chops on a flat surface and cut a pocket in each with a sharp boning knife. Mix together the hot boudin, ham, chopped bell pepper, onion, and egg and stuff into the pork chop. Don't worry about sealing the opening because the egg will act as a binder to keep the stuffing in place. Preheat the oven to 375° F. In a pie tin or shallow plate combine the herbs and spices with the bread crumbs. Beat together the oil and mustard, and brush generously on each chop, then coat it with the bread crumb mixture. Place the chops on a rack above a roasting pan or in a lightly oiled baking dish. Bake for 45 minutes, or until the internal temperature of the chops reads 155–160° F. Serve immediately. Makes 4–6 servings

Serve these spicy pork chops with an aromatic Riesling from Alsace or Oregon.

· veal chop and andouille étouffée ·

Étouffée is the French Creole word for smothered, and it describes a style of slow braising in a flavorful and spicy sauce. Many of Louisiana's favorite dishes are cooked this way.

1 tsp. plus a pinch black pepper
2 tsp. paprika
¾ tsp. plus a pinch cayenne
2 tsp. plus a pinch dried thyme
1 tsp. dried basil
2 tsp. salt
6 large veal chops, ½ to ¾ lb. each
1 tbsp. butter
¼ c. peanut oil
¼ c. all-purpose flour
Pinch ground sage
2 c. finely chopped onion
½ c. finely chopped celery

¼ c. *each* finely chopped red and
  green bell pepper
¼ lb. andouille or other spicy smoked
  sausage, coarsely chopped
¼ lb. tasso or smoked ham, finely
  diced
2 tbsp. chopped garlic
1 c. finely chopped green onions or
  scallions
2 c. rich chicken or veal stock
4 tbsp. tomato paste
Tabasco to taste

Mix together the teaspoon of black pepper, paprika, ¾ teaspoon cayenne, 2 teaspoons thyme, basil, and salt. Rub this spice mix all over the veal chops. Heat the butter and 1 tablespoon of the peanut oil in a heavy 12-inch skillet over medium-high heat. Add the veal chops and brown for 5 minutes on each side. Transfer the chops and any juices to a platter.

In the same heavy-bottomed pan, make a medium-brown roux (see page 77) with the remaining peanut oil and flour. Add a pinch each of black pepper, cayenne, thyme, and sage. Immediately remove the pan from the heat, and add the onion and celery. Put the pan back over medium heat. Continue stirring and scraping the pan until the vegetables are soft, about 5 minutes. The roux will continue to darken. Add the bell peppers, andouille, and tasso, and cook for 2–3 minutes more, until the peppers are wilted. Add the garlic and green onions and

Other favorite ingredients in étouffées are crawfish, shrimp, chicken, and game.

cook for 2 more minutes. Put in the stock and tomato paste, and stir well to make smooth. Add the veal chops and any juices. Bring the pot to a boil, then reduce to a simmer. Cover and cook over low heat for an hour, or until the veal is quite tender. Remove the veal chops to a heated platter and reduce the sauce so it coats a spoon. Adjust the seasoning with salt, pepper, and Tabasco. Pour the sauce over the chops and serve with lots of plain rice.

Makes 6 servings

hot sausage po' boy ·

New Orleans, a city that takes its food quite seriously, has come up with a humble name for one of the city's greatest dishes, the po' boy sandwich. It can be made with humble ingredients such as fried potatoes or with dramatic and elegant fillings such as fried oysters or soft-shelled crab. Some of the best are made with chaurice, or "Hot Sausage" as it's called in New Orleans.

What makes a great po' boy? First the bread. It must be very fresh, soft inside with a slightly chewy crust. The crust can't be too hard or the filling will come oozing out with the first bite. The sausage and other ingredients must be of the highest quality and freshness.

And then there's the fixins'. Usually the sandwich maker will ask how you want your po' boy. "Fully dressed" means the works — finely shredded lettuce or cabbage, mayonnaise, Creole mustard, sliced dill pickles, and sometimes tomatoes, along with very thinly sliced red onions.

4 6-inch sections of French bread
4 links chaurice or other spicy fresh
  sausage, such as hot Italian
½ c. Creole Mustard–Mayonnaise
  Sauce

3 c. finely shredded cabbage or
  lettuce
12–15 dill pickle slices
½ red onion, thinly sliced (optional)
1 large tomato, sliced (optional)

Preheat the oven to 350° F. Warm the French bread for 10 minutes. In a heavy skillet, fry the sausages for 15 minutes over medium heat, turning the links so they brown evenly. Slice the bread in half lengthwise, and spread generously with Creole Mustard–Mayonnaise Sauce on both sides. On one side heap the shredded cabbage or lettuce and lay over it the pickle slices, and onion and tomato, if using. Place a split hot sausage on top, close up the sandwich as best you can, and get to work.

Makes 4 servings

· Creole mustard– mayonnaise sauce ·

½ c. Creole or Dijon mustard
¼ c. homemade or good commercial
  mayonnaise
½ tsp. Worcestershire sauce
Tabasco or other hot sauce to taste
   Mix ingredients thoroughly.
Makes ¾ cup

· Cajun carbonara ·

Carbonara is an Italian classic normally made with pancetta or with smoked bacon. Substituting tasso adds a whole new flavor dimension and yields a lot less grease.

¾ lb. spaghettini or other fine pasta
2 tbsp. butter
¼ lb. tasso cut into thin strips, or
   andouille, diced
1 c. whipping cream

1 egg, lightly beaten
½ c. freshly grated Parmesan cheese
Salt, pepper, and Tabasco to taste
¼ c. finely chopped green onions or
   scallions

This last-minute dish is very quick and simple to prepare and it's guaranteed to get rave reviews from your guests.

Cook the spaghettini as per directions on the package. While it is cooking, make the sauce. In a large heavy frying pan, melt the butter over medium heat. Add the tasso and fry for 2–3 minutes. Pour in the cream and bring to a boil. Reduce to a simmer and cook for 2 minutes. Remove from the heat, cool for 2–3 minutes, and then stir in the egg and the Parmesan cheese. Taste for salt, pepper, and Tabasco. Toss pasta well with the sauce. Garnish with the green onions and serve immediately. Makes 4 servings

· chaurice baked with mashed potatoes ·

This simple dish not only makes use of leftover mashed potatoes, but is good with many types of spicy sausages such as hot Italian or Spicy Country Sausage.

2 lbs. chaurice or other spicy sausage
4 c. leftover mashed potatoes (see
   opposite page)

2 c. finely chopped green onions or
   scallions
1 egg, beaten

In a 2–3-quart pot bring 6 cups of water to a boil. Add the chaurice, cover, and remove from the fire. Let the sausages poach in the water for 20 minutes. This step can be done a day ahead, and the sausages refrigerated until use.

Preheat the oven to 375° F. Arrange the sausages on the bottom of a baking dish. Combine the mashed potatoes and green onions, and cover the sausages with this mixture. Spread the beaten egg over the potatoes. Bake for 30 minutes, until the top is golden brown.
Makes 6–8 servings

This recipe derives originally from The *Picayune's* Creole Cook Book, *published in New Orleans in 1901.*

·white beans with pickled pork and pickled-pork sausages·

If you haven't made your own Pickled Pork or Pickled-Pork Sausages, don't fret. Use ham and smoked sausage, as suggested below.

1 lb. navy or small white beans
1½ qts. chicken or beef stock
¾ lb. Pickled Pork (see page 58) or ham (make sure the piece includes some fat), cut into 1-inch dice
2 tbsp. bacon fat or butter (optional)
1 onion, chopped
1 carrot, chopped
2 ribs celery, chopped
½ green or red bell pepper, chopped
1 tbsp. chopped garlic

1 tsp. black pepper
3 bay leaves
½ tsp. cayenne
½ tsp. dried oregano
½ tsp. dried thyme
1½ lbs. Pickled-Pork Sausage (see page 59) or other smoked sausage, such as andouille, country sausage, or kielbasa
1 c. chopped green onions or scallions
Cooked rice

Soak the beans in water to cover by 3–4 inches overnight. Next day, drain, and put the beans in a 6–8-quart pot or Dutch oven. Add the stock and bring to a boil over high heat. Reduce the heat to a simmer while you prepare the meats and vegetables. Stir the pot occasionally to prevent the beans on the bottom from burning. Cook slowly for 1 hour, then add vegetables.

Wash down this hearty dish with some cold Dixie beer, Pilsner Urquell or Yuengling Pilsner from New Jersey.

In a heavy 12-inch skillet, fry the pickled pork over medium heat to render some of the fat. If the meat is too lean, add bacon fat or butter as needed. Brown for about 10 minutes. Add the onion, carrot, and celery, cover, and cook for 10 more minutes, stirring occasionally. Add the bell pepper and garlic, and cook for 2 minutes. Mix the meat and vegetables with white beans, along with the pepper, bay leaves, cayenne, oregano, and thyme. Continue to cook slowly for about 30 minutes, or until the beans become tender and the liquid begins to thicken. If the mixture becomes too dry, add more stock or water. At this point you can refrigerate the beans overnight.

Panfry the sausages, turning them often to brown evenly. Drain on paper towels and slice them into ½-inch rounds. Add to the beans along with the chopped green onions. Cook for 5–10 more minutes. Serve over rice. Makes 5–6 servings

·mashed potatoes·

3 lbs. russet potatoes, peeled and quartered
8 tbsp. (1 stick) butter
About 1 c. milk
About 1 c. half-and-half
Salt and pepper to taste

Boil potatoes for 25 minutes or until soft. Drain and mash coarsely with butter. Using electric mixer, beat potatoes, adding milk and half-and-half until desired consistency. Add salt and pepper to taste.
Makes 6–8 servings

· ya ca mein ·

In a New Orleans neighborhood, well beyond the terminal stage of decline and long past Desire, sits Sam's Pool Hall. It's a gathering place for people with plenty of free time to play pool, pass the time of day, drink beer, and eat cheap and satisfying food. And like most New Orleans bars, Sam's is heavy on the cheap and satisfying. Spicy, rib-sticking vegetable-beef soups are the house specials. These soups are substantial, to say the least. They are more like stews — usually thick enough to stand a spoon up in — and are basically one-pot meals.

This hearty soup/stew is a favorite at Sam's, and represents the little-known Chinese influence in New Orleans cooking. Like many full-flavored soups or stews, this dish is best made a day ahead so the flavors can mellow. Add the bean sprouts just before serving, and ladle the stew over Chinese soup noodles. At Sam's, the soups are always served with a bottle of hot pepper sauce just in case they are not fiery enough.

¼ c. olive oil
¼ lb. tasso or smoked ham, diced
¾ lb. andouille or other spicy smoked
   sausage, diced

· **Spice rub** ·
1 tsp. salt
2 tsp. freshly ground black pepper
2 tsp. paprika
½ tsp. cayenne
1 tsp. dried oregano
1 tsp. dried thyme
½ tsp. ground sage

....

2 oxtails (about 4 lbs.), cut into
   sections, or 4 lbs. beef short ribs, or
   a mixture of both
½ c. all-purpose flour
1 large onion, chopped
3 medium leeks, chopped and well
   washed

3 ribs celery, chopped
5 medium carrots
1 green bell pepper, chopped
2 tbsp. minced garlic
5–6 c. beef stock, preferably
   homemade
½ c. Chinese soy sauce
3 bay leaves
6 small turnips, quartered (about 4 c.)
½ lb. mushrooms, sliced
½ lb. fresh Chinese noodles or other
   fresh pasta, such as tagliarini
½ lb. bean sprouts

· **Garnishes** ·
Oriental sesame oil
1 c. finely chopped green onions or
   scallions
1 c. coarsely chopped fresh cilantro
   (optional)
Tabasco to taste

Heat the olive oil over medium heat in a 4–6-quart Dutch oven. Add the tasso and andouille and fry for 5 minutes, stirring occasionally. When brown, transfer the smoked meat to a platter and save. Leave any fat in the pot.

Mix the salt, pepper, paprika, cayenne, oregano, thyme, and sage in a medium-sized bowl. Put in the oxtails and/or short ribs and coat with the spice mix. Turn up the heat to medium-high, and add the meat in 2–3 batches to the Dutch oven. Do not overcrowd. Brown for about 5 minutes per side and remove.

When you have browned all the meats, remove and reserve, leaving any fat in the pot.

Reduce the heat to medium, and whisk in the flour to make a brown roux (see page 77). When the roux is light brown, the color of peanut butter, remove the pot from the heat and add the onion, leeks, and celery and 2 of the carrots, finely chopped. Stir until the vegetables are well coated. This will stop the roux from continuing to cook. Place the vegetable-roux mixture back over medium heat and continue to stir until the vegetables are soft, about 10 minutes. Add the bell pepper and cook for another minute. Put in the garlic, and stir in the stock and soy sauce so that they blend well with the vegetables and the roux. Add the meat and bay leaves and bring to a boil. Reduce to a simmer and cook, covered, for 2–3 hours, until the meat is tender. Quarter the remaining carrots lengthwise, and cut into 2-inch pieces. Add them to the pot along with the turnips, tasso, and sausage. Cover and cook for 20 minutes more. Add the mushrooms and cook 5 minutes. Taste the meat. It should be quite tender. If not, cook 15 minutes more, or until done. At this point the Ya Ca Mein can be cooled and refrigerated. Remove surface fat and reheat.

To serve, cook the Chinese noodles or fresh pasta in salted boiling water for 1 or 2 minutes, or until tender. Drain. Place about ½ cup of noodles in a large shallow soup bowl. Add the bean sprouts to the Ya Ca Mein, and ladle over the noodles, making sure each serving has plenty of oxtails or short ribs and vegetables. Sprinkle about 1 teaspoon sesame oil over each serving and allow guests to add their own green onions, cilantro, if desired, and Tabasco.

Makes 6–8 servings with leftovers

· gumbo z'herbes ·

This zesty mix of greens and spices is a Lenten favorite in Louisiana, and is usually made without any meat or seafood. We've made it a bit more sinful (and delicious) with the addition of andouille and tasso. The combination of aromatic, sweet, and bitter greens (use whatever greens you can find in your market) with the smoky meats is irresistible, and what the hell, you can always give up margarine, TV commercials, imitation maple syrup, low-cal frozen tofu, and white bread for Lent anyway, just to compensate.

1 bunch each turnip greens, collard greens, mustard greens, spinach, watercress, and beet greens, or other greens of your choice
⅔ c. peanut oil
⅔ c. all-purpose flour
3 c. chopped onions
3 ribs celery, chopped
8 c. chicken stock
¾ lb. andouille or Louisiana-Style Smoked Sausage, Pickled-Pork Sausage, or good-quality smoked sausage, cut into ½-inch dice
½ lb. tasso or smoked ham, cut into ½-inch dice

1 green bell pepper, chopped
2 tbsp. chopped garlic
4 c. shredded cabbage
1 c. finely chopped green onions or scallions
2 bay leaves
1 tsp. dried thyme
2 whole cloves
⅛ tsp. allspice
1 tsp. dried basil
½ c. Pernod or other anise-flavored liqueur
Salt and black pepper to taste
Cooked rice

Wash the greens thoroughly, remove any tough stems and discard. Chop the greens coarsely. In a heavy pan, make a light-brown roux with the oil and flour, the color of peanut butter (see page 77). Add the onions and celery and cook, stirring until the vegetables are soft, about 10 minutes. Meanwhile bring the chicken stock to a boil in a 4–5-quart pot. Add the andouille, tasso, green pepper, and garlic to the vegetable and roux mixture and continue to cook for 5 more minutes. Now whisk this mixture into the boiling stock. Put in the greens, cabbage, green onions, spices, and Pernod. Bring the gumbo to a boil and reduce to a simmer. Cook gently for 45 minutes. Remove about 2 cups of the solids, and puree them in a food processor. Return the puree to the pot and stir well. Taste for salt and pepper. Serve the gumbo over rice. Makes 8–10 servings

Filé powder and oysters poached in a bit of the liquid can be passed to guests for them to add to the gumbo, if desired.

smothered cabbage
with andouille and tomato ·

This dish can be used as a side dish, but if you add another half pound of andouille, it is substantial enough to serve as a main course.

½ lb. andouille or other spicy smoked
   sausage, cut into ¼-inch dice
8 tbsp. (1 stick) butter or bacon fat
2 medium onions, thinly sliced
½ c. diced carrots
1 tbsp. minced garlic
1 head cabbage, quartered, cored,
   and shredded
2 bay leaves

¾ c. rich chicken or beef stock
¼ c. dry sherry
1 tsp. dried thyme
½ tsp. cayenne
4 tomatoes, peeled and coarsely
   chopped
Tabasco to taste
Salt and pepper to taste

· Louisiana ·

Brown the andouille in butter or bacon fat in a 4–6-quart pot over medium heat for 2–3 minutes. Add the onions and carrots, and cook, covered, for 10 minutes, or until the onions begin to color lightly. Add the garlic, cabbage, and bay leaves. Cover, and cook, stirring occasionally, until the cabbage is well coated and begins to wilt, about 10 minutes. Pour in the stock and sherry and stir well to deglaze the bottom of the pot. Add the thyme and cayenne along with the tomatoes, cover, and cook at a low heat for 10 more minutes, until the cabbage is quite tender. Season to taste with Tabasco, salt, and pepper. Keep warm until served.

Serve with a dark beer, along with some crusty bread.

Makes 8 servings

· oyster and andouille stuffed eggplant ·

Half an eggplant makes a substantial portion as a main course. If the small Japanese eggplants are available in your area, you can stuff them and use the dish as a first course or hors d'oeuvre.

2 medium eggplants
½ c. olive oil
4 tbsp. (½ stick) butter
¾ lb. andouille or other spicy smoked sausage, finely chopped
½ lb. tasso or smoked ham, finely chopped
2 c. finely chopped onion
½ c. finely chopped red or green bell pepper
½ c. finely chopped green onions or scallions

2 tbsp. minced garlic
1 12-oz. jar oysters or 18 shucked fresh oysters, coarsely chopped into ½-inch pieces
½ tsp. *each* dried oregano, basil, and thyme
½ tsp. Worcestershire sauce
⅔ c. freshly grated Parmesan cheese
1–1½ c. coarse dried bread crumbs
Tabasco to taste
Salt and black pepper to taste

Preheat the oven to 400° F. Cut each eggplant in half lengthwise and score the cut side in a crisscross pattern with a knife. Brush the eggplant generously with olive oil all over and place cut side down on a sheet pan. Bake for 10 minutes and then turn the eggplants over. Brush with more oil if needed and continue to bake until the eggplants are quite soft, about 20 minutes. Remove the eggplants and set aside. Reduce the oven to 350° F.

In a large frying pan melt the butter over medium heat, then add the andouille, tasso, and onion. Cook over medium heat until the onion is soft and the meat is beginning to brown, about 10 minutes. Add the bell pepper, green onions, and garlic and cook 5 minutes. Add the oysters to the pan and cook for 2 minutes. Remove the pan from the heat and transfer the contents to a bowl. Scoop out the pulp from the eggplant, being careful not to rip the skin, and coarsely chop the pulp, then add to the bowl along with the herbs and Worcestershire sauce. Add ½ cup of the Parmesan cheese and reserve the rest.

A great lunch or picnic dish — delicious hot, cold, or at room temperature.

Mix in enough bread crumbs to bind the mixture — it should remain moist. Season with salt, pepper, and 6–8 drops of Tabasco. Generously stuff each eggplant half, using up all the dressing. Sprinkle on the remaining cheese and bake for 30 minutes, or until the cheese begins to brown. Makes 6–8 servings

· mushroom, tasso, and chaurice dirty rice ·

This is a great side dish to liven up an otherwise bland meal. Try it with pork, grilled fish, or chicken.

2 tbsp. butter
½ lb. chaurice or other spicy sausage, coarsely chopped
¼ lb. tasso or smoked ham, coarsely chopped
¼ lb. chicken gizzards and/or hearts, finely chopped or ground
1 medium onion, finely chopped
1 rib celery, finely diced
1 leek, split in half and thinly sliced
1 medium green bell pepper, finely chopped

¼ lb. mushrooms, thinly sliced
1 tbsp. minced garlic
½ tsp. cayenne
1 tsp. dried thyme
½ tsp. dried sage
¼ lb. chicken livers, coarsely chopped
2 c. long-grain rice
2¼ c. chicken stock
Salt and pepper to taste

· Louisiana ·

In a large skillet or Dutch oven melt the butter over medium-high heat. Add the chaurice, tasso, and giblets and fry them for 5–7 minutes, until the giblets are no longer red. Add the onion and celery and cook, stirring occasionally, for 5 minutes, or until the vegetables are soft. Add the leek, green pepper, mushrooms, and garlic, cover, and cook 5 minutes, stirring occasionally. At this point all the vegeta-

Good for lunch with a salad of bitter greens.

bles should be soft. Stir in the cayenne, thyme, sage, and chicken livers. Continue to cook, stirring frequently for 3 minutes, until the liver is no longer red. Stir in the rice so it is completely coated with the meats and vegetables, add the stock, and bring everything to a boil. Adjust seasoning with salt and pepper, cover, and reduce the heat to a low simmer. Cook for 20 to 30 minutes, until the rice is tender and all the liquid is absorbed. Makes 6–8 servings.

THE **N**ORTHEAST

· the American stewpot ·

SOUPS

Minestrone

Italian zucchini soup

Chum botta

Portuguese kale soup

APPETIZERS & PASTAS

Skewered Tuscan sausage and chicken livers

Stuffed quahogs

Asparagus and sausage tortiere

Tuscan sausage frittata

Cannelloni

Bolognese sauce

Italian sweet fennel sausage and porcini pasta

Quick and easy pastas

MAIN DISHES

Steamed clams with linguiça

Clam and smoked sausage hash

Joe Molinari's eggplant and sausage "lasagna"

Italian street barbecue — grilled sausage and vegetables

Italian sausage, chicken, and ricotta pie

Chicken breasts stuffed with sausage, spinach, leeks, and ham

Italian sausage and pheasant pie

Quick and easy sautés

Puerto Rican chicken, rice, and sausage stew

Lamb shoulder stuffed with hot Italian sausage in porcini sauce

Loukaniko with lamb and spinach

Pastitsio — macaroni and cheese with a sausage surprise

Cotechino with lentils

Rolled flank steak stuffed with Italian sausage, basil, and Swiss cheese

Franco's bagnet Piemontese

Tuscan sausage and cannellini beans

Cholent

Brian's maple beans

Butternut squash stuffed with sausage, apple, and chestnuts

HOT LINKS & COUNTRY FLAVORS

merica is a country of immigrants. The gateway ports of the Northeast received the greatest flow of exiles in the nineteenth and early twentieth centuries, but the process began with the Pilgrims, and continues today. These new Americans bring with them their languages, dress, and customs, and especially their foods that make this part of the country a rich stew of diverse ingredients and flavors.

This diversity is evident on the streets of northeastern cities today, and in bars, cafés, and restaurants. New York and Boston are among the best cities in the United States for street food, especially sausages. Walking through Greenwich Village or Boston's North End, Spanish Harlem or Coney Island, you come across a mind-boggling variety of foods sold from sidewalk carts or hole-in-the-wall lunch counters of every ethnic persuasion. And among the blintzes and blinis, taquitos, fried plantains, roast chestnuts, shaved ice, knishes, kishkes, and souvlaki, you'll find sausages of every type imaginable.

Some would say that the quintessential New York sausage is the frankfurter or Coney Island hot dog. After all, what can compare to standing on tiptoe as a kid at the sauerkraut table at Nathan's in Coney Island, hot frank firmly gripped in the left hand, slathering khaki-brown mustard down the length of the dog, then covering all, bun included, with the hot and tangy kraut? But then there's strolling down Bleecker Street in Greenwich Village on a muggy Saturday evening in summer, stopping at a lunch counter where the rich smoke of Italian sausage, garlic, pepper, and anise swirls out into the street. Juice drips through your fingers as you walk down the sidewalk, munching the sandwich of sausage, peppers, and onions, wondering where it was Bob Dylan played for the first time, and if that's De Niro or only his cousin over there at the café, gesturing elegantly over the cappuccino. Or what about eating Greek loukaniko sausages and *mezedes*, drinking ouzo and retsina, and dancing to the wild *rembetika* music of bouzoukis and accordions, at the old Pantheon on Ninth Avenue, a few blocks up from Times Square? Or putting down huge platters of linguiça

and clams at the Fado night club on East 14th Street, where they sang those sinuous Portuguese blues all night long? Or snacking on *piononos,* plantain, and spicy sausage fritters, at that Puerto Rican café on Lexington Avenue where the tall girl with the dark eyes added even more spice with her lively smile?

Sausages from all over the world came into American cuisine through the great ports of the Eastern Seaboard, and added life and seasoning to the cooking of New York and New England.

The Northeast incorporates a true mix of cultures in its cooking. The Indians first, as in other regions, provided the base of corn, squash, game, fish, and other native ingredients. Pilgrims and other early English settlers built on the native cuisine, amalgamating indigenous foods and techniques with European ingredients and recipes.

From the beginning, though, the region was open to a great variety of culinary influences. French Canadians drifted down from the North, and brought with them *tourtière* and other specialties of *les habitants.* Seafaring New Englanders brought back the spices and flavors of foreign ports. Germans and Eastern Europeans arrived and spread out through the towns and countryside, bringing with them their many sausages. Italians, Greeks, and other southern Europeans opened restaurants in the cities and small towns. The Portuguese came early to the northeastern seaboard to fish for cod along the Great Banks, and stayed to create communities in Massachusetts and Rhode Island that even today maintain their language, customs, and links to the mother country.

All these ethnic groups have left their traces in the rich cuisine of the northeastern United States, and their various sausages have helped to enrich both home and restaurant cooking throughout the region. The basic Yankee sausage of ground pork, sage, black pepper, and spices is based on the ubiquitous English recipe found in Hannah Glasse's and other early cookbooks. Italian, Greek, Portuguese, and other sausages are found in dishes that are popular from Maine to Staten Island. The Portuguese have had a special influence on the regional cuisine, especially in New England. Their flavorful combinations of spicy sausage and seafood seem uniquely suited to the seaborne riches of the Northeast, and their highly seasoned dishes

HOT LINKS & COUNTRY FLAVORS

such as Steamed Clams with Linguiça (see page 126) or Portuguese Kale Soup (see page 117) can stand side by side with baked beans (see Brian's Maple Beans, page 142) as regional specialties. In cities like New York, Boston, and Providence, the Italian communities offer a wide range of regional sausages from the mildly flavored luganega, cotechino, and Tuscan-style sausages to spicier, hotter versions from farther south. These sausages combine beautifully with poultry as in our Chicken Breasts Stuffed with Sweet Fennel Sausage, Spinach, Leeks, and Ham (see page 131) and Italian Sausage and Pheasant Pie (see page 132). Italian sausage and pasta is, of course, a natural pairing, and our Cannelloni (see page 122) and Bolognese Sauce (see page 123) show how tasty this combination can be. Other recipes, from Greek Loukaniko with Lamb and Spinach (see page 136) to Puerto Rican Chicken, Rice, and Sausage Stew (see page 134), show how the flavor of the varied sausages used by the Northeast's lively ethnic mix provides an undertone of spice and excitement to the region's cuisine.

Each village, town or region in Italy seems to have a slightly different accent, in both language and food. The sausages of Italy are as rich and variegated as its culture, and much of the attraction of Italy's sausages, and its people, is found in just this diversity. The standard sweet Italian and hot Italian sausages available in most American cities today offer just a hint of the unbounded variety of Italian sausages.

In America, Italians, like most immigrant groups, tended to form neighborhoods from regions in the old country. *Paisano* means, literally, a person from the same "countryside," and New York's Little Italy could easily be subdivided into Little Sicily, Calabria, or Tuscany, with each region's distinctive sausages sold in the pork stores and restaurants of each neighborhood. Below we give recipes for some of these individually styled sausages of Italian regions and American neighborhoods. Like most Italians, we'll talk more in "dialect" than "polite Italian," and try to preserve some of the lively diversity of Italy's sausages and sausage dishes as they are found today in Italian-American restaurants and home kitchens.

· spicy hot Italian sausage ·

This spicy sausage is the one you're most likely to find sizzling on a grill at the Feast of San Gennaro or at a lunch counter in New York's Little Italy. Try it grilled, with fried peppers and onions, or poached and sliced on top of homemade pizza.

3 lbs. pork butt	1 tbsp. red pepper flakes
¾ lb. pork back fat	2 tsp. freshly ground black pepper
1 tbsp. minced garlic	2 tbsp. anise-flavored liqueur such as
4 tsp. kosher salt	Sambuca (optional)
2 tbsp. anise or fennel seed	¼ c. cold water
1 tsp. cayenne	Medium hog casings

For details on making sausage, see page 332.

Combine the pork, fat, and all other ingredients except the water and casings in a large bowl. Grind everything through a ⅜-inch plate. Moisten with water, and squeeze and knead the mixture until everything is well blended. Stuff into medium hog casings, and tie into 5-inch links. Will keep 3 days in the refrigerator, 2–3 months frozen. Makes 4 pounds

Drink a big, rough red wine with this, like an old-style California burgundy or a Barbera d'Alba from Piedmont.

·Tuscan sausage·

Tuscany is famous for its wines and olive oils, and also for its delicately flavored sausages. What comes through here is not the heat and spice of the South, but rather the subtle aromas of herbs, tomatoes, and wine. The best match for these complex and richly flavored sausages is a medium-bodied Chianti Classico from Tuscany.

3 lbs. pork butt
½ lb. pork back fat
2 tsp. kosher salt
½ c. chopped sun-dried tomatoes
  packed in olive oil
4 anchovy fillets, finely chopped
2 tsp. coarsely ground black pepper

¼ c. minced fresh basil or 2 tsp. dried
2 tbsp. chopped fresh oregano or
  ¾ tsp. dried
Pinch allspice
½ c. Chianti or other dry red wine
Medium hog casings

For details on making sausage, see page 332.
Grind the pork meat through a ⅜-inch plate, the fat through a ¼-inch plate. In a large bowl, knead the meat, fat, and all the remaining ingredients except the casings together until the mixture is well blended. Stuff into casings and tie into 6-inch links. Will keep 3 days in the refrigerator, frozen for 2–3 months.
Makes 4 pounds

Tuscan sausage accents the flavors of chicken and squab very nicely, and can be used in any dish where a mild flavor is desired.

· Festa di San Gennaro: New York's Little Italy ·

At the Feast of San Gennaro on Mulberry Street in New York's Little Italy, there's music and laughter, and Italian in every dialect from Sicilian to Toscano, Friulano to Calabrese. Everybody's out on the streets celebrating the saint's day with feasting, talk, and good times. Sausages of virtually every region in Italy are grilled at sidewalk stands, with smells of garlic, peppers, onions, and olive oil everywhere. At one stand there's aromatic Tuscan sausage flavored with sun-dried tomatoes, basil, and wine; at another, Barese sausage, redolent with anise, Pecorino cheese, garlic, and oregano.

With glasses of rough, homemade Zinfandel in our hands, we order spicy Sicilian sausages from an old man whose dark face is wrinkled and creased from years of smiles and sun. He pricks the skins with a long, thin knife, and lays the sausage carefully on the hot grill over glowing coals. The sausages smoke and jump on the grill, aromas of garlic, pepper, and fennel billowing up. With one deft movement he flips them over and to the side. He tosses a handful of sliced onions and peppers into a blackened frying pan, and pours in green-gold olive oil from an old wine bottle.

HOT LINKS & COUNTRY FLAVORS

As the peppers and onions sputter in the oil, he splits two rolls and lays them down along the far side of the grill. Suddenly, the old man smiles and nods to us, scoops up the peppers and onions on one side of the roll, the sausage on the other, wraps them together in paper, and hands them to us. He watches us carefully as we bite into the sandwiches. Spicy pork, garlic and hot pepper, fennel and onions all come together in a rush of flavors and textures. We gulp down big juice glasses full of fiery, slightly sweet Zinfandel, look into his bright, ancient eyes, and smile back.

· Italian sweet fennel sausage ·

This mildly flavored sausage is perfumed with the scents of fennel, allspice, and oregano, and is the sweet Italian sausage of your neighborhood delicatessen. Use it wherever you want a pleasant fresh sausage with a touch of garlic, spices, and herbs.

3 lbs. pork butt
¾ lb. pork back fat
4 garlic cloves, minced
4 tsp. kosher salt
2 tbsp. fennel seed

1 tbsp. freshly ground black pepper
⅛ tsp. ground allspice
1 tsp. dried oregano
½ c. dry red wine
Medium hog casings (optional)

For details on making sausage, see page 332.

A wonderful quick dinner: grill sausages with eggplant and thick slices of red onion sprinkled with olive oil; serve with a full-bodied Merlot from California or northern Italy.

Grind the pork and fat together through a ⅜-inch plate. Add the garlic, salt, spices, and red wine. Mix well with your hands. Shape into patties, or stuff into casings and tie into 5-inch links. Keeps 3 days refrigerated, 2–3 months frozen. Makes 4 pounds

· Barese-style sausage ·

This popular sausage made in the style of Bari in southern Italy contains cheese. Its lively, aggressive flavors make it a favorite in Italian neighborhoods in New Orleans. Don't store this sausage too long in the refrigerator or freezer, as the cheese can become quite strong with age and overpower the other flavors.

2 lbs. lean pork butt
1 lb. lean beef chuck
1 lb. pork back fat
1 c. (about 4 oz.) cubed Pecorino or
  Romano cheese
1 tbsp. freshly ground black pepper
1 tbsp. ground fennel seed

1 tbsp. finely chopped garlic
1 tbsp. kosher salt
1 tbsp. red pepper flakes
¼ c. chopped fresh flat-leaf parsley
½ c. dry red wine
Medium hog casings

For details on making sausage, see page 332.

In a large bowl, toss together the meat, fat, and cheese, and grind through a ⅜-inch plate. Add the remaining ingredients except the casings, and knead the mixture well. Stuff into casings and tie into 4-inch links. Keeps for 2–3 days in the refrigerator, 1–2 months frozen. Makes 4½ pounds

· luganega ·

This mild but flavorful sausage is popular in northern Italy where hot pepper, fennel, and garlic aren't as appreciated in sausages as they are farther south. Aromatic spices like nutmeg, coriander, and cinnamon, fragrant herbs like sage and marjoram, and often a light touch of lemon peel make this sausage an interesting and unusual addition to many bean and pasta dishes. It also makes an original and delightful breakfast sausage.

Luganega is usually stuffed into sheep casings and coiled, unlinked, in the refrigerator or display case. It is cut to order, and used in the casings or as a bulk sausage.

3 lbs. pork butt	½ tsp. dried marjoram
¾ lb. pork back fat	1 tsp. sugar
4 tsp. kosher salt	1 tsp. minced garlic (optional)
¼ tsp. freshly grated nutmeg	1 tsp. grated lemon peel (optional)
½ tsp. ground coriander	2 tbsp. chopped fresh flat-leaf parsley
2 tsp. freshly ground black pepper	¼ c. dry white wine or vermouth
Pinch cinnamon	¼ c. water
¼ tsp. ground sage	Sheep casings

For details on making sausage, see page 332.

Mix all the ingredients, except the wine, water, and casings, in a large bowl, and grind through ¼-inch plate. Moisten the mixture with the wine and water. Knead thoroughly until everything is well blended. Stuff into sheep casings, coiling the sausage as you go. Keeps 2–3 days refrigerated, 2–3 months frozen.
Makes 4 pounds

For considerably more flavor, be sure to grate the nutmeg fresh for each batch.

· cotechino ·

Cotechino is a delightfully aromatic, large boiling sausage that lends flavor to beans, lentils, and soups (see Cotechino with Lentils, page 138). Cooked pork skin is added to give this sausage body and a firm texture.

1 lb. pork skin cut from the ham, belly, or back
3 lbs. pork butt
½ lb. pancetta
¼ lb. pork back fat
4 tsp. kosher salt
1 tbsp. coarsely ground pepper
½ tsp. dried thyme
¼ tsp. ground sage
¼ tsp. dried marjoram or oregano

½ tsp. ground bay leaf (use blender or spice mill)
¼ tsp. pure vanilla extract
Pinch *each* ground allspice, cinnamon, ginger, and freshly grated nutmeg
2 tsp. sugar
1 tsp. curing salts (see page 343) (optional)
½ c. dry white wine
Large beef casings

For details on making sausage, see page 332.

Place the pork skin in a 2–3-quart pot, cover with water, and bring to a boil. Reduce the heat, cover, and simmer for about 45 minutes, or until the skin is soft. Drain and cool under running water. The skin must be completely cool or it will clump up when ground. Mix together with all the ingredients, except the wine and casings. Grind through a ¼-inch plate. Moisten the mixture with white wine and knead until all the ingredients are well blended. Stuff into large casings, and tie into large links, 7–8 inches long. Air-dry the sausages on a rack for 2–3 days in the refrigerator or, if you are using curing salts, at room temperature, before cooking. To poach cotechino, simmer slowly (in 160–180° F water) for 1–1½ hours. Keeps 4–5 days refrigerated, 2–3 months frozen. Makes 4 pounds

When stuffed into a boned pig's foot, this becomes zampone, a specialty of Modena in northern Italy.

There's some discussion, to say the least, among sausage fanciers about the origin and composition of that American favorite, the hot dog. One school of thought maintains that New York's all-beef, kosher-style frankfurter is, if not the first, certainly among the best versions of this legendary and succulent delicacy. And having enjoyed more New York franks than we can begin to remember from Coney Island to Times Square, who are we to disagree?

But we are not including a recipe for an all-beef frankfurter in this section — not because we don't like the New York style, but because it is difficult to make an acceptable version of this sausage in the home. Preparing frankfurters requires emulsifying the beef, fat, and spices with ice and water, an arduous task involving special equipment — and most homemade attempts to re-create the Coney Island–style hot dog are pallid compared with the original. You can come pretty close in flavor, but most homemade all-beef hot dogs don't have that satisfying pop when you bite through the casing and the hot juices burst into the mouth. We tried numerous versions, none very successfully, and frankly we'd just as soon send out to the nearest Nathan's.

But hot dog lovers should not despair! We have included a toothsome frank recipe in the Midwest section (see page 154), based on the German knockwurst or frankfurter, that uses a savory mix of pork, beef, and spices — and it's much more tasty than any of our all-beef versions.

That said, we do have a delicious recipe for a peppery, Romanian-style beef sausage similar to those served in restaurants and delicatessens along New York's Second Avenue.

· Romanian Jewish beef sausage ·

This all-beef sausage is loaded with garlic and black pepper, and is a staple at such famous Romanian kosher restaurants as Sammy's in New York. Use it in a number of traditional recipes in place of plain beef brisket to perk up the flavors and provide a dash of spiciness (see our Cholent recipe, page 141).

The sausage can be left raw or air-dried, and poached before serving. Or it can be cold smoked, and then poached. If you opt for air-drying or cold smoking you must use the curing salts in the recipe (see "Note on Nitrites," page 343).

3 lbs. lean beef chuck

1¼ lbs. fatty beef, such as short ribs
  or plate

¼ lb. beef suet or other firm beef fat

5 tsp. kosher salt

1 tbsp. coarsely ground black pepper

2 tsp. ground coriander

Pinch *each* ground allspice, ground
  bay leaves, and ground cloves

1 tsp. dry mustard

2 tbsp. whole yellow mustard seed

2 tbsp. minced garlic

2 tsp. sugar

1 tsp. curing salts (if air-drying or cold
  smoking, see page 343)

½ c. water

Lamb or beef casings

For details on how to make sausage, see page 332.

Grind the lean beef through a ⅜-inch plate, the fatty beef and fat through the ¼-inch plate. In a large bowl, mix the ground meats with all the other ingredients, except the water and casings. Add enough water to allow you to work the spices in, and knead until all the ingredients are well blended.

If you are going to leave the sausage fresh, then stuff into lamb casings. If you are going to air-dry or cold smoke the sausage, then use the larger beef casings. For fresh sausage, tie into 5-inch lengths. For air-dried or smoked, make 6–7-inch links. To cold smoke: air-dry overnight and smoke 6–8 hours. For air-drying: air-dry up to 3 days in front of a fan, with a drip pan underneath to catch any liquid. Poach smoked or air-dried versions of this sausage in 180° F water for 30 minutes before serving. Keeps for 2–3 days in the refrigerator, 2–3 months frozen. Makes 4–5 pounds

This hearty sausage is delicious grilled or as part of a boiled dinner with brisket, cabbage, potatoes, onions, and carrots.

If you've ever sat at a table in a Greek café next to the Aegean on a bright afternoon and ordered an ouzo or a glass of retsina, you'll know about the wonderful custom called *mezedes*. These little snacks are considered an indispensable accompaniment to drinks, and usually include olives, some sharp white cheese like feta or kefalotiri, a bite or two of chewy octopus, and a chunk of grilled loukaniko, the flavorful Greek sausage.

· loukaniko ·

Loukaniko is not only a tasty snack before dinner, but like most fully flavored sausages, it can be a savory addition to many chicken, meat, or pasta dishes. It is sometimes made entirely with pork, sometimes with a mix of pork and lamb, or pork and beef. We use pork and lamb, but you should feel free to experiment.

¼ c. olive oil
1 c. chopped onions
2 lbs. pork butt
1 lb. lean lamb shoulder
¾ lb. pork back fat
4 tsp. kosher salt
1 tsp. freshly ground black pepper
1 tbsp. minced garlic
2 tsp. dried oregano or 1 tbsp. chopped fresh oregano

1 tsp. dried thyme or 2 tsp. chopped fresh thyme
1 tbsp. ground coriander
2 tbsp. grated orange zest
½ c. dry white wine (use retsina, if you like the flavor)
Medium hog casings

For details on making sausage, see page 332.

Heat the olive oil in a heavy skillet over medium heat. Put in the onions, cover, and cook until they are translucent, stirring occasionally, about 10 minutes. Spread the onions on a plate and chill them quickly in the freezer for about 15 minutes. In a large bowl, mix the onions with all the other ingredients except the wine and the casings. Grind everything through a ¼-inch plate. Add the wine, and knead well until all the ingredients are blended together. Stuff into medium hog casings and tie into 6-inch links. Loukaniko will keep 3 days in the refrigerator, 2–3 months in the freezer. Makes 4–5 pounds

Serve as part of mezedes, *the traditional Greek appetizers, accompanied with ouzo. Loukaniko also provides spice and flavor in traditional Greek dishes like pastitsio (see page 137).*

The Portuguese are great lovers of sausage, and their tangy linguiça and spicy chouriço are delicious combined with seafood and fish. Both sausages are great for sandwiches or appetizers, and add lots of flavor to bean and pasta dishes, stews, and casseroles.

· linguiça ·

Linguiça is one of a family of smoked sausages that are coarse in texture and usually fairly spicy. Other similar sausages, such as kielbasa, andouille, and smoked country sausage, are the backbone of country cooking all over the world, and are found in many dishes and almost every tradition. The Portuguese are particularly passionate about their sausages, and use them in a wide variety of dishes. They realize how much flavor and excitement sausages such as linguiça can add to even the simplest dish.

3 lbs. pork butt
½ pound pork back fat
4 tsp. kosher salt
3 tbsp. high-quality paprika,
  Hungarian or Spanish
1 tbsp. minced garlic
3 tbsp. red wine vinegar

1 tbsp. freshly ground black pepper
½ tsp. dried marjoram
½ tsp. dried oregano
Pinch ground coriander
1 tsp. curing salts (if cold smoking,
  see page 343)
Wide hog casings

For details on making sausage, see page 332.

Separate all the external fat from the pork and refrigerate it along with the back fat. Cut the lean meat into strips, and liberally coat it with all the remaining ingredients except the casings. Pack the meat into a plastic tub or stainless steel bowl, cover, and refrigerate it overnight to marinate. The next day, grind the lean pork through a very coarse (⅜ or ½ inch) plate, then grind the fat through a ¼-inch plate. In a large bowl, mix the lean meat and fat along with any liquid and spices still remaining from the marinade. Knead and squeeze the mixture until all the ingredients are thoroughly blended. Stuff into wide hog casings, and tie into 10-inch links. If you are going to dry and cold smoke the sausage, use the curing salts in the mix. If you intend to hot smoke the sausages, you can leave the cure out. Follow directions on page 340 for drying and smoking. Keeps 1 week refrigerated, 2–3 months frozen. Makes 3 pounds

Linguiça, split and grilled with sliced onions, and served on a French roll, makes a world-class sandwich. It's also a favorite with scrambled eggs or in an omelette.

· Portuguese chouriço ·

This sausage is similar to linguiça, but a different spice mixture and a bit of cayenne give it more heat.

3 lbs. pork butt
½ lb. pork back fat
4 tsp. kosher salt
3 tbsp. high-quality paprika,
   Hungarian or Spanish
1 tsp. cayenne
1 tbsp. minced garlic
3 tbsp. red wine vinegar

1 tsp. freshly ground black pepper
½ tsp. dried marjoram
1 tsp. ground cumin
½ tsp. ground coriander
1 tsp. curing salts (if cold smoking,
   see page 343)
Wide hog casings

For details on making sausage, see page 332.

Separate all the external fat from the pork and refrigerate it along with the back fat. Cut the lean meat into strips, and liberally coat it with all the remaining ingredients except the casings. Pack the meat into a plastic tub or stainless steel bowl, cover, and refrigerate it overnight to marinate. The next day, grind the lean pork through a very coarse (⅜ or ½ inch) plate, then the fat through a ¼-inch plate. In a large bowl, mix the lean meat and fat along with any liquid and spices still remaining from the marinade. Knead and squeeze the mixture until all ingredients are thoroughly blended. Stuff into wide hog casings, and tie into 10-inch links. If you are going to dry and cold smoke the sausage, use the curing salts in the mix. If you prefer to hot smoke the sausage, leave them out. Follow the directions on page 343 for drying and smoking. Keeps 1 week refrigerated, 2–3 months frozen. Makes 3 pounds.

Use chouriço in recipes where you want plenty of spicy flavor — our Puerto Rican Chicken, Rice, and Sausage Stew (page 134), for example.

New England country cooks have long made a flavorful sausage from the traditional English mix of ground pork, sage, and black pepper, but they've added a few ingredients of their own. These often include exotic spices brought in by their seafaring ancestors, and they sometimes add their native oysters to the mix. The combination of oysters and pork sounds a bit odd, but the flavors go together beautifully.

· Yankee sage sausage ·

This recipe, adapted from Judith and Evan Jones's *The L. L. Bean Book of New New England Cookery,* is another regional variation of the basic American sage-flavored sausage. Ginger and cloves give the sausage a bit more spice than usual, and the mix of herbs contributes a lovely aroma. Use it in any recipe calling for fresh country-style sausage.

3 tbsp. finely chopped or dried and
   crumbled fresh sage, or 2–3 tsp.
   ground sage
3 lbs. pork butt
½–¾ lb. pork back fat
3½ tsp. kosher salt
1 tbsp. coarsely ground black pepper
¼ tsp. cayenne

¼ tsp. dried summer savory
¼ tsp. dried marjoram
¼ tsp. dried thyme
⅛ tsp. ground ginger
Pinch ground cloves
½ c. cold water
Sheep or medium hog casings
  (optional)

For details on making sausage, see page 332.

To dry fresh sage: spread the leaves on a cookie sheet and bake at 350° F for a few minutes, until the leaves are dry and you can crumble them in your hands.

Grind the meat and fat through a ¼-inch plate. In a large bowl, mix the meat, fat, and spices with the cold water. Knead and squeeze the mixture until thoroughly blended. You can stuff the meat into sheep or medium hog casings, but it is quite good as bulk sausage. Simply form the meat into thick ½-pound rolls, wrap, and refrigerate or freeze. Keeps 2–3 days refrigerated, 2–3 months frozen.

Makes 4 pounds

Judith and Evan Jones suggest drying fresh sage in a warm oven before crumbling it into the sausage mixture to give a lovely sage perfume and flavor.

· oyster and pork sausage ·

Sausage and oysters might sound like an odd combination, but they pair up beautifully. The salty tang of the oyster and the spice and liveliness of sausages combine on the palate in a startling and delicious way. We've taken this pairing a step farther, though, and actually combined oysters and meat in a sausage. In early New England, oysters were very cheap and plentiful. These days, they are a bit more dear, but all you need here is a 12-ounce jar or a dozen and a half fresh oysters. This also makes a great stuffing for steak or thick pork chops, and is an excellent substitute for oysters in the Gold Rush classic, Hangtown Fry.

1½ c. shucked fresh oysters (about 18) or a 12-oz. jar
½ lb. pork shoulder
½ lb. beef suet
2 c. fresh white bread crumbs
2 tsp. fresh lemon juice
⅛ tsp. ground allspice
¼ tsp. freshly grated nutmeg

½ tsp. freshly ground black pepper
2 tsp. kosher salt or to taste
½ tsp. dried thyme
½ tsp. Tabasco
Medium hog casings
2 tbsp. butter
1 tbsp. peanut oil

For details on making sausage, see page 332.

Grind the oysters, pork, and beef suet through a ¼-inch plate. In a large bowl, mix together thoroughly all the ingredients except the casings, butter, and oil. Fry a small patty, and taste for seasonings. Add more spices, salt, or pepper as desired. Stuff into hog casings and tie into 5-inch lengths.

Prick the sausages, and poach in simmering (180° F) salted water for 10–15 minutes, until firm. Cool. You can refrigerate the sausages at this point for 2–3 days until you are ready to eat them, or freeze them for up to 3 months. To serve, brown over medium heat for 5 minutes on both sides in butter and oil.

Makes 2–3 pounds

Serve with new potatoes roasted with garlic, onions, and anchovies, and a green salad with lemon and walnut oil dressing, along with a full-bodied, dry California Chenin Blanc.

· minestrone ·

The version of this wonderful soup that most of us grew up with was thick and flavorful. In a traditional minestrone, however, the vegetables are usually overcooked, and the pasta more of a thickener than an individual ingredient. In the following recipe, we've tried to make a similarly thick and rib-sticking soup, but with plenty of flavor still in the vegetables.

Serve this soup with lots of freshly grated Parmesan cheese sprinkled on top and a loaf of crusty sourdough bread for a satisfying supper.

½ lb. dried kidney beans, soaked
  overnight
3–4 qts. beef or chicken stock
1 c. lentils
1 c. tomato puree
1 c. dry red wine
1 c. chopped onions
1 c. carrots cut into ¾-inch pieces
1 c. celery cut into ¾-inch pieces
2 tbsp. chopped garlic
1 tsp. dried basil or 2 tbsp. chopped
  fresh basil
½ tsp. dried oregano or ½ tbsp.
  chopped fresh oregano

1 bunch spinach or chard, chopped
  (2 c.)
1 lb. hot or sweet Italian sausage,
  sliced in ½-inch rounds
2 c. zucchini, cut into ¾-inch pieces
1 c. chopped fresh parsley, flat-leaf
  preferred
1 c. dried shell pasta or elbow
  macaroni
Salt and pepper to taste
Freshly grated Parmesan cheese

Drain the soaked beans. Bring the stock to a boil in a 6–8-quart pot. Add the beans, reduce to a simmer, and cook 2 hours, partially covered. Add the lentils and cook for 30 minutes more, or until the beans and lentils are done. Add the tomato puree, wine, onions, carrots, celery, garlic, basil, oregano, and spinach. Cook for 15 minutes.

Fry the sausage in a heavy skillet over medium heat for about 5–7 minutes, until lightly browned. Add to the soup along with the zucchini, parsley, and pasta. Cook until the pasta is *al dente*. Minestrone is at its best the next day, so if you can, cool it, then refrigerate overnight. When reheated, the soup should be about thick enough for a spoon to stand up in it. Season with salt and pepper and serve hot with lots of freshly grated Parmesan cheese.

Makes 10–12 servings

Minestrone can be made up a day ahead — the flavors will mellow and the soup will thicken in the refrigerator.

·Italian zucchini soup·

This soup recipe is a boon to the home gardener who is experiencing run-away zucchini production, or a family suffering from zucchini burnout.

1 tbsp. fruity olive oil
½ lb. luganega or other mildly
   flavored Italian sausage, sliced in
   ½-inch rounds
¼ lb. fat trimmings from prosciutto,
   finely chopped, or ¼ lb. pancetta,
   finely chopped (optional)
2 medium onions, finely chopped
2 ribs celery, finely chopped
3 tbsp. minced garlic
3 qts. chicken or beef stock

3 ripe tomatoes, peeled, seeded, and
   chopped
1½ c. raw rice, preferably arborio
1½ lbs. small zucchini, thinly sliced
1 tbsp. chopped fresh oregano or
   1 tsp. dried
¼ lb. prosciutto or ham, cut into thin
   strips
Salt and pepper to taste
½ c. freshly grated Parmesan cheese

In a heavy 5–6-quart stockpot or Dutch oven, heat the olive oil over medium-high heat. Add the sausage and fry 5–7 minutes, until lightly browned, turning a few times. Remove the sausage, and put the optional prosciutto fat or pancetta in the oil remaining in the pan. Fry until the fat is rendered. Add the onions, celery, and garlic. Cover the pot and reduce the heat to medium. Cook the vegetables until they just begin to color, about 10 minutes. Pour off most of the fat, and discard. Add the stock and chopped tomatoes. Bring to a boil, and then reduce to a simmer. Add the rice, cover, and cook 25 minutes, or until the rice is done to your taste. Put the sausages back in the pot, along with the zucchini, oregano, and prosciutto. Cook, covered, 5 minutes. Season with salt and pepper. Serve in individual bowls with lots of Parmesan cheese. Makes 8 servings

Here's one more delicious and sneaky way to get zucchini on the table.

· chum botta ·

This "recipe" was a family favorite of Paul Camardo's, an assistant cook of mine at Poulet. It is a hearty soup/stew that can be inspired by leftovers. Use whatever is lurking around the refrigerator — scraps of prosciutto, salami, or ham, some tasty sausage, vegetables, etc.

4 qts. beef or chicken stock
1 lb. leftover pieces of prosciutto,
   coppa, ham, or salt pork
2 tbsps. whole fennel seed
3 medium boiling potatoes, cut into
   1-inch chunks
1 medium onion, coarsely chopped
4 ribs celery, cut into 1-inch chunks
½ head cabbage, coarsely chopped
2 medium carrots, coarsely chopped
2 lbs. luganega, sweet fennel or other
   mild Italian sausage, cut into 1-inch
   rounds

2 bunches of greens (mustard, kale,
   turnip, chard, spinach, etc.)
   coarsely chopped, about
   2 pounds total
½ lb. green beans
1 head garlic, chopped
4 tbsp. chopped fresh basil or
   2 tsp. dried
Salt and black pepper to taste
Freshly grated Parmesan cheese

A great way to use up leftovers — come up with your own mix of ingredients. Ham bones or rinds, celery root, leeks, just about any kind of greens could all be tossed into the pot.

Bring the stock to a boil, and add the meat, coarsely chopped, and the fennel seed. Reduce the heat, and simmer for 1 hour, uncovered. Add the potatoes, onion, celery, cabbage, and carrots, and cook gently for 20 minutes more. Place the sausage in a large skillet, and brown lightly to render some of the fat. Add the sausage to the pot along with the chopped greens, green beans, garlic, chopped basil, and salt and pepper to taste. Cook for an additional 10 minutes, or until all the vegetables and meats are tender. Serve in large individual bowls. Sprinkle with Parmesan cheese, and enjoy. Makes 12 servings, with leftovers

· Portuguese kale soup ·

This simple and delicious soup is found all along the New England seacoast where Portuguese fisherfolk have been settling since the seventeenth century. It's a popular favorite in Portugal, where it's called *caldo verde* or green soup. The full, rich flavors combine the spice of sausage with the satisfying bitterness of the greens. If you can't find kale, use any other slightly bitter green such as collard, turnip, mustard, chard, or a combination. For the sausage, Portuguese linguiça and chouriço, either alone or mixed, work best, but almost any spicy smoked sausage will give you the zip you need. We used kidney beans, but garbanzos, pea beans, or just about any dried bean tastes fine in this adaptable, easy, and tasty soup.

1 lb. linguiça and/or chouriço, cut into ¼-inch rounds
1 tbsp. olive oil
1 c. chopped onions
1 medium carrot, diced
1 tbsp. chopped garlic
6 c. chicken or beef stock
4 ripe tomatoes, peeled, seeded, and chopped, or 1 c. canned Italian-style tomatoes, drained and chopped

1½ lbs. potatoes, sliced into ¼-inch rounds
1 lb. kale or other greens, thoroughly washed, stems discarded, and leaves cut in ½-inch strips
1½ c. cooked or canned kidney beans, drained and rinsed
Salt and pepper to taste

Brown the sausage in olive oil in a heavy pot over medium heat for about 5 minutes. Remove with a slotted spoon and reserve. Add the onions and carrot, and cook until soft, about 10 minutes. Add the garlic, stock, tomatoes, and potatoes. Bring the soup to a boil, reduce heat, and then simmer for 10 more minutes. Add the browned sausage, shredded kale, and the cooked beans. Cover and cook about 5 minutes more, until the potatoes are tender and the kale still has a little hint of crunch. Season with salt and pepper. Makes 6–8 servings

Serve this for dinner with hot home-made bread, a flavorful cheese like Asiago or dry Jack, and a big red California Syrah or Portuguese Dao.

· skewered Tuscan sausage and chicken livers ·

The rich flavors of chicken liver and bacon merge beautifully with the aromatic sausage. A big and buttery Sonoma County Chardonnay would make a stunning combination here, or a smoky white Burgundy from Meursault.

1 lb. chicken livers, each liver
  separated into 2 lobes
¼ lb. thinly sliced bacon or pancetta
1 lb. Tuscan or other mild Italian
  sausage, each link cut into 5 pieces
1 tsp. minced garlic

2 tbsp. balsamic vinegar
2 tbsp. virgin olive oil
½ tsp. dried tarragon
¼ tsp. salt
¼ tsp. pepper

Wrap each piece of chicken liver in bacon or pancetta. Prepare skewers by alternating pieces of bacon-wrapped liver and sausage. In a small bowl, mix all the remaining ingredients. Brush the skewered meats with half the marinade; reserve the rest in a separate bowl. Place the skewers over medium-hot coals in a covered barbecue and grill, turning frequently, until the sausage and liver are firm, but the liver is still pink inside, about 10–12 minutes. An instant-read thermometer inserted in the end of a sausage should read 160° F. Transfer to a platter and pour over the reserved marinade. Makes 4 servings

A terrific first course for a barbecue or sit-down picnic. Serve with grilled Belgian endives and some Italian herb bread for a satisfying lunch or light supper.

· stuffed quahogs ·

Quahog is the Indian name for clam, but on the Eastern Seaboard the name refers to large, tough clams 4–6 inches in diameter that are best chopped up for chowders, sauces, or stuffings. This dish can also be made with canned minced clams and baked in a casserole or in ramekins. If you do it this way, you might want to jazz up the flavors a bit with some bottled clam juice, sherry, and a bit more hot sauce.

12 large hard-shelled clams, 4–6 inches in diameter, or 2 6½-oz. cans minced clams
4 tbsp. butter
¼ lb. linguiça, finely chopped
½ c. chopped onion
1 tsp. chopped garlic
¼ c. chopped green onions or scallions

½ tsp. dried thyme
¼ c. chopped fresh parsley
¼ tsp. dried marjoram
1½ c. fresh bread crumbs made from French bread
Bottled clam juice or dry sherry
Salt and pepper to taste
Tabasco to taste (optional)

Wash and scrub the clam shells thoroughly. Shuck the clams, straining and reserving any liquid. Wash the clam bodies to remove any sand and wash the inside of each shell under running water. Pat the shells and clams dry. Finely chop the clams in a food processor or meat grinder. Omit above steps if using minced clams.

Preheat the oven to 400° F. Melt 2 tablespoons of the butter over medium heat in a heavy skillet, and put in the linguiça and onion. Cover, cook for 5 minutes, then stir in the garlic, green onions, thyme, parsley, and marjoram. Cook, uncovered, an additional minute. Remove from the heat and stir in the clams and the strained juices along with the bread crumbs, and mix until well blended. If the mixture is too dry, add a little bottled clam juice or dry sherry. Taste for salt and pepper, and add optional Tabasco to taste. Melt the remaining butter and lightly brush the insides of 12 of the deepest cleaned shells. If you are using canned clams, oil a small casserole or individual ramekins. Fill each of the shells, ramekins, or the casserole

On the West Coast, Pismo or other large clams can be used for this recipe.

with the stuffing and drizzle the remaining butter over the top. Arrange the stuffed shells or ramekins on a baking dish and bake in the upper third of the oven for 10–15 minutes, until the tops are nicely browned. Bake the casserole for 20–25 minutes. Makes 6 servings as a main course, 12 as appetizers

· asparagus and sausage tortiere ·

Loni Kuhn, one of the *grandes dames* of our San Francisco cooking scene, has been running a cooking school from her home for more than ten years. Although she teaches everything from Mexican to Moroccan, her first love has always been Italian food. This savory pizzalike custard makes a perfect appetizer or light main course. Loni says to be sure to use real Italian Fontina. It's much better than any other version, and it will really make a difference in the dish's flavor.

2 lbs. pencil-thin asparagus
8 tbsp. (1 stick) softened butter
1 loaf day-old, chewy white bread, such as San Francisco sourdough or Italian bread, crusts removed and thinly sliced
¾ lb. mild Italian sausage like sweet fennel, Tuscan, or luganega, removed from casings

12–14 oz. Italian Fontina cheese, sliced, rind removed
4 egg yolks
1 c. heavy cream
¼ tsp. salt
¼ tsp. white pepper
Pinch freshly grated nutmeg
Freshly grated Parmesan cheese

Butter 2 14-inch pizza pans. Trim the asparagus to fit the radius of the pan. Bring 3–4 quarts salted water to a boil. Put in the asparagus and cook until crisp-tender, about 2 minutes. Plunge them into cold water, drain, and pat dry. Butter the bread slices and, buttered side down, completely cover the bottom of the pan, fitting the pieces together like a jigsaw puzzle with *no gaps*.

Fry the sausage over medium-high heat. Use a fork to crumble the meat as it browns. After about 5 minutes, remove and drain. Discard the grease.

Place a thin layer of sliced Fontina over the bread, and then a layer of asparagus, radiating with the tips facing toward the center. Top with another layer of Fontina, and divide and sprinkle half the sausage on the top of each pan. You can prepare the tortiere several hours ahead to this point.

Preheat the oven to 375° F. Beat the egg yolks, cream, salt, pepper, and nutmeg together lightly. Carefully pour the egg mixture over the surface of the 2 tortieres. Sprinkle with grated Parmesan. Bake for about 25 minutes until the custard has set and the top is golden brown. To make sure the tortieres brown evenly, switch pans on the oven shelves halfway through the baking.

Makes 10–12 servings as a first course, 6 as a main course

· Tuscan sausage frittata ·

This recipe was given to us by Lonnie Gandara, a superb cook, cooking teacher, and cookbook writer. A frittata is a thick, pancake-like omelette that can incorporate many types of vegetables and meats. It is a great way to use the odds and ends of leftovers.

1 lb. zucchini, shredded
Salt
2 tbsp. olive oil
½ lb. Tuscan sausage or other mild
  Italian-style sausage, removed from
  casings
1 medium onion, finely chopped
1 red bell pepper, chopped
2 cloves garlic, minced

¼ lb. mushrooms, sliced
6 eggs, beaten
6 oz. freshly grated Parmesan cheese
  (1½ cups)
1 medium bunch Swiss chard,
  blanched and chopped
¼ c. chopped fresh parsley
Pinch salt and pepper

Toss the shredded zucchini in a generous amount of salt. Place it in a colander and let the liquid drain off for at least 30 minutes and up to an hour. Wash off the salt, and squeeze out the remaining liquid. Preheat the oven to 350° F.

Heat 1 tablespoon of the olive oil in a heavy 10-inch skillet over medium-high heat. Brown the sausage and onion, stirring and breaking up the meat, until the onions are soft, about 10 minutes. Add the bell pepper, garlic, and mushrooms, and cook for 3 minutes more. Drain off the fat.

In a large bowl, mix together the beaten eggs, the sausage/vegetable mixture, Parmesan cheese, zucchini, chard, parsley, salt, and pepper. Oil a skillet or baking dish with the remaining olive oil. Pour in the egg mixture, and bake 40–45 minutes until the eggs are set, and the frittata is firm. Or you can cook the frittata slowly for 5–7 minutes, covered, in an oiled heavy skillet until the bottom is done, and then finish by placing under the broiler for 2–3 minutes. Makes 4–6 servings as a main course, 10–12 as an hors d'oeuvre

Bake or fry a frittata in a skillet; it is equally delicious hot or cold.

· cannelloni ·

Cannelloni can be made from crêpes, fresh pasta sheets, or dried cannelloni shells. They make a wonderful first course, lunch or light supper.

1 lb. Italian sausage (sweet Italian, Tuscan, Barese-style, or luganega), removed from casings
1 c. finely chopped onions
1 bunch spinach (about 1 lb.), stems removed and discarded, chopped
2 tsp. dried basil or 2 tbsp. chopped fresh basil
1 c. finely chopped cooked chicken, veal, pork, or turkey

1 c. ricotta cheese
½ c. freshly grated Parmesan cheese
3 c. Bolognese Sauce (see opposite page)
Salt and pepper to taste
16 cooked (*al dente,* slightly underdone) cannelloni pasta shells or equivalent crêpes
2 c. shredded mozzarella (8–10 oz.)

We used leftover chicken here, but cooked veal, pork, or turkey are also delicious.

Fry the sausage meat in a heavy 12-inch skillet over medium-high heat. Use a fork to crumble the meat. After about 5 minutes, add the onions and cook 5 minutes more, then put in the spinach and basil, cover, and cook until wilted, stirring occasionally. Remove from the pan and drain off excess liquid.

In a large bowl, combine the sausage/spinach mixture with the chicken, ricotta, ¼ cup of the Parmesan, and 1 cup of the bolognese sauce. Mix well until all the ingredients are blended. Taste for salt and pepper.

Carefully stuff into precooked cannelloni shells or spoon about ½ cup of the filling onto each of the crêpes and roll up.

Preheat the oven to 350° F. Lightly oil a baking pan and arrange the cannelloni on it, leaving a little space between each. Spoon bolognese sauce over the top of each. Sprinkle with mozzarella and then with the remaining Parmesan. Bake for 15–20 minutes, until the sauce is bubbly and the filling is quite hot.

Makes 6–8 servings

· Bolognese sauce ·

Unlike the standard Italian-American red sauce, this recipe uses no ground beef, but instead contains sausage and ground chicken giblets. We think the giblets make a difference, but if they're not available or your kids say "Yuck!," you can use hamburger in place of the "insides."

¼ lb. finely chopped pancetta or salt pork (optional)

4 mild Italian sausages, preferably the sweet fennel type, removed from casings

½ lb. ground chicken or duck giblets (gizzards and hearts)

1 medium onion, finely chopped

1 medium carrot, finely chopped

1 rib celery, finely chopped

2 tbsp. minced garlic

2 c. whole milk

2 c. beef stock

6 c. chopped tomatoes, either
 4 c. fresh Roma tomatoes, peeled, seeded, and chopped, with
 2 c. canned tomato puree, or
 6 c. canned crushed tomatoes in puree

1 c. dry red wine

2 tsp. dried basil

Salt and pepper to taste

In a large heavy pot or Dutch oven, brown the optional pancetta or salt pork over medium-high heat, stirring frequently until the fat is rendered and the pieces are a golden color, about 5 minutes. Add the sausage meat and giblets, crumbling them with a fork as they brown for about 3 minutes. Add the onion, carrot, and celery, and cook, covered, until the vegetables are soft, about 5 or 6 minutes. Put in the garlic, milk, and stock. Bring to a boil and cook, uncovered, over medium-high heat, until most of the liquid is absorbed, stirring occasionally, about 30 minutes. Add the tomato mixture, wine, and basil. Bring to a boil, reduce the heat to a simmer, and cook, uncovered, until the sauce is thick enough to coat a spoon. This should take about ½–¾ hour. Taste for salt and pepper.

Makes 2–3 quarts

Use this versatile sauce on everything from pasta to pizza. It freezes well, so you might want to make up a double batch.

This simple and satisfying dish tastes great served over a good-quality dried Italian pasta. We prefer tagliarini or spaghetti, but just about any will do as well. Accompany this with a salad of bitter greens, *bruschetta* — French bread toasted and rubbed with garlic and extra-virgin olive oil — and a bottle of Dolcetto d'Alba or California Charbono.

1 oz. dried porcini mushrooms

1 tbsp. olive oil

1½ lbs. Italian Sweet Fennel Sausage (see page 104), Spicy Hot Italian Sausage (see page 100), or other good-quality Italian sausage

½ c. beef stock

1 c. dry wine, white or red

4 cloves chopped garlic

1 lb. ripe tomatoes, peeled, seeded, and roughly chopped, or 2 c. canned Italian-style tomatoes, drained and chopped

1 tsp. dried basil or 2 tbsp. chopped fresh basil

Salt and pepper to taste

1 lb. of your favorite dried pasta, cooked

Freshly grated Parmesan cheese

Our Italian Sweet Fennel Sausage is a perfect match with the earthy flavors of dried mushrooms, but almost any Italian sausage is delicious here.

Pour 2 to 3 cups of boiling water over the porcini. Cover and let the mushrooms steep for at least 30 minutes or up to several hours. Drain, and reserve liquid.

In a heavy 12-inch skillet fry the sausages over medium heat, turning them occasionally, for 10–15 minutes until nicely browned. Transfer to a plate and pour off the accumulated fat. Pour the stock and wine into the pan, and bring it to a boil, scraping up any brown bits from the bottom of the pan. Add the garlic, tomatoes, and basil, and bring to a boil. Add the sausages and porcini. Strain the reserved porcini liquid through a paper towel or coffee filter into the pan, taking care to keep out any dirt or sand. Reduce the heat to a simmer, and cook, uncovered, 30 minutes, or until the sauce begins to thicken slightly. Taste for salt and pepper, and serve over cooked pasta. Garnish with grated Parmesan. Makes 4–6 servings

· quick and easy pastas ·

Sausage and pasta are a perfect match. You can pair virtually any type of sausage with any of the many fresh or dried pastas available today. Each sausage provides a unique flavor, and the different shapes and forms of pasta offer endless combinations.

If unexpected guests show up for dinner or you are tired after a long day, all you need is some sausage in the freezer and some dried pasta on the shelf, and you can whip up a simple but delicious meal in minutes.

For 1 lb. of dried pasta (enough to feed 4 people generously), you'll need ½ to ¾ lb. of sausage removed from the casings and chopped coarsely. While you are cooking the pasta, fry the sausage in a skillet until it is no longer pink. Drain off and discard the grease. To make a quick and easy sauce: add some liquid (½ c. wine or 1 c. of cream or 1 c. of stock or 1 c. of chopped tomatoes), perhaps a few sun-dried tomatoes, sliced mushrooms, or blanched spring vegetables, or any combination of the above. Cook the sauce down over a high flame until it just begins to thicken. Taste for salt and pepper and mix the sauce with the cooked, drained pasta. Sprinkle some freshly grated Parmesan cheese on top and enjoy!

· Other Quick Pasta Ideas: ·

▶ Sauté chopped smoked sausage, add peas and cream.

▶ Sauté Italian sausages with parboiled crookneck squash, zucchini, broccoli, and chicken stock.

▶ Fry spicy sausages with chopped beet greens, garlic, and olive oil.

▶ Fry some spicy sausages with garlic and bitter broccoli rabe.

· steamed clams with linguiça ·

In Portugal this dish is called a *cataplana*, which refers to the dome-shaped pan it is traditionally cooked in. The shape of the pan is such that once the clams have opened, their juices will run down into the rest of the ingredients. If you want to be really authentic, you can probably find a *cataplana* at a specialty cookware supplier. You can accomplish the same effect, however, by stirring the clams thoroughly once they have opened. Use either linguiça or chouriço, depending on how spicy you want the dish, or a combination of the two.

1 lb. linguiça and/or chouriço, sliced into ½-inch rounds

¼ lb. smoky ham, prosciutto, or lean smoky bacon, diced

2 tbsp. olive oil

3 c. thinly sliced onions

½ c. chopped red or green bell pepper

2 tbsp. chopped garlic

½ tsp. red pepper flakes

2 tsp. Spanish or Hungarian paprika

1 c. ripe tomatoes, peeled, seeded, and coarsely chopped, either fresh or canned Italian style

1 c. dry white wine

1 c. bottled clam juice or chicken stock

1 c. chopped fresh parsley, flat-leaf preferred

2 bay leaves

1 tbsp. chopped fresh basil or 1 tsp. dried

48 Little Neck or Cherrystone clams, or small mussels, thoroughly washed and scrubbed

Salt and black pepper to taste

Tabasco to taste

Brown the sausage and ham in the olive oil in a Dutch oven or large heavy skillet over medium-high heat. Stir frequently until the fat is rendered and the meat is lightly browned. Add the onions and cook, covered, for 5 minutes, stirring occasionally. Put in the bell pepper and garlic and cook, covered, for 2 or 3 minutes more. Stir in the red pepper flakes, paprika, tomatoes, wine, and clam juice or stock. Bring everything to a boil, and add the parsley, bay leaves, and basil. Reduce to a simmer and cook for 10 minutes. Put the clams into the pot, and cook, covered, for 10–15 minutes, or until the shells have opened. Thicker-shelled clams will take longer. Discard any clams that don't open. Stir the pot well to distribute the clam juices. Taste for salt, pepper, and Tabasco. Serve the clams in shallow soup bowls with plenty of sauce and soup spoons, as well as forks. Makes 6 servings

Serve with crusty French bread and a light white wine like Portuguese Vinho Verde or Italian Soave.

· clam and smoked sausage hash ·

The spicy flavors and rich texture of smoked sausage go beautifully with clams. This dish can stand alone as a delicious lunch or light supper, or you can serve it as a first course over long slices of sautéed zucchini. Served with poached eggs and homemade rye toast, this also makes a great brunch; or pair it with a green salad with bits of fried pancetta and red bell pepper for a hearty lunch or dinner.

4–5 oz. chopped smoked sausage
2 tbsp. butter
1 c. finely chopped onion
2 c. freshly shucked or canned
  chowder-type clams, finely
  chopped, or small, tender clams,
  coarsely chopped

4 c. cold cooked boiling potatoes,
  diced
½ tsp. dried thyme
¼ c. chopped fresh parsley
Salt and black pepper to taste
2 tbsp. chopped green onions or
  scallions

In a heavy, well-seasoned skillet or nonstick frying pan, brown the sausage in the butter over medium heat, about 3–5 minutes, shaking the pan frequently. Add the onion and cook for 5 minutes until soft. Shake the pan occasionally to keep the meat and onion from sticking. Stir in the clams, potatoes, thyme, and parsley. Sprinkle with black pepper. Pat the surface to form a smooth cake. Fry 10–15 minutes, shaking the pan once in a while to keep the hash from sticking. When the bottom of the hash is nicely browned, place a warm platter on top of the pan. Quickly invert the pan while holding the platter firmly so that the hash cake is presented browned side up. Taste a corner for salt and pepper and sprinkle on more if needed. Garnish with green onions. Makes 4–6 servings

Use any variety of heavily smoked sausage such as linguiça, chouriço, andouille, kielbasa, Smoked Country Sausage, or Louisiana-Style Smoked Sausage.

· Joe Molinari's eggplant and sausage "lasagna" ·

This is a family recipe that fed a whole houseful of Italians one warm and friendly summer evening in upstate New York. Calling the dish "lasagna" is stretching the term a bit, since there are no lasagna noodles in the dish, but rather layers of eggplant, sausage, cheese, and mushrooms. But we figure if the Molinari family can get away with calling it lasagna, so can we!

2 medium-large eggplants, peeled and cut into ¼-inch slices lengthwise
1 c. olive oil
2 lbs. luganega, hot Italian sausage, or other Italian sausage, sliced into ½-inch pieces
2 medium onions, chopped
4 tbsp. chopped garlic
¼ tsp. fennel or anise seed

1 tsp. dried basil or 2 tbsp. chopped fresh basil
½ lb. sliced mushrooms
2 8-oz. cans tomato puree
1 c. dry white wine
Salt and pepper to taste
1 lb. mozzarella, thinly sliced
½ lb. Parmesan, freshly grated

Preheat the oven to 375° F. Dip each eggplant slice in olive oil, drain, and bake the slices on sheet pans for 20–30 minutes, until soft. Use more olive oil if needed. Set aside while you prepare the sauce.

In a large, deep skillet or Dutch oven, brown the sliced sausages over medium-high heat for 10 minutes, stirring and scraping the bottom of the pan. Remove the sausages and set aside. Add the onions and garlic to the fat left by the sausages, and cook for 5 minutes, stirring frequently, until the onions are soft. Put in the fennel, basil, and mushrooms, and fry 2–3 minutes more. Add the tomato puree and wine. Bring everything to a boil, and then reduce the heat to a simmer. Cook, uncovered, for 30 minutes, and then return the sausages to the skillet. Cook 10 minutes more until the sauce has thickened a bit. Taste for salt and pepper. Adjust the oven temperature to 350° F.

The key to success with this hearty dish is to slice the eggplants thinly and then bake the slices until they are completely soft. Any variety of Italian sausage will do, but we think the aromatic spices of luganega go beautifully with eggplant.

To assemble the lasagna, place a layer of eggplant on the bottom of a 9 x 13 x 2-inch baking pan. Cover with the sausage and sauce, followed by sliced mozzarella and grated Parmesan. Continue layering ingredients, ending with a layer of cheese on top. The lasagna can be made ahead to this point and refrigerated overnight. Bake for 20–30 minutes, until the sauce is bubbly and the cheese melted. Let the lasagna rest 10 minutes before slicing and serving.
Makes 6–8 servings

·Italian street barbecue—
grilled sausage and vegetables·

While it's nice to wander down Mulberry Street during the Festa di San Gennaro sampling the grilled sausages as you go, you can come pretty close in your own backyard, on the deck, or in the kitchen with this Italian sausage and vegetable barbecue. We suggest a mix of half hot and half mild Italian sausages, but you can cook any types that you, your family, and friends prefer. A nice start to your own *festa* might be our Skewered Tuscan Sausage and Chicken Livers wrapped in bacon (see page 118).

Offer both white and red wines to your guests: a spicy Pinot Bianco from the Alto Adige region in Italy's Alps, and an earthy Chianti Colli Senesi or California Barbera.

· **Marinade** ·
¼ c. fresh lemon juice
½ c. fruity olive oil
3 cloves garlic, minced
2 tbsp. chopped fresh basil or 1 tbsp. chopped fresh marjoram
½ tsp. salt
½ tsp. pepper
....
1 red bell pepper, quartered lengthwise and seeded

1 green bell pepper, quartered lengthwise and seeded
1 yellow bell pepper, quartered lengthwise and seeded
4 Japanese eggplants, split lengthwise
1 large red onion, cut into ½-inch slices
4 mild Italian sausages
4 hot Italian sausages
8 crusty French or Italian rolls

Whisk together the lemon juice, olive oil, garlic, fresh herbs, salt, and pepper in a large bowl. Toss the vegetables into the bowl and rub them with the marinade so they are generously coated. Remove the vegetables, shaking off any excess marinade into the bowl. Save the marinade. Grill the vegetables over medium coals in a covered barbecue kettle or under a broiler. Place the sausages on the grill and cover immediately. If any flaming occurs, douse the flames with a spray of water. Turn the sausages and vegetables frequently. The vegetables are done when they are tender but still firm. Transfer them to a serving platter when they are cooked. Serve the vegetables warm or at room temperature. The sausages are done when firm or when an instant-read thermometer inserted through the end registers 160° F. Transfer the sausages to the platter and keep warm.

Cut the French rolls in half and brush with the reserved marinade. Pour the remaining marinade over the platter of sausages and grilled vegetables. Have your guests make their own sandwiches, choosing their own sausage and vegetable combination. Makes 4–6 servings

· Italian sausage, chicken, and ricotta pie ·

This substantial lunch or dinner entree is a good way to use leftover roast chicken or turkey.

¾ lb. mild Italian sausage such as
    sweet Italian, Tuscan, or luganega,
    removed from casings
1 tbsp. olive oil
1 medium onion, finely chopped
1 tbsp. minced garlic
¼ lb. dry coppa, finely chopped
2 c. diced cooked chicken or turkey
1 bunch spinach, cooked, drained,
    and chopped (about ½ lb.)
1 lb. ricotta cheese

½ c. freshly grated Parmesan cheese
1 c. chopped fresh parsley
1 tsp. dried basil or
    2 tbsp. chopped fresh basil
2 eggs, beaten
Salt and pepper to taste
1 recipe Edy's Foolproof Pie Dough
    (see page 64)
1 egg mixed with 1 tbsp. water, milk,
    or cream for egg wash

Another example of how leftovers can be more exciting the second time around.

Lightly brown the sausage meat in olive oil in a heavy medium skillet over medium-high heat for 5 minutes, crumbling the sausage as it browns. Transfer it to a large bowl, leaving the fat in the pan. Put the onion and garlic in the pan, and fry until the onion is soft, about 5 minutes. Transfer to the bowl. Add the coppa, chicken or turkey, spinach, ricotta, Parmesan, parsley, basil, and eggs to the bowl. Mix well, and season with salt and pepper.

Preheat the oven to 425° F. Roll out a circle of dough about 3–4 inches larger than a 9 x 2-inch springform pan. Line the pan with the dough, pressing it against the bottom and sides. Fill with the sausage and cheese mixture, spreading it evenly. Roll the remaining dough into a 10-inch circle, place over the top of the pan, and seal the edges. Trim off any excess dough, and cut steam vents in the top. Brush with egg wash, place the pie on a sheet pan, and bake for 15 minutes. Reduce the heat to 350° F, and continue to bake the pie until the top is golden, about 30–40 minutes more. Cool for 10 minutes before serving.

Makes 8 servings

· chicken breasts stuffed with sausage, spinach, leeks, and ham ·

This satisfying dish offers elegance and rich and complex flavors as a main course with pasta. Cold and sliced, it makes a delicious lunch or appetizer.

· Stuffing ·

1 lb. sweet fennel or other mild Italian sausage, removed from casings

1 c. finely chopped leeks

2 large shallots, finely chopped

¼ lb. smoked ham or smoked sausage such as linguiça, finely chopped

½ to 1 c. day-old bread crumbs

¼ c. freshly grated Parmesan cheese

1 bunch spinach (1 lb.), washed, blanched, and coarsely chopped

3 tbsp. chopped fresh parsley

1 egg

Salt and pepper to taste

....

6 chicken breasts (about 3 lbs.), boned with skin left intact

1 c. all-purpose flour

2 tbsp. butter

2 tbsp. olive oil

½ c. dry white wine

2 cloves minced garlic

1 lemon, juice only

1 tbsp. capers

Fry the sausage in a 12-inch skillet over medium heat for 5 minutes. Add the leeks, shallots, and ham. Cover and cook until the leeks are soft, about 10 minutes, stirring occasionally. Transfer the mixture to a large bowl and stir in ½ cup bread crumbs, Parmesan cheese, spinach, 2 tablespoons of the parsley, and egg. If the stuffing is too moist, add more bread crumbs. Taste for salt and pepper.

Cut a pocket into each breast and stuff generously with the dressing. You don't have to seal the pocket because the egg binds the mixture and should keep it in place. Dredge each breast in flour.

Heat the butter and oil in a heavy 12-inch skillet over medium heat. Put in the chicken breasts skin side down and cook until golden, about 5–7 minutes. Turn and cook 5–7 minutes more. Pour off any fat and add the white wine. Bring to a boil and scrape up any bits stuck to the bottom of the pan. Cover, reduce heat to a simmer, and cook 10 minutes. Transfer the chicken to a serving platter and cover it with foil to keep warm while you finish the sauce. Turn the heat to medium-high. Add garlic and cook 1 minute, stirring continuously and scraping up all the bits that have stuck to the bottom of the pan. Add the lemon juice, capers, and remaining tablespoon of parsley, and cook for 1 additional minute. Taste for salt and pepper. Pour the sauce over the chicken and serve. Makes 4 servings

Serve with a crisp white Gavi from Piedmont in Northern Italy or a spicy Alexander Valley Sauvignon Blanc.

· Italian sausage and pheasant pie ·

Serve this elegant dish with a salad of cold broccoli and cauliflower spears, garnished with strips of roasted red bell peppers, and dressed with extra-virgin olive oil and lemon juice. A Chardonnay from California or Italy's Alto Adige region is the perfect accompaniment.

½ oz. dried porcini mushrooms

4 c. chicken stock

2 tbsp. unsalted butter

½ lb. luganega or other mild Italian sausage

2–3-lb. pheasant or chicken, cut into 6 pieces

Salt and pepper

½ c. all-purpose flour

1 oz. mild dry coppa or prosciutto, finely chopped

1 pheasant or chicken liver, finely chopped

1 small carrot, finely chopped

1 rib celery, finely chopped

3 shallots, finely chopped

1 c. finely chopped leeks, white part only

3 cloves garlic, chopped

1 c. dry white wine

½ c. crème fraîche or sour cream

1 lb. puff pastry (use your favorite recipe, or frozen pastry)

1 egg mixed with 1 tbsp. water, milk, or cream for egg wash

Soak the dried mushrooms in 2 cups of boiling water to cover for at least 30 minutes or up to 2 hours. When they are soft, strain the liquid through cheese-cloth or a coffee filter into the stock, and reserve the mushrooms.

Melt the butter in a heavy large pan. Add the sausages whole, and brown them for about 10 minutes over medium heat. Remove with a slotted spoon and set aside. Sprinkle the pheasant or chicken pieces with salt and pepper, and dredge in flour. Fry them in the fat remaining in the pan until lightly browned, about 5–7 minutes a side. Remove, and pour off all but 3 tablespoons of the fat. Put in the chopped coppa and liver, and cook over medium heat for 2–3 minutes. Add the chopped vegetables and garlic, and cook for 5–10 minutes more, until they are soft, but not colored. Put in the wine, chicken stock, and porcini, and deglaze the pan. Bring to a simmer and add the pheasant or chicken pieces in a single layer. Cover and cook at a simmer for 20 minutes. Remove the cover, and cook for another 25 minutes, or until the bird is tender and the sauce has begun to thicken. Remove the pheasant. If the liquid in the pan is not thick enough (it should be the consistency of heavy cream), reduce it over high heat. If it is too thick, add more stock or wine. When it has thickened, add the crème fraîche or sour cream. Cut the sausage into 1-inch rounds and add to the pot. Adjust the salt and pepper. Return the pheasant to the sauce and cool everything thoroughly in the refrigerator a minimum of 2 hours or overnight.

A great centerpiece for a buffet or special dinner party.

Preheat the oven to 425° F. To assemble the pie, place the braised pheasant, sausage, and sauce in an ovenproof casserole large enough to hold everything with about 2 inches to spare on top. Roll out the puff pastry ¼ inch thick and large enough for about 2–3 inches to drape over the sides of the casserole. Let the pastry rest on a sheet pan for 30 minutes or more in the refrigerator. Mix together the egg wash, and paint the top 2 inches of the outside of the casserole with this mixture. Drape the pastry over the casserole, and press the overhang against the outside edge to make a seal with the egg wash. Don't press down too firmly. Brush the crust with more egg wash, and bake for 25–30 minutes until the top is deep gold in color. When serving, give each person a piece of pastry, some pheasant, sausage, and plenty of the delicious sauce. Makes 4–6 servings

· quick and easy sautés ·

Sausage is so delicious that one of the best ways to serve it is sautéed, using a bit of wine or stock to deglaze the pan to make a sauce, and adding some mushrooms, garlic, scallions, or bell peppers for flavor and texture.

Sautéing is a quick and convenient way to cook for a small group of people as only 1–4 portions are cooked at a time in the hot pan.

The key to successful sautés is to cut all the ingredients into bite-sized pieces, and not to crowd the sauté pan. Here is a simple recipe that you can embellish with numerous variations. Sauté about 1 lb. of diced or sliced sausage in a little hot oil, pour off excess fat, deglaze the pan with 1 c. of stock or wine, add 1 c. of chopped mushrooms, onions, garlic, etc., and reduce the sauce slightly over high heat.

You can mix the sausage with some other diced meat such as skinless chicken or veal, or use other vegetables such as green or red bell peppers, green beans, or peas. In fact, any vegetable that requires little cooking or has been precooked will work well in a sauté. In place of wine, you can use stock, clam juice, lemon juice, cream, or a combination of cream and stock. Cream-based sautés are particularly good as pasta sauces.

· Puerto Rican chicken, rice, and sausage stew ·

We call this a stew, but the dish is meant to be on the soupy side. Use a full-flavored, smoked sausage such as Portuguese chouriço or linguiça, Spanish chorizo, andouille, or smoked country sausage. This dish is wonderful with black bread spread with a fresh cheese like *queso fresco* or pot cheese, and a salad of oranges and marinated red onions.

¾ lb. smoked sausage, sliced into
   ¼-inch rounds
2 tbsp. olive oil
1 tbsp. chopped fresh oregano or 1
   tsp. dried oregano
2 cloves garlic, chopped
1 tsp. salt
½ tsp. black pepper
1 tsp. paprika
1 3½-lb. chicken, cut in 8–10 pieces
   (2 wings, 4 breast pieces, 2 legs,
   2 thighs)
1 c. thinly sliced onion
½ c. chopped green or red bell
   pepper or mild chile, such as
   Anaheim or poblano

6 medium tomatoes, peeled, seeded,
   and chopped, or 2 c. canned Italian-
   style tomatoes, drained and
   chopped
5–6 c. chicken stock
2 c. converted or long-grain rice
½ lb. fresh green beans, cut into
   2-inch pieces and blanched in boiling
   water for 5 minutes
½ c. grated sharp cheese, such as
   Manchego, Asiago, or Parmesan
20 pimiento-stuffed green olives
1 tbsp. capers
1 canned or fresh fire-roasted
   pimiento, cut into ½-inch strips
Lemon wedges

Brown the sausage in the olive oil in a heavy pot or 2–3-quart Dutch oven over medium heat for about 5 minutes, until the fat is rendered. Remove with a slotted spoon and set aside. With a mortar and pestle make a paste of the oregano, garlic, salt, pepper, and paprika. Rub this all over the chicken pieces and fry them in the hot fat until golden brown, about 10–15 minutes, turning once. Don't crowd the pan, but fry 3 or 4 pieces of chicken at a time, transferring them to a platter as they brown. Pour off all but 2 tablespoons of the fat. Add the onion to the remaining fat, stirring frequently. After about 5 minutes put in the bell pepper, and cook for a few minutes more until the onion is soft, but the pepper still firm. Return the sausage to the pot along with the tomatoes, stock, and chicken. Bring everything to a boil, and then reduce to a simmer. Cover the stew and cook for 20 minutes, until the chicken is tender. Stir in the rice, making sure it is covered with liquid. If not, add more stock. Bring to a boil, reduce to a simmer, cover, and cook 20–25 minutes. When the rice is cooked, but the mixture is still somewhat soupy (if not, add more stock), stir in the green beans, grated cheese, olives, and capers, and simmer for 5 minutes. Arrange the pimiento strips on top. Cook for 2 minutes more to heat everything thoroughly. Adjust the seasonings, and serve right from the pot.
Makes 6 servings

This lively stew cries out for a flavorful beer such as Red Stripe or Anchor Steam or a full-bodied white wine from Catalonia such as Torres' Gran Viña Sol.

· lamb shoulder stuffed with
hot Italian sausage in porcini sauce ·

This hearty dish combines the spice and heat of the sausage, the smoky flavor of dried wild mushrooms, the aromas of mint and rosemary, and the subtle sweetness of lamb. Try this with a Cabernet or Merlot from northern Italy, or a full-bodied Australian Cabernet Sauvignon.

2 oz. dried porcini mushrooms
4–5 lb. lamb shoulder, boned
Salt and pepper to taste
6 shallots, finely chopped
2 tsp. minced garlic
1 tsp. finely chopped fresh rosemary
2 tsp. finely chopped fresh mint
1 lb. hot Italian sausage, removed
    from casings

¾ c. dried bread crumbs
1 tsp. salt
1 tsp. pepper
1 large egg
2 tbsp. olive oil
1 carrot, finely chopped
1½ c. beef stock
2 c. dry red wine such as Cabernet
3–4 sprigs fresh rosemary

Cover the porcini mushrooms with 3 cups of boiling water and soak for at least 30 minutes or up to several hours. Strain the soaking liquid through a fine sieve and reserve. Rinse the mushrooms.

Preheat the oven to 350° F. Sprinkle the lamb with salt and pepper. Set aside. In a bowl mix 2 tablespoons of the shallots and 1 teaspoon of the garlic, with the rosemary, mint, sausage, bread crumbs, salt, pepper, and egg. Finely chop about 4 tablespoons of the mushrooms and add them to the bowl. (Save the rest of the mushrooms for the sauce.) Using your hands or a wooden spoon, mix the stuffing until all of the ingredients are well blended. Stuff into the pocket left by the lamb bones, then close the pocket with skewers or tie with string. The stuffed shoulder should be flat, but will be fairly sloppy and uneven. Not to worry, since the final dish will be presented in slices and will look beautiful.

A wonderful Italian dinner with Oven-Roasted Garlic-Rosemary Potatoes (see page 352) and fresh broccoli sautéed in olive oil.

Heat the olive oil in a heavy 12-inch Dutch oven over medium-high heat. Put in the stuffed shoulder, fat side down, and brown for 10 minutes, turning the lamb over once. Remove the lamb and set aside. Reduce the heat to medium. Add the remaining shallots and the chopped carrot. Cover and cook for 5 minutes over medium heat. Add the rest of the garlic and mushrooms, and cook for 1 minute. Pour in the stock, wine, the soaking liquid from the mushrooms, and add a sprig of fresh rosemary. Bring everything to a boil. Put in the lamb, fat side up. Cover the pot and transfer it to the oven. Cook for 2 hours, or until meat is quite tender. Remove the lamb from the oven and transfer it to a heated platter. Degrease the sauce and reduce it over high heat until it becomes syrupy. Taste for salt and pepper. Slice the lamb in ¾-inch slices and arrange them on a platter. Pour the sauce over the lamb and add rosemary sprigs as a garnish.

Makes 4–6 servings, with leftovers

· loukaniko with lamb and spinach ·

Like many peasant dishes, this can be either a soup or a stew. We've given proportions that lean more toward a hearty, thick stew, but if you prefer soup, just add a little more stock or red wine. Serve by itself, or with a rice pilaf with currants and pine nuts.

1 lb. loukaniko sausage (see page 109), left whole, or any mild sausage like Italian fennel or luganega

2 tbsp. fruity olive oil, preferably Greek

2 lbs. lamb shoulder cut into 1½-inch cubes

Salt and pepper to taste

2 c. chopped onion

1 medium carrot, diced

1 tbsp. chopped garlic

4 c. beef or lamb stock

1 c. dry red wine

2 c. diced potatoes

2 bunches spinach (2 lbs.), stems removed and discarded, thoroughly washed, and coarsely chopped

1 tsp. dried dill or 1 tbsp. fresh

1 tbsp. fresh mint or ½ tsp. dried

Fresh mint and/or parsley to garnish

Yogurt

In a 3–4-quart Dutch oven or heavy pot, brown the sausages in the olive oil over medium heat, turning occasionally, for about 10 minutes. Remove and set aside.

Put the lamb in the pot, sprinkling it lightly with salt and pepper, and brown it in the hot fat for 5–7 minutes. Remove and set aside. Add the onion, carrot, and garlic. Reduce the heat to medium, cover the pot, and cook for about 10 minutes, stirring a few times. Add the stock and wine, and bring to a boil. Put the lamb back in the pot, cover, and cook over a slow flame for 45 minutes. Taste the lamb to make sure it's tender enough. If not, you can simmer the stew for another 15 minutes or so until it is done. Add the diced potatoes and let them simmer for 15 minutes. Then add the chopped spinach, the sausages (either whole or cut up, as you prefer), along with the dill and mint. Let the stew cook for another 5 minutes just to warm everything through and blend the flavors. Taste a potato to make sure it is tender. Season with salt and pepper, and garnish with chopped fresh mint and/or parsley, and a dollop of plain yogurt. Makes 6–8 servings as a main course, 8–10 as a soup

Kokkinelli, a light red retsina, is delightful with this dish; if you don't like the taste of resin, try a lighter California Pinot Noir or Gamay Beaujolais.

· pastitsio — macaroni and cheese with a sausage surprise ·

Pastitsio is one of the basics of Greek country cooking. This recipe is a glorified and tasty version of the rich pasta dish that includes sausage as a spicy surprise. If you can't find loukaniko or you don't feel like making your own, just substitute some sweet fennel or other mild Italian sausage.

1 lb. Italian ziti or dried elbow macaroni

4 tbsp. olive oil

¾ lb. loukaniko or sweet fennel or other Italian sausage, removed from casings

1 lb. lean lamb shoulder, cut into ½-inch dice

Salt and pepper to taste

2 c. chopped onions

5 ripe tomatoes, peeled, seeded, and chopped, with 1 c. tomato puree, or 2 c. canned Italian-style plum tomatoes with 1 c. tomato puree

1 tsp. chopped garlic

⅛ tsp. cinnamon

⅛ tsp. ground allspice

½ c. fresh bread crumbs

1 egg, lightly beaten

· Cream sauce ·

2 tbsp. butter

½ c. all-purpose flour

4 c. milk

½ tsp. salt

Pinch freshly grated nutmeg

6 eggs, beaten until frothy

1 c. grated Kefalotiri, Asiago, Kasseri, or other sharp cheese

Cook the pasta in plenty of water until it is *al dente* or just barely done. Drain it in a colander, and cool under running water. Coat the pasta with about 1 tablespoon of olive oil to keep it from sticking together while you make the sauce.

For the tomato and sausage sauce, heat the remaining olive oil in a heavy skillet over medium-high heat, and brown the sausage, breaking up the meat with a fork as you go. After about 5 minutes, when it is nicely browned, remove the sausage with a slotted spoon and drain on a paper towel. Add the lamb to the hot fat, and sprinkle lightly with salt and pepper. After it is lightly brown, about 5 minutes, toss in the onions and cook for another 5 minutes, or until they are soft and translucent. Add the tomatoes, bring to a boil, and reduce to a simmer. Add the garlic, spices, sausage, and meat. You can add a little tomato juice or water if the sauce is too thick. Cook for 30 minutes over a low flame, then remove the pan from the heat. Stir in ¼ cup of the bread crumbs along with the beaten egg.

A substantial lunch or dinner with a salad of tender lettuce and bitter greens with Greek olives and marinated red onions—a great dish for a crowd of guests. Serve with cold retsina or a crisp Mâcon Blanc.

While the tomato sauce is cooking, you can prepare the cream sauce. In a heavy saucepan, melt the butter over medium heat. Stir in the flour and cook for 1 or 2 minutes, until the flour and butter are smoothly blended together. Remove from the heat and whisk in the milk, salt, and nutmeg. Return to the heat and continue to whisk until the sauce is thick and creamy, about 5 minutes. Remove from the heat and gradually whisk in the 6 beaten eggs.

Preheat the oven to 375° F. Oil a large casserole or 9 x 13-inch baking

dish with olive oil. Sprinkle the bottom with the remaining bread crumbs. Spread half the pasta over the crumbs and cover it with all of the tomato-sausage sauce. Cover this with half the cream sauce and sprinkle with half the grated cheese. Make another layer of the remaining pasta. Pour over the rest of the cream sauce, and the remaining cheese. Bake, uncovered, for 45 minutes until the top is lightly golden and bubbly. Cut the pastitsio into squares and serve.
Makes 8–10 servings

· cotechino with lentils ·

Earthy lentils and aromatic cotechino seem made for each other. Serve with a full-bodied California Barbera, plenty of sourdough French bread, and zesty Franco's Bagnet Piemontese (see opposite page).

2 cotechino sausages (1½–2 lbs. total)
5 c. chicken or beef stock
1 c. dry white wine
1 lb. lentils
2 c. canned Italian tomatoes, chopped
2 bay leaves
2–3 sprigs fresh rosemary or 2 tsp. dried

2 medium onions, chopped
1 carrot, chopped
1 rib celery, chopped
1 tbsp. chopped garlic
½ c. chopped fresh parsley
Salt and pepper to taste
Franco's Bagnet Piemontese

Place the sausages, stock and wine in a large pot or Dutch oven. Bring to a boil. Add the lentils, tomatoes, bay leaves, and rosemary. Simmer, uncovered, for 30 minutes. Add the vegetables and garlic, and continue to simmer until the lentils are tender, about another ½ hour. Taste for salt and pepper. Remove and discard the rosemary sprigs and bay leaves. Cut the cotechino into ¼-inch slices. Place the lentils in a shallow serving bowl, mix in the cotechino and parsley, arranging a few slices on top. Ladle some Bagnet Piemontese over the slices and pass extra to guests. Makes 6–8 servings

Easy to make up the day before— it's even better reheated.

· rolled flank steak stuffed with
Italian sausage, basil, and Swiss cheese ·

Serve this dramatic and delicious dish with fried polenta and a salad, along with a Vino Nobile di Montepulciano or a gutsy Zinfandel from California's Sierra foothills.

1 flank steak (about 1½ pounds)
10–12 fresh basil leaves
4 thin slices Swiss cheese
2–3 links sweet fennel or other mild
   Italian-style sausage
Salt and pepper to taste
3 tbsp. olive oil

1 large onion, thinly sliced
8 whole cloves garlic, peeled
1 c. dry red wine, like Zinfandel
½ c. red wine vinegar
½ c. beef stock
2 bay leaves

Preheat the oven to 350° F. Lay the flank steak on a flat surface and cover it with basil leaves, reserving 2–3 leaves for the sauce. Place slices of Swiss cheese on top, enough to cover the surface of the leaves. Place whole sausages lengthwise down the center and roll the steak around them, then tie with kitchen string. Lightly salt and pepper the roll.

Heat the olive oil in a heavy 12-inch Dutch oven or high-sided skillet over high heat. Add the rolled steak, seam side up, and brown for 5–7 minutes. Remove the steak and add the onion. Cover, and reduce the heat to medium. Cook the onion for 15 minutes, stirring occasionally, until it turns light brown. Add the garlic and cook for a minute more. Add the wine, vinegar, stock, bay leaves, and the rest of the basil. Put the steak back in, seam side up. Bring everything to a boil, cover, and place it in the oven. Cook for 1 hour, or until the meat is tender. Remove the steak to a heated platter. If the sauce is too watery, reduce it over high heat until it becomes slightly syrupy. Slice the steak into 10–12 ¾-inch slices, arrange on a heated platter, pour the sauce over, and serve.
Makes 4–6 servings, with leftovers

· Franco's bagnet Piemontese ·

A piquant sauce that's wonderful with cotechino, boiled beef, chicken, or veal—an old recipe of chef Franco Dunn's family.
3 cloves garlic
2-oz. can anchovies
6 sun-dried tomatoes packed in olive
   oil
2 bunches Italian flat-leaf or regular
   parsley (1 lb.)
1–1½ c. extra-virgin olive oil (the
   best you can afford)

¼ c. balsamic vinegar (ditto)
Salt and pepper to taste
   In food processor, process garlic, anchovies, and sun-dried tomatoes for 30 seconds. Add parsley and pulse to chop roughly. Add olive oil and balsamic vinegar, pulse to blend in. Don't puree. Taste for salt and pepper. Will keep 5–7 days refrigerated in a closed jar. Makes 2–3 cups

· Tuscan sausage and cannellini beans ·

This dish uses the wonderfully rich and heavy cannellini beans of Northern Italy, accented by the flavors of aromatic Tuscan sausage and fresh fennel. It's a hearty and satisfying dish, and typical of Tuscan country cooking at its rustic best. You can substitute luganega or Italian sweet fennel sausage for the Tuscan type. If you can't find cannellini beans, navy or Great Northern beans will do.

1 lb. dried cannellini, Great Northern or navy beans, soaked overnight, and drained
2 qts. rich chicken stock
2 bay leaves
1½ lbs. Tuscan-style sausage or other mild Italian sausage
1 c. diced onion
1 c. diced carrot
1 medium fennel bulb, diced
¼ c. virgin olive oil

2 tbsp. chopped garlic
¼ c. chopped fresh parsley
1 bunch chard (about 1 lb.), stems removed and discarded, washed, and roughly chopped
1 c. fresh basil leaves or 2 tsp. dried basil
Salt and pepper
Freshly grated Parmesan cheese (optional)

In a large stockpot or Dutch oven, cover the soaked and drained beans with the stock. Bring to a boil, and then reduce to a simmer. Add the bay leaves.

Brown the sausages whole in a heavy large skillet over medium heat, turning occasionally. Remove and reserve. Add the onion, carrot, and fennel to the fat remaining in the pan, along with a little olive oil if necessary. Cover and cook for 10 minutes. Add 1 tablespoon each of the garlic and parsley. Remove from the heat. After the beans have cooked an hour, add the vegetable mixture to the pot. Continue to simmer, uncovered, for 1–1½ hours.

If fresh fennel isn't available, add a little extra chopped parsley and a generous pinch of ground fennel seed or an ounce or two of Pernod for the anise flavor.

When the beans are tender, slice the sausage into 1-inch rounds. Add them to the beans along with the remaining garlic, the chard, and basil. Cook for 3–5 minutes. Stir in the olive oil. Taste for salt and pepper. Serve in large individual bowls, garnished with the remaining parsley, and allow guests to add Parmesan if desired. Makes 8 servings

cholent ·

This substantial meat and bean dish came about because of the strict Jewish observance of the Sabbath that doesn't allow any cooking from sunset Friday to sunset Saturday. Orthodox Jewish cooks would prepare the cholent on Friday, and bring it down to the village or neighborhood baker before sunset. Left in the warm oven overnight, the cholent would be ready for the noonday Sabbath meal. It can be made with only beans and flavorings, but it usually includes meat of some sort, most often beef or lamb. In our adaptation we use Romanian beef sausage and lamb shanks. This is still traditional, since as with many peasant dishes, there are as many versions of cholent as there are cooks who make it.

2 tbsp. chicken fat (schmaltz) or olive oil
1 lb. Romanian beef sausages (whole)
4 lamb shanks, cut into 8 pieces
Salt
1 tsp. black pepper
Pinch each ground ginger and cumin
2 tsp. Hungarian paprika
3 large onions, coarsely chopped

1 rib celery, coarsely chopped
2 bay leaves
4 c. chicken stock
3–4 c. dry white wine
½ lb. dried lima beans, soaked overnight, washed, and drained
½ lb. lentils
1 c. pearl barley

Preheat the oven to 250° F. In a 4–6-quart Dutch oven with a tight-fitting lid, heat the chicken fat or olive oil over medium heat. Put in the sausages, and cook them for 5 minutes, turning often to brown evenly. Don't worry if they are not completely cooked. Remove the sausages, and put the lamb shanks in the fat in the pan. Lightly sprinkle them with some of the salt, pepper, ginger, cumin, and paprika. Brown for 10 minutes or so, turning often. Remove, and add the onions and celery. Cover and cook until the onions begin to brown, about 10 minutes, stirring frequently. Put in the remaining spices and the bay leaves, along with the sausages and the lamb. Pour in the stock and wine. Add the limas, lentils, and barley. Make sure the meat rests on a layer of beans and is covered with more beans. Bring everything to a boil. Cover the casserole, and put it in the oven. Bake for 3½ hours at 250° F. Check every hour or so to see whether the liquid has been absorbed or the beans are tender. Adjust the liquid level and cooking times accordingly. Remove bay leaves before serving. Makes 6–8 servings

Cholent is similar to cassoulet, another traditional bean dish that requires slow cooking.

· Brian's maple beans ·

Brian Stack grew up in Fitchburg, Massachusetts, in a Polish-American family. They made this New England classic with kielbasa or linguiça, but any good-quality, lean smoked sausage will work fine. In New England, the small white beans are called pea beans. You can also use white navy beans. Brian recommends serving this with old-fashioned frankfurters or bratwurst, cole slaw and Cornbread (see page 151) or Johnnycakes.

1 lb. pea beans or other small white
    beans
¾ c. ketchup or chili sauce
⅓ c. maple syrup
1 tbsp. prepared brown mustard like
    Gulden's
3 tbsp. molasses

½ lb. linguiça, chopped
½ lb. salt pork or bacon, or a
    combination of both, washed and
    diced
1 medium onion, chopped
Salt and pepper to taste

Pick over and rinse the beans. Cover with 2–3 inches of water and bring to a boil for 2 minutes. Remove from the heat. Cover, and let stand for 2 hours.

Use grade B maple syrup if you can find it—it's darker and richer than grade A.

Drain the beans. Cover with 2–3 inches of fresh water in a large pot or Dutch oven. Add the ketchup, maple syrup, mustard, and molasses. Bring to a boil and reduce to a simmer.

Cook the sausage and salt pork in a heavy skillet, stirring occasionally, over medium heat for about 5 minutes to render some of the fat. Add the onion and cook 5 minutes more. Pour off most of the fat, and then add the mixture to the beans. Cover and cook over low heat on the top of the stove until the beans are quite tender, about 2–3 hours. Add more liquid as needed. You can serve as is, or you can pack the beans into a bean pot or casserole, refrigerate them overnight, and then bake them, covered, in a 350° F oven for 45 minutes to an hour. This allows the flavors to mellow and mature. Add more water if needed during baking. Taste for salt and pepper and serve.

Makes 8–10 servings as a side dish

butternut squash stuffed with sausage, apple, and chestnuts ·

Of all the winter squashes, we think butternut has the finest taste and texture. It is rarely fibrous and stringy, and its sweet and buttery taste lives up to its name. This recipe is adapted from Judith and Evan Jones' *The L. L. Bean Book of New New England Cookery*. Chestnuts are used instead of bread crumbs to bind the mixture together, adding a subtle nuttiness that mixes nicely with the butternut flavors. You can substitute acorn squash, if butternut is unavailable.

2 medium butternut squash, about
   1 lb. each
4 tbsp. butter
2 tbsp. maple syrup
Pinch *each* cinnamon and freshly
   grated nutmeg
¼ tsp. salt
¼ tsp. pepper

1 small green apple such as Pippin or
   Granny Smith, cored, peeled, and
   finely chopped, about 1 c.
8–10 cooked chestnuts (see page
   346), finely chopped
Salt and pepper to taste

· **Stuffing** ·

1 lb. Yankee Sage Sausage (see page
   112) or other good bulk sausage

Preheat the oven to 350° F. Cut each squash in half lengthwise, and scoop out the seeds and fibrous material. Melt the butter. Stir in the maple syrup, cinnamon, nutmeg, salt, and pepper. Add 1 or 2 tablespoons of this mixture to the hollow center of each squash and brush it on the cut surface of the squash. Reserve the rest. Bake the squash, uncovered, cut side up, for about 40 minutes, or until the flesh is partially cooked.

Meanwhile, prepare the stuffing. In a large bowl, mix the sausage, apple, and chestnuts. Remove the squash from the oven, and pour the liquid from the hollow of each half into this mixture. Scoop out some of the partially cooked flesh from the squash shells to expand the cavity. Chop this roughly and mix into the stuffing. Taste for salt and pepper. Pile equal amounts of the stuffing into each shell. Generously brush the squash with the remaining melted butter and maple syrup. Cover

This sweet and savory stuffing highlights the squash wonderfully.

the squash with aluminum foil and bake 35–45 minutes. The squash can be stuffed a day ahead and kept in the refrigerator until ready to bake. You should add 5 or 10 minutes to the baking time if the squash is cold. Makes 4 servings as a main course, 8 or more as a side dish, if you cut each stuffed squash in half.

THE MIDWEST
· the heartland ·

Ukrainian beef and pork sausage

Minnesota potato sausage

Iowa farm sausage

Michigan Dutch farmer's
sausage

APPETIZERS,
SNACKS,
& SOUPS

Sausage and cornbread bites

Beef and sausage piroshki

Takoma Park pelmeni

Shirred eggs and sausage

Quick and easy sandwiches

German white bean soup

Cornbelt chowder

Second Street sauerkraut soup

Cold beet, cucumber, and
kielbasa soup

Polish sausage, mushroom,
and barley soup

Solianka, a Russian soup with meat,
sausage, prunes, and cucumbers

New Year's Eve borscht

MAIN
DISHES

Deep dish chicken and sausage pie
with biscuit crust

Rabbit or chicken paprikash

Brats braised with beer and onions

Rouladen: Shaker-style stuffed
flank steak

Beef and sausage stew with potato
dumplings

Pennsylvania Dutch schnitz und knepp

Family favorite ham and
sausage loaf

Lazy Hungarian goulash

Bigos or Polish hunter's stew

Calves' liver and sausage,
Hungarian style

Hungarian stuffed cabbage

Sausage, mashed potato, and
cabbage casserole,
or bubble and squeak

SIDE DISHES

Braised cabbage and sausage

Smoked kielbasa and red cabbage

"The spinach"

Potato casserole with
sausage and cheese

Hot potato and sausage salad

Potato, sausage, and leek gratin

Simple home-style scrapple

he Midwest is America's heartland, a vast, rich, and fertile region that supplies the nation, and much of the world, with its wheat, corn, soybeans, and hogs. The poet Carl Sandburg called Chicago the "Hog Butcher for the World" and that wasn't entirely hyperbole. Down the Midwest's rivers and across its lakes flows an immense treasure of grain and livestock that is processed and shipped from the great midwestern cities and ports. Chicago, first and foremost, but Cincinnati, Cleveland, Milwaukee, Minneapolis/St. Paul, St. Louis, and other cities are all immense food processors that transform and market the agricultural riches of America's great central plain.

This bountiful region with its rich and fecund soil has always been an attraction to the land-starved peasants of Europe. From the late eighteenth century when settlers pushed through the Alleghenies and first looked down on this green sea of forest and plain, pioneers carved out farms and planted crops in the dark, virgin soil. The first settlers were Scotch-Irish from the poor uplands of Virginia and Carolina, but they were soon followed by immigrants from northern Europe: Germans seeking freedom of worship, Poles and Bohemians looking for land and a decent life for their families, Hungarians fleeing the aftermath of revolution and political persecution, Scandinavians dreaming of lush pastures.

And they brought their own traditions and food with them. Just as in other regions, immigrants to the Midwest grafted their culinary traditions onto American roots, and adapted native cuisines to what they grew on their new land.

The American base was the same as in other regions. The first farmers brought corn and the pig, then wheat, rye, barley, and other grains when the new settlers spread out across the great plains of Kansas, Iowa, and the Dakotas. All this abundance nourished the cities, and the feedlots of Chicago, Omaha, and Kansas City soon supplied meat to a hungry nation. The great packing houses of Armour, Swift, and others, combined with the new technology of refrigerated train cars, offered America, and the world at large, a seemingly unlimited supply of pork and beef. In the late nineteenth and early twentieth century, the farmers of the Midwest and the great food processors and shippers of the cities transformed America and its cuisine.

German immigrants formed large communities in the major cities, and the neighborhoods of Chicago, Cleveland, Cincinnati, Milwaukee, and other cities were soon filled with markets, butcher shops, delicatessens, and restaurants that dispensed hearty food, sausages, beer, and *Gemütlichkeit*. German butchers introduced to America the art of fine sausage making that included a staggering array of sausages from every region of Germany. Many of these traditional sausages like braunschweiger, leberwurst, knockwurst, and the ubiquitous frankfurter joined the mainstream of American cooking and became popular favorites of families from all ethnic backgrounds.

German sausage-making traditions go back a long way—to the beginnings of agriculture and pastoralism in Europe. One of the requirements of the harsh climate in northern Europe is the "Great Killing" that takes place every fall, when all animals that are not essential for breeding new stock are killed off before the onset of winter. It was the lack of fodder during the cold months, as well as the preservative effect of the cold weather, that engendered a rich tradition of meat preservation and sausage making in northern Europe, and especially Germany.

The *Schlachtplatte* offered in German restaurants in Milwaukee and Chicago reflects this tradition and hearkens back to the *Schlachtfest,* when all the parts of the slaughtered pig (*schlachten* means "to slaughter or butcher" in German) were offered to families that helped with the butchering. The variety of German sausages seems to be inexhaustible. Usingers of Milwaukee, one of the premium German-style sausage makers in America, offers more than fifty different sausages in its retail store, including gothaer cervelat, summer sausage, mettwurst, teewurst, landjaeger, theuringer blood sausage, bierwurst, hessische landleberwurst, hildesheimer liver sausage, jagdwurst, knockwurst, holsteiner, bratwurst, and fritzies, to name but a few.

Sausages are used in a wide variety of German-American dishes and are often paired with cabbage, sauerkraut, and potatoes in traditional recipes like Hot Potato and Sausage Salad (see page 200), Second Street Sauerkraut Soup (see page 171), and Braised Cabbage and Sausage (see page 197).

An important tradition in American cooking is found among the Pennsylvania Dutch, a community that came early to William Penn's Philadelphia colony from Moravia, the Palatinate, and other parts of Germany, seeking religious tolerance. Mennonites, Amish, and the Moravian

HOT LINKS & COUNTRY FLAVORS

Brotherhood took root in the rich, deep soil of Pennsylvania, and created a great American cuisine. Anyone who has ever visited the Lancaster market can testify to the abundance and plentitude of Pennsylvania Dutch farms. Pale pink mounds of sage-flavored farmer's sausage, coils of mahogany-colored smoked sausage, spicy Lebanon bologna, colorful pickles, chow chows and relishes, heaps of bright green beans, mounds of tomatoes, melons and squash, pies of every description, pale yellow aged cheeses, pots of white farmer's cheese, and hand-churned butter in tubs and bowls, all presided over by cheerful, glowing womenfolk and serious men who dress plain but cook tasty are reflective of a culture that loves and respects good food.

Eastern Europeans also have a cuisine that uses sausage as an important element in many traditional dishes. Polish sausage or kielbasa has become an American favorite, and versions of this garlicky smoked sausage are found in supermarkets and butcher shops throughout the United States. In the ethnic neighborhoods of the Midwest, however, a wide range of kielbasa can be found—from lightly spiced, fresh versions (see our recipe for Fresh Kielbasa, page 161), to coarse-textured smoked sausages with plenty of garlic, spices, and pepper (see Smoked Kielbasa, page 165). Other Eastern European nationalities offer their own special sausages such as Hungarian Paprika Sausage or Debrecini (see page 166), Pork and Liver Sausage with Slivovitz (see page 167), and Ukrainian Beef and Pork Sausage (see page 168).

Immigrants from Scandinavian countries have enriched American cuisine by their skills with cheese and other dairy products. Wisconsin Cheddar is deservedly world famous, along with other cheeses like brick and Limburger that were developed by the enterprising dairy farmers of the Midwest. Hearty food has always been a part of Scandinavian culture, and Minnesota Potato Sausage (see page 169) is no exception.

Midwestern farmers raise some of the finest pigs in the world, and are proud of their own version of American sage and black pepper sausage. Whether in link or bulk form, sausage is found in farm towns and cities throughout the region, on the table for breakfast with hotcakes and biscuits, or in homey dishes like meat or ham loaf (see our recipe for Family Favorite Ham and Sausage Loaf, page 191) or casseroles (see Potato Casserole with Sausage and Cheese, page 199).

· Sheboygan brats (fresh farm bratwurst) ·

Folks in the Midwest take their bratwurst very seriously, especially in Wisconsin up around Sheboygan, home of the Sheboygan brat. In fact, in Sheboygan they take their bratwurst so seriously that they have an annual Bratwurst Festival where thousands upon thousands of brats are grilled and eaten with onions and mustard on the famous Wisconsin hard rolls. And nobody is shy about washing down these savory sausages with foaming steins of the locally brewed beer.

In Germany and throughout the German communities of Wisconsin, Minnesota, and the Midwest, this savory sausage is often made on farms, and is usually consumed fresh. Many U.S. sausage makers sell bratwurst already cooked, and then it's simply poached or steamed in most Wisconsin taverns and bars.

Steamed brats can be mighty tasty, especially with some kraut or onions, hot mustard, and a stein of cold beer, but we think you get more flavor if you start out with the raw sausage, and grill it over charcoal or under a broiler.

1½ lbs. pork butt	1 tsp. ground mace
1 lb. veal shoulder	1 tsp. ground caraway seeds
½ lb. pork back fat	½ tsp. ground ginger
1 tbsp. salt	½ c. milk
1 tsp. sugar	Medium hog casings
1 tsp. freshly ground black pepper	

For details on sausage making, see page 332.

Mix the meats, fat, and all the seasonings in a large bowl and grind everything finely through the ⅛-inch plate. Add the milk and knead until the spices are well mixed in with the meat. Stuff into medium hog casings and tie into 5-inch links. You can leave the brats raw or poach them for 20 minutes. Refrigerated, the sausages will keep for 3 days, frozen for 2 months.

Makes about 3 pounds

Use fresh bratwurst in any recipe in this chapter that calls for mildly flavored sausage.

·smoked bratwurst·

Although similar spices are used in both the fresh and smoked versions of bratwurst, the smoked variety has a rich and smoky flavor. Make smoked bratwurst with all pork or a combination of pork and beef. Experiment a bit with different proportions of meats until you find the taste and texture you like. We like about 4 parts pork to 1 part beef, but taste for yourself.

2½ lbs. pork butt, or 2 lbs. pork butt and ½ lb. beef chuck
½ lb. pork back fat
2 tsp. minced garlic
1 tbsp. coarsely ground mustard seed
½ tsp. freshly grated nutmeg
1 tsp. ground mace
1 tsp. dried sage

1 tbsp. coarsely ground black pepper
1 tbsp. kosher salt
2 tsp. sugar
¾ tsp. curing salts (optional) (see "Note on Nitrite," page 343)
½ c. water
Medium hog casings

For details on sausage making, see page 332.

Mix the meat, fat, and all the seasonings in a large bowl, and grind everything through a ¼-inch plate. Add the water, and the optional curing salts if you intend to cold smoke the sausages. Knead and squeeze the mixture to blend all the ingredients thoroughly. Stuff into medium hog casings, and tie in 5–6-inch links. If you choose to cold smoke the brats, use curing salts and air-dry the sausages in front of a fan overnight. Cold smoke for 12–24 hours (see "Smoking," page 340). Bratwurst can also be hot smoked very successfully. Hot smoke to an internal temperature of 155° F (see page 341). These sausages will keep 1 week refrigerated, 2 months frozen. Makes about 3 pounds

Use this sausage in any recipe in the book that calls for smoked sausage.

· cold beer, hot brats ·

It's a muggy
Wisconsin night
in late summer somewhere
outside Sheboygan. A red neon sign
looms through the darkness, "Cold Beer Hot
Brats." We're on our way to the Sheboygan
Bratwurst Festival, and our '55 Buick Road-
master (affectionately termed The Wurstmo-
bile) lurches off the highway into yet
another parking lot. We pile into the tavern
for a taste test of Sheboygan brats and the
inevitable accompaniment, foaming steins of
cold Wisconsin lager.

A long, dimly lit bar stretches back into
the darkness. Men in shirtsleeves nurse tall
seidels of pale golden beer, beads of moisture
clinging to the sides of the glasses. Nobody's
saying much, staring into the mirrors
flanked by naked nymphs and angels, watch-
ing the neon beer signs revolve, waiting for a
cool breeze off the river.

We pick a spot at the bar and wave the
bartender over. "Beer and brats," we say.
"Doubles all around, with the works." He
nods, smiling.

The beer arrives first, pale and clean,
with the bitter tang of hops in the nose, the
rich sweetness of malt across the palate. As
we sip our beers, we all find ourselves staring
into the ornate mirrors, dreaming of bratwurst, of ancient festivals, the works.

A flurry of activity erupts in the quiet
bar. Heads turn, suddenly smiling, as the
bartender's wife (mother, girlfriend, sister)
sweeps up behind us, balancing plates on her
plump and lovely arms; blonde hair piled up
around her face, red cheeks, pale blue eyes,
cheerful and bold and beautiful, saying, "You
the boys ordered brats, doubles, works all
around?"

She lays the plates down along the bar.
Two grilled brats bulge between halves of the

hard roll; a slice of pale white onion sticks out underneath; hot brown mustard, coarse-ground with horseradish, opens up the sinuses; long thin slices of sour dill pickles crisscross the brats. This is the best of Sheboygan's wursts: a double brat with the works!

The first question, as with any good sausage sandwich, is the mode of attack. That is to say, how to get all these gustatory wonders into your mouth with a minimum of hassle and a modicum of dignity. At the first bite, however, all hopes of decorum and clean shirts fade. You just open your mouth as wide as you can, and bite down.

And suddenly it all becomes clear. Why everyone seems so peaceful here, so happy. As the spiced juicy meat mingles with the sweet onions, hot mustard, and sour pickles you experience a kind of heavenly harmony, a clear perception of rightness, of how things should be. "This might just be the ultimate sausage sandwich," I say, sipping my beer pensively. "It can't get any better than this."

· Chicago-style hot dogs ·

There's a lot of argument about where in Europe the hot dog originated —
some say Frankfurt (frankfurter), others Vienna (wiener), while others relate
it to the Czechoslovakian párky or French *saucisse de Strasbourg*. There's
even debate as to where it first appeared in America: St. Louis in the 1880s,
the Bowery or Coney Island in New York, or even Chicago or Cleveland.

But one thing nobody is willing to argue about is that the hot dog has
long been the most popular and famous American sausage. Whether you're
munching one of Nathan's Famous Franks with sauerkraut and brown mustard, a Chicago hot dog with the works, an L.A. chile dog or even a "chien
chaud" on the Champs Elysées stuffed into a hollowed-out baguette with
Gruyère, you know that you are eating *the* American sausage.

We do know that a German butcher named Feltman opened up a
sausage stand in Coney Island in the 1870s, and his "hot dachshund sausages" soon become the rage of that popular, and then fashionable, resort.
And on an April afternoon at the Polo Grounds in 1901, cartoonist Tad Dor-
gan christened the sausage in a bun the "hot dog" (he couldn't spell
"dachshund"). In 1916, Nathan Handwerker, a former Feltman's employee,
opened Nathan's Famous Franks and has sold, literally, millions of his spicy
frankfurters over the years. Now we have frankfurters of types that would
make old Mr. Feltman blanch: skinless franks, all-beef franks, old-fashioned
franks, corn dogs, and bagel dogs, and even chicken hot dogs (ugh!). For
juicy texture and plenty of taste, however, we don't think you can beat the
original mixture of pork, beef, and spices.

Unlike the other sausages in this book, the hot dog is an emulsified
sausage, which means you must achieve a completely homogeneous mixture
of meat and fat to make a successful sausage. To do this without the aid of
chemicals such as phosphates, extenders like dried milk, and the special
mixers found in sausage factories can be a bit tricky. It's easy enough to
combine ground meat and spices, but if you don't achieve an emulsion, you
don't have a hot dog. When you bite into a juicy hot dog, the sausage should
pop when you break the casing. It should be succulent and juicy without
being watery. If you don't get the emulsion right, the hot dogs will be dense
and grainy, even though the taste may be passable.

So before you set off to whip up your own bunch of juicy hot dogs let
me tell you of our experiences:

Try number one looked like the right homogeneous mixture when I
stuffed them into the casings. They were nice and plump, and about 8 inches
long. I poached them and they looked just fine. I drained them and left them
to cool in the sink while I went to the store to pick up some buns, beer, and
condiments. Thirty minutes later I returned with some friends to taste my
efforts. When we looked into the colander, we all had a bit of a shock. My
lovely hot dogs had shrunk to about 3 inches long and half their original

HOT LINKS & COUNTRY FLAVORS

diameter. Biting into one was like trying to eat an eraser, grainy, dry, and dense. Back to the drawing board!

Batch number two was also a failure. The meat was overprocessed and became too warm. The fat separated out and the result was a mess when I tried to cook the franks.

Try number three finally brought success because I paid very close attention to temperature and processing times, both of which are critical for achieving a stable emulsion. Once all the meats and fats are ground, you must chill them well in the refrigerator. To emulsify the meat and fat, you will need an instant-read thermometer and a large and powerful food processor. The temperature of the mixture must not rise above 60° F at any time during the processing. This is accomplished by adding crushed ice to the mixture, and processing in short intervals of 15 seconds. So good luck!

¾ lb. pork butt	¼ tsp. ground mace
½ lb. beef chuck	½ tsp. ground coriander
¼ lb. pork back fat	¼ tsp. ground cardamom
1 tbsp. light corn syrup	¼ tsp. ground cumin or ground
2 tsp. sweet Hungarian paprika	celery seed
1 tsp. dry mustard	1½ tsp. salt
1 tsp. minced garlic	1–2 c. crushed ice
½ tsp. finely ground black pepper	Sheep casings

For details on sausage making, see page 332.

Grind well-chilled meats and fat through the finest plate of your meat grinder (⅛ or ¼ inch) into the smallest size possible to help emulsify the mixture. Chill for 30 minutes in the refrigerator or 15 minutes in the freezer.

Mix together all the spices and salt. Add half the meat and fat mixture to the bowl of a large food processor. Put in half the spice blend, half the corn syrup, and ½ cup of crushed ice. Process in 15-second spurts for a total of 1–1½ minutes. After each 15 seconds of processing, stop the machine, and check the temperature of the meat mixture to make sure it is under 60° F. If not, add a tablespoon or more of crushed ice. The key is to process the mixture until it has a homogeneous appearance. There should not be any visible particles of fat, and the mixture should look like a stiff pink paste. Transfer to a bowl and refrigerate while you process the second half of the meat, fat, corn syrup, and spices, repeating the same procedure, including the crushed ice. Use a spatula or wooden spoon to mix together the two batches. Stuff into sheep casings and tie into 6-inch links. Poach the hot dogs in 160–180° F water for 20–25 minutes, or until they are firm. Remove and cool under running water.

To rewarm the hot dogs, bring a pot of water to a boil. Put the hot dogs in, cover the pot, and remove from the heat. Let the sausages stand for 10 minutes and enjoy. Makes 1½–2 pounds

· bockwurst ·

This mild-flavored white sausage is very popular in German neighborhoods throughout the Midwest. It is great tavern food, eaten with some tangy German-style mustard, crusty bread, and a stein of cold lager beer. Bockwurst's rich but delicate flavor is perfect for dishes like our Deep Dish Chicken and Sausage Pie with Biscuit Crust (see page 184), or Pennsylvania Dutch Schnitz und Knepp (see page 190).

½ c. finely chopped leeks or onions
1 tbsp. butter
1 lb. pork butt
1 lb. stewing veal or veal shoulder
½ lb. chicken breast or thigh with skin left on
½ lb. pork back fat
Pinch ground ginger
1 tsp. ground mace

½ tsp. finely ground white or black pepper
4 tsp. salt
1 c. milk
1 egg, beaten
½ c. finely chopped green onions or scallions, or chives
¼ c. chopped fresh parsley
Medium hog casings

For details on sausage making, see page 332.

Cook the leeks or onions in the butter, covered, over medium heat for about 10 minutes until they are quite soft and translucent. Set aside and reserve.

Mix the pork, veal, chicken, and fat with the seasonings, and grind through a ⅛-inch plate into a large bowl. Add the cooked leeks or onions along with the milk, egg, green onions or chives, and the parsley. Using a wooden spoon, beat the mixture until everything is well blended. Chill the sausage meat in the refrigerator for at least 30 minutes, and then stuff it into medium hog casings. Tie into 6–7-inch links, and poach in lightly salted water at 180° F for 20–25 minutes, or until the sausage is firm. Cool under running water. Refrigerated, the poached sausage will keep 3 days, frozen for 2 months. Makes about 4 pounds

Like most German-style sausages, bockwurst is delicious grilled, as well as poached and then browned in butter.

· hunter's sausage ·

This hearty sausage has an ample, smoky flavor from the bacon, and a nice lift in its aromas and taste from the spices and mustard. Hunter's sausage is excellent grilled and served with a coarse-grained mustard, or braised with beer and onions (see page 186).

2 lbs. pork butt
1 lb. lean smoked bacon
1 tsp. kosher salt
2 tsp. coarsely ground black pepper
1 tsp. ground coriander
2 tsp. minced garlic
1 tsp. freshly grated nutmeg

½ tsp. ground ginger
2 tsp. sweet Hungarian paprika
2 tsp. dry mustard
1 tbsp. whole yellow mustard seeds
½ c. water
Medium hog casings

For details of sausage making, see page 332.

Grind the pork and bacon through a ¼-inch plate. Mix the ground meat with the remaining ingredients, except the casings, and knead until all the spices are thoroughly blended with the meat. Stuff into medium hog casings, and tie into 6–7-inch links. Dry the sausages, uncovered, in the refrigerator for 1 or 2 days. Poach in water at 180° F for 25 minutes. Cool and refrigerate. The poached sausages will keep for 3–4 days in the refrigerator, 2 months in the freezer. Makes about 3 pounds

Use anywhere you want a subtle smoky flavor or to replace kielbasa in any of our recipes.

· quick summer sausage ·

The most likely explanation of the name is that making summer sausage was a way to preserve highly perishable meat during the summer months in the days before refrigeration. The tangy flavor of summer sausage is caused by a natural fermentation of the chopped meat. Commercial producers actually add a starter culture of lactobacillus to get the fermentation started. Home sausage makers simply rely on the natural process of fermentation to flavor and preserve the meat.

Commercial summer sausage is air-dried in temperature- and humidity-controlled aging rooms. Home sausage makers should air-dry the sausage at cool temperatures, below 70° F. The sausage should dry slowly and evenly, so that the outside doesn't dry too quickly and the interior stays moist. Often, homemade summer sausage has to hang for as long as 2–3 months before it is completely dry and ready to eat. This takes an inordinate amount of patience, so we offer a quicker method that produces very good results.

We suggest you air-dry the sausage for 2 days in a cool, airy place so that the flavors can develop and some fermentation occur. Then you can smoke the sausage for 24 hours in a warm smokehouse or smoker at temperatures between 115° and 130° F. This will partially cook the sausage and help to firm it. If you want it drier and tangier, continue to hang it at cool room temperatures or in the refrigerator until the desired level of hardness is reached.

2 lbs. lean beef chuck, very cold
¼ lb. salt pork, frozen, only partially
  defrosted
¾ lb. pork butt, frozen, only partially
  defrosted
1½ tsp. ground coriander
1 tsp. dry mustard
2 tbsp. whole mustard seed
3 tsp. cracked black pepper
1 tbsp. sugar

½ c. dry red wine
½ tsp. ground ginger
2 tsp. minced garlic
3 tsp. kosher salt
1 tsp. curing salts (see "Note on
  Nitrites," page 343)
⅛ tsp. *each* ground allspice and
  freshly grated nutmeg
½ c. water
Wide beef casings

For details on sausage making, see page 332.

Grind the beef through a ¼-inch plate and the prefrozen salt pork and pork through a ⅛-inch plate. Make sure that all the meats and fats are very cold. In a large bowl, mix the ground meats with all the other ingredients, except the casings, being careful not to overmix and heat up the fat and meat. Stuff the sausage meat very tightly into wide beef casings, tie with a string into two 8–10-inch links, drape over a clean pole or smoke stick, and air-dry in a cool and airy place for 2 days. Then cold smoke them at 115–130° F for 24 hours. If you want a harder sausage, air-dry the sausage for 2–3 more days, or until it is dry enough for your taste. Another method to dry the sausage further is to bake it for about 1 hour in a very slow oven or water smoker at a temperature of less than 200° F. Cool and slice thinly to eat. Refrigerated, Quick Summer Sausage keeps for about 1 month; frozen, 2 months. Makes 2½ pounds

To make Quick Summer Sausage safely, you must use curing salts, and you must freeze the salt pork and pork butt for at least 2 weeks at no higher than 0° F to eliminate any possibility of trichinosis.

· garlic, pork, and ham cervelat ·

Cervelat is a large sausage that is often eaten as a cold cut, or it is boiled and then used either hot or cold in various dishes. Cervelat used as a cold cut is usually air-dried for several days until it is semi-dry, and therefore must include curing salts. In our recipe, either air-dry the sausage overnight at cool room temperature, in which case you need the curing salts, or dry it uncovered for a few days in the refrigerator and leave the cure out.

Whether you air-dry the cervelat or dry it in the refrigerator, you will need to poach it before eating. Once it is poached, you can eat it hot or cold. Cervelat goes especially well with potatoes. We particularly like it with home fries or in vinaigrette potato salad (see page 200), but it also tastes delicious with some cheesy mashed potatoes or German potato pancakes.

1¾ lbs. pork butt	½ tsp. ground mace
1 lb. smoked or boiled ham	½ tsp. ground cumin
¼ lb. pork back fat	Pinch ground cloves
3 tbsp. minced garlic	2 tsp. kosher salt
1 tsp. ground coriander	½ tsp. curing salts (optional) (see
2 tsp. coarsely cracked pepper	"Note on Nitrites," page 343)
1 tsp. finely ground black pepper	½ c. water or white wine
½ tsp. dried savory	Wide beef or hog casings

For details on sausage making, see page 332.

Grind the pork and ham through a ⅜-inch plate and the pork fat through a ¼-inch plate. Mix the ground meats and fat with the other ingredients, except the casings, and knead until everything is well blended. Stuff into wide beef or hog casings (beef is preferred since it is easier to peel off before eating the sausage). Tie into 6-inch links. If you intend to air-dry the sausages at room temperature, be sure to include the curing salts. If you dry the sausages in the refrigerator, you can leave them out. An alternative method is to dry them at room temperature for a day, and then 2 days in the refrigerator. In this case, you should use curing salts to be on the safe side.

To poach cervelat, bring a large pot of lightly salted water to a boil. Add the sausages, and reduce the heat to the lowest setting. Maintain the poaching water at a temperature between 160 and 180° F for 40–50 minutes, depending on how thick the sausages are. They should reach an internal temperature of 155° F. Eat the cervelat as is, or cool under running water, refrigerate, and eat the cold sausage sliced. To reheat, place the sausages in simmering water and cook for 15 minutes until heated through. Keep 1 week refrigerated, 2 months frozen. Makes 2½–3 pounds

Hot or cold, fried, baked, or mashed, the earthy flavor of potatoes melds nicely with this garlicky, richly flavored sausage.

· Lebanon bologna ·

Lebanon bologna is more like summer sausage than bologna, and this wonderfully spicy smoked sausage is a far cry from the pallid and tasteless bologna of the supermarket shopping case. Named for the Pennsylvania Dutch town of Lebanon, this all-beef sausage has a pleasantly coarse texture and a smoky, robust flavor. One bite of real Lebanon bologna and you know why Pennsylvania Dutch cooks are ranked among the finest in America, and why their rich and satisfying cuisine is one of the glories of American cooking.

Lebanon bologna is best cold smoked, which means you should use curing salts. It is usually sliced and eaten cold, although it can also be diced to provide flavor for soups and stews (see Cornbelt Chowder, page 178).

2¾ lbs. lean beef chuck
¼ lb. beef plate or other cut of fatty
  beef
1 tbsp. kosher salt
1 tbsp. sugar
1 tsp. curing salts (see page 343)
1 tsp. dry mustard

2 tsp. paprika
¼ c. light corn syrup
1 tbsp. coarsely ground black pepper
½ tsp. ground mace
1 tsp. ground ginger
½ c. cold water
Wide beef casings

For details on sausage making, see page 332.

Dice the meat into 1-inch pieces. Toss with the salt, sugar, and curing salts and pack into a bowl. Cover and cure in the refrigerator for 2 days. Mix the meat chunks with the remaining ingredients except the water and casings. Grind through a fine plate (⅛–¼ inch) into a large bowl. Add the water and any liquid produced during the curing period. Mix everything well and stuff the sausage meat into wide beef casings. Tie into 8-inch links and air-dry in a cool place in front of a fan overnight. Cold smoke for 24 to 36 hours. Lebanon bologna can then be air-dried at cool room temperature until firm, about a week, or left to dry unwrapped, for 2 weeks or more in the refrigerator. Keeps 4 weeks refrigerated.

Makes 2½ pounds

One of the great lunches of all time: Lebanon bologna on homemade black bread with hot mustard and a slice of raw sweet onion, along with a glass of full-bodied dark beer, such as Yuengling Porter or Prior's Double Dark.

· fresh kielbasa ·

Kielbasa is the Polish word for sausage in general, and in Poland, a country that loves its sausage and pork products, there are many varieties of kielbasa, both fresh and smoked. When the Poles immigrated to America's heartland, they brought along their love of sausages and their skills in making them. In the neighborhoods of Chicago and other large Midwestern cities, kielbasa or "Polish sausage" became popular, and then, as its reputation grew, eventually made its way into American kitchens generally. Now Polish sausage, along with the frankfurter and Italian sausage, has become a classic American sausage, and is found in virtually every region and style of American cooking.

Most Polish sausage sold in American supermarkets and delis is a smoked, smooth-textured type, but if you are lucky enough to live near a Polish butcher shop, you should be able to find the fresh variety. In Poland and Polish communities in the United States, fresh kielbasa is often made at home or on the farm during the pig-killing in the fall. Use this sausage in any recipe calling for a fresh mild sausage. Like bratwurst, it is great grilled and eaten on a hard roll with coarse mustard and onions.

2¼ lbs. pork butt	2 tsp. coarsely ground black pepper
¾ lb. pork back fat	½ tsp. ground coriander
2 tbsp. finely chopped garlic	1 tbsp. kosher salt
2 tsp. dried marjoram	½ c. water
1 tsp. dry mustard	Medium hog casings

For details on sausage making, see page 332.

Grind the meat and fat together through a ¼-inch plate. In a large bowl, mix the ground meat with all the remaining ingredients, except the casings. Knead the mixture until everything is well blended. Stuff into medium hog casings, and tie into 6-inch links. Refrigerated, the sausage will keep 3 days, frozen for 2 months. Makes about 3 pounds

Like most farmhouse recipes for country sausage, there are many versions of Fresh Kielbasa, but almost all contain substantial amounts of garlic, black pepper, and aromatic herbs.

· Polish wedding, Chicago ·

On a warm Sunday in spring it's pleasant to walk down the sidewalks of Chicago's Northside beside small neat houses with white picket fences, daffodils and crocuses along the pathways, past groceries with signs in Russian and Polish, butcher shops with "Fresh Kielbasa Here" painted on the windows in whitewash.

We're on our way to the wedding a Polish-American friend invited us to last night. "You want kielbasa, by God," he shouted in the bar of the huge German restaurant in the Loop, "come to my cousin's wedding. You'll eat more kielbasa than you ever thought existed in this world, or the next one too," and toasted us with a foaming stein of dark German draft.

So today we're searching for the wedding party in the parish hall just behind St. Casimir's church. And then we hear, pulsing in the still air from afar like the trumpets of Krakow to wandering pilgrims, the polka! We follow the sounds of accordions, tubas, trum-

pets, and drums down the street, turn the corner, and suddenly we're there.

The party is outside in the schoolyard next to the church, the band is perched on a make-shift stage hung round with flags and bunting, the air seems to shake with the music. Everybody's dancing, young and old: women in embroidered dresses, their blond braids whirling; old ladies in black,

waltzing with men who wear serious mustaches and low-brimmed hats; boys in leather jackets shuffling around the edge of the swirl with girls in short skirts and bee-hive hairdos; little girls dancing with each other, eyes wide and serious amid the laughter.

All around the schoolyard, tables are piled high with food, and a band of women with kerchiefs and flowered aprons moves back and forth from the parish hall with platters and bowls. Galvanized washtubs full of ice hold kegs of beer, bottles of wine and vodka, root beer and orange soda. Old men with bright cheeks and pale eyes are drinking straw-colored vodka from tiny glasses, beaming at the dancers, nodding their heads to the rhythms.

It's a sausage lover's dream: chunks of grilled smoked kielbasa are laid on heaps of red cabbage; small fresh sausages, brown and crisp, nestle on mounds of sauerkraut; brightly painted bowls are filled with aromatic goulash and bigos — the Polish hunter's stew made with sausage, game, and wild mushrooms; a roast suckling pig glistens, festooned with coils of sausages, surrounded with spiced apples and plums; roast potatoes circle pale pink hams.

We pile our plates high and talk with

women in aprons and men with ruddy cheeks about the feast and how the traditional dishes are cooked. Everybody has an opinion and a different ingredient, and we find out about juniper-smoked sausages from the Tatra Mountains, pickled hams and smoked bacon from the plains, kielbasa from War-saw, from Krakow, and from the butcher just down the block.

The party really gets going after the sun goes down, with tasting and talking, beer and vodka, and polka after polka far into the night. Then suddenly it's quiet, and an old man starts to sing a *tzigane,* a mournful gypsy song. A violin picks up the tune in the darkness. We sip *zubrowka* and dream of mountains and of horses cantering down the passes under a smuggler's moon.

· smoked kielbasa ·

This recipe gets pretty close to the real kielbasa that you can still find in small butcher shops in Polish neighborhoods from Chicago to Buffalo. Unlike the ubiquitous "Polish sausage" found in American supermarkets, authentic kielbasa is coarse in texture, quite smoky, and very garlicky in flavor, making it a wonderful addition to dishes of all types. It is also delicious grilled and served with coarse-grained mustard, a sweet and sour red cabbage cole slaw, and potatoes roasted with garlic and rosemary (see page 352).

Serve smoked kielbasa with a crisp, hoppy lager like Pilsner Urquell, a hearty California Petite Sirah or a full-bodied Châteauneuf-du-Pape.

1½ lbs. pork butt
1 lb. beef chuck
½ lb. pork back fat
2 tbsp. finely chopped garlic
1 tbsp. sweet Hungarian paprika
2 tsp. coarsely ground black pepper
½ tsp. dried marjoram
½ tsp. ground coriander

½ tsp. freshly grated nutmeg
1 tsp. curing salts (optional) (see page 332)
1 tbsp. kosher salt
2 tsp. sugar
½ c. water
Medium hog casings

For details on sausage making, see page 332.

Grind the pork through a ⅜-inch plate, the beef and fat through a ⅛- or ¼-inch plate. Add all the remaining ingredients, except the casings, and knead the meat until everything is well blended. Stuff into medium hog casings, and tie into 8-inch links. An alternative is to stuff the sausage meat into wide hog or beef casings about 24 inches long, and tie the two ends together with string to form a large ring.

If you are going to cold smoke the sausage, be sure to include the curing salts in the mixture. Then air-dry the sausage in front of a fan overnight, and cold smoke it for at least 12 hours. Or you can hot smoke the sausage (see page 341) and leave the curing salts out. Smoked kielbasa will keep refrigerated for 1 week, frozen for 2 months. Makes 2–3 pounds

We prefer to add curing salts and to cold smoke kielbasa, but very good results can be had by leaving the cure out and hot smoking the sausage.

· Hungarian paprika sausage (debreceni) ·

Hungary, like its Eastern European neighbors, is a sausage-eating country. Hungarian dry salami is deservedly world famous, and Hungarians enjoy a wide range of sausage, bacon, and smoked meats. What really sets Hungarian cooking apart, however, is the liberal use of paprika—the ubiquitous ground red pepper that varies from sweet to hot—in traditional dishes such as chicken or veal paprikash, pörkölt, and gulyás or goulash. And paprika is always found in the wonderful sausages made on farms and in villages at the pig-killing in autumn.

In Midwestern ethnic neighborhoods, it seems as though every butcher has his own variation, but any way you make it, debrecini will contain lots of paprika and a goodly amount of garlic. Often these paprika sausages are air-dried to intensify and develop the flavors. If you choose to air-dry the sausage, hang it in a cool place until it is firm. This usually takes several days, depending on temperature. If you do air-dry debrecini, don't forget to use curing salts in the recipe. You can then cold smoke or hot smoke the sausage (see page 338), or leave it fresh.

3 tbsp. sweet Hungarian paprika	1 tbsp. kosher salt
1½ tbsp. finely chopped garlic	1 tsp. sugar
½ tsp. ground coriander	1¾ lbs. pork butt
2 tsp. coarsely ground black pepper	¾ lb. beef chuck
⅛ tsp. *each* ground ginger and allspice	½ lb. pork back fat
1 tsp. curing salts (optional) (see page 343)	½ c. water
	Medium hog casings

For details on sausage making, see page 332.

Mix the spices, seasonings, and sugar together and rub all over the strips of pork, beef, and pork fat. Cover and refrigerate for 2 hours or overnight. Grind everything through a ¼-inch plate into a large bowl. Add the water, and any liquid remaining from the spice marinade. Knead and squeeze the meat until everything is well blended. Stuff into medium hog casings, and tie into 8-inch links. Be sure to include the optional curing salts if you are going to air-dry or cold smoke the sausage. Air-dry in front of a fan overnight and cold smoke for 8–12 hours. Otherwise you can dry the sausages lightly by refrigerating them, unwrapped, overnight. Or you can hot smoke the sausage (see page 341). Air-dried or smoked debrecini will keep refrigerated for 1 week, the fresh for 3 days. Frozen, all types will keep for 2 months. Makes 2½–3 pounds

As with other peasant sausages, there are many versions — fresh, smoked, or air-dried — of Hungarian paprika sausage, or debrecini.

· pork and liver sausage with slivovitz ·

These aromatic and flavorful sausages are delicious when cold smoked, but they can also be enjoyed fresh or air-dried. They use slivovitz, the fiery Yugoslavian plum brandy, as a flavoring, and its fruity, heady aromas blend beautifully with the liver and spices. We used beef liver here, since it is easier to find, but the stronger flavors of pork liver provide a little more resonance with the brandy.

1 c. finely chopped onions
1 tbsp. oil
2 lbs. pork butt with some fat
1 lb. pork or beef liver, poached until firm, about 5 minutes
1 tsp. dried thyme
¼ cup slivovitz or kirsch
1 tsp. curing salts (optional) (see page 343)

4 tsp. kosher salt
2 tsp. freshly ground black pepper
½ tsp. ground ginger
½ tsp. ground allspice
¼ tsp. freshly grated nutmeg
½ c. water
Medium hog casings

For details on making sausages, see page 332.

Cook the onions, covered, in the oil for 5 minutes until they are translucent. Grind the pork, liver, and onions through a fine (⅛–¼ inch) plate. Add the remaining ingredients, except the casings, and moisten with enough water to blend everything well. Stuff into medium hog casings, and tie into 7-inch links. Air-dry the sausages overnight in a cool place and cold smoke them for at least 8 hours. The sausage can also be used fresh, either poached or raw, according to recipes. You should use curing salts if you air-dry or cold smoke the sausages; you can leave them out if you are going to use the sausages fresh. They will keep fresh 2–3 days refrigerated, smoked up to 1 week in the refrigerator, frozen 2 months.

Makes 3 pounds

This mix of slivovitz, palinka, or other fruit brandies with spices, liver, and meat is typical of peasant sausages brought to the United States by immigrants from Austria, Hungary, Czechoslovakia, and Yugoslavia.

· Ukrainian beef and pork sausage ·

Slavic countries in Eastern Europe share a common heritage of garlicky beef and pork sausages similar to kielbasa. Kielbasa, or "sausage" in Polish, is the most famous, but you can find many other delicious fresh and smoked sausages in the Slavic neighborhoods of midwestern cities and towns. This Ukrainian version uses a bit more beef than pork, but you can vary these proportions to suit your own tastes. Again, as with smoked kielbasa, we prefer to cold smoke this sausage, which means some curing salts should be included in the recipe. But good results can be had by hot smoking and leaving the curing salts out. You could also leave the sausage unsmoked and use it in any dish where you want a lightly smoky flavor.

1½ lbs. beef chuck
¼ lb. beef plate or other fatty cut of
  beef
1 lb. pork butt
½ lb. smoked bacon
1 tsp. coarsely ground pepper
1 tbsp. sweet Hungarian paprika
2 tbsp. cracked black pepper
1 tbsp. chopped garlic
1 tsp. dried marjoram

2 tsp. whole mustard seed
½ tsp. ground coriander
½ tsp. ground ginger
2 tsp. kosher salt
1 tsp. curing salts (optional) (see
  page 343)
2 tsp. sugar
½ c. water
Medium or wide hog casings

For details on sausage making, see page 332.

Grind the beef through a ⅜-inch plate, the pork and bacon through a ¼-inch plate. Mix the ground meats and all the remaining ingredients, except the casings, in a large bowl, kneading the mixture with your hands until everything is well blended. Stuff into medium or wide hog casings. If you are using curing salts and intend to cold smoke the sausages, air-dry them overnight in front of a fan, and then cold smoke them for 12–24 hours. Otherwise hot smoke the sausages to an internal temperature of 155° F (see page 341). You can also leave the sausages raw and unsmoked. The raw sausage will keep for 3 days refrigerated, smoked versions up to 1 week. Frozen, the sausages will last 2 months. Makes 2–3 pounds

Bacon contributes a pleasantly smoky tang to this tasty sausage, even when served fresh.

· Minnesota potato sausage ·

The many commercial varieties of this Swedish sausage sold throughout Minnesota and Wisconsin tend toward the bland and boring. When they say potato, potato it is, with very little of anything else in the sausage. Our version uses a bit more meat, and a variety of mild spices to wake up the taste buds. Potato sausage is a real favorite for breakfast, since its texture and flavors are similar to hash. It goes beautifully with poached or fried eggs, especially with a few thin pancakes with some lingonberry or red currant jam on the side. And don't forget some strong black coffee, flavored with a little cardamom seed, and if it's Sunday brunch, perhaps just a touch of Aquavit.

To cook Minnesota Potato Sausages, place them in a heavy covered skillet in about ¼-inch of water. Cook over medium heat until the water evaporates. Continue to fry the sausages for about 10 more minutes until they are nicely browned, turning them occasionally.

⅓ lb. pork skin
1½ lbs. pork butt
1 lb. beef chuck
½ lb. pork back fat
2 lbs. boiling potatoes, peeled, covered in water with a little vitamin C (ascorbic acid) or lemon juice added to prevent browning
2 medium onions

1½ tbsp. kosher salt
2 tsp. dry mustard
1 tsp. ground allspice
2 tsp. fresh marjoram or 1 tsp. dried
2 tsp. ground caraway seeds
1½ tsp. coarsely ground black pepper
Water as needed
Medium hog casings

For details on making sausage, see page 332.

Cover the pork skin with water and bring to a boil. Cover the pot and reduce the heat to a simmer. Cook for 30–40 minutes until the skin is soft. Cool under cold running water, and set aside.

Grind the meats, fat, raw potatoes, onions, and pork skin through a ¼-inch plate into a large bowl. Add the remaining ingredients, except the casings, and knead until everything is well blended. Moisten with a little water if needed to aid mixing. Stuff into medium hog casings, and tie into 5–6-inch links. Poach in 180° F water for 40 minutes. Remove and cool. Refrigerated, the sausage will keep for 3 days, frozen for 2 months.

Makes about 5 pounds

Pork skin adds texture and flavor — the next time you cook a fresh ham or pork shoulder, cut the skin off before cooking and freeze it, or ask your butcher for some. You can also use the rind from slab bacon.

· somewhere in Iowa ·

We're somewhere in Iowa, driving east just before dawn, the first light glimpsed through the tall corn that lines the road. It's definitely time for coffee and breakfast after a long night on the road, but will anything be open at 4:00 a.m. on a summer morning?

The sun's just coming up as we enter the town: neat brick houses, carefully tended lawns, trees shading quiet streets. There's no problem finding someplace open for breakfast at this early hour. Here on the main street, four cafés are bustling. Pickup trucks fill the lots and the streets in front; there are men in overalls and baseball caps sitting on fenders and talking, crowded at tables just inside the windows.

The smell of sweet cinnamon rolls and frying pork sausage billows out onto the street from the air conditioners. We sniff our way to the most crowded (and most fragrant) restaurant, the neon sign says "Home Style Cooking—Buffet."

Inside it's all friendly pandemonium with large, firmly smiling women in flowered aprons keeping everyone happy and all the coffee cups filled. Flats of eggs are stacked neatly beside grills almost hidden under mounds of home fries. Sausage patties sizzle next to constantly depleted and replenished stacks of pancakes. Trays of hot, sticky cinnamon rolls emerge with regularity from the ovens. This is the heartland. We have arrived in breakfast country. A waitress waves us to a table. As we sit down, suddenly the day looks better, and the journey not so long.

·Iowa farm sausage·

Here is another example of the basic American sage and pork sausage, this time with a bit of garlic, fresh parsley, and just enough hot red pepper to give the sausage a mild zing. Sausage like this is made all through the American Midwest on farms and in small butcher shops.

2¼ lbs. pork butt
¾ lb. pork back fat
2 tsp. ground sage
¼ cup finely chopped fresh parsley
1 tsp. dried thyme
1 tsp. dried basil
1 tsp. red pepper flakes

2 tsp. coarsely ground black pepper
1 tsp. ground ginger
½ tsp. minced garlic
¼ c. finely chopped onion
1 tbsp. kosher salt
¼ c. water

For details on sausage making, see page 332.

Grind the meat and fat together through a ⅛- or ¼-inch plate. Mix the ground meat with all the remaining ingredients, and knead the mixture until everything is well blended. Package the bulk sausage in plastic wrap. Refrigerated, this fresh sausage will keep for 3 days, frozen for 2 months.

Makes about 3 pounds

This makes the quintessential American breakfast sausage patty. Leave in bulk form, and freeze in packets in large enough to feed your family for one meal.

· Michigan Dutch farmer's sausage ·

Many Dutch immigrants settled in Michigan and became successful dairy farmers. This mild sausage is typical of what you might find in small butcher shops or farms in Dutch communities in and around Grand Rapids. Use it in any recipe in this chapter calling for a mildly flavored sausage. It is also a good replacement for fresh bratwurst or bockwurst. Once made, the sausage can be left raw or poached. We prefer to poach it, and then grill or brown it in butter.

1 lb. pork butt
½ lb. pork back fat
¾ lb. veal shoulder
¾ lb. beef plate or chuck
1 tsp. ground coriander
½ tsp. ground ginger
½ tsp. ground mace
½ tsp. dried thyme

1 tsp. coarsely ground black pepper
1 tbsp. kosher salt
2 tsp. dry mustard
1 tsp. sugar
½ tsp. ground cardamom
½ c. water
Medium hog casings

Served with buttered parsley potatoes, fresh Blue Lake green beans with bacon, and a stein of Amstel or Heineken light lager, this aromatic sausage makes a hearty lunch or dinner.

For details on sausage making, see page 332.

Grind the pork through a ¼-inch plate, the pork fat, veal, and beef through a ⅛-inch plate. Mix the ground meats with all the remaining ingredients, except the casings, and knead until everything is well blended. Stuff into medium hog casings, and tie into 5-inch links. Poach in a large pot of 180° F water for 20 minutes or until the sausage reaches an internal temperature of 155° F. Cool under running water, and refrigerate. The sausage will keep for 3 days in the refrigerator, 2 months frozen. Makes about 3 pounds

· sausage and cornbread bites ·

These flavorful appetizers are delightful before dinner with cocktails or with a dry sparkling wine. The key to success is to choose a large enough pan so that the cornbread batter is just thick enough to cover the sausages. This way, these delicious baked snacks turn out light and crisp, not heavy and bready. You can use just about any lean smoked sausage for these easy-to-make tidbits.

1 c. yellow cornmeal
¼ c. all-purpose flour
2 tbsp. sugar
½ tsp. salt
1½ tsp. baking powder
4 tbsp. (½ stick) melted butter
2 tbsp. melted shortening
1 egg, beaten

¾ c. milk
¼ c. chopped green onions or
   scallions, or chives
¼ c. shredded sharp Cheddar cheese
½ lb. lean smoked sausage, such as
   smoked bratwurst, kielbasa,
   smoked country sausage, or
   linguiça, cut into ⅜-inch rounds

Preheat the oven to 400° F. Into a large bowl, sift the cornmeal, flour, sugar, salt, and baking powder. Into another bowl, stir together the melted butter, shortening, and egg, and add the milk. Pour this wet mixture into the dry ingredients, and beat until well blended and smooth, about 1 minute. Do not overbeat. Stir in the green onions or chives, and the cheese.

Cover the bottom of an 8 x 12-inch baking pan with rows of the sausage rounds; each piece should be almost touching the next. Spread the cornbread batter carefully over the rounds, being careful not to move them. Bake in the center of the oven for 30 minutes, or until the bread pulls away from the edges of the pan and has a golden color. Invert the pan over a cutting board, and cut into squares with a piece of sausage at the center of each. Makes 30–40

The cornbread is just great on its own — among the best we've ever eaten. To make crusty cornbread muffins, leave out the green onions and cheese, and add 1 more tablespoon of shortening to the batter.

· beef and sausage piroshki ·

My grandmother always served piroshki with cabbage borscht. When I was growing up, it was one of my favorite meals. I would get excited as soon as I stepped into my grandmother's house because the appetizing aroma of piroshki baking is overwhelming. As soon as they came out of the oven and were put out on a board to cool in the kitchen, I'd sneak around the back door and grab one. I'd eat it while it was much too hot and burn my mouth. I still love piroshki, and with the simple cream cheese pastry in this recipe, they are easy to make and foolproof.

Easy Cream Cheese Dough

· Filling ·

2 onions, finely chopped
2 tbsp. butter
1 lb. lean ground beef
1 lb. fresh kielbasa, or other fresh
    sausage, removed from casings

2 hard-boiled eggs, chopped
2 tsp. fresh chopped dill or 1 tsp. dried
Salt and pepper to taste
2 tbsp. rich chicken or beef broth

....

1 egg beaten with 1 tbsp. water for
    egg wash

Make the dough.

Preheat the oven to 450° F. To make the filling, cook the onions in the butter over medium heat until they are soft and transparent, about 5 minutes. In a bowl, mix them thoroughly with all the other ingredients, except the egg and water.

Roll out the dough to ⅛-inch thickness. Cut out circles 4 inches in diameter, then place 2 tablespoons of filling to one side of the center of each circle. Brush the edges lightly with the egg wash. Fold the dough over and press the edges together. Piroshki can be frozen at this point. Brush each finished piroshki with the egg wash, and bake for 30 minutes or until lightly browned. Cut into one to make sure the meat is completely cooked. Makes 20

If you have fresh kielbasa, it is the perfect sausage here. If not, use any mild-flavored fresh sausage such as fresh bratwurst or hunter's sausage.

· easy cream cheese dough ·

8 oz. cream cheese
8 tbsp. (1 stick) unsalted butter
2 c. unbleached all-purpose flour
Pinch salt
Cream the cheese and butter together, blend in flour and salt. Form dough into a ball, cover, and chill 30 minutes before using.

· Takoma Park pelmeni ·

The hardest thing about these savory little dumplings is getting yourself to stop eating them. I first made pelmeni in Takoma Park, a tree-shaded suburb of Washington, D.C., so naturally I've named them Takoma Park pelmeni. Although I'm not Russian Orthodox, I celebrated Russian Easter each year because it was an excuse to hold a great party and feast on Russian delicacies. Everybody made special dishes, and we ate and drank all day and long into the evening. Many of the dishes were appetizers, part of the Russian zakuski that includes such delights as blinis and caviar, herring, grilled sausage, beet salad, cold chicken, and, of course, pelmeni.

Using cilantro in the recipe is by no means traditional, but I think it adds a nice flavor. If you don't have fresh kielbasa, use any mild fresh sausage such as bratwurst or hunter's sausage.

¾ c. finely chopped onion	1 tsp. cracked black pepper
2 tbsp. butter	1 tbsp. lemon juice
1 lb. ground beef	1 package (about 100) won ton skins
½ lb. fresh kielbasa or other garlicky fresh sausage	2 qts. chicken stock or water
	· **Garnish** ·
½ tsp. salt	Chopped fresh dill or dried dill
2 tsp. fresh dill or ½ tsp. dried	Sour cream
¼ c. chopped fresh cilantro (optional)	

To make the filling, cook the onion in the butter in a small pan over medium heat until soft but not colored, about 5 minutes. In a bowl, mix the onions with all the remaining ingredients except the won ton skins and stock, and knead until everything is well blended together. Fry a sample, and taste for salt and pepper.

To make the pelmeni, place about 1 teaspoon of this filling in the center of each won ton wrapper. Fold the wrapper over the filling, and seal the edges with a finger dipped into a little water. Crimp the 2 corners of each half circle together. Pelmeni can be frozen for up to 2 months at this point.

To cook the pelmeni, bring the stock or water to a boil, add the pelmeni in batches of 25, and simmer for about 5 minutes until they are tender and the filling is cooked through. Transfer with a slotted spoon to serving bowls, and garnish with dill and sour cream. Makes about 100, or 6–8 servings as a main course, 12 or more as appetizers

Eat Takoma Park pelmeni as is for an appetizer with sour cream or yogurt on the side, or serve them in the broth as a soup or main course.

· shirred eggs and sausage ·

Use any recipe for sage sausage in this book (see page 112), or any high-quality store-bought bulk sausage. This simple egg preparation makes a great brunch or hearty breakfast.

⅔ lb. bulk sage sausage
4 eggs
2 tbsp. heavy cream

¼ c. grated sharp Cheddar cheese
1 tbsp. chopped chives (optional)

Serve it with home fries or Potato Casserole (see page 199; omit the sausage) and homemade Buttermilk Biscuits (see page 26).

Preheat the oven to 350° F. Make 4 sausage patties about 3 inches in diameter, and fry for about 5 minutes on each side until they are nicely browned. Drain on paper towels, and place 2 patties into individual ramekins or shallow bowls. Gently break the eggs over the sausage patties. Pour the cream over the eggs and sprinkle with the grated cheese. Bake in a pan of water for 15–20 minutes or until the eggs are set, and the topping has begun to brown. Sprinkle with the optional chives, and serve. Makes 2 servings

· quick and easy sandwiches ·

What could be simpler or tastier than a juicy, flavorful sausage tucked into a roll with some sliced onions, peppers, hot mustard, and whatever else you might have on hand? There are unlimited possibilities for sausage sandwiches, so experiment and try them on your family and friends. Instead of mustard, dress the sandwich with Lee Coleman's Rémoulade Dressing (see page 353); combine sausage with seafood, sautéed eggplant, or grilled vegetables. Let your leftovers and your imagination be your guide.

Just about every region in America has its favorite sausage sandwich, and we've included plenty in the book: Hot Sausage Po' Boy from Louisiana (see page 85), Italian sausage with pepper and onions in the Northeast (see page 100), Grilled Southwest Sausage "Sandwich" with Chiles and Cheese in the Southwest (see page 221), and Baguette Stuffed with Sausage and Chard in the New American section (see page 308).

Even the hot dog, America's favorite sausage by far, has its own regional variations: in New York it is eaten on steamed rolls with sauerkraut, raw onions, and brown mustard; in Chicago, it is consumed with mustard, chopped tomato, chopped pickles, onions, and cheese; in Los Angeles it is preferred cut open, grilled, and eaten with chili, cheese, and onions.

· German white bean soup ·

Bean soups are quite popular in Germany as well as in German neighborhoods throughout the United States, and sausages provide much of the flavor and character of these hearty soups. Just about any type of mild or lightly smoked German-style sausage works well, and in a pinch you can use good-quality hot dogs or knockwurst. The addition of cabbage and leeks gives this soup a particularly savory flavor, unlike any bean soup you may have tried.

½ lb. Great Northern beans or other dried white beans, soaked overnight and drained
2 bay leaves
1 c. chopped fresh parsley
2 qts. of chicken stock
1 carrot, sliced into ¼-inch rounds
½ small head cabbage, finely chopped

2 leeks, split, cleaned, and sliced
½ lb. fresh bratwurst, Michigan Dutch Farmer's Sausage, or fresh kielbasa
½ lb. smoked kielbasa or cervelat, sliced
¼ tsp. freshly grated nutmeg
Salt and pepper to taste

In a large soup pot or Dutch oven, cook the beans with the bay leaves, ¾ cup of the parsley, and the chicken stock for 45 minutes to an hour, or until the beans are tender but still whole. Add the carrot, cabbage, and leeks, and cook 15 minutes more. Pan-fry the fresh bratwurst or other fresh sausages whole to render some of the fat and make the sausages easier to slice. Cool briefly, and slice into ¾-inch rounds. Put in the fresh and smoked sausages, the nutmeg, salt, and pepper, and cook an additional 15 minutes until some of the beans are beginning to break up in the soup. Serve in bowls, garnished with the remaining parsley.
Makes 8 servings

Like most bean dishes, this flavorful soup is even better made up a day ahead and rewarmed.

· Cornbelt chowder ·

Corn chowder is a popular soup all through the heartland, and in New England and the South as well. Recipes often contain bacon or salt pork, but we've substituted a highly smoked sausage instead. Summer sausage or Lebanon bologna has more complexity and depth of flavor than bacon or salt pork, and a lot less fat. If these sausages aren't available, use smoked kielbasa or any good-quality smoked sausage.

The key to this dish is the freshness of the corn. Ideally you should try to make this chowder at the height of the corn season when the ears can be freshly picked and are perfectly sweet. At other times of the year use frozen corn rather than out-of-season fresh corn, because the frozen has a sweeter taste.

½ lb. smoked sausage, such as Lebanon bologna, summer sausage, or smoked kielbasa, diced
2 tbsp. butter
1 medium onion, finely chopped
½ c. chopped celery
1 fresh pimiento, red bell or other sweet red pepper, seeded and chopped
2 medium red potatoes, peeled and diced
4 c. chicken stock
2 bay leaves

⅛ tsp. ground cumin
2 sprigs fresh thyme or ½ tsp. dried
4 c. garden-fresh corn kernels (from about 4 ears) or frozen corn
2 c. half-and-half
2 egg yolks
2 tbsp. cornstarch
1 c. buttermilk
Salt, pepper, and Tabasco to taste

· Garnish ·

2 tbsp. butter
Chopped chives

In a large pot or Dutch oven, fry the sausage in the butter over medium heat. Add the onion and celery, and cook until soft, about 10 minutes. Add the fresh pimiento or red bell pepper, and potatoes, and sauté briefly. Pour in the stock. Bring to a boil, reduce heat, and simmer. Cook with the bay leaves, cumin, and thyme for 5–10 minutes until the potatoes and peppers are tender. Add the corn and any milky juices, along with the half-and-half. Cook for 1–2 minutes until the corn is tender but still full of flavor. Whisk the egg yolks and the cornstarch into the buttermilk. Stir ½ cup of the soup into this mixture, and then add back to the soup off the fire, stirring well. Heat without boiling to thicken. Taste for salt, pepper, and Tabasco. Serve with a bit of butter and chopped chives in each bowl. Makes 5–7 servings

Use fresh corn if you can and be sure to scrape the cobs with the dull side of the knife after you slice the kernels off to get all that delicious milky juice into the chowder.

Second Street sauerkraut soup ·

You may wonder why some of the dishes in this book are named after streets. That's because when I was a graduate student, I moved around a lot. Every time I came up with a good dish, I'd write the recipe down and name it after the street where I was living at the time. Since I moved so often, no dish ever ended up with the same street name, but now that I've lived in the same house in the hills above Berkeley for nine years, this method doesn't work so well anymore. Maybe I'll start naming dishes after my cats.

½ lb. ham in 1 piece
1 lb. sauerkraut, drained and lightly washed
1 tsp. caraway seeds
1 bay leaf
3 c. beef or chicken stock
½ medium head cabbage, shredded
½ bunch collard greens or kale, coarsely chopped
2 medium potatoes, grated
1 leek, split, cleaned, and sliced

1 carrot, chopped
1 tsp. fennel seed
1 tbsp. sweet Hungarian paprika
1 tbsp. tomato paste
½ lb. smoked sausage such as smoked bratwurst, kielbasa, Ukrainian Beef and Pork Sausage, or knockwurst, sliced
Salt and pepper to taste

· **Garnish** ·
Sour cream

To a large pot or Dutch oven, add the ham, sauerkraut, caraway seeds, bay leaf, and the stock. Cover, and cook over medium heat for 1¼ hours. Put in all the remaining ingredients except the sausage, and cook, covered, for an additional ½ hour. Remove the ham, and dice it. Add the diced ham and the sausage to the pot, and cook for 10 minutes more. Taste for salt and pepper. Serve the soup in individual bowls with a spoonful of sour cream on top. Makes 8 servings

Buy the best-quality sauerkraut you can, preferably from a German or Eastern European deli. If you use canned sauerkraut, it's a good idea to rinse it lightly in cold water as it can be a bit too salty.

· cold beet, cucumber, and kielbasa soup ·

This hearty cold soup makes a perfect summer lunch with some dark rye bread and sweet butter. You might also enjoy a small bowl as a first course of the evening meal.

2 c. julienned beets, canned or freshly cooked

1 c. beet cooking liquid

2 c. beef stock

1 c. diced smoked kielbasa or Ukrainian Beef and Pork Sausage

¼ c. lemon juice

2–3 c. sour cream or yogurt, or a mixture of both

1 cucumber, peeled, seeded, and diced

2 green onions or scallions, thinly sliced

1 tbsp. chopped fresh dill

¼ tsp. ground bay leaf (use blender or spice mill)

2 hard-boiled eggs, chopped

Salt and pepper to taste

· **Garnish** ·

Sour cream or yogurt

Fresh dill

Lightly smoked sausage adds a savory flavor to this classic Eastern European soup.

If you are using fresh beets, cook them in 1½ cups of water for 10 minutes until tender, and add them and their cooking liquid to the stock. If using canned beets, add the beets and juice to the stock, and proceed with the recipe. Add the sausage, and cook it with beets for 5 minutes in the stock. Cool and stir in the remaining ingredients. Chill the soup at least 3 hours, or overnight. Serve in chilled soup bowls garnished with a dollop of sour cream or yogurt and a sprinkling of fresh dill. Makes 4–6 servings

· Polish sausage, mushroom, and barley soup ·

My mother made a big deal about Scotch broth, a meat and barley soup that she'd make up in prodigious quantities every two years or so and freeze. That was my first experience with barley soup, and after a while I somehow lost my enthusiasm.

Many years later in a Polish neighborhood restaurant in Toronto, I ate a barley and mushroom soup that was included with the dinner (I wouldn't have ordered it if it wasn't). It was spicy, satisfying, and wonderfully rich. From then on I was hooked on barley soups, especially ones that used dried mushrooms and kielbasa.

Either smoked or fresh kielbasa works well in this recipe. If you prefer the smoky flavor, then use smoked kielbasa or another smoked sausage. You could also use a mild but flavorful sausage like bockwurst or bratwurst.

½ c. pearl barley, soaked overnight and drained
¼ lb. chicken gizzards, finely diced, or ¼ lb. beef stew meat, diced
1 bay leaf
½ tsp. dried marjoram
2 qts. chicken or beef stock
1 medium onion, finely chopped
1 c. thinly sliced leeks
1 carrot, diced
1 rib celery, diced

1 oz. dried Polish or porcini mushrooms, soaked for 2 hours in 3 c. boiling water
½ lb. fresh mushrooms, sliced
½ lb. fresh or smoked kielbasa or other mild sausage, chopped
2 eggs
1 c. sour cream
Salt and pepper to taste
· Garnish ·
Fresh dill

Cook the barley, gizzards, bay leaf, and marjoram in the stock in a large pot for 45 minutes. Put in the chopped onion, leeks, carrot, and celery. Add the soaked mushrooms and their liquid. Make sure that you leave any sand from the mushrooms behind, by either decanting the liquid carefully from the bowl or straining through a coffee filter or cheesecloth. Cook the soup for 20 more minutes, and then put in the fresh mushrooms and sausage. Cook for 10 additional minutes, or until the barley is completely tender.

Some recipes for this popular Eastern European soup call for beef, but we prefer to use chicken gizzards, and of course, sausage.

Beat together the eggs and sour cream in a bowl. Ladle a cup of soup into this mixture and whisk until it is well blended. Add the sour cream–egg mixture to the soup over very low heat or off the heat, stirring well and taking care not to let the soup boil. Taste for salt and pepper. Serve the soup garnished with fresh dill.
Makes 6–8 servings

· solianka, a Russian soup with meat, sausage, prunes, and cucumbers ·

This hearty Russian soup/stew makes a perfect one-pot meal for those cold winter evenings. The combination of meat, sausage, prunes, and cucumbers might sound a bit unusual, but they all go together amazingly well. The prune/meat combination is common in many Eastern European dishes and lends a savory sweetness to many recipes.

6 c. beef or chicken stock
1½ lbs. beef or veal stew meat or a combination of both, cut into 1-inch chunks
2 bay leaves
4 tbsp. (½ stick) butter
1 medium onion, thinly sliced
3 tomatoes, peeled, seeded, and chopped
2 tbsp. tomato paste
¾ lb. smoked kielbasa or Ukrainian Beef and Pork Sausage, sliced in ½-inch rounds

4 cucumbers, peeled, seeded, sliced, and lightly salted
10 pitted prunes, soaked in hot water
12 black Kalamata olives, pitted and sliced
2 tsp. capers
Salt and pepper to taste

· **Garnish** ·
Lemon slices
Fresh dill or parsley
Sour cream or yogurt

Bring the stock to a boil in a large soup pot, and put in the meat and bay leaves. Reduce the heat to a simmer, and cook, uncovered, for 1½ hours. Meanwhile, heat the butter in a heavy frying pan over medium heat, and cook the onion for 5 minutes until soft. Add the tomatoes, tomato paste, and the sausage. Simmer for 10 minutes. Remove the grease, and add the contents of the pan to the soup, along with the cucumbers, prunes, olives, and capers. Cook for 2–3 minutes, and taste for salt and pepper. Serve in individual bowls garnished with lemon slices, dill and sour cream or yogurt. Makes 6 servings

Use a mild smoked sausage for this dish such as smoked kielbasa, Ukrainian Beef and Pork Sausage, or smoked bratwurst.

· New Year's Eve borscht ·

I call this recipe New Year's Eve borscht, because its bright red and green colors are reminiscent of the Christmas/New Year's holidays, and I often serve this hearty one-pot meal at my own New Year's gatherings. Borscht is popular throughout Eastern Europe. Depending on region and nationality, ingredients and spellings may differ, but the taste is always satisfying. Use a garlicky smoked sausage such as kielbasa, German garlic sausage, or cervelat.

2 lbs. beef chuck, cut into 1-inch chunks
3 qts. beef stock
2 c. coarsely chopped onions
4 carrots, coarsely chopped
1 celery root, peeled and cut into julienne strips
1 lb. boiling potatoes, coarsely diced
4 ribs celery, coarsely chopped
2 c. chopped Italian-style canned tomatoes

2 lbs. cabbage, coarsely shredded
2 leeks, coarsely chopped
½ lb. parsnips, diced
4 beets, diced, with greens, sliced
1 lb. garlicky sausage, such as smoked kielbasa or cervelat
2 tsp. caraway seeds
Salt, pepper, and red wine vinegar to taste
1 c. sour cream
Fresh or dried dill

In a large soup pot, bring the meat and stock to a boil, lower the heat and simmer, uncovered, for 1 hour. Add all the vegetables except the beet greens, and simmer 30 minutes more. Add the sausage and cook 5 minutes. Put in the beet greens and the caraway seeds and simmer vigorously for 5 more minutes. Taste for salt and pepper, and add a little red wine vinegar if you like a slight tang. Serve in large soup bowls, garnished with sour cream and dill.
Makes 12–16 servings

If beet greens aren't available, use chard, kale, or other greens.

· deep dish chicken and sausage pie with biscuit crust ·

This is a satisfying version of a Sunday-dinner favorite throughout the Midwest. The flaky baking powder biscuit crust is also a great recipe for biscuits.

4–5 lb. stewing or roasting chicken

2 qts. chicken stock

24 pearl onions or ¾ lb. boiling onions, peeled

12 baby carrots or ½ lb. medium carrots cut into ½-inch pieces

3 ribs celery, cut into ¾-inch pieces

½ lb. fresh or frozen peas, or ¾ lb. 2-inch-long asparagus tips with tender stem cut into 1-inch pieces

½ lb. small mushrooms, left whole

4 tbsp. (½ stick) butter

⅓ c. flour

1 c. heavy cream or half-and-half

Salt and pepper to taste

1 lb. mild fresh sausage, such as bockwurst, Michigan Dutch Farmer's Sausage, bratwurst, or Iowa Farm Sausage, in links

1 recipe Baking Powder Biscuit Crust

Cook the chicken in the stock until tender, 1–1½ hours. Remove from stock and cool. Cook the onions, carrots, and celery for 7–10 minutes in the stock and remove. Take the chicken meat from the bones and reserve. Cook the peas or asparagus and mushrooms for 2 minutes in the stock and remove.

Melt the butter in a saucepan, stir in the flour and cook gently 2–3 minutes. Whisk in 4–6 cups of the stock along with the cream or half-and-half to make a rich chicken gravy. If it is too thick, add more stock. Season with salt and pepper. Fry the sausages whole for 5 minutes until firm, then cut into ¾-inch rounds.

Preheat the oven to 425° F. To assemble the pie, roll out the baking powder biscuit crust ½ inch thick and large enough to cover the surface of the pie. Arrange the cooked chicken, the sliced sausage, and the parboiled vegetables in a deep casserole or baking dish. Pour in the chicken gravy. Cover with the crust, and bake 20–30 minutes, or until golden brown. Makes 8 servings

· baking powder biscuit crust ·

This easy and delicious recipe comes from Cynthia Scheer in *Regional American Classics.*

2 c. all-purpose flour

1 tbsp. baking powder

½ tsp. salt

Pinch sugar

8 tbsp. (1 stick) cold unsalted butter

¾ c. half-and-half or ½ cup half-and-half with ¼ cup heavy cream

4 tbsp. (½ stick) melted unsalted butter

Mix first four ingredients. Cut in cold butter until mixture resembles coarse crumbs. Pour in half-and-half, blend gently. Knead soft dough four or five times on floured surface to form ball. Sprinkle lightly with flour.

Roll or pat out ½ inch thick. For deep dish pie: place over filling, brush with butter, bake at 425° F for 20–30 minutes until brown. For biscuits: cut 2½-inch circles, place on ungreased cookie sheet, brush lightly with butter. Bake for 20–30 minutes at 425° F until golden brown.

· rabbit or chicken paprikash ·

We prefer to make this dish with rabbit, as its firm flesh takes well to the robust flavors. It can also be made with chicken, pheasant, partridge, veal chops, or pork. Serve with homemade noodles, spaetzle, or boiled dumplings to sop up the sauce.

¼ lb. salt pork, diced
½ lb. debreceni sausage or kielbasa, diced
2–3 lb. rabbit, or 3–4 lb. chicken, cut into 8 pieces, or 2 pheasants or 2 partridges, quartered
Spice Rub (see below)
1 medium onion, sliced
1 medium carrot, diced
1 c. sliced leeks (optional)
1 shallot, finely chopped
1 tbsp. minced garlic
2 red or yellow bell peppers, sliced
¼ c. Hungarian sweet paprika
1 c. dry red or white wine
3 tbsp. tomato paste
1 c. chicken stock
2 tbsp. flour
1 c. sour cream
Salt and pepper to taste

In a large skillet or Dutch oven, fry the salt pork over medium heat until it turns a light brown and most of the fat is rendered. Add the sausage and fry for another 5 minutes. Remove the meats and reserve. Leave the fat in the pan. Rub the rabbit or chicken pieces thoroughly with the spice rub. Brown the rabbit or chicken in the fat, turning the pieces occasionally so they color evenly. Do not overcrowd the pan. As the pieces brown, transfer them to a platter. Pour off all but 2 tablespoons of the fat, and add the onion, carrot, leeks, if using, and shallot. Cover the pot, and cook for 10 minutes, stirring the vegetables from time to time. Stir in the garlic and peppers, and cook for 2 more minutes. Add the paprika, and stir until everything is well coated. Put in the wine, tomato paste, and stock. Bring it all to a boil and add back the rabbit or chicken, the sausage, and salt pork. Reduce the heat to a simmer, and cook, covered, for 30 minutes. Check to see if the rabbit or chicken is tender. If not, cook longer. Transfer the rabbit or chicken pieces to a warm platter. Degrease the sauce and cook until it begins to thicken slightly. Mix together the flour and sour cream, and stir into the sauce. Cook for 1 minute. Taste for salt and pepper. Pour the sauce over the rabbit or chicken, and serve with noodles, spaetzle, or dumplings covered with the sauce.
Makes 4–6 servings

An earthy, flavorful Côtes du Rhône or Madiran from southern France would be a great match here or a big Hungarian red wine like Szekszardi Voros or Egri Bikaver.

· spice rub ·
This flavorful spice rub is delicious on poultry, pork, or veal.

1 tsp. salt
1 tsp. pepper
1 tsp. Hungarian sweet paprika
1 tsp. dried marjoram
1 tsp. chopped fresh rosemary
Combine and rub thoroughly over meat before braising or roasting.

· brats braised with beer and onions ·

Wisconsin is justifiably famous for its bratwurst and its beer. And it's no coincidence that these two hearty German specialties go well together. There are as many recipes for braising bratwurst in beer as there are types of bratwurst, and many call for sweet spices like cloves, allspice, or some sugar in the braising liquid. These can be very tasty, but we prefer the flavors of coarse German mustard and onions with the spicy sausages.

Another popular variation is to cook the sausages for 10 to 15 minutes until the beer evaporates, and then brown the brats in the pan or grill them over charcoal.

1 lb. fresh bratwurst, Hunter's Sausage or other mild sausage	2 bay leaves
1 large onion, sliced	1 tbsp. coarse German-style mustard
12 oz. dark German beer	4 kaiser or other hard rolls

Any way you cook them, brats are delicious served on a crusty roll with plenty of old-fashioned mustard and a foaming stein of what made Milwaukee famous.

Brown the bratwurst for about 10 minutes in a heavy skillet large enough to hold all the sausages at once, turning them occasionally as they brown. Remove the sausages and all but 3 tablespoons of fat. Add the onion, cover the pot, and cook over medium-high heat for 10 minutes, stirring frequently until light brown. Pour in the beer, and scrape up any brown bits clinging to the bottom of the pan. Put the sausages back in the pan, along with the bay leaves. Partially cover and cook over moderate heat for 15 minutes. Stir in the mustard, and cook until the liquid has begun to thicken slightly. Serve the brats, split down the middle, on a roll with the onions and sauce, and a pot of hot mustard on the side. Makes 4 servings

· rouladen: Shaker-style stuffed flank steak ·

The Shakers flourished throughout the Midwest as well as in the South and New England in the nineteenth century, and the sect contributed much to America's folk arts and crafts. In addition to spare and beautiful furniture, tools, and buildings, they left many delicious recipes for traditional dishes that often reflect their German origin.

Stuffed meat dishes have a long legacy in German cooking. This stuffed steak called rouladen is still very popular today in German-American homes and restaurants. We recommend a mild sausage such as Iowa Farm Sausage, Bratwurst, Michigan Dutch Farmer's Sausage, or bockwurst for the stuffing.

2–2½ lb. flank steak

· Stuffing ·

1 carrot, diced
½ c. diced onion
½ c. diced celery
4 tbsp. (½ stick) butter
¾ lb. mild fresh sausage, removed
   from casings
2 c. diced day-old bread
1 egg

Salt and pepper to taste
2 tbsp. olive oil
2 onions, thinly sliced
1 carrot, sliced
1 rib celery, sliced
Pinch *each* ground sage, ground
   ginger, and freshly grated nutmeg
1 c. beef or chicken stock
1 tbsp. coarse German-style mustard
Cider or red wine vinegar

....

Prepare the flank steak for the stuffing by cutting a pocket lengthwise in the steak with a long, thin knife, or have your butcher do it for you.

To make the stuffing, cook the diced carrot, onion, and celery in the butter over medium heat in a covered frying pan for 10 minutes, until they're soft and aromatic. Add the sausage meat and fry for about 5 minutes more, breaking up the meat with a fork. Pour off all but about 2 tablespoons of the fat. Put the vegetable/sausage mixture in a bowl along with the bread cubes and egg, and mix until well blended, then stuff into the pocket of the flank steak.

By using sausage in the rouladen stuffing, you produce not only a delicious stuffed steak but a wonderfully savory sauce.

Seal the pocket with skewers or sew to close. Sprinkle the meat with salt and pepper. Brown the steak in the olive oil in a heavy casserole or Dutch oven over medium heat, about 5 minutes on each side. Transfer to a platter, and put the sliced onions, carrots, and celery in the pot. Cover and cook for 5 minutes. Sprinkle the vegetables with the sage, ginger, and nutmeg, return the steak to the pot, add stock, cover, and cook in a 350° F oven for 1¼ hours, or until the steak is quite tender.

Remove the steak to a heated platter. Degrease the sauce, stir in the mustard, and reduce until the sauce just coats a spoon. It should not be too thick. Season with salt, pepper, and a little vinegar to taste — you want a slightly tart sauce. Slice the stuffed steak into ½-inch slices, and nap the slices with the sauce. Serve the rest in a bowl on the side.

Like so many other hearty dishes, this is best made a day ahead. To reheat, slice the steak first, and warm the slices gently in the sauce on the top of the stove or in a microwave. Makes 6 servings, with leftovers

· beef and sausage stew with potato dumplings ·

This stew is hearty fare for cold winter evenings. It is typical of the stews eaten in German areas throughout the heartland from Pennsylvania to Nebraska, the stick-to-the-ribs dishes that have helped many a farmer's family get through the long cold nights on the Great Plains.

We prefer a mild-flavored sausage such as fresh bratwurst, but Hunter's Sausage and other fresh sausages will work well. If you are feeling lazy you can leave out the dumplings (what a shame, though!), and just add some diced boiling potatoes for the last 20 minutes of cooking.

1½ lbs. fresh bratwurst

2 tbsp. butter or bacon fat

3 lbs. beef stew meat, cut into 2-inch cubes

1 medium leek, chopped

2 medium onions, chopped

1 rib celery, finely chopped

1 medium carrot, diced

2 c. beef or veal stock

½ c. cider vinegar

1 tbsp. sweet Hungarian paprika

1 tsp. caraway seeds

2 bay leaves

1 tsp. dried marjoram

½ tsp. ground ginger

1 lb. small boiling onions, peeled

1 lb. carrots, peeled and cut into 2-inch pieces

1 small celery root, peeled and cut into 2-inch pieces (optional)

1 parsnip, peeled and cut into 2-inch pieces

Salt, pepper, and sugar to taste

Potato Dumplings (see opposite)

This dish makes a complete meal in itself, but a loaf of good, heavy rye bread and a glass or two of dark Munich-style lager would be welcome on the table.

In a large heavy pot or Dutch oven, fry ½ pound of the sausage, removed from its casings, in the butter or bacon fat over medium heat for 5 minutes. Add the meat, and brown the pieces on all sides, about 10 minutes. Put in the leek, chopped onions, chopped celery, and diced carrot, and cook for 5 more minutes, stirring occasionally. Cover the meat and vegetables with the stock and cider vinegar. Add the paprika, caraway seeds, bay leaves, marjoram, and ginger. Cover the pot and simmer for 40 minutes. Cut the remaining sausage into ¾-inch rounds, and add them to the pot, along with the carrot chunks, celery root, if using, and parsnips. Simmer 25 minutes more or until the meat and vegetables are tender. Season to taste with salt, pepper, and sugar.

While the stew is cooking, make the dumplings, and add them to the stew. Cover and cook gently for 15 minutes. *Do not peek* for at least 15 minutes. Sample a dumpling to see if they are cooked. If still doughy, cover and cook a little longer. Makes 6–8 servings

· potato dumplings ·

1½ lbs. potatoes, boiled and peeled
½ c. fresh bread crumbs
2 eggs, beaten
2 tbsp. milk
2 tsp. minced onion
¼ c. flour
1 tbsp. chopped fresh parsley
Salt and pepper to taste

Grate or rice potatoes. Add remaining ingredients (reserve 1 tablespoon flour), mix well. Taste for salt and pepper. Form into walnut-sized balls, dust with remaining flour, drop into the simmering stew or soup. Cover and cook gently 15 minutes. Makes 24

Pennsylvania Dutch schnitz und knepp (braised sausage, apples, and dumplings)

This one-pot meal is one of the classics of Pennsylvania Dutch cooking, but it is so simple, homey, and downright flavorful that it is bound to become a favorite in your family. Use any mildly flavored sausage here, such as Iowa Farm Sausage, fresh bratwurst, Hunter's Sausage, Michigan Dutch Farmer's Sausage, or bockwurst.

· Dumplings ·
2 c. all-purpose flour
1 tbsp. baking powder
½ tsp. salt
3 tbsp. melted butter
1 egg
¾ c. milk (enough to bind the dough)

1 lb. mild fresh sausage links
1 tbsp. butter
1 c. dried apples
2 c. apple cider
2 c. chicken stock
1 tbsp. molasses
3 tbsp. cider vinegar

To make the dumplings, mix together the flour, baking powder, and salt. Add the melted butter and egg, and mix in just enough milk to form a soft dough. Set aside.

In a large high-sided frying pan with a lid, brown the whole sausages in the butter over medium heat. Pour off any excess fat, and add the dried apples, cider,

Dried apples work best because they hold up better during braising and have a more intense flavor than fresh.

stock, molasses, and cider vinegar. Partially cover the pan, and simmer for 10–15 minutes, making sure there is enough liquid to cover the sausages and apples.

Spoon heaping tablespoons of the dumpling dough over the surface of the mixture in the pan. Cover and simmer for 10 minutes more, and don't peek while they are cooking. The dumplings are done when they are firm but puffed up and fluffy. A toothpick inserted into the middle should come out clean. If they are not done, cover, and cook for an additional minute or two until ready. Makes 4–6 servings

·family favorite ham and sausage loaf·

This wonderful meat loaf is delightfully easy to prepare, and a delicious family dish. This is another recipe from Loni Kuhn, whose own family has been enjoying this loaf for years. In fact, Loni's son Steven loves this dish so much that he requests it for birthday dinners. And, although Loni is a very accomplished cook with a vast repertoire of elaborate and exotic dishes, this simple preparation is the family favorite. Like all good meat loaf recipes, this makes great sandwiches cold the next day.

Use a sage-flavored breakfast sausage in this recipe. Any of the basic American sage sausage recipes from this book will do fine, or buy some good bulk sausage from a reliable butcher. For the ham, use a mildly smoked ham, preferably one that is not too salty. If you are feeling lazy, ask the butcher to grind it for you.

2 lbs. mildly smoked ham, ground
1½ lbs. Iowa Farm Sausage or other
  sage-flavored bulk sausage
1 medium onion, chopped
1 c. milk
1 c. day-old bread crumbs
2 eggs, beaten

· **Basting sauce** ·
½ c. brown sugar
¼ c. cider vinegar
1½ tbsp. brown mustard such as
  Gulden's

Preheat the oven to 350° F. Mix all the meat loaf ingredients in a large bowl, kneading the mixture until everything is well blended. Free-form it into a loaf on a baking pan.

Before baking, make a ¼-inch deep crosshatch pattern on top of the loaf by pressing the handle of a wooden spoon flat across the surface of the meat. This provides little gullies to hold the basting sauce on the loaf.

To make the basting sauce, mix all the ingredients together thoroughly; divide between two bowls and set one aside. Using the sauce in the other bowl, brush generously over the meat before baking and baste four or five times while cooking.

Bake the loaf for 1¼ hours, until it is firm and the top is nicely browned. Slice into ½-inch slices and serve each slice with a generous amount of sauce from the reserved bowl on top. Makes 6–8 servings

It's simple to make up some bulk sausages especially for this recipe in a food processor or grinder — you'll get a leaner and more flavorful sausage than the store-bought variety.

·lazy Hungarian goulash·

This rich goulash is made in one pot without the addition of any liquid. The thick, wonderful gravy comes from the natural meat juices and the vegetables alone. It is great made up a day ahead, and rewarmed.

The recipe came to us from a smart Hungarian woman who knew how to make great meals for a huge family with very little effort. The dish can easily be increased to feed a large crowd.

1 lb. paprika sausage or smoked kielbasa, sliced into ¾-inch rounds
2 c. chopped onion
3 lbs. beef chuck, cut into 2-inch chunks
1 lb. pork, cut into 2-inch chunks
½ c. sweet Hungarian paprika
1 tbsp. dried marjoram

6 cloves garlic, minced
5 canned Italian-style tomatoes, roughly chopped
3 red, green, or yellow bell peppers, or fresh pimientos, or a combination, coarsely chopped
1 tsp. *each* salt and freshly cracked black pepper

Cook the sausage in a heavy Dutch oven or casserole with a tight-fitting lid over medium-high heat for 5 minutes, add the onion and cook 10 more minutes, stirring occasionally. Add the remaining ingredients and stir well.

Preheat the oven to 350° F. Cover the pot very tightly, using foil for a seal underneath the lid. Simmer the goulash on the stove top for 10 minutes. Place the pot in the oven and cook for 2 hours, stirring every 30 minutes, until the meat is quite tender and a rich gravy has been formed. Taste for salt and pepper. This dish reheats well, and is best made a day or two ahead. Remove any congealed fat before reheating and serving. Makes 8 servings

Serve with noodles or boiled potatoes, buttered green beans, and a hearty red Syrah from the Rhône, California, or Australia.

· bigos or Polish hunter's stew ·

Bigos is one of the great peasant dishes of the world. It was originally a hunter's stew filled with the bounty of the forest: venison, wild mushrooms, and game birds, all cooked together with sausages, cabbage, and wine. Today, most people don't have access to such game, however, and Bigos is most often made with store-bought ingredients. Wild mushrooms, usually dried, are an integral part of the dish even today, and are available in Polish or Italian delis as dried mushrooms or porcini. Sausage is essential also, and usually includes a fresh and a smoked version.

1 oz. dried porcini or dried Polish mushrooms

1 medium onion, sliced

2 medium leeks, split and thinly sliced

1 medium carrot, chopped

6 tbsp. (¾ stick) butter

1 tbsp. chopped garlic

½ head cabbage, cored, quartered, and shredded

2 tbsp. sweet Hungarian paprika

½ lb. fresh kielbasa, sliced

½ lb. smoked kielbasa, sliced

½ lb. beef stew meat, cut into 1-inch cubes

½ lb. venison or lamb stew meat, cut into 1-inch cubes

½ lb. pork, cut into 1-inch cubes

Salt to taste

1 tsp. coarsely ground black pepper

2 c. beef or chicken stock

1 c. dry red wine

1 lb. sauerkraut

1 c. Roma tomatoes, peeled, seeded, and chopped

4 bay leaves

2 whole allspice

· **Garnish** ·

Sour cream

Soak the dried mushrooms in 2 cups boiling water for at least 30 minutes. In a large heavy pot or Dutch oven, cook the onion, leeks, and carrot in 4 tablespoons of the butter for 5 minutes. Stir in the garlic and cabbage, cover, and cook until the cabbage has wilted, about 5 minutes. Sprinkle with the paprika and cook for 1 more minute.

In a heavy frying pan brown the sausages over medium-high heat for 5 minutes in the remaining butter. Remove with a slotted spoon, and reserve. Sprinkle the meats with salt and pepper. Brown the pieces of meat in batches in the fat remaining in the pan, being careful not to overcrowd — this should take about 10 minutes. Remove the meats as they brown, and add to the vegetables. Deglaze the frying pan with the stock, and add this to the vegetables along with the red wine, sauerkraut, tomatoes, mushrooms and their strained liquid, the bay leaves, and allspice. Bring everything to a boil, lower to a simmer, cover, and cook for 1 hour. Add the reserved sausages, and cook, uncovered, for 15–20 minutes more, or until all the meats are tender. Taste for salt and pepper. Serve the bigos in big shallow bowls, garnished with sour cream. Makes 6–8 servings, with leftovers

A hearty red wine is a must with bigos: a Hungarian Egri Bikaver (Bull's Blood), a Rhône Crozes-Hermitages, or an Amador County Zinfandel.

· The Midwest ·

· calves' liver and sausage, Hungarian style ·

We realize that you may want to make this savory dish but might not have some Pork and Liver Sausage with Slivovitz on hand. Don't despair. You can easily substitute another Eastern European type such as kielbasa or bratwurst.

1¼ lbs. calves' liver or beef liver, thinly sliced and cut into ½-inch strips

1 c. flour mixed with ½ tsp. salt, ½ tsp. finely ground black pepper, ¼ tsp. ground ginger, 1 tsp. sweet Hungarian paprika

2 tbsp. oil

¼ lb. Hungarian Paprika Sausage (see page 166), sliced into ½-inch rounds

½ lb. Pork and Liver Sausage with Slivovitz (see page 167), sliced into ½-inch rounds

1 large onion, thinly sliced

1 fresh pimiento or red bell pepper, thinly sliced

1 tbsp. sweet Hungarian paprika

½ c. chicken or beef stock

½ tsp. dried marjoram

½ c. sour cream

Lemon juice, salt, and pepper to taste

Dredge the liver strips in the seasoned flour. Heat the oil in a large, heavy skillet and fry over medium-high heat for 1–2 minutes on a side. Remove and reserve. Fry the sliced sausages in the same pan for about 5 minutes, and remove with a slotted spoon. Add the onion and cook, covered, over medium heat for about 15 minutes, or until it begins to color. Add the pimiento or red bell pepper and the paprika and fry for 1 minute more. Put the stock and marjoram in the pan along with the cooked sausage, and cook, uncovered, for 10 minutes. Return the liver to the pan, and cook for 1–2 minutes more until it is firm and just cooked through. Remove the pan from the heat. Stir in the sour cream and taste for lemon juice, salt, and pepper. Serve over egg noodles. Makes 6 servings

This dish is wonderful with home-made egg noodles or spaetzle tossed in butter, accompanied with a tall glass of Pilsner Urquell, perhaps the world's finest lager.

· Hungarian stuffed cabbage ·

Just about every country in northern and eastern Europe has a version of stuffed cabbage, and recipes for this hearty peasant dish are like folk songs — similar in general content, but wonderfully different in details. Stuffed cabbage almost always features a spicy meat or sausage filling, and most renditions are mighty tasty. But our favorite way of preparing the dish is the way the Hungarians do it — baked over sauerkraut with a tangy tomato-paprika sauce.

You can use just about any mild-flavored fresh sausage for stuffed cabbage, such as paprika sausage, fresh kielbasa, Hunter's Sausage, or fresh bratwurst. We prefer fresh kielbasa or paprika sausage in this Hungarian recipe.

1 lb. ground chuck
1 lb. paprika sausage, fresh kielbasa,
   or other fresh sausage, removed
   from the casings
1½ c. finely chopped onion
2 c. cooked rice
2 eggs
3 tbsp. sweet Hungarian paprika
½ tsp. ground caraway seed
½ tsp. salt
1 tsp. coarsely ground pepper
2 medium heads cabbage, cored

· **Sauce** ·
1 c. tomato puree
1 c. beef or chicken stock
2 tbsp. sweet Hungarian paprika
½ lb. smoked kielbasa, diced
1–2 tbsp. tomato paste
....
1½ lbs. sauerkraut, washed briefly
   and drained
1 c. sour cream
Salt and pepper to taste

In a large bowl, knead the ground beef, sausage, onion, cooked rice, and eggs together with the paprika, caraway, salt, and pepper until well blended.

Bring enough water to cover the cabbage to a boil in a large pot. Add the whole heads of cabbage and cook for 10 minutes. Using a large fork, stab a head of cabbage from the bottom, remove it, cool slightly under running water, then gently peel off as many leaves as you can, one at a time. Put the cabbage back in the pot, and cook for a few more minutes until it is soft enough for you to peel off a few more layers of leaves. Continue the process with both heads until you get down to the small inner leaves. Set the separated leaves and what remains of the heads aside while you make the sauce.

If you have a favorite stuffed cabbage recipe of your own, try adding some fresh sausage like kielbasa or bratwurst to the stuffing. You should be pleasantly surprised by the increase in flavor and liveliness.

Put the tomato puree, stock, paprika, and diced kielbasa into a saucepan, and bring to a boil. Stir in just enough tomato paste to give the sauce body. Reserve and keep warm.

To make the stuffed cabbage rolls, place about ⅔ cup filling in the center of each of the largest leaves. Fold in the sides, and roll the leaves up. Continue this process until all the filling is used (the smaller leaves will need less filling).

Preheat the oven to 325° F. Finely shred any remaining leaves and the unused centers of the cabbage heads. Lay the shredded cabbage and sauerkraut on the bottom of a 9 x 12-inch baking pan. Put the cabbage rolls on top, seam side down. Repeat the process if you need another pan. Pour the sauce over the rolls. Cover with foil, and bake in the oven for 1½ hours, or until the cabbage rolls are quite tender. Transfer the rolls to a warm platter. Drain the juices into a saucepan, and spoon the kraut and shredded cabbage over the rolls. Reduce the sauce by boiling until it is just syrupy. Off the fire, stir in the sour cream. Taste for salt and pepper. Spoon the sauce over the kraut-covered rolls, and serve. Makes about 18–24 cabbage rolls, enough for 8 servings, with leftovers

· sausage, mashed potato, and cabbage casserole (bubble and squeak) ·

This dish is inspired by leftover mashed potatoes, not in itself one of the world's more inspiring substances. But once you start making this dish, you'll be mashing extra (with plenty of milk or cream) just for the leftovers.

4 c. mashed potatoes (see page 87)
1 small head cabbage, cored and
　quartered (1½–2 lbs.)
1½ lbs. bulk sage sausage, smoked
　sausage, or other sausage
1 onion, finely chopped
1 c. finely chopped leeks

1 c. finely chopped green onions or
　scallions
½ tsp. Tabasco (optional)
½ tsp. dried dill
Salt and pepper to taste
Bread crumbs

The type of sausage isn't essential. Each will impart its own unique flavor to the dish, so vary the recipe to suit what you have on hand.

Place the mashed potatoes in a large bowl. Cook the cabbage in salted water until tender, about 20 minutes. Drain and chop finely. Add to the potatoes.

While cooking the cabbage, brown the sausage. If you are using fresh bulk sausage, break it up as it cooks. For smoked sausage, finely chop it before frying. If the sausage is on the lean side, you may need to add a little butter or oil to the pan. Cook until the sausage is lightly browned, 5–10 minutes, depending on the type. Add the onion and leeks, and cook 5 minutes more. Drain the mixture and add it to the potato-cabbage mixture. Add 2 tablespoons of the sausage drippings for flavor. Add the chopped green onions, Tabasco, and dill and mix well. Taste for salt and pepper. Preheat the oven to 375° F. Spoon the mixture into a greased casserole or baking dish. Sprinkle generously with bread crumbs and bake for 30–40 minutes uncovered until the top is golden and the center is bubbly. Makes 6–8 servings

braised cabbage and sausage ·

Depending on the amount of sausage, this dish can be a side dish or main course. If you use it as a side dish, serve it with roast pork, pork chops, or roast fowl. If you use it as a main dish, cut the sausage in large chunks and serve about a third of a pound of sausage per person.

¼ lb. bacon, diced
¼ lb. salt pork, diced
2 onions, thinly sliced
1 carrot, sliced
2 lbs. shredded cabbage
2 tbsp. sweet Hungarian paprika
1 lb. sauerkraut, rinsed and drained
½ tsp. caraway seeds

¼ tsp. dried thyme
1 tsp. cracked black pepper
2 c. water, beef or chicken stock, white wine, or a combination
½–¾ lb. Kielbasa, Smoked Bratwurst, or other smoked sausage
Salt and pepper to taste

Fry the bacon and salt pork over medium-high heat in a Dutch oven or casserole until crisp, about 5 minutes. Pour off all but 2 tablespoons of the fat. Add the onions, carrot, and cabbage. Cover and cook, stirring frequently, until the cabbage has wilted and the onions are soft, about 10 minutes. Add the paprika, and cook 1 minute more. Put in the sauerkraut, caraway seeds, thyme, pepper, and the liquid, cover, and cook at a simmer for 45 minutes or up to an hour. Add the sausage, and cook 10 minutes more. Remove any grease from the casserole before serving. This dish is delicious when made up in advance and reheated, or you can serve it right from the stove. Makes 6–8 servings as a side dish, up to 8 as a main course with 2½ pounds of sausage

Use any of the smoked sausage from this chapter: Smoked Kielbasa, Smoked Bratwurst, or any other good country-style smoked sausage.

· The Midwest ·

· smoked kielbasa and red cabbage ·

The sweet and sour flavors of the red cabbage marry beautifully with the robust, smoky taste of the kielbasa.

½–2 lbs. smoked kielbasa, diced or
   sliced (see note)
2 tbsp. butter
2 medium onions, thinly sliced
2–3 lb. head of red cabbage,
   quartered, cored, and shredded
2 green apples, peeled, cored, and
   diced

¼ c. cider vinegar
½ c. beef or chicken stock
2 bay leaves
1 tsp. curry powder
½ tsp. dried marjoram
Salt and pepper to taste

Use ½ pound of diced kielbasa for a side dish, 2 pounds sliced sausage for a main course.

Brown the sausage in the butter in a Dutch oven or high-sided skillet over medium-high heat for about 5 minutes, turning occasionally. Add the onion and cook until lightly colored, about 10 minutes. Stir in the rest of the ingredients. Cover and reduce the heat to medium. Simmer for about 30 minutes, stirring occasionally. Add more stock if needed. Taste for salt and pepper. Makes 6–8 servings as a side dish, 4–6 as a main course

· "the spinach" ·

This is another simple and wonderful recipe from Loni Kuhn, a good friend and gifted cook. This way of preparing spinach became so popular in the Kuhn household that it was simply referred to as "The Spinach." Any smoked country-style sausage will work well in this dish. Try smoked kielbasa, linguiça, Smoked Country Sausage, or smoked bratwurst.

2 tbsp. butter
¾ lb. smoked sausage, diced
1 large onion, chopped
1 tbsp. flour
⅛ tsp. freshly grated nutmeg
1 tsp. minced fresh rosemary or
   ½ tsp. dried

¾ c. milk
1 chicken bouillon cube, crumbled
2 bunches fresh spinach (about
   2 lbs.), washed and roughly
   chopped
Salt and pepper to taste

In a heavy 12-inch skillet or Dutch oven, melt the butter over medium heat. Add the sausage and cook for 5 minutes to render some fat, but do not brown the sausage. Add the onion and continue to cook until pale gold in color. Drain off excess fat. Add the flour and stir until the onion is well coated. Add the nutmeg and rosemary, and fry briefly for 1 minute, stirring constantly. Add the milk, and cook, stirring constantly, until the sauce thickens. Add the bouillon cube and spinach. Simmer for 2–3 minutes until the spinach has wilted and is just barely cooked. Taste for salt and pepper. This dish can be made ahead, or refrigerated overnight and rewarmed on top of the stove or in the oven the next day.

Makes 4–6 servings as a side dish

Good-quality smoky bacon is a fine substitute for the sausage.

potato casserole with sausage and cheese ·

Elevate this rich and savory side dish to a main course simply by increasing the amount of sausage. It's particularly satisfying with eggs for breakfast or brunch (see Shirred Eggs and Sausage, page 176).

½ lb. Michigan Dutch Farmer's
    Sausage or other mild sausage such
    as Iowa Farm Sausage, fresh
    bratwurst, or kielbasa, removed
    from casings or in bulk
3 tbsp. butter
1 c. heavy cream

3 eggs
1¼ lbs. cream cheese
½ tsp. *each* salt and pepper
1¼ lbs. Swiss cheese, grated
2 lbs. boiling potatoes, peeled and
    grated

Brown the sausage meat in a small heavy skillet for about 5 minutes over medium heat. Drain the grease and transfer the sausage to a bowl. In a food processor or electric mixer, cream together 2 tablespoons of the butter with the cream, eggs, and cream cheese. Add this to the bowl with the sausage, along with the salt, pepper, Swiss cheese, and freshly grated potato (do this at the last minute to avoid discoloring). Butter a 9 x 12-inch baking dish with the remaining butter, and spread the potato mixture over the surface. It should be no more than 1 inch thick to insure proper cooking and browning.

Place the pan in a preheated 350° F oven and bake, uncovered, for 1 hour. If the top is becoming too brown, cover loosely with foil. Cut into serving-sized squares and serve. Makes 6–8 servings as a side dish

This is even better when made ahead. To rewarm, cut into serving-sized squares, wrap in foil, and warm in a 350°F oven or heat on a platter in the microwave.

· hot potato and sausage salad ·

This delicious potato salad is best eaten warm. If you have any leftovers, rather than eating them cold, fry the salad in a heavy pan until lightly brown. This results in delectably tangy home fries.

2 lbs. small red boiling potatoes
1 tbsp. salt
6 tbsp. cider vinegar
½ c. finely chopped red onion
½ c. finely chopped green onions or
   scallions
¼ c. finely chopped fresh parsley
¾ lb. cervelat, Smoked Bratwurst,
   Smoked Kielbasa, or other smoked
   sausage, cut into ¼-inch dice

6 tbsp. olive oil
1 clove garlic, minced
¼ tsp. cayenne
1 tbsp. Dijon mustard
½ tsp. cracked black pepper
6 drops Tabasco
Salt to taste

Use a German-style garlic cervelat, smoked bratwurst, smoked kielbasa, or any good-quality smoked sausage for this dish.

In a large pot, cover the potatoes with water, add 1 tablespoon of salt and bring to a boil. Cover and cook for 20–30 minutes, or until a knife inserted into a potato meets no resistance. Drain the potatoes, and when cool enough, cut each in half. Cut each half into ¼-inch slices and put in a large bowl. Sprinkle them with 3 tablespoons of the cider vinegar. Add the red onion, green onions, and parsley.

In a heavy pan, fry the sausage pieces in the olive oil until they begin to brown. Remove with a slotted spoon and add to the potatoes. To the fat remaining in the pan, add the garlic, cayenne, mustard, remaining cider vinegar, black pepper, and Tabasco. Bring to a boil while whisking continuously. This should loosen any sausage bits, and produce a smooth creamy dressing. Salt to taste. Pour the dressing over the sausages and potatoes, and mix lightly. Serve immediately. Makes 6–8 servings

· potato, sausage, and leek gratin ·

The earthy flavors of potato, sausage, and leeks seem to go perfectly with each other, and are combined in a wide variety of traditional casseroles, soups, and stews. This recipe, adapted from *The L. L. Bean Book of New New England Cookery* by Judith and Evan Jones, can be served as a side dish or a main course, depending on how much sausage you include. To convert the recipe below into a main dish, just double the amount of sausage. Use a mild-flavored sausage here such as smoked kielbasa, smoked bratwurst, or linguiça.

4 tbsp. (½ stick) butter
4 c. diced unpeeled red potatoes
1 c. finely chopped leeks, white part only
½ c. finely chopped green onions or scallions
Salt and pepper to taste

2–3 tbsp. flour
½ lb. chopped smoked kielbasa, or other smoked sausage
Milk to cover
½ c. bread crumbs

· **Garnish** ·
Chopped chives

Butter a casserole or baking dish. Spread half the potatoes, leeks, and green onions in the bottom and sprinkle with salt, pepper, and half the flour. Add all the sausage, and then spread the remaining potatoes, leeks, and green onions on top. Sprinkle with salt, pepper, and the remaining flour. Pour over enough milk to just cover the mixture in the pan, and sprinkle the bread crumbs over the top. Dot with butter. Bake in a 375° F oven, covered, for 1 hour, until the potatoes are tender. Remove the cover, and bake for 15–20 minutes more until the top is brown. Sprinkle with chopped chives just before serving. Makes 4–6 servings

· simple home-style scrapple ·

Many recipes for this hearty Pennsylvania favorite call for the long cooking of a pig's head, or trimmings such as pig's feet, ears, or tails, with the addition of cornmeal at the end. Our simpler and, we think, tastier version combines good-quality bulk sausage with cornmeal and seasonings to form a loaf which can be sliced and fried for breakfast or lunch. Use fresh sage sausage from any of the recipes in this book (see index) or a good commercial product.

1½ lbs. fresh sage-flavored sausage, in bulk
1 medium onion, finely chopped
1¼ c. cornmeal
3 c. rich beef, pork, or chicken stock

1 tsp. dried sage
½ tsp. dried thyme
1 tsp. coarsely ground black pepper
Salad oil to oil loaf pan
1 tbsp. butter

Bulk sausage is easily made at home in a food processor and provides more flavor and less fat than store-bought.

Fry the sausage for about 3 minutes to render some of the fat, breaking the meat apart with a fork as it browns. Remove with a slotted spoon, and discard all but 2 tablespoons of the fat. Add the chopped onion to the pan and cook for 5 minutes over medium heat. Meanwhile cook the cornmeal in lightly boiling stock, following the instructions on the box, stirring frequently, for 20 minutes. Add the onion and sausage, along with the sage, thyme, and black pepper. Cook for 10 minutes more.

Pour the mush into a lightly oiled 9 x 5 x 2½-inch loaf pan and chill in the refrigerator overnight. To serve, fry ½-inch slices of the scrapple in a little butter for about 5 minutes per side over medium-high heat. Makes about 3–4 pounds

THE SOUTHWEST

· a fiery, complex cuisine ·

MAKING THE SAUSAGES

Chorizo

New Mexico chicken, pork, and roasted chile sausage

El Paso beef, pork, and chile sausage

Santa Fe spicy chicken, pork, and cilantro sausage

Texas smoky link

BREAKFAST DISHES & APPETIZERS

Salsas and guacamole

Chilequiles de chorizo (tortilla and chorizo pie)

Huevos con chorizo

Spicy empanadas

Sausage wrapped in
cabbage leaves

Grilled Southwest sausage
"sandwich" with chiles
and cheese

Quick and easy appetizers

SALADS
& SOUPS

Tom Blower's nopalito and
bell pepper salad

Karl's Tex-Mex rice salad

Smoked sausage and black
bean salad

Phyllis's wilted spinach salad
with crispy chorizo

Tortilla, vegetable, and
chorizo soup

MAIN
DISHES

Southwest mixed grill:
shrimp and marinated pork
with orange-chile adobo

Rice with shrimp and chorizo

Chimichangas with Santa Fe
spicy chicken, pork, and
cilantro sausage

Turkey pie with chile
cornbread crust

Chile and chorizo cornbread

Navajo lamb stew

Tex-Mex chili

Pork and chorizo pozole

New Mexico chicken, pork, and
roasted chile sausage in
chile verde

Stacked cheese and chorizo
enchiladas

Robin's black bean chili

Poblano chiles stuffed with
New Mexico chicken, pork, and
roasted chile sausage

Grilled Anaheim chiles
with cheese and chorizo stuffing

Tex-Mex red enchilada
sauce

Chorizo-stuffed potatoes

n the past few years the fiery and complex cooking of America's Southwest has been recognized as one of our most exciting regional cuisines. An amalgam of Indian, Mexican, and "Anglo" influences has produced an array of delicious and increasingly innovative dishes, from the fashionable restaurants in Dallas, Fort Worth, and Denver to the small cafés and restaurants of Taos, Tucson, and Santa Fe, and in the kitchens of talented home cooks all across the southern plains and high plateaus of Texas, New Mexico, Arizona, and Colorado. Using traditional foods such as chiles, beans, corn, chicken, pork, and game, this new generation of southwestern cooks has built upon the past to create a vibrant and exciting style of cooking.

It wasn't always so. A decade or so ago, if you asked for southwestern cooking, you most likely would have received a blank stare at first, followed by a "Mexican" meal of bland chili con carne or a limp enchilada surrounded by some tired refried beans and tasteless "Spanish" rice. Like much of the best modern American cooking, the new southwestern cuisine is grounded in the discovery of our ethnic and regional roots. It is a return to an earlier and more authentic style of cookery that depends on fresh and natural ingredients, carefully and respectfully prepared.

The dishes Southwest cooks are making today differ in many ways from the often frugal and spare foods of a harder, less affluent time, but they share the same basic ingredients: corn—blue, white, or yellow, fresh, parched, or made into hominy; beans of every color and flavor; chiles ranging from mild to scorching; pork, fresh or cured, smoked, or ground into sausage; range-fed beef, lamb, and game; farmyard chickens; squash, tomatoes, and onions from thirsty gardens; herbs like oregano, wild mint and pungent *epazote* from the high plains.

The landscape of the Southwest is beautiful, but harsh. From the peaks of the Sangre de Cristo range north of Santa Fe to the high plateaus of Big Mountain and the Four Corners, from the barren Jornada del Muerte and Llano Estacado to the valleys of the Rio Grande, Pecos, and Gila rivers, eking out a living from this land has never been easy. Native Americans, whether pueblo dwellers like the Hopi or Zuni, or nomadic hunters and pastoralists like the Navajo, Apache, or Comanche, made the best of what they could grow and hunt. Their foods were similar to those of other native peoples to the east and north: corn and game, squash and beans. But their lives were leaner and drier, and there was less margin for comfort or error. The coming of the Spaniards brought European foods such as pork, beef, chickens, herbs, rice, and vegetables, and these were quickly incorporated into the indigenous cooking of the Southwest.

Corn, the American staple, was the basic food throughout this region as in almost every other. Cooked fresh or "green" when it ripened during the short harvest period, it was most often dried on the cob for preservation over winter months. Corn was ground into meal and boiled with water for *atole,* a kind of gruel, or made into a thin paste and fried on a hot flat stone for *pik,* the paper-thin Indian bread. Dried corn was leached with lime from the ashes of fires to make *nixtamal,* or hominy, that was eaten fresh or ground into masa dough to make tortillas and tamales. Corn, still the mainstay of southwestern cooking, combines with a wide variety of ingredients in traditional dishes.

Beans are another staple of southwestern cooking, and are served with almost every meal. Pinto beans are the most popular variety throughout the region, and families in many rural areas seem to exist largely on a diet of frijoles or boiled pinto beans and tortillas. The combination is a healthy one, and when spiced up with chiles, and rounded out with cheese and a little meat and vegetables, southwestern cooking can provide a well-balanced and lively diet for very little money. Black beans are also popular and can be found in dishes such as Robin's Black Bean Chili, with chiles and smoked sausages (see page 237), and Smoked Sausage and Black Bean Salad (see page 224). Kidney beans and garbanzos are also found in a variety of dishes like the ubiquitous chili con carne of roadside diners, in the famous three-bean salad of church potlucks, and in soups, stews, and salads from Galveston to Tombstone.

The often bland flavors of corn and beans are given life and energy by an array of seasonings, led by an astonishing variety of chiles. This family of highly flavored peppers (*Capsicum annuum*) spread north from Mexico to the Indians of the Southwest in pre-Columbian times. Many types of chiles were used in the sophisticated cuisine of the Aztecs of central and northern Mexico, and over two hundred can be distinguished today in Mexican cookery. Southwestern cooks take advantage of the widely varied levels and gradations of flavor and piquancy of the many types of chiles, and often use these differences as signatures of specific dishes and styles of cooking.

Chiles are used in every stage of their development from green to red ripe to dried. Dried chiles are ground and mixed with herbs like cumin and oregano to make the ubiquitous chile powder blend found on supermarket shelves throughout America. Large mild green chiles are often stuffed with cheese and other ingredients and served as vegetables or entrees like our Grilled Anaheim Chiles with Cheese and Chorizo Stuffing (see page 239) and Poblano Chiles Stuffed with New Mexico Chicken, Pork, and Roasted Chile Sausage (see page 239). Smaller, hotter varieties like jalapeños and serranos are chopped and mixed with tomatoes, onions, and the aromatic fresh herb cilantro to make spicy salsas (see page 216), the main condiments found on southwestern tables. Bright red dried chiles hang in long strings called *ristras* from the eaves of New Mexican adobes, and are soaked in hot water and pureed to make the ever popular Tex-Mex Red Enchilada Sauce (see page 239). For a discussion of types and hotness levels of many of the chiles used in southwestern cooking, along with information about handling and preparation of chiles, see page 208.

Pork, fresh or cured, has been one of the most important sources of protein in the Southwest since the coming of Europeans in the sixteenth century. Salted, smoked, or made into sausage or chorizo, pork was most often the meat that flavored the dried beans and corn during the winter months. Chorizo is found in a myriad of southwestern dishes including the breakfast favorite of fried tortilla strips in a spicy chile and sausage sauce, Chilequiles de Chorizo (see page 217). The German influence on sausage making is seen mostly in Texas around the towns of New Braunfels and Castroville. Our Texas Smoky Link (see page 214) shows how the German traditions of sausage making blended with local ingredients and tastes.

Beef and lamb are popular meats, and are served in many traditional dishes. Shredded beef or *machacha* is a common stuffing for tacos and burritos, and lamb is found throughout the region, especially where the Navajo influence is felt. Our venison or lamb and chorizo Tex-Mex Chili (see page 233) and Navajo Lamb Stew (see page 232) provide a taste of these hearty, traditional foods. Game still finds a place on southwestern tables, both in the home and increasingly in fashionable restaurants. Chicken, duck, and turkey are featured in many dishes, including our New Mexico Chicken, Pork, and Roasted Chile Sausage (see page 210), Santa Fe Spicy Chicken, Pork, and Cilantro Sausage (see page 214), and Turkey Pie with Chile Cornbread Crust (see page 230).

· chiles ·

· Types of chiles ·

There are many varieties of fresh or dried chiles used in the Southwest, ranging from mild to very hot. We give suggestions for specific chiles in the recipes, but you should feel free to substitute, depending on what is available in your market, and your tolerance for heat.

Here are some of the main types usually found in Hispanic markets and neighborhoods (in ascending order of hotness):

Anaheim · Large, mild green chile often stuffed as in Grilled Anaheim Chiles with Cheese and Chorizo Stuffing (see page 239). Also called California chile.

New Mexico · When green, similar to Anaheim. Dried red chiles are found in *ristras* (long strings of chiles), and used in sauces and for chile powder.

poblano · Large green chile similar to above. Also called pasilla. When dried, called ancho — used widely in sauces and for chile powder.

mulato · Medium-hot green chile similar to poblano. Chocolate brown when dry, with rich flavor. Substitute ancho.

jalapeño · Hot green chile used fresh or pickled (*en escabeche*) in sauces or for garnish. Dried red version is smoky, fiery chipotle, often packed in adobo sauce.

serrano · Small green chile, even hotter than jalapeño. Used in salsas and for dishes with emphatic heat levels.

· Handling chiles ·

Much of the heat is found in seeds and white inner membranes, so removing these will tone down chiles. Be careful when handling chiles, as they can burn eyes or sensitive skin: wear rubber gloves, wash hands afterwards.

· Peeling chiles or peppers ·

To peel green chiles (as well as bell peppers), fire-roast under broiler or over open flame until skin is charred and put in plastic or paper bag for 15 minutes to steam. Scrape skin off under running water. Soak dried chiles in hot water until soft and puree in food processor.

You can make your own chile powder using dried chiles in a blender (be careful not to inhale dust — it can be irritating) or buy ground New Mexico, California, or ancho chiles from Hispanic markets or mail order (see page 357). Most commercial chile powder blends include oregano and cumin; Gebhardt is the best widely available blend.

Canned green chiles are good alternatives to fresh, or use fire-roasted and peeled bell peppers and add heat with cayenne, red pepper flakes, or hot sauce.

· chorizo ·

Chorizo is the general Spanish word for sausage, so it can be a bit confusing when you find the word referring to different types of sausages made in Spain, Mexico, South America, and (with slightly differing spellings) in Portugal (chouriço) and Louisiana (chaurice).

The Mexican version usually contains ground pork mixed with lots of cumin, pure chile powder, and fresh hot peppers such as serrano or jalapeño. Again, as with many peasant sausages, there are variations depending on the place of origin or family traditions. Some chorizos contain cinnamon, others tequila, some are served fresh and lightly spiced, others are dried, pungent, and decidedly funky. The recipe below is a basic one that you should feel free to vary and add your own personal touch to. Use chorizo as a filling for enchiladas or tacos, in sauces, or fried with eggs or rice.

Since it's usually used in bulk, chorizo is an easy sausage to make in a food processor. Wrap ½- to 1-pound quantities in foil, label, and freeze until needed.

1½ lbs. pork butt
½ lb. pork back fat
1 tbsp. New Mexico or other ground dried chile powder
½ tsp. coarsely ground black pepper
¼ tsp. ground coriander
1 tsp. ground cumin
½ tbsp. whole cumin seed

½ tsp. cayenne
1 tbsp. sweet Hungarian paprika
2 tsp. kosher salt
¼ c. red wine vinegar
1 bunch fresh cilantro, chopped (optional)
1 fresh serrano, jalapeño or other hot chile, seeded and chopped

For details on making sausage, see page 332.

Grind the meat and fat through a ¼-inch plate or in batches in a food processor. Put the ground meat and fat in a bowl, and add the spices, salt, vinegar, cilantro, if using, and chile. Mix together with your hands, and chill overnight. Package for the freezer or use in 2–3 days. Refrigerated, chorizo will keep 3 days, frozen 2 months. Makes 2 pounds

We prefer to use pure ground dried chile powders — found in most Hispanic markets. If unavailable, use a good-quality commercial chile powder blend.

· The Southwest ·

· 209 ·

· New Mexico chicken, pork, and roasted chile sausage ·

Small game birds thrive in the piñon scrub of the New Mexican highlands, and they are often included in the savory dishes of the region. This delicious mixture of fowl, pork, and chiles gives you a taste of the hearty cooking of the high desert. Use the sausage wherever you want the spicy flavors of southwestern cooking.

1 red bell pepper or fresh pimiento

2 green poblano, Anaheim, California, or other mild fresh chiles

1 green jalapeño or other hot fresh chile

1–1½ lbs. chicken breast, boned and skinned

1½ lbs. pork butt

1 lb. pork back fat

4 tsp. kosher salt

1 tsp. minced garlic

1 bunch fresh cilantro, coarsely chopped (1 c.)

1 tbsp. ground New Mexico chile powder

2 tbsp. sweet Hungarian paprika

¼ tsp. cayenne

1 tbsp. ground cumin

1 tsp. ground coriander

2 tsp. freshly ground black pepper

⅓ c. red wine vinegar or lime juice

¼ c. cold water

Medium hog casings

For details on making sausage, see page 332.

Fire-roast and peel the peppers (see page 208), and then seed and chop them coarsely. All the peppers combined should yield about 2 cups. Cool them in the refrigerator while you grind the meat.

Grind all the meats and fat through a ⅜-inch plate. Mix with the peppers, salt, garlic, cilantro, spices, vinegar, and water. Knead the mixture thoroughly until all the ingredients are well blended. Do not overmix. Chill for at least 1 hour or overnight. Stuff the sausage meat into medium hog casings, and tie into 5-inch links. Refrigerated, the sausage keeps 3 days, frozen for 2 months.

Makes 4–5 pounds

These are marvelous grilled, but also make an excellent stuffing for small birds like quail, squab, or game hens, or a filling for chimichangas and empanadas (see pages 229 and 219).

El Paso beef, pork, and chile sausage ·

Dark beer and aromatic spices give this zesty sausage a unique flavor that goes well with lamb or game birds. It is also excellent grilled, or used to make empanadas (see page 219), tamales, or tacos. Leave the sausage in bulk or stuff into casings.

1¼ lbs. beef chuck
1¼ lbs. pork butt
½ lb. pork back fat or beef fat
1 tbsp. kosher salt
1 tbsp. chopped garlic
1 tsp. coarsely ground black pepper
1 tsp. red pepper flakes
1 tbsp. pure ground New Mexico chile powder

1 tbsp. ground achiote seed or Hungarian paprika
2 tsp. sugar
1 tbsp. ground cumin
⅛ tsp. cinnamon
⅛ tsp. ground cloves
1 c. dark Mexican or German beer
Medium hog casings

For details on making sausage, see page 332.

Grind all the meat and fat through a ¼-inch plate. In a large bowl, blend the ground meats with the remaining ingredients except the casings. Chill for an hour before stuffing, so the beer can be completely absorbed into the meat. Stuff into medium hog casings, and tie into 5-inch links. Mellow, uncovered, in the refrigerator overnight. Keeps 3 days refrigerated, 2 months frozen. Makes 4 pounds

The achiote seeds in the recipe are more for color than flavor and can be replaced with deeply colored sweet Hungarian paprika.

· fiesta in the Sangre de Cristo mountains ·

Two red-tailed hawks ride high in a thermal, drifting up in widening circles as we break out of the hills and down into the Chimayo Valley just north of Santa Fe. The landscape changes quickly from the hard beauty of the uplands with its piñon scrub and cactus, red rocks and arroyos, to valley fields bright with the deep brassy green of chile plants, the soft wide leaves of pumpkins, squash, and melons. Fruit trees and cottonwoods cluster near water. Nearby, adobe houses are the color of dry earth, their pale walls threaded with bright red *ristras,* strings of chiles, hanging from the eaves. Dirt roads like streams of brown water cut through the green fields. Two children riding a burro wave and laugh as we pass. The clear autumn light flavors everything like a spice.

We're on our way to a fiesta up in the foothills of the Sangre de Cristo mountains, named for how the red of the sunset seems like Christ's blood on the slopes. It's a harvest festival to honor the corn and the beans, the chiles ripening red-green under the leaves; a dance for what this hard earth gives. Apart from a good time and celebration, we're looking for the sausages we've heard about in Santa Fe and Taos. Great sausages up there in

the hills, we're told: chorizos of wonderful spice and depth; sausages made from wild pigs and birds fed on piñon nuts, smoked with the aromatic woods of the high desert.

As we rise up from the valley, the sun is bright on the rocks, shadows beginning to lengthen. We turn suddenly into the village tucked in the edge of the canyon, a white church with a plaza, a cluster of houses up against the hills. In the central square there's a riot of color, bands and dancing, and smoke from the cooking rises up all around the edge.

The dancers swirl through the plaza: Moors and Christians, mustachioed Conquistadores and warriors in masks and feathers battle across the square. We stroll among the food stands. Old women are making tortillas, cooking them quickly on *comals,* filling them with chorizo and chiles. Sausages sputter on hot grills next to salsa in bright terra-cotta bowls. *Cabritos* smoke on spits over glowing coals in the gathering dark. We order tacos and cold beer with lime, and watch the mariachis playing under the streetlights. Young girls smile and stroll around the square on the arms of their mothers. The young men are drinking beer, boisterously singing the first lines of love songs as they strut by in the other direction.

We wander around the plaza as the night goes on, sampling sausages, chiles stuffed with cheese and chorizo, bowls of steaming pozole and venison chili, spicy empanadas, and chimichangas. The *corridos* (songs of the border, danger, and love) are starting up as we drive away. We can hear them a long time as we head down the mountain under the bright, cold harvest moon.

· Santa Fe spicy chicken, pork, and cilantro sausage ·

The flavors of this lively sausage come from fresh chiles, lime, and cilantro. It is wonderful grilled or used in any recipe that calls for spicy fresh sausage.

1½ lbs. chicken thighs, boned and skinned
1 lb. pork butt
½ lb. pork back fat
1 jalapeño or other hot green chile, seeded and finely chopped
¼ c. seeded and finely chopped poblano or other mild green chile

2 tbsp. minced garlic
¼ c. tequila
1 c. chopped fresh cilantro
¼ c. lime juice
1 tbsp. kosher salt
1 tsp. coarsely ground black pepper
Medium hog casings

For details on making sausage, see page 332.

Grind the chicken through a ⅜-inch plate, the pork and pork fat through a ¼-inch plate. Mix the ground meats and fat with the remaining ingredients except the casings, and knead until everything is well blended. Stuff into medium hog casings, and tie into 5-inch links. Refrigerated, the sausage will keep 3 days, frozen up to 2 months.

Makes 3 pounds

This recipe was inspired by Mark Miller's Yucatan Sausage at the Coyote Cafe in Santa Fe. Limes, tequila, and jalapeño give it an exotic character, lighter than our New Mexico Chicken, Pork, and Roasted Chile Sausage.

· Texas smoky link ·

Sausage making in Texas goes back to the days of the Lone Star Republic, when Germans and Alsatians emigrated to the new country in large numbers, particularly around the towns of Castroville and New Braunfels. What began as food for immigrant communities soon became popular with the rest of the early settlers. Sausages became one of the staples of a traditional Texas barbecue.

Texas smoked sausages are made with beef and pork; vary the proportions to suit your taste. Hot smoke or cold smoke the sausages, depending on your preference and attitude towards using curing salts.

2 lbs. pork butt	1 tbsp. coarsely ground black pepper
½ lb. beef chuck	2 tsp. red pepper flakes
½ lb. pork back fat	1 tsp. curing salts (optional) (see page
1 tsp. ground coriander	343)
2 tsp. ground cumin	½ c. water
2 tsp. chopped garlic	4 tsp. kosher salt
Pinch *each* ground allspice and cloves	Wide hog casings

For details on making sausage, see page 332.

Grind the pork through a ⅜-inch plate. Grind the beef and pork fat through a ¼ inch plate. Mix the ground meats with all the remaining ingredients except the casings. Add the curing salts if the sausage is to be cold smoked (see page 338). Stuff the sausage into wide hog casings, and tie into 8-inch links. If cold smoking, air-dry overnight in a cool place, and smoke the sausage for at least 12 hours. Otherwise, dry overnight, uncovered, in the refrigerator, and hot smoke the sausages to an internal temperature of 155° F. Refrigerated, the sausage will keep for 1 week, frozen for 2 months. Makes 3–4 pounds

Tangy smoked links and grilled meats are served at many a Texas get-together with spicy barbecue sauce, side dishes like chili and frijoles, and a wide variety of salsas and salads (see pages 216 and 222–225).

· The Southwest ·

· salsas and guacamole ·

Salsas and guacamole are natural accompaniments to Southwest cooking. Here are some of our favorites. We prefer to chop the ingredients by hand, but you can use a food processor. Just be careful not to puree everything.

· Salsa cruda ·

½ c. minced onion, red or yellow
2 jalapeño or other hot green chiles, seeded, or 2 tsp. crushed dried red chile
1 Anaheim or other mild green chile, fire-roasted and peeled (see page 208)
1 poblano or other mild green chile, fire-roasted and peeled
½ c. chopped fresh cilantro
1 large ripe tomato, chopped (about 1 c.)
¼ c. lime or lemon juice
Salt to taste

   Chop ingredients and mix together. Keeps 3–5 days refrigerated. Makes 2 cups

· Salsa verde ·

1 large clove garlic
6 tbsp. fresh cilantro
1 small jalapeño or other hot green chile, seeded
½ medium onion
8 fresh tomatillos, husks removed and parboiled, or a 16-oz. can
½ tsp. salt
2 tbsp. lime juice or to taste

   Finely chop garlic, cilantro, chile, onion, and tomatillos. Mix with salt and lime juice. Keeps 3–4 days in refrigerator. Makes 1 cup

· Guacamole ·

2 large avocados, peeled
½ c. Salsa Cruda
Lime juice to taste
Salt to taste

   Mash avocados, mix with salsa cruda and lime juice. Taste for salt. Keeps 1–2 days refrigerated. Makes 2 cups

chilequiles de chorizo (tortilla and chorizo pie) ·

Tortillas are an essential part of the Mexican and southwestern diet, so they are never thrown away, even when stale. The challenge is finding ways to use up leftover tortillas, but chilequiles is the usual answer. This substantial and delicious dish is often served with scrambled eggs for breakfast on Sunday morning to use up the last of the week's tortillas, but it is good anytime for lunch or dinner with a salad.

2 tbsp. olive oil
3–4 fresh Anaheim or other mild
  green chiles
6–8 tomatillos, husks removed and
  parboiled 5 minutes, or a
  16-oz. can
2 medium onions
4 cloves garlic
1 bunch fresh cilantro
1 or more c. chicken stock
Salt and pepper to taste

1½ lbs. chorizo or other fresh
  Southwest sausage, in bulk or
  removed from casings
2 c. finely chopped onions
16 corn tortillas cut into sixths
Oil for deep-frying
6 c. shredded Jack cheese

· Garnishes ·
Avocado slices
Fresh cilantro sprigs

To make the sauce, coarsely puree the olive oil, chiles, tomatillos, onions, garlic, and cilantro in a food processor. Combine with the chicken stock in a saucepan and simmer for 5 minutes. Taste for salt and pepper, and reserve.

Fry the chorizo over medium-high heat, breaking up the meat with a fork, for about 5 minutes. Pour off all but about 2 tablespoons of the fat, add the finely chopped onions, and cook another 5 minutes, until the onions are soft.

Meanwhile deep-fry the tortilla wedges in batches for 1–2 minutes, until they are crisp but not brown. Drain well on paper towels.

To assemble the chilequiles, oil a 3–4-quart casserole. Make layers of tortilla chips, chorizo, Jack cheese, and sauce. Repeat until all the ingredients are used. Press down with a plate, making sure all the solids are covered with liquid. Otherwise, add more stock. Cover with foil, and refrigerate overnight so that the tortillas absorb the liquid. The next day, remove the plate, and sprinkle the top with more shredded Jack cheese. Bake, covered, in a pre-heated 350° F oven for 45 minutes. Garnish with avocado slices and cilantro sprigs. Makes 5–6 servings

Use any of the fresh spicy sausages from this chapter or any good-quality Mexican-style chorizo. Serve chilequiles with plenty of fresh salsa (see opposite page).

· huevos con chorizo ·

This hearty breakfast is a favorite in fine restaurants and greasy spoons from Beaumont, Texas, to Albuquerque, New Mexico. Served with refried beans and hot tortillas, huevos con chorizo makes a substantial brunch or light supper.

Use any of the spicy fresh sausages in this chapter or a good store-bought chorizo. Be sure to drain the sausage thoroughly before mixing it with the eggs.

½ lb. chorizo or other spicy sausage, in bulk or removed from casings

2 tbsp. chopped green onions or scallions

1 mild green chile like Anaheim or poblano, fire-roasted and chopped, or 1 canned fire-roasted green chile, chopped

3–4 eggs, lightly beaten

· **Garnishes** ·

Salsa Cruda (see page 216)

Sour cream

Fry the chorizo in a heavy small skillet for 5 minutes over medium-high heat, crumbling the meat as it cooks. Add the green onions and chile, and cook for 2 more minutes. Pour off all but about 2 tablespoons of the fat and transfer the chorizo mixture to an omelette pan. Add the eggs over high heat, and scramble them until done to your taste, or let them set, fold over into an omelette, and serve on a warm platter. Garnish with sour cream and salsa. Accompany with refried beans, with cheese melted on top, and with warm tortillas. Makes 2–3 servings

Depending on your preference, you can let the eggs set in the pan to make an omelette or you can stir them to make scrambled eggs.

spicy empanadas ·

These spicy meat-filled turnovers have many variations, and have become a very popular snack throughout the Southwest. They are great at parties or before dinner served with an array of Mexican beers or a sparkling wine from Spain or California. In this version we suggest a piquant chorizo, raisin, and potato stuffing. You should feel free to experiment with fillings depending on your tastes, and what you have on hand. Just make sure that the turnovers are packed with plenty of spice and flavor.

1½ lbs. chorizo or El Paso Beef, Pork, and Chile Sausage, removed from casings
2 c. finely chopped onions
1 c. diced potatoes (¼-inch dice)
¼ c. red wine vinegar
½ c. Tex-Mex Red Enchilada Sauce (see page 239)
½ c. raisins
½ c. chopped fresh cilantro (optional)
1 recipe Edy's Foolproof Pie Dough (see page 64), or Easy Cream Cheese Dough (see page 174)
1 egg mixed with 2 tbsp. water for egg wash

In a heavy large skillet, fry the sausage meat and onions together for about 5–7 minutes over medium-high heat until the onions are soft, and the fat is rendered. Pour off most of the fat. Add the potatoes, vinegar, enchilada sauce, and raisins. Reduce the heat to moderate, simmer, and cook until the potatoes are tender and most of the sauce has been absorbed, about 15 minutes. Add a little water if the potatoes are not quite done by the time the sauce is absorbed, and cook a bit longer. Skim any fat from the surface and cool the mixture in the refrigerator completely before assembling the empanadas. The filling can be made up a day ahead of time and refrigerated until used.

To assemble the empanadas, stir the optional cilantro into the filling, and roll out the dough to a thickness of ⅛ inch. Cut out 6-inch circles and place about ⅓ cup of filling in the center of each. For hors d'oeuvre–sized empanadas, cut 3-inch circles, and use 2–3 teaspoons of filling. Fold the dough over the filling to make half-moon-shaped turnovers and crimp the edge well with a fork or dough crimper. Place the empanadas on an ungreased baking sheet.

Preheat the oven to 400° F. Brush the empanadas with the egg wash and bake both sizes until the dough is golden and they give off a wonderful aroma, about 20 minutes. Makes 12 large, about 36 small

Make empanadas ahead of time, freeze, and then bake them directly from the freezer. Add an extra 5 minutes or so to the baking time. This empanada filling also works well in tamales, tacos, or enchiladas.

· sausage wrapped in cabbage leaves ·

These easy-to-make hors d'oeuvres can be made with many types of sausage, but we prefer the spicy flavors of our New Mexico Chicken, Pork, and Roasted Chile Sausage.

2 lbs. New Mexico Chicken, Pork,
   and Roasted Chile Sausage (see
   page 210) (about 8 links)
16 large cabbage leaves
1 c. milk

1 egg
Salt and pepper to taste
2 c. all-purpose flour
4 c. or more peanut oil
Lime wedges for garnish

For contrast, you might want to make some of these with a spicy sausage (see pages 209, 211, and 214) and some using a mild Italian or fresh herb sausage (see pages 112 and 254).

Pierce the sausage links with a skewer or sharp fork and poach in lightly salted water that is just below the simmer point (about 160° F) for 10 minutes. Remove and cool. While the sausages are cooling, simmer the cabbage leaves in water until they are tender, about 10 minutes. Drain the cabbage and cut each leaf in half. Cut each sausage in half crosswise, and wrap in the half leaf of cabbage, folding in the edges and ends to make a tight bundle. Secure with a wooden toothpick.

    Mix together the milk and egg, lightly salt and pepper the cabbage rolls, then dip them into the egg/milk mixture. Roll in flour, and fry in hot oil that is at least ½ inch deep in a heavy skillet. Cook in the hot oil, turning once until brown, about 5 minutes per side. Drain the rolls on paper towels and serve with lime wedges. Makes 8 hors d'oeuvre servings

· grilled Southwest sausage "sandwich" with chiles and cheese ·

This simple but delicious grilled "sandwich" is a wonderful way to eat any of the fresh spicy sausages in this chapter.

8 El Paso Beef, Pork, and Chile
  Sausages or other spicy sausages
4 Anaheim or other mild green chiles,
  split in half and seeded
¾ lb. Jack cheese, cut into ¼ x 1 x 3-
  inch pieces, about 16 chunks in all
8 flour tortillas

· Garnishes ·
1 bunch cilantro, leaves only
2 limes, quartered

Grill the sausages and chiles in a covered barbecue kettle over medium heat, turning frequently. When the chiles are brown and soft, transfer them to a platter. The sausages are done when they are firm and have an internal temperature of 160° F, about 10–15 minutes. Remove them from the grill and keep warm.

Just right for a hot-weather barbecue served with a light Mexican lager such as Corona or Pacifica and slices of lime.

Place 2 chunks of cheese in each tortilla, add a piece of grilled chile, and fold in half. Grill in the covered barbecue for 1–2 minutes per side, or bake in a 400° F oven until the cheese becomes soft but not runny. To serve, insert a sausage into each chile-and-cheese-filled tortilla. Let each person garnish with cilantro leaves and squeezes of lime. Makes 4–6 servings

· quick and easy appetizers ·

Sausages make the perfect easy appetizer. All you have to do is make sure they are cooked, and cut them into bite-sized pieces. Your guests can serve themselves with toothpicks or fingers, and dip the savory bites into interesting sauces, mustards, chutneys, or flavored mayonnaises. You can be more elaborate, if you wish, arranging the sausages on skewers with aromatic vegetables, meats, or seafoods. Or you can use sausage meat as a savory filling for pastries, empanadas, small tamales, and other hors d'oeuvres.

Sausage bites coated with crisp bread crumbs make a delicious appetizer or cocktail snack. Use a mildly flavored, precooked sausage such as bratwurst, bockwurst, sweetbread boudin, rabbit boudin, boudin blanc, or veal sausage. Cut the sausage into 1-inch chunks, brush generously with a sweet mustard, roll in dried bread crumbs, and broil 3–4 inches from the flame for 2–3 minutes, turn and broil 1–2 minutes more until crisp and brown.

· Tom Blower's nopalito and bell pepper salad ·

This crunchy salad provides a cool contrast to the spicy food of the Southwest. Serve it as part of the Southwest Mixed Grill (see page 227) or as a side dish with enchiladas (see page 236). It also makes a simple and satisfying meal when served with any of the spicy sausages in this chapter, grilled or fried.

Tom Blower is a professional chef who has cooked in restaurants from Louisiana to California, and is well versed in many facets of American regional cuisine.

1 lb. chorizo
½ head leaf lettuce
1 red onion
1 large green bell pepper
1 large red bell pepper
1 bunch radishes
⅓ c. olive oil
Juice from 3–4 limes (about ½ c.)
2 tsp. minced garlic
½ 15-oz. jar nopalitos

2 fresh jalapeño or other hot green chiles, seeded
1 bunch cilantro
1 large avocado
2 large tomatoes or 1 basket cherry tomatoes

· Garnish ·

2 c. crumbled *queso fresco* or fresh chèvre (optional)

In a heavy skillet, fry the sausage meat for 5–7 minutes over medium-high heat to render the fat. Transfer to a sieve over a bowl to drain.

Line a large salad bowl with clean, dry leaf lettuce. Slice the onion. Remove the seeds from the bell peppers, and slice approximately the same size as the onions. Thinly slice the radishes. At this point the salad ingredients can be covered and refrigerated until ready to serve.

Just before serving whisk the olive oil into the lime juice, pouring the oil in a slow, steady stream. Add garlic. Rinse the nopalitos, dice the chiles very finely, and chop the cilantro. Mix these with the sliced onions, peppers, radishes, and the reserved chorizo, and toss thoroughly with the dressing.

Cut the avocado and tomatoes in 1-inch cubes (if using cherry tomatoes, cut in half), add to the other vegetables, and mix gently. Place in the lettuce-lined bowl. Garnish with a crumbled soft cheese like *queso fresco* or fresh chèvre, if desired. Makes 6–8 servings

Nopalitos are cactus pads cut into strips and pickled in brine. They can be found in Mexican specialty stores or obtained from mail order (see page 357). They are usually quite salty and should be rinsed well before using. If they seem a bit exotic for your neighborhood, substitute fresh, lightly salted cucumbers.

· Karl's Tex-Mex rice salad ·

Rice salads make satisfying one-course lunches or great side dishes for a buffet. They are best served when the rice is freshly cooked and still a bit warm, or at room temperature. They can be made a day ahead and refrigerated, but try to let the salad warm to room temperature before serving.

Karl Kuhnert was a very talented sous chef at Poulet, a popular restaurant and charcuterie in Berkeley, where I was the head chef. He did a great job with the day-to-day operation of the kitchen. He contributed this zesty recipe, and later went on to run his own deli kitchen before his untimely death.

¾ lb. chorizo or El Paso Beef, Pork, and Chile Sausage, removed from casings

½ c. pine nuts

4 c. freshly cooked converted rice

2 Anaheim or poblano chiles, fire-roasted and diced (see page 208)

1 red bell pepper, fire-roasted and diced (see page 208)

1 c. diced Fontina, Jack, or Swiss cheese

1 bunch cilantro, chopped (1 c.)

6 green onions or scallions, thinly sliced

1 basket cherry tomatoes, cut in half

1 tsp. minced garlic

6 tbsp. olive oil

¼ c. fresh lime juice

Salt and pepper to taste

In a heavy skillet, fry the sausage over medium-high heat for 5–7 minutes until most of the fat is rendered and the meat begins to brown. Break the meat up with a fork into ¼-inch pieces as it cooks. Transfer the cooked sausage to a sieve set over a bowl to drain off the fat. Toast the pine nuts in a dry pan until they are light brown, shaking the pan as they color. Transfer to a bowl, and reserve.

In a large bowl, mix the rice with all but ¼ cup of the sausage, the chiles, bell pepper, cheese, cilantro, green onions, and all but 12 of the half tomatoes. Combine the garlic, oil, and lime juice and add to salad. Toss and taste for salt and pepper. Garnish the salad with the remaining cherry tomato halves, the toasted pine nuts, and the remaining chorizo. Makes 4 servings for lunch, 6–8 as part of a buffet

Converted rice is best for salads because it doesn't get soggy. Basmati rice is a good alternative, as its characteristic nutty flavor adds an interesting note.

· smoked sausage and black bean salad ·

Any smoked sausage such as our Texas Smoky Link, andouille, or Smoked Country Sausage will work well in this hearty salad. It's smoky, simple, and delicious.

1 lb. smoked sausage, diced
1½ c. vinaigrette (see page 353)
4 c. cooked black beans
1 red onion, finely chopped
1 red bell pepper, diced

1 jalapeño or other hot green chile,
    finely chopped
1 tsp. minced garlic
2 c. chopped fresh cilantro or flat-leaf
    Italian parsley

In a heavy skillet, fry the sausage over medium-high heat until the fat is rendered, about 5–7 minutes. Discard the fat. Add the vinaigrette to the beans while they are still hot. Cool, and mix in the sausage and the remaining ingredients. Makes 4–6 servings

· Phyllis's wilted spinach salad with crispy chorizo ·

Wilted spinach salads have become very popular in restaurants throughout the country. They are usually made with a dressing containing some hot bacon fat poured over the greens and crisp bacon for garnish. Instead of bacon, we've used cooked chorizo to give this simple salad a completely new dimension.

⅓ lb. chorizo or El Paso Beef, Pork, and Chile Sausage, removed from casings
1 bunch spinach (about 1 lb.) thoroughly washed and dried
2 c. (loosely packed) bitter greens such as radicchio, arugula, dandelion, or watercress (optional– if not used, double amount of spinach)
½ c. thinly sliced red onions
1 c. julienned jícama root (optional)

½ red or yellow bell pepper, diced

· **Dressing** ·
1 tbsp. red wine vinegar
1 tbsp. lime juice
1 small clove garlic, minced
1 tbsp. chorizo fat
3 tbsp. olive oil
1 tsp. Tabasco or other hot sauce
Salt and pepper to taste

· **Garnish** ·
1 small orange, peeled and sliced into thin rounds

Fry the sausage in a small skillet over medium-high heat for about 10 minutes, crumbling the meat with a fork as it browns, until the fat is rendered and the bits of sausage are crisp. Drain in a sieve placed over a bowl, and reserve 1 tablespoon of the fat. Place all the greens, well washed and dried, in a large salad bowl along with the vegetables.

To prepare the dressing, pour the vinegar and lime juice into the pan in which the chorizo was cooked. Cook over medium heat for 30 seconds and scrape up any browned bits from the bottom of the pan with a spoon. Add the garlic, and gradually whisk in the reserved chorizo fat and olive oil. Add the Tabasco and adjust for salt and pepper. Immediately pour over the salad. Arrange the cooked chorizo and orange slices on top, toss well, and serve.

Makes 4–6 servings

Phyllis Steiber is an inventive cook who has plenty of opportunities to devise new ways to cook with sausage as she is a member of the Aidells Sausage Company.

· tortilla, vegetable, and chorizo soup ·

Soups garnished with freshly fried tortilla strips are very popular in Mexican-American neighborhoods throughout the Southwest. This soup was never officially a recipe when I made it at Poulet — I just put it together with whatever vegetables I had on hand. The only constants were the chicken broth, chorizo, and the fried tortillas. Depending on the season and what we had in the refrigerator, we used zucchini, green beans, spinach, crookneck squash, cabbage, or even shredded lettuce. But no matter what ingredients we used, everybody seemed to loved the soup.

2 lbs. chorizo or El Paso Beef, Pork, and Chile Sausage, removed from casings
4 medium onions, chopped
6 c. chicken stock
1 28-oz. can peeled whole tomatoes and liquid, coarsely chopped, or 3½ cups peeled and chopped fresh tomatoes
1 16-oz. can garbanzo beans, washed and drained
1 tsp. dried oregano
1 tsp. ground cumin
2 Anaheim chiles, fire-roasted, peeled, and chopped (see page 208)

1 red bell pepper, fire-roasted, peeled, and chopped (see page 208)
1 tbsp. chopped garlic
4 c. diced zucchini
1 10-oz. box frozen corn or about 2 c. fresh corn, cut from cob
Juice from 3–4 limes (about ½ c.)

· **Garnishes** ·

Fried tortillas, about 5 strips per serving
2 c. grated Jack cheese
½ c. chopped green onion or scallion
Fresh cilantro leaves (about 4–5 per serving) (optional)
Lime wedges

Peek into the fridge or take a walk in the garden for inspiration — use up your leftovers in this substantial and easy-to-prepare soup.

Brown the chorizo in a heavy large pot or Dutch oven over medium-high heat until the fat is rendered, about 5–7 minutes. Remove all but 3 tablespoons of the fat from the pan, and add the onions. Sauté for 3–5 minutes until they are translucent and soft. Pour in the chicken broth, and add the tomatoes and their liquid, the garbanzos, oregano, and cumin. Bring everything to a boil, and then reduce to a simmer. Add the chiles, bell pepper, garlic, zucchini, corn, and lime juice to the soup, and simmer until the vegetables are done, about 5 minutes. Ladle into bowls, and let guests add their own garnishes. Makes 8 servings

·Southwest mixed grill: shrimp and marinated pork with orange-chile adobo·

Barbecuing and grilling are very popular throughout the Southwest. The marinade here is also wonderful for that new American fast-food sensation, fajitas. Marinate strips of skirt steak or pork in this marinade overnight, and you'll have the best fajitas you've ever tasted. Serve with plenty of hot tortillas, a tangy Mexican beer like Bohemia or Carta Blanca, and our wilted spinach salad (see page 225).

· Marinade ·

Juice from 1 juice orange, preferably tart (½ c.)

Juice from 2 limes (¼ c.)

3 cloves garlic, minced

1 tsp. salt

1 jalapeño or other hot green chile, seeded and finely chopped

⅓ c. olive oil

1 tbsp. minced orange zest (optional)

....

2 lbs. country spareribs, or 1 chicken, cut up for grilling

½ lb. large shrimp (8–10)

1½ lbs. New Mexico Chicken, Pork, and Roasted Chile Sausage or Santa Fe Spicy Chicken, Pork, and Cilantro Sausages (6 links), or other spicy fresh sausage

Cooked rice or Rice with Shrimp and Chorizo (see page 228)

· Garnishes ·

Salsa Cruda (see page 216)

Guacamole (see page 216)

Lime wedges

Chopped fresh cilantro

Hot tortillas (corn or flour)

Mix all the marinade ingredients together, and remove ½ cup to marinate the shrimp later. Put the spareribs or chicken in the marinade, and marinate for at least 2 hours at room temperature or overnight in the refrigerator.

The next day prepare the spinach salad, salsa, and guacamole. Marinate the shrimp for 30–60 minutes in the reserved marinade. Light a charcoal fire in a covered grill. Grill the pork or chicken 30 minutes over medium heat with the grill covered, turning frequently. Cooking times here are only estimates; test with a meat thermometer. Pork and sausage are done at 160° F, chicken at 170° F. Grill the sausage for 10 minutes, and the shrimp for 5 minutes, turning them frequently. Keep the grill cover on to prevent flare-ups, and use a spray bottle of water to dampen any flames. Serve the meat and shrimp on a large platter over rice with garnishes and hot tortillas.

Makes 6 servings

A lot of the fun of serving (and eating) this delicious mixed grill is in the array of sauces and garnishes you can present with it (see page 216).

· rice with shrimp and chorizo ·

In Mexico and throughout the Southwest, a large and wonderful variety of rice dishes called *sopas secas* or "dry soups" can be found. This version includes chorizo, peas, and shrimp.

1 lb. chorizo or El Paso Beef, Pork, and Chile Sausage, removed from casings
1 c. finely chopped onion
1 tsp. chopped garlic
2 c. long-grain rice
1 c. Tex-Mex Red Enchilada Sauce (see page 239) or canned tomato sauce

2 c. chicken stock
1 c. frozen peas
2 fire-roasted mild chiles, chopped (see page 208)
1 lb. peeled raw shrimp

· **Garnishes** ·
Sliced avocado
Sliced radishes
Fresh cilantro

In a Dutch oven or heavy pot, fry the sausage over medium-high heat, crumbling the meat with a fork as it cooks, for about 5 minutes. Pour off the fat, leaving about 3 tablespoons in the pot. Add the onion and garlic, and fry them for 5 minutes, stirring frequently. Add the rice, and stir it until well coated with the onion/sausage mixture. Pour in the enchilada sauce and stock. Cover and cook 15 minutes, until the rice is almost done. Stir in the peas, chiles, and shrimp. Cover and cook 5 minutes more until the rice is tender and fluffy, and the shrimp are just cooked. Garnish with sliced avocado, radishes, and cilantro leaves.

Makes 4–6 servings as a main course, 8–10 as a side dish

Delicious served as a main course or side dish — a great accompaniment to grilled chicken or pork.

· chimichangas with Santa Fe spicy chicken, pork, and cilantro sausage ·

Chimichangas, flour tortillas stuffed with a savory filling and deep-fried, are very popular throughout the Southwest, especially in Arizona. These crisp cousins to the burrito are filled with shredded beef, chicken, sausage, or a combination of all three, generously doused with salsa and garnished with sour cream, jalapeños *en escabeche*, sliced radishes, and guacamole. The inspiration for our version comes from Joan and Michael Goodwin, authors of several cookbooks on southwestern and spicy cuisine.

1½ lbs. Santa Fe Spicy Chicken, Pork, and Cilantro Sausage or other spicy fresh sausage, removed from casings
1 medium onion, finely chopped
1 c. diced fresh tomato
1 c. grated Jack cheese
1 c. chopped fire-roasted (see page 208) mild chiles (optional)
½ c. chopped fresh cilantro (optional)

6 flour tortillas (regular-sized), very fresh
Vegetable oil for deep-frying
· **Garnishes** ·
Salsa
Jalapeños
Sliced radishes
Guacamole
Sour cream

Fry the sausage meat over medium-high heat in a heavy skillet for 5–7 minutes, crumbling it with a fork as it cooks. With a slotted spoon, transfer the cooked sausage meat to a bowl. Add the onion to the fat remaining in the pan, and cook until transparent, about 5 minutes. With a slotted spoon add the onion to the bowl, along with the tomato, cheese, and the optional chiles and cilantro. Mix well.

To assemble the chimichangas, lay each tortilla flat, and divide the filling into 6 equal amounts (each portion should be about ⅔ cup). Place filling in the center of each tortilla. Fold the sides over the filling, and then roll the tortilla. Secure with wooden toothpicks. Repeat until all the tortillas are filled.

Put about an inch of vegetable oil in a heavy, high-sided skillet, and heat to about 350° F. To test the oil, drop in a small bread cube. It should brown in about 1 minute. Fry 2 chimichangas at a time, seam side down, until they are light brown and crisp, regulating the heat so as not to burn them. This should take about 1 minute. Using a metal spatula or slotted spoon, turn the chimichangas over, and fry on the other side for another minute. Lift them out and drain on paper towels while you fry the remaining batches. Remove the toothpicks and serve with garnishes. Makes 6 servings

We prefer Santa Fe Spicy Chicken, Pork, and Cilantro Sausage, but any of the spicy fresh sausages in this chapter would do well as a filling, by themselves, or combined with beef or chicken. Mexican beer is the perfect match for chimichangas.

· The Southwest ·

· 229 ·

· turkey pie with chile cornbread crust ·

This dish not only makes delicious use of leftover turkey or chicken, but it tastes immeasurably better than any tamale pie you've ever tasted. It is a relative of that grammar school cafeteria favorite — but with a lot more interest and flavor. Moreover, the filling is versatile — leftover pork, veal, or duck also tastes wonderful tucked under a savory cornbread crust.

½ c. blanched almonds
5 cloves garlic, peeled but left whole
¾ lb. chorizo or other spicy fresh
   sausage, in bulk or removed from
   casings
1 large onion, finely chopped
1 c. crushed tomatoes in puree
1 c. turkey or chicken stock
2 tsp. ground coriander
Pinch cinnamon
½ c. chopped canned green chiles or
   2 fresh Anaheims, fire-roasted,
   peeled, and chopped (see
   page 208)

2 tbsp. chile powder blend
½ tsp. salt
¼ c. bread crumbs
3–4 c. diced cooked turkey or
   chicken
Pepper to taste
1 recipe Chile and Chorizo Cornbread
   (see opposite page), without the
   chorizo

To use fresh chicken or turkey thighs, poach for 45–60 minutes in lightly salted water or stock until tender. Cool, bone, skin, and chop coarsely.

In a small heavy frying pan, toast the almonds and garlic cloves, shaking the pan continuously until the nuts are lightly browned and the garlic is beginning to color. Transfer to a food processor and process until finely chopped but not pureed. Set aside.

In a large heavy skillet or Dutch oven, fry the chorizo over medium-high heat for about 5 minutes, crumbling it with a fork as it browns. Add the onion and continue to cook 5 minutes more, stirring frequently. Put in the tomatoes, stock, coriander, cinnamon, chiles, chili powder, and salt. Bring everything to a boil, and then reduce to a simmer. Cook 10 minutes. Add the garlic/nut mixture, and just enough bread crumbs to thicken the sauce. Stir in the poultry. Taste for salt and pepper. Set aside to cool, or refrigerate overnight.

When you are ready to bake the pie, put the filling into a 3–4-quart casserole and cover with the chile cornbread batter. Bake at 400° F for 45 minutes to 1 hour, or until the crust is golden. Serve at once. This dish rewarms well and is excellent as leftovers. Makes 6 servings

· chile and chorizo cornbread ·

Just about every book we've ever seen on Southwest cooking includes a recipe for one of the spicy cornbreads of the region. Once you've tasted one, you'll know why — they are really delicious. This version is more of a pudding than a bread because it is quite moist and cheesy in texture. It makes a wonderful side dish to replace potatoes or rice, or it is quite satisfying eaten as a light entree or lunch with a salad of fresh young greens. Use this recipe without the chorizo to top our Turkey with Chile Cornbread Crust (see opposite page).

½ lb. chorizo
3 tbsp. melted butter (if not using chorizo)
1 c. yellow cornmeal
1 tbsp. baking powder
2 c. grated sharp Cheddar cheese
2 eggs, lightly beaten
1 c. sour cream or yogurt

1 8-oz. can creamed corn
4 fresh Anaheim chiles, fire-roasted, peeled, and chopped (see page 208)
1 fresh jalapeño chile, seeded and finely chopped, or 1 4-oz. can green chiles, chopped
½ tsp. salt

Fry the chorizo in a heavy skillet over medium-high heat for 5 minutes to render some of the fat. Put the sausage meat and 3 tablespoons of the fat in a large bowl. If you leave out the chorizo, add 3 tablespoons of melted butter. Stir in the remaining ingredients, reserving ¾ cup of the cheese for sprinkling on before baking. Mix all the ingredients thoroughly.

Preheat the oven to 350° F. Generously butter a 1½-quart casserole or 9 x 9-inch baking dish or 10-inch heavy skillet. Spoon in the cornbread batter. Sprinkle the top with the reserved cheese, and bake for 45–55 minutes until the cornbread turns golden and smells wonderful. Makes 6–8 servings

It's a good idea to make an extra pan of this rich bread, because it rewarms so nicely. Just cut serving-sized squares, wrap them in foil, and bake at 350° F for 15 minutes, or microwave them unwrapped for a minute or two.

· navajo lamb stew ·

Out on the Navajo reservation, this savory stew could be made with any of the tougher cuts of mutton, goat, or venison, but for us city folks, lamb shanks or neck work very well. Little or no liquid is used in the recipe, and the meat slowly steeps in the tomatoes, chiles, and its own natural juices.

3 dried mulato and 3 ancho chiles, or
   6 ancho chiles (see page 208)
6–8 cloves garlic
3 medium onions, roughly chopped
2 bay leaves
1 tsp. dried oregano
1 tsp. ground cumin
½ tsp. salt
1 tsp. coarsely ground black pepper
4 lbs. whole lamb shanks or lamb neck
   cut into 2-inch pieces

1 lb. chorizo or El Paso Beef, Pork,
   and Chile Sausage, removed from
   casings
6 canned Italian-style tomatoes,
   coarsely chopped
2 1-lb. cans white hominy
3 c. winter squash (butternut,
   banana, or pumpkin), peeled and cut
   into 1½-inch dice

Soak the dried chiles in boiling water to cover for 10 minutes. Drain, reserving water, and remove the stems and seeds. In a food processor, puree the chiles with the garlic, onions, bay leaves, oregano, cumin, salt, and pepper, adding a teaspoon of the reserved soaking water. Place the lamb in a bowl and cover with the puree. Cover the bowl with plastic wrap and marinate the lamb for 2 hours at room temperature or overnight in the refrigerator.

Preheat the oven to 350° F. Place the lamb, sausage meat, and all the marinade in a heavy casserole or Dutch oven with a tight-fitting lid. Stir in the tomatoes and hominy. Cover the casserole with foil and put on the lid. Place in the middle of the oven and bake for 1½ hours, or until the meat is tender. Add water if the sauce is too thick. Add the winter squash and cook 20 minutes more until the squash is tender. Degrease the sauce, and taste for salt and pepper. Serve with rice and warm corn tortillas. Makes 4–6 servings

Use any type of winter squash — we prefer butternut or banana squash.

· Tex-Mex chili ·

In Texas, and in other parts of the Southwest, they take their chili very seriously. Questions like whether or not to add beans, ground meat versus chopped, fresh chiles or powder can lead to strong words and high dudgeon at chili cook-offs and festivals. We've added sausage to a traditional Texas chili from Michael and Joan Goodwin in *Regional American Classics*.

1½ lbs. chorizo or El Paso Beef, Pork, and Chile Sausage, ¼ lb. removed from casings

½ lb. Texas Smoky Link (see page 215) or other smoked sausage, diced

2 large onions, finely chopped

2 tbsp. chopped garlic

2 Anaheim, poblano, or other mild green chiles, fire-roasted, peeled, and chopped (see page 208)

2 jalapeño, serrano, or other hot green chiles, seeded and minced

2 lbs. venison, lamb, beef, or pork, or any combination, cut into ½-inch dice

1 28-oz. can whole tomatoes or crushed tomatoes in puree

1 can beer (12 oz.)

1 c. stock or water

2–3 tbsp. good commercial chile powder blend like Gebhardt's

2 tsp. ground cumin

½ tsp. dried oregano

1 tsp. sugar

2 tbsp. masa harina or cornmeal

3 tbsp. cider vinegar

Salt, pepper, and vinegar to taste

· **Garnishes** ·

Shredded Cheddar cheese

Chopped red onion

Sliced avocado

In a large Dutch oven or heavy pot, brown about ¼ pound of the chorizo or El Paso sausage over medium-high heat, crumbling the meat with a fork as it cooks, for about 5 minutes. Add the diced smoked sausage, and cook for 2 minutes more. Reduce the heat to medium and stir in the onions. Cook until soft, about 5 minutes. Add the garlic and chiles, and fry for 5 minutes, stirring occasionally. Put in the diced meat and cook over medium heat until no longer pink, stirring constantly. Pour in the tomatoes, beer, and stock or water and add chile powder to taste, cumin, oregano, and sugar. Bring to a boil, reduce to a simmer, and cook for an hour. Add more stock or beer if the chili becomes too thick.

You don't need venison to be authentic here — beef, pork, or lamb will work just as well. Feel free to improvise with whatever comes to mind—chili cooks have been known to toss just about anything into a "bowl of red," from goat haunch to diced rattlesnake.

Meanwhile, slice the remaining chorizo or El Paso sausages into 1-inch rounds and fry over medium-high heat for 5 minutes in a heavy frying pan to render some of the fat. Drain the fat and add the sausage. Cook 15 minutes or until tender.

In a small bowl make a paste of the masa harina or cornmeal with the vinegar and about ½ cup of liquid from the chili. Stir this into the pot and cook 10 minutes. Taste for salt, pepper, and vinegar and serve or refrigerate overnight.

Serve the chili over cooked rice or with cooked beans. Garnish with cheese, onions, and avocado slices. Makes 8–10 servings

· pork and chorizo pozole ·

Janet Fletcher is a talented writer with several cookbooks under her belt in addition to her weekly restaurant reviews in the *Oakland Tribune*. She is also a versatile cook, whose repertoire stretches from appetizers to Italian feasts. She recommends making this dish a day ahead. It's great for cold weather.

3½ lbs. country-style spareribs, sawed into 2-inch pieces (ask the butcher to do this)
1 onion, sliced
3 cloves garlic, crushed
10 black peppercorns
2 bay leaves
1 lb. chorizo or El Paso Beef, Pork, and Chile Sausage, removed from casings
1 onion, minced
2 cloves garlic, minced
1 poblano or Anaheim chile, fire-roasted, peeled, and chopped (see page 208)

½ jalapeño chile, chopped
1 tsp. dried oregano
1 tsp. ground cumin
1 tbsp. flour
2 tomatoes, diced
3 tbsp. minced fresh cilantro
1½ c. cooked whole hominy
Salt and freshly ground pepper to taste

· Garnishes ·
2 c. shredded cabbage
20 cilantro sprigs
Lime wedges

Put the spareribs, sliced onion, crushed garlic, peppercorns, and bay leaves in a large pot, add 8 cups of water, and simmer over medium-high heat. Skim off any foam that collects on the surface, lower the heat, and simmer for 40 minutes, skimming if necessary. Drain, discard vegetables and herbs, and reserve the pork and broth separately.

Fry the chorizo over medium heat, crumbling the meat as it cooks. Place in a sieve over a bowl to drain off the fat. Put 3 tablespoons of the fat into a large pot or Dutch oven over medium heat. Add the minced onion and garlic along with the chiles, oregano, and cumin, and cook, stirring constantly, until the onion and chiles are soft, about 10 minutes. Stir in the flour and cook for 3 more minutes. Put in the spareribs, tomatoes, cilantro, and 5 cups of the pork broth (save any remaining broth). Bring everything to a simmer, reduce the heat, and cook, partially covered, until the pork is very tender, about 45 minutes. Add the hominy, and cook for 15 minutes more. Cool and chill in the refrigerator.

This recipe for pozole — a spicy hominy stew — comes from Janet's little gem of a book Grain Gastronomy, *published by Aris Books.*

The next day, lift off any solidified fat, and reheat the soup, adding a little more broth if necessary. Taste and adjust seasonings, adding salt and pepper as necessary. Serve in large bowls with a mound of cabbage in each, a few sprigs of cilantro, and lime wedges. Makes 4–6 servings

· New Mexico chicken, pork, and roasted chile sausage in chile verde ·

Chile verde is usually made by braising chunks of pork slowly with green chiles and tomatillos, and is often used in burritos or served over rice. This easy-to-make chile verde gains much of its flavor from the spicy sausages — it's delicious by itself or in enchiladas with sour cream.

1½ lbs. New Mexico Chicken, Pork, and Roasted Chile Sausage or Sante Fe Spicy Chicken, Pork, and Cilantro Sausage
1 medium onion, finely chopped
2 cloves garlic, chopped
1 tsp. ground cumin
1 c. chicken stock
6 canned or parboiled and peeled tomatillos, finely chopped
6 Anaheim or poblano chiles or other mild fresh green chiles, fire-roasted, seeded, peeled, and chopped (see page 208), or a 7-oz. can green chiles, seeded and chopped
1 bunch cilantro or flat-leaf Italian parsley
Salt, pepper, and lime juice to taste

In a dry skillet, brown the sausages whole over medium heat for about 5 minutes on a side. Remove and let them cool a bit. Cut into ½-inch-thick rounds, or, if you intend to use the chile verde in enchiladas, dice the sausage.

In the fat remaining in the skillet, cook the onion and garlic until soft, about 10 minutes. Mix in the cumin and add the stock and tomatillos. Bring to a boil, add the chiles, and reduce the heat to a simmer. Discard any roots from the cilantro or parsley, and finely chop the stems. Add to the pot and cook 10 more minutes, then put in the sausage. Coarsely chop the cilantro or parsley leaves, reserve about ¼ cup for a garnish, and add the remainder to the pot. Cook for 5 more minutes. Taste for salt, pepper, and add enough lime juice to give a tang to the sauce. Garnish with the remaining cilantro or parsley and serve. Makes enough for 6 burritos or 12 enchiladas or 4 servings as a main course over rice

· stacked cheese and chorizo enchiladas ·

Stacked enchiladas are quicker and easier to put together than the rolled kind. You can use up stale tortillas and you eliminate the messy (and calorie adding) step of frying the tortillas first in oil. This type of enchilada originates in the state of Sonora in northern Mexico, and is very popular in neighboring New Mexico. We prefer to use the New Mexico or Santa Fe chicken and pork sausages here, but chorizo also works well.

¾ lb. New Mexico Chicken, Pork, and Roasted Chile Sausage, Santa Fe Chicken, Pork, and Cilantro Sausage, or other spicy sausage, removed from casings
1 c. chopped onions
½ c. thinly sliced green onions or scallions
3 fire-roasted mild green chiles like Anaheim or poblano, chopped (see page 208)

2 c. chopped fresh cilantro (optional)
4 c. shredded Jack cheese
3 c. Tex-Mex Red Enchilada Sauce (see page 239)
12 corn tortillas

· **Garnishes** ·
Sour cream (optional)
Sliced green onions or scallions

In a heavy frying pan, fry the sausage over medium-high heat for 5 minutes, breaking the meat up as it cooks. Pour off excess fat. Combine the cooked sausage with the onions, green onions, chiles, optional cilantro, and 3 cups of the shredded cheese.

To assemble the enchiladas, heat the sauce in a 10-inch pan. Grease the bottom of a baking pan. Dip a tortilla in the warm sauce to coat it and place it flat in the baking pan. Spread a layer of the sausage/cheese filling over the tortilla, and top with another sauce-coated tortilla. Repeat the process until the stack is as high as you wish (6 tortillas high is about the limit). Build another stack, or make a number of 2- or 3-high stacks, depending on your preference. Sprinkle on the remaining cup of cheese, and bake at 375° F, until the cheese is melted. Larger stacks take more time in the oven, about 30 minutes; smaller stacks, about 20 minutes. The enchiladas can also be made up a day ahead, and refrigerated until the final baking. Add an extra 7 minutes to the baking time if they start out cold. Garnish with optional sour cream and green onions. Makes 4–6 servings

Stack the enchiladas high and cut into wedges, or use 2 or 3 tortillas for individual portions — either way is great for brunch garnished with a fried egg and salsa.

Robin's black bean chili ·

Robin Cherin, who patiently and carefully tested all the recipes for this cookbook, has contributed one of her favorites. The combination of chorizo and smoked meats gives this chili a wonderful, savory taste. Robin usually uses tasso, but this recipe works quite well with the Texas Smoky Link from this chapter. Any high-quality smoked sausage or tasso will do just fine in this deliciously spicy chili. The chorizo should be extra-lean or use a high-quality store-bought variety.

4 c. dried black beans, picked over, soaked overnight, and drained
1 bay leaf
1 tsp. dried epazote (optional)
¾ lb. chorizo
½ lb. Texas Smoky Link (see page 215), other smoked sausage, or tasso
2 tbsp. olive oil
2 large onions, chopped
4 large cloves garlic, chopped
1 red bell pepper, fire-roasted, peeled, and chopped (see page 208)
1 green bell pepper, fire-roasted, peeled, and chopped
1 Anaheim chile, fire-roasted, peeled, and chopped

2 fresh jalapeño chiles, seeded, and finely chopped, or 2 chipotle chiles packed in adobo sauce (Herdez brand), chopped (optional)
1 tsp. ground cumin
1 tbsp. sweet Hungarian paprika
1 tbsp. chopped fresh oregano or 1 tsp. dried
3 c. canned crushed tomatoes in puree
Salt and pepper to taste

· **Garnishes** ·
Grated cheese
Sour cream
Fresh cilantro
Salsa Cruda (see page 216)

Rinse the beans well and put into a large pot. Cover with water 4–5 inches above the beans. Bring to a boil and add the bay leaf and optional epazote. Reduce the heat, cover, and simmer 1–1½ hours until the beans are tender. Drain the beans, reserving 2 cups of the cooking liquid, and set aside.

Brown the chorizo and smoked sausage in a large pot or Dutch oven in the olive oil over medium-high heat. Stir with a fork to break up the chorizo, and cook for about 5 minutes. Add the onions and garlic and cook 5 minutes more, stirring frequently. Add the peppers and chiles, including the chipotles in adobo if you are using them, along with the cumin, paprika, oregano, and tomatoes. Put in the beans and 1 cup of the reserved liquid. Bring everything to a boil, reduce to a simmer, and cook, uncovered, for 45 minutes, until the liquid begins to thicken. If it is too thick, add more reserved bean liquid. Taste for salt and pepper. Serve over rice. Pass the various garnishes and let the guests add their own.

Makes 8–10 servings

Epazote — a pungent herb found in Mexican groceries and from mail order sources (see page 357) — is especially good with black beans, but definitely an acquired taste. You can substitute oregano or leave it out altogether.

poblano chiles stuffed with New Mexico chicken, pork, and roasted chile sausage

Poblano chiles have a rich peppery flavor and are preferred for this dish, but you could also use Anaheim or green New Mexico chiles. If fresh chiles are hard to come by in your area, substitute green or red bell peppers. Anaheims tend to run a bit smaller than poblanos, so use two per serving.

Serve with our Rice with Shrimp and Chorizo (page 228), sliced avocado, and refried beans. Use any of the fresh sausages from this chapter or a lean commercial chorizo.

6 large poblano chiles, 12 Anaheim chiles, or 6 bell peppers, tops removed
1 tbsp. olive oil
1 c. finely diced onion
1 tsp. minced garlic
2 lbs. New Mexico Chicken, Pork, and Roasted Chile Sausage (see page 210) or chorizo, removed from casings
1 c. cooked rice
1 c. crumbled *queso fresco* or diced Jack cheese
1 egg

· **Sauce** ·
3 c. coarsely chopped Italian-style tomatoes with juice
1 tbsp. minced garlic
2 tbsp. pure New Mexico chile powder
¼ tsp. salt
½ tsp. coarsely ground black pepper

· **Garnish** ·
1 bunch cilantro, coarsely chopped (1 c.) (optional)

Blanch the chiles in a large saucepan of boiling, well-salted water for 10 minutes. Remove and cool under running water. Reserve.

In a heavy frying pan, heat the olive oil over medium heat. Put in the onion and fry until soft, about 10 minutes. Add the garlic. Remove from the heat and transfer to a bowl. Mix the sausage with the onion and garlic, along with the cooked rice and cheese. Add the egg and blend everything together with your hands. Let the mixture cool for 5 minutes and then stuff it into the chiles.

If you're fortunate enough to live near a Mexican market, use the delicious fresh Mexican cheese, queso fresco, instead of Jack cheese.

Put the sauce ingredients into a small nonreactive pan and bring to a boil. Reduce the heat and simmer the sauce uncovered for 10 minutes. Preheat the oven to 350° F. Pour the sauce on the bottom of a glass or enamel baking dish and arrange the stuffed chiles on their sides. Cover the dish with foil and bake for 30 minutes. Remove the foil and bake for an additional 10 minutes. Spoon the sauce over the chiles and serve garnished with optional cilantro.

Makes 4–6 servings

grilled Anaheim chiles with cheese and chorizo stuffing ·

Grilled or baked, these simple stuffed chiles make a complete meal, or a delicious side dish with fish or grilled chicken. They are also excellent eaten cold with a lemony vinaigrette or salsa.

1 lb. chorizo, in bulk or removed from
   casings
½ c. bread crumbs
½ lb. shredded Jack cheese

2 c. ricotta or *queso fresco*
10–12 large Anaheim chiles
Oil

Sauté the chorizo until the fat is rendered, about 5 minutes. Drain in a sieve over a bowl and cool. Mix with the bread crumbs and cheeses. Blanch the chiles in boiling salted water for 5 minutes, drain, and cool. Carefully cut a slit from the top of the chile lengthwise halfway down to make an opening for the stuffing. Stuff with the chorizo mixture, being careful not to split the chile. Close the opening with wooden toothpicks. Brush with oil and grill over a hot fire until dark brown, about 8 minutes per side, or bake in a 350° F oven for 30 minutes. Serve with Salsa Cruda. Makes 4 servings

Serve hot or cold with Salsa Cruda (see page 216) and a pale Mexican lager for a wonderfully spicy lunch or light dinner.

· Tex-Mex red enchilada sauce ·

One of the foundations of Tex-Mex cooking — use for enchiladas, tacos, tamales, empanadas, etc. Make double or triple this recipe; it keeps for 2–3 weeks in the refrigerator, or freeze in 1- or 2-cup batches for later use.

2 tbsp. olive oil
1 onion, chopped
2 tbsp. chopped garlic
2 tbsp. flour
½ c. high-quality chile powder
   blend, such as Gebhardt's
1 14-oz. can tomato puree
1 14-oz. can tomato sauce
1 28-oz. can red chile sauce (also
   called enchilada sauce)
¼ c. red wine vinegar
1 c. water

Heat olive oil over medium heat. Add onion and garlic and cook 10 minutes, stirring occasionally. Stir in flour and chile powder, cook 2 minutes, scraping pan. Add other ingredients, bring to a boil, stirring. Reduce to a simmer, and cook, uncovered, 30 minutes, stirring occasionally, until desired thickness. Makes 6–8 cups

· chorizo-stuffed potatoes ·

The native populations of Latin America were enjoying this delicious staple long before the Conquistadores arrived. In many South American countries, potatoes are stuffed and then eaten as a main course or an appetizer. This Southwest variation is a main course, but it can also serve as an appetizer using smaller potatoes. These potatoes can be made up a day ahead, refrigerated, and then baked just before you want to eat them.

4 very large baking potatoes
4 tbsp. butter
½ c. *each* cooked diced carrots and peas
2–3 diced canned green chiles or fire-roasted fresh green chiles (see page 208)

1½ c. cooked chorizo, drained
½ c. grated Jack cheese
1 c. Simple Béchamel Sauce, yogurt, or sour cream
Grated Parmesan cheese

Bake the potatoes until soft, about 45 minutes at 400° F, and cut them in half lengthwise. Hollow them out carefully, and mash the potatoes with the butter. Gently stir in the vegetables, chiles, chorizo, and grated Jack cheese. Pile the mixture into the shells. Spoon béchamel, yogurt, or sour cream over each potato.

The potatoes can be refrigerated at this point. Place on a baking sheet and bake for 35 minutes in a 400° F oven if cold, less if at room temperature. Top with grated Parmesan cheese for the last 5 minutes of baking.

Makes 4 servings

· simple béchamel sauce ·
1½ tbsp. butter
1½ tbsp. flour
1 c. milk
Salt and pepper to taste

Melt butter, stir in flour, and cook over medium heat for 3 minutes. Whisk in milk and cook 5 minutes, or until thickened. Season to taste with salt and pepper.

Makes 1½ cups

THE WEST COAST
· where sea meets land ·

Betsy's savory cheesecake

Sausages in sherry

Loni Kuhn's crusty rolls with chard and sausage

Sheepherder's omelette of wild greens, potatoes, and chorizo

Salinas Valley braised stuffed lettuce

SALADS & SOUPS

Mushroom, provolone, and smoked sausage salad

Priscilla's wilted salad of savoy cabbage, pears, and sausage

Cold Chinese noodles and sausage with sesame dressing

Quick and easy salads

Winter vegetable, sausage, and chestnut soup

Won ton soup

Japantown miso soup with pork and shiitake sausage

MAIN DISHES

Chinese braised stuffed fish

Grilled or steamed fish with smoky black bean sauce

Crab and Italian sausage cioppino

Braised squid stuffed with Basque chorizo and prosciutto

Asian sausage and shark kebabs

Salmon sausage in champagne sauce

California quail and artichokes in lemon sauce

Grilled turkey paupiettes

Anzonini's chicken livers and chorizo

Sausage, red pepper, and eggplant stir-fry

Chinatown crépinettes braised with Napa cabbage

Artichoke and sausage ragù

Basque sheepherder's lamb stew

Oakland barbecue with Franco's sauce

John King's Asian barbecue

he continent ends here at the edge of the Pacific, and dwellers along this rugged and beautiful coast have always looked to the sea. Currents bring warm water close inshore, the rivers sweep nourishment into the depths, and waters off Monterey Bay, Puget Sound, Coos Bay, and San Diego harbor are teeming with fish and seafood. Each morning before dawn the small boats set out from the wharves and harbors, and return at evening heavy with halibut and salmon, Dungeness crab or spiny lobster, rock cod, sea bass, and grouper. This bountiful harvest of the sea can be found in our Seattle's Pike Place Salmon Sausage (page 247) and Crab and Italian Sausage Cioppino (page 273).

But the coast, with its spacious harbors and ports like San Francisco, San Diego, Los Angeles, Portland, and Seattle, gives more than just nourishment. It also brings trade and immigration, the influences of other cultures and all the rich complexities that create great cities and marketplaces. Cooking along the West Coast is eclectic, borrowing elements from all the countries that contribute to its rich ethnic mix.

The Asian influence on West Coast life and cooking is immense. Ever since gold rush days, Chinese immigrants have been important as cooks in West Coast restaurants, both Oriental and American. The great Chinese tradition of careful preparation and impeccably chosen ingredients is one of the most powerful elements in West Coast cooking. The delicate and flavorful way Chinese cooks handle fish and seafood, which are so much a part of West Coast life, has inspired dishes such as Chinese Braised Stuffed Whole Fish (see page 271) and Grilled or Steamed Fish with Smoky Black Bean Sauce (see page 272). Their ability to keep vegetables crisp, fresh, and full of character, often combined with aromatic sausages, can be seen in dishes such as Chinatown Crépinettes Braised with Napa Cabbage (see page 282) and Winter Vegetable, Sausage, and Chestnut Soup (see page 268). Other Asian traditions are becoming increasingly popular along the coast, with Japanese, Thai, Cambodian, and Vietnamese cooks influencing

many dishes. Our Japantown Pork and Shiitake Mushroom Sausage (see page 249) and Asian Sausage and Shark Kebabs (see page 276) are good examples of how West Coast cooks incorporate and blend a wide array of Asian elements into their foods.

The fishing boats that ply the waters off the coast from San Diego to Seattle are still piloted mostly by Italians. San Francisco's Fisherman's Wharf is a somewhat gaudy tourist attraction today, but if you push through the vendors of gimcracks and geegaws and the flocks of eager visitors shivering in their Hawaiian shirts and Bermuda shorts, you can still see a real fishing fleet set out each morning. San Francisco's North Beach, a neighborhood just uphill from the wharf, is still filled with small Italian restaurants serving cioppino, a savory fisherman's stew. The West Coast's love affair with garlic, fresh herbs, and tomatoes owes much to the passion for food of its Italian population.

The Spanish influence is strong, especially in California and Nevada, derived from the Mexican heritage as well as the large number of Basques who came to herd the region's sheep. Basque restaurants and hotels that cater to these hearty eaters are found all over the West, and they serve great quantities of wonderful food at very cheap prices. For the flavor of Spanish Basque cooking, try our Nevada Basque Chorizo (see page 253), Sheepherder's Omelette of Wild Greens, Potatoes, and Chorizo (see page 262), Braised Squid Stuffed with Basque Chorizo and Prosciutto (see page 275), Basque Sheepherder's Lamb Stew (see page 284), and Anzonini's Chicken Livers and Chorizo (see page 280).

Because of the mild climate and the casual lifestyle of coast dwellers, outdoor cooking—grilling fish, seafood, meat, or poultry—is the most popular style of cooking. Our West Coast Barbecue (see page 286) gives you the flavor of this outdoor style. Salads too have long been an integral part of coastal cookery. Priscilla's Wilted Salad of Savoy Cabbage, Pears, and Sausage (see page 265) and Mushroom, Provolone, and Smoked Sausage Salad (see page 264) show how fresh, crisp produce, often in original combinations, is a constant presence on dinner tables throughout the West.

Sausage is popular with West Coast cooks, and we enjoy many of the ethnic and traditional sausages found throughout America. Italian sausage is a favorite with cooks in San Francisco, often paired with pasta. You can find succulent potato sausages in Portland and rich seafood sausages in Seattle. Oakland's great barbecue joints offer the fiery and smoky Oakland

hot link. In San Francisco's Chinatown you'll see the aromatic sweet *lop cheong* sausages whose flavors inspired our Asian sausage recipes; Philippine butchers in Daly City make delicious luganesa; Portuguese communities in San Leandro and Santa Clara consume huge quantities of linguiça. Cooks throughout the region, especially in Latino neighborhoods such as San Francisco's Mission District, Chula Vista, and East L.A., use plenty of chorizo, both the Mexican and Spanish type.

One of the reasons that West Coast cooks have contributed so much to the revival of good cooking in America is this rich mix of influences and abundant cornucopia of ingredients. Creative chefs in West Coast kitchens are constantly drawing on the varied traditions of coastal cookery, and combining the resources of sea and land in new and exciting ways. This spirit of adventure, the love of fresh pure products, and healthy eclecticism can be a model for cooks everywhere.

· Chinatown crépinettes ·

Lion's head, a succulent meatball made from pork and aromatic seasonings, is one inspiration for these savory sausages. Another is *lop cheong*, the thin, mahogany-red sausages you see hanging in Chinese pork butchers' windows. The fragrant seasonings used in both dishes — five spice powder, cinnamon, star anise — add a subtle, sweet undertone to the sausage, making it especially good in braises or stir-fries.

We prefer to wrap the sausage meat in the veil-like caul fat of the pig to make crépinettes, but you could just as easily leave it in bulk. Substitute patties of the sausage meat wherever we call for crépinettes, or leave it in bulk to use as a seasoning with vegetables or rice. You could also stuff the sausage into sheep casings and twist it into links.

3 lbs. pork shoulder
½ lb. pork back fat
2 bunches cilantro or flat-leaf parsley, coarsely chopped (about 2 cups)
4 green onions or scallions, finely chopped
2 tsp. minced garlic
4 tsp. kosher salt
1 tsp. freshly ground black pepper

2 tsp. Szechuan peppercorns, roasted and ground
2 tsp. Chinese five spice powder or 2 tsp. ground star anise
Pinch cinnamon
¼ c. Chinese rice wine or Madeira
1 lb. caul fat, soaked (optional), or small sheep casings (optional)

For details on making sausage, see page 332.

Grind the meat and fat through a ⅜-inch plate. Mix the meat and fat with the other ingredients (except caul fat or sheep's casings), and blend everything together thoroughly with your hands. Chill the sausage meat for at least an hour or overnight. For crépinettes, spread out sheets of the lacy caul fat and cut into 6-inch squares. Wrap each square around ⅓ cup of the meat mixture. Shape into ovals and fry or grill over charcoal. For bulk sausage, divide the sausage meat into serving-sized portions and freeze for later use. To make links, stuff the mixture into small sheep casings and tie into 6-inch links. Sausage meat will keep 2–3 days in the refrigerator, 2 months frozen. Makes 3½ pounds

Five spice powder is widely available in Asian grocery stores.

Seattle's Pike Place salmon sausage ·

Fish and seafood sausages are popular these days because their subtle and delicious flavors suit the modern taste for lighter dishes. In addition, many diners feel that fish sausages are low in calories, although most recipes do call for goodly amounts of cream. While fish sausages may seem trendy, they are really similar to the quenelles, or fish dumplings, of classic French cuisine. The best are light in texture and subtly seasoned to accent the flavor of the fish and seafood.

The trick to making perfect fish sausages is to have all the ingredients well chilled so that they will stay light and properly absorb the cream. Serve these delicate sausages, inspired by the beautiful array of salmon and seafood at Seattle's Pike Place market, warm with a Champagne Sauce (see page 277), or cold with our Tidewater Tartar Sauce (see page 27).

1½ lbs. fresh salmon, boned and skinned
2 egg whites, well chilled
1⅓ c. heavy cream, well chilled
2 tsp. kosher salt
½ tsp. finely ground white pepper
1 tsp. sweet Hungarian paprika
¼ tsp. freshly grated nutmeg
½ c. finely chopped fresh parsley
¼ c. chopped mushrooms or ½ oz. dried cèpes or porcini mushrooms, soaked in hot water for 1 hour, coarsely chopped

1 c. scallops, cut into ½-inch chunks
¼ c. fresh shrimp cut into ¼-inch pieces, or ¼ c. lobster meat cut into ¼-inch pieces
3 tbsp. Pernod or other anise-flavored liqueur
½ tsp. ground fennel seed
3 tbsp. minced green onion or scallions, or chives
2 tbsp. fresh tarragon or chervil or 2 tsp. dried tarragon
Sheep casings (optional)

Put the food processor bowl and metal blade into the freezer for at least 30 minutes before beginning. Cut about 1 pound of the salmon into ¾-inch chunks, the remainder into ¼-inch pieces. Freeze the large pieces for 15 minutes and refrigerate the others for the same amount of time.

In the food processor, using the metal blade, process the partially frozen large chunks of salmon until smooth. With the motor running, gradually add the egg whites until they are incorporated. Then pour in the cream in a steady stream until blended. Add the salt, pepper, paprika, and nutmeg.

Transfer the salmon puree to a bowl and stir in the small salmon chunks along with the parsley, mushrooms, scallops, and the shrimp or lobster meat. Add the Pernod, fennel seed, green onions or chives, tarragon or chervil, and stir well. Make a small ball of the mixture, and poach in simmering water for 5 minutes. Taste and correct the salt, pepper, and other seasonings.

Stuff the mixture into sheep casings (not hog — they're too coarse), and tie into 5-inch links. Alternatively, spread the fish sausage on lightly oiled plastic wrap and roll into a long cylinder, approximately 1 inch in diameter. Tie the ends with string.

Bring a large pot of lightly salted water to a boil. Add the sausage and adjust the heat to just below a simmer, about 180° F. Poach the small links 15 minutes, the larger plastic-wrapped sausage 25 minutes. Remove the plastic wrap carefully before slicing. Eat immediately or serve cold. The linked sausage can be reheated by poaching for 5–7 minutes in 180° F water. This sausage keeps 2–3 days refrigerated, but does not freeze well. Makes 2–3 pounds

· Chinese pork and shrimp sausage ·

Pork and shrimp are often mixed as a stuffing for dim sum, the popular steamed dumplings served in the sometimes palatial teahouses of San Francisco's Chinatown. This sausage of ours has a bit more flavor and spice than the typical dim sum filling and can be used in a wide variety of dishes. You can grill and eat it by itself, either stuffed in casings or left in bulk and then formed into patties.

2 lbs. pork shoulder
½ lb. shrimp, peeled and deveined
½ lb. pork back fat
4 tbsp. Chinese soy sauce
2 tsp. finely chopped fresh ginger
1 tsp. minced garlic
¼ c. sweet sherry

¼ c. finely chopped green onions or
    scallions, or Chinese garlic chives
½ tsp. Chinese chile paste (available
    in Chinese groceries or specialty
    shops), or 2–3 dashes of hot sauce
    such as Tabasco
Medium hog casings (optional)

For directions on sausage making, see page 332.

Grind the pork, shrimp, and fat through a ¼-inch plate into a large bowl. Add the remaining ingredients, except the casings, and knead the mixture until everything is well blended together. Stuff into medium hog casings or leave in bulk for patties or meatballs, or to use as a filling. Keeps 3 days refrigerated, 2 months frozen. Makes 3 pounds

This richly flavored sausage is a great filling for won ton, egg rolls, pot stickers or any type of meat-filled dumpling — or it can be turned into delicious small meatballs as a garnish for Chinese soup or braised with turnip or mustard greens.

· Japantown pork and shiitake mushroom sausage ·

All along the West Coast and in Hawaii there are large Japanese-American communities, some going back many decades. Many Japanese dishes have joined the mainstream of American cooking, like teriyaki, tempura and, increasingly, sushi and sashimi. The style, flavor, and seasonings of Japanese cooking are found all over the West Coast in restaurants and in home kitchens, and the visual beauty and aesthetic balance of this great cuisine have had a great influence on creative chefs everywhere.

You can use this aromatic sausage in bulk to stuff won tons or pot stickers (see pages 269, 257), called gyoza in Japanese kitchens. Or you can stuff the meat into casings for grilling to eat as is or use in Priscilla's Wilted Salad of Savoy Cabbage, Pears, and Sausage (see page 265).

½ oz. dried shiitake mushrooms (4–6)
2 lbs. pork shoulder
¾ lb. chicken thighs, boned, but with skins
¼ lb. pork back fat
4 tbsp. Japanese-style soy sauce or shoyu

1 tsp. sugar
¼ c. mirin, sake, or sweet sherry
1 tbsp. Oriental sesame oil
1 tsp. finely chopped or grated fresh ginger
2 tbsp. rice vinegar
1 tsp. finely grated lime or lemon zest
Medium hog casings (optional)

For directions on sausage making, see page 332.

Soak the mushrooms in hot water for 30 minutes. Remove and discard the tough stems; drain and chop the mushrooms finely.

Grind the pork, chicken, and fat through a ¼-inch plate. Add the shiitake mushrooms and all the other ingredients, except the casings. Mix to blend well, and stuff into medium hog casings or leave in bulk. Refrigerated, sausage will keep 3 days; frozen, 2–3 months. Makes 3½ pounds

These slightly sweet sausages incorporate some of the ingredients that make Japanese food so rich and satisfying: shiitake mushrooms, mirin or sweet cooking sake, shoyu or Japanese-style soy sauce, fresh ginger, and roasted sesame oil.

· West Coast market:
bounty of the sea and land ·

The market cascades down the hill to the water, an incredible profusion of shops and stands, noise and laughter, hagglers and hawkers using all the languages of the coast —English, Spanish, Chinese, Italian, Thai, Basque. As we walk down the steep streets shopping for the evening's cioppino, we pass rows of glistening fish laid out on beds of shaved ice, bright silver salmon—kings, cohos, chinooks—one splayed open, pale pink against the ice; tiny sand dabs and other flatfish—rex sole, flounder; huge brown halibut with bulging eyes, grouper, ling cod and black cod, "red snappers" and other rockfish, pug-nosed cabezon, fat golden perch, greenlings and sea trout, the rich harvest of the Pacific. Tanks hold crawling piles of live crabs with cooked Dungeness crabs stacked neatly nearby among heaps of prawns and gleaming squid, dark green octopus sprawled here and there on the ice. Clams and mussels, oysters of every size and shape are piled in baskets lined with kelp. Pale swordfish steaks rimmed with black skin, fillets of

salmon, sole, butterfish, translucent hunks of shark and mounds of cooked, pink bay shrimp line the display cases inside the shops. We pick out crabs and prawns, clams and mussels, good-sized chunks of shark and halibut for tonight's fisherman's stew.

Farther downhill we pass Italian delis with loops of sausage and salami hanging in the windows. Chinese pork butchers offer *lop cheong*—air-dried, long and twisted mahogany-colored sausages—bright red *cha shao,* and red-brown Smithfield hams. Spanish and Mexican markets have long tables with rows of green and red chiles artfully arranged, jars of spices and chile powder, dried chorizos hanging from the ceiling among the brightly colored *piñatas* and long strings of dark red chiles. Outside the Chinese poultry shops, cages hold live chickens, quail, squab, and guinea hens, all squawking and fluttering, feathers scattering up the street in the brisk sea breeze.

When we arrive at the vegetable stands it's hard to know where to start. We need tomatoes, onions, garlic, fresh basil, and fresh oregano for the stew. Deep red tomatoes fill bins on either side of the street in all sizes and shapes from fat, round Beefsteaks to pear-shaped Romas. We can see heaps of tiny yellow cherry tomatoes and papery green tomatillos dotted here and there. The produce seems to stretch out for blocks: green beans — Blue Lake, Kentucky Wonder, Chinese long beans; broccoli—

bright green mixed with exotic purple and yellow types; eggplants — glossy black and plump ones alongside deep purple Japanese and Chinese eggplants, and small, round, pale Thai varieties. We can choose lettuces and greens of every color and shape; fresh herbs; onions large and small — green, yellow, white, and red; pink Mexican garlic or white garlic from Gilroy; leeks from Sacramento and the slopes of the Cascades; gray-green artichokes from coastal valleys.

We trudge back uphill carrying bags of fish and seafood, sausages and vegetables, the sun going down behind us into the Pacific, the sounds and smells of the market borne inland on the freshening wind.

HOT LINKS & COUNTRY FLAVORS

Nevada Basque chorizo ·

Spanish or Basque chorizo is very different from the more common Mexican variety. The Spanish style is milder, less *picante*, and is often air-dried or smoked to concentrate and intensify the flavors.

If properly air-dried and/or smoked, this sausage doesn't need refrigeration. As a result, dried, smoked chorizo became a staple in the diet of Basque sheepherders who tended their flocks far from civilization and electricity. Since most of us (and even the sheepherders most likely) do have refrigerators these days, you have your choice of air-drying the chorizo and using curing salts, or leaving the curing salts out and hot smoking the sausage. If you choose the latter route, however, you should store the chorizo in the refrigerator, where it will keep for 10 days to 2 weeks.

2½ lbs. pork shoulder
½ lb. beef plate or chuck
¼ c. dried New Mexico chile puree
½ c. sweet Spanish or Hungarian paprika
¼ c. minced garlic
2 tsp. sugar
2 tsp. coarsely ground black pepper

Pinch ground cloves
3 tbsp. dry red wine
1 tsp. curing salts dissolved in ¼ c. water (optional) (see "Note on Nitrites," page 343)
4 tsp. kosher salt
Medium to wide hog casings

For directions on sausage making, see page 332.

Grind the pork and beef through a ⅜-inch plate. Add the remaining ingredients, except the casings, and mix well, kneading the meats and spices until everything is thoroughly blended. Stuff into medium to wide hog casings, and tie into 10-inch links. If you've added the curing salts you can then air-dry the sausages in a cool place until they are firm. This may take as long as 2–3 weeks. Alternatively, you can leave the curing salts out, and hot smoke the sausages until their internal temperature reaches 160° F. After hot smoking, you can store them for up to 2 weeks in the refrigerator or in the freezer for up to 2 months. Air-dried chorizo will keep for several months in the refrigerator. Makes 2–3 pounds

Small amounts of spicy Nevada Basque Chorizo will liven up beans, soups, stews, and, of course, the delicious rice dish, paella.

· New Mexico chile puree ·

To make a small amount, soak one mulato or ancho chile in boiling water to cover for 10 minutes. Drain, reserving water, and remove stems and seeds, then puree in a food processor, adding a teaspoon of the reserved soaking water.

· California white wine and herb sausage ·

The mild climate of most of the West Coast encourages local cooks to grow their own fresh herbs and vegetables. One of the great pleasures of cooking is walking out into your garden and picking fresh produce for your family's dinner. Chervil, tarragon, and basil are summer herbs in California, but many of the better produce markets in urban areas carry them year round.

1½ lbs. pork shoulder
½ lb. pork back fat
1 tsp. coarsely ground black pepper
2 tsp. kosher salt
2 tsp. minced garlic
1 tsp. chopped fresh sage or ½ tsp. dried
1 tsp. chopped fresh thyme or ½ tsp. dried

1 tsp. chopped fresh marjoram or ½ tsp. dried
¼ c. chopped fresh parsley
2 tbsp. chopped fresh herbs such as chervil, tarragon, and basil, in any combination
½ c. dry white California wine
Medium hog casings

For directions on sausage making, see page 332.

Grind the meat and fat through a ¼-inch plate. In a large bowl, mix the meat and fat with all the other ingredients except the casings, kneading well to blend everything thoroughly. Stuff into medium hog casings and tie into 5-inch links. Makes 2½ pounds

If you can't find fresh herbs, just substitute ½ teaspoon dried tarragon and ½ teaspoon dried basil. Don't bother with dried chervil, though; it has none of the subtle charm of the fresh herb.

HOT LINKS & COUNTRY FLAVORS

· Oakland hot links ·

Sometimes you can smell them for blocks away when the wind is right, and you speed the car up to get to the barbecue joint a little quicker. As you get closer your mouth starts to water, and you know that in just a few minutes you'll be chomping down on one of the great sausages in the world: a barbecued Oakland Hot Link. Smoky and spicy, barbecued Hot Links make for good eating on a French roll with lots of tangy Franco's Barbecue Sauce (see page 287) or tucked into a pot of beans or a mess of boiled greens with cornbread.

½ lb. pork shoulder	1 tsp. cayenne
1½ lbs. beef chuck	Pinch *each* ground allspice,
1 lb. pork back fat	cardamom, cloves, coriander,
1½ tbsp. kosher salt	cinnamon
2 tbsp. finely chopped garlic	1 tbsp. coarsely ground black pepper
1 tbsp. sweet Hungarian paprika	2 tsp. sugar
½ tsp. dried sage	½ c. ice water
1 tsp. dried marjoram	Medium hog casings

For directions on sausage making, see page 332.

Grind the meats and fat through a ⅜-inch plate. Mix the ground fat and meats with the other ingredients (except casings), kneading well with your hands until everything is well blended. Stuff into medium hog casings, and tie into 6-inch links. Dry overnight on a rack in the refrigerator. Hot smoke, following the directions on page 341, until the internal temperature of the sausages is 150–160° F. Refrigerated, Oakland Hot Links will keep for 4–5 days, frozen for 2 months. To reheat sausages, grill on a covered barbecue for 3–5 minutes a side. Serve with plenty of Franco's Barbecue Sauce. Makes 3½ pounds

A cold beer, a couple of Hot Links, R&B blasting on the jukebox, the sun going down into San Francisco Bay — letting the good times roll in Oakland.

· mini egg rolls ·

If you've made some of the Asian sausages in this chapter, you can put together these egg rolls quickly and simply. And if you haven't made some already, don't worry. Since the sausage meat doesn't have to be stuffed into casings, you can easily whip up a batch in your food processor. If you are in a hurry, or not feeling particularly ambitious, just mix up some of our quick Asian sausage (see margin page 270), and you're ready to roll.

4 dried shiitake mushrooms
½ lb. Chinese Pork and Shrimp
   Sausage (see page 248) or other
   Asian sausage from this chapter, in
   bulk or removed from casings

½ carrot, julienned or shredded
2 c. coarsely chopped fresh bean
   sprouts
48 square won ton wrappers
Oil for deep-frying

Quick, easy, and delicious! Won ton wrappers, available in Chinese groceries and many supermarkets, are perfect for these hors d'oeuvre–sized egg rolls. We used our Chinese Pork and Shrimp Sausage, but any of the Asian sausage recipes will work just as well.

Soak the dried shiitake mushrooms in hot water to cover for at least 30 minutes, remove, discard stems, and shred the caps. Mix together the sausage meat, carrot, bean sprouts, and shredded shiitake mushrooms. Place 1 or 2 teaspoons of the filling in a 2–3-inch-long roll across the diagonal of each won ton wrapper. Lift the point of the lower triangle over the filling. Fold each of the edges of this triangle, one at a time, over the filling and press down firmly. Moisten the exposed top triangle with a little water to seal, and roll the filling up in it to form a small, tight roll. Place the egg rolls on a platter when you have rolled them. If you are not going to fry them within a half hour, cover with plastic wrap and refrigerate.

Heat 2–3 inches of oil in a wok or small heavy pan until it reaches 375° F. Test the temperature by frying a sample egg roll; the oil should bubble and spatter as soon as you add it. Fry 6–8 rolls at a time in the hot oil for 3–5 minutes, until they are golden brown and crisp. Drain the egg rolls on paper towels. Transfer to a heated platter and serve at once. Makes about 48

· my pot stickers ·

Pot stickers are a popular appetizer or party snack and make a great accompaniment with soup. If you have some sausage in the fridge, as I usually do, they are quick and easy to put together. Any of our Asian-style sausages will work well here. Try the Chinatown Crépinettes, Japantown Pork and Shiitake Mushroom Sausage, the Chinese Pork and Shrimp Sausage, or the quick Asian sausage (see pages 246, 249, 248, and 270).

½ lb. Chinatown Crépinettes, Japantown Pork and Shiitake Mushroom Sausage, or other Asian-style sausage from this chapter, removed from casings

2 c. finely shredded Napa or green cabbage

½ c. chopped fresh cilantro

¼ c. finely chopped green onions or scallions

1 tsp. Chinese brown bean paste (optional)

20 –24 round pot sticker (won ton) wrappers

3 tbsp. peanut oil

⅔ –1⅓ cups water or stock

Thoroughly mix together the sausage, cabbage, cilantro, green onions, and optional bean paste. Put 1 tablespoon or more of this filling in the center of a wrapper, fold it over to make a half moon. Brush edges with a little water and pinch the edges together. Make 4 or 5 small pleats along the curved side, then pinch the 2 pointed ends together tightly to seal.

Heat the oil in a heavy 12-inch nonstick or cast-iron frying pan over medium heat. Put the pot stickers in, seam side up, and fry for 2–3 minutes until the bottoms are lightly browned. Pour in ⅔–1 cup water or stock, and cover the pan. Cook the pot stickers over medium heat for 10–15 minutes or until the liquid has evaporated. Check to see that the bottoms of the pot stickers are nicely browned and the dough is tender. If they are not brown, fry them, uncovered, for 1 or 2 more minutes. If the dough isn't tender, add another ⅓ cup of liquid, cover, and cook until the liquid has evaporated. Serve at once. Makes 20–24

The Japanese version of this savory dumpling, called gyoza, *is a little smaller with a thinner wrapper. Both types are delicious served with rice vinegar, soy sauce, and Chinese hot chile oil.*

· Marty's marvelous Marin mushrooms ·

To many Americans, Marin County epitomizes California's laid-back life-style with shingled cottages tucked away among the eucalyptus groves, red-wood decks and hot tubs, and, of course, the ever-popular peacock feathers. While not everyone has the peacock feathers, a lot of people who appreciate food, wine, and the good life live in Marin, and Marty's Parties of Marin helps them enjoy themselves. Marty and Betsy Rosenbloom run a catering operation that is well-organized and professional, and provides genuinely original, delicious party food. This stuffed mushroom recipe is a favorite appetizer or party snack.

24 large mushroom caps
¼ c. olive oil
4 cloves garlic, minced
4 green onions or scallions, finely chopped
2 tbsp. mirin or medium-sweet Madeira
½ tsp. coarsely ground black pepper
2 tsp. fresh lemon juice

1 lb. California White Wine and Herb Sausage (see page 254) or other fresh sausage, removed from casings
¼ c. bread crumbs
6 tbsp. freshly grated Parmesan cheese
¼ c. fresh goat cheese (optional)

Clean the mushrooms with a damp cloth, and carefully remove and chop the stems. Heat 2 tablespoons of the olive oil in a skillet over medium-high heat, and fry the chopped stems, garlic, and green onions for about 5 minutes, stirring frequently. Add the wine and cook until it evaporates. Transfer the stuffing to a bowl and sprinkle with the black pepper and lemon juice.

In the same pan, fry the sausage meat for about 5 minutes, crumbling with a fork, until it is no longer pink. Add this to the bowl and stir in the bread crumbs, and all but 2 tablespoons of the Parmesan cheese, along with the goat cheese if you are using it. Divide the mixture into 24 equal portions and stuff the mushrooms, mounding the stuffing up and pressing it lightly into the cavities with your fingers. At this point the mushrooms can be wrapped and refrigerated until they are ready to be cooked.

These stuffed mushrooms are simple to prepare, can be made in advance, and are very appealing. We used our California White Wine and Herb Sausage, but almost any savory fresh sausage will contribute its own flavor and character. A mild fresh chèvre from France or California can add extra zest.

Preheat the oven to 375° F. Brush the mushrooms with the remaining 2 tablespoons of olive oil and sprinkle with the rest of the Parmesan cheese. Bake for 10 minutes or until the mushrooms soften and the tops begin to brown.

Place the mushrooms under a broiler for 1–2 minutes to finish browning the tops, and serve at once. Makes 24 mushrooms, 6–8 cocktail servings

· Betsy's savory cheesecake ·

Betsy Rosenbloom, the other half of Marty's Parties of Marin, is both a superb party organizer and an accomplished baker. On her party menus, Betsy regularly includes savory cheesecakes because they are simple to make and always a great success.

½ c. chopped Oakland Hot Links (see page 255), andouille, or other spicy smoked sausage
1 tbsp. butter
¼ c. finely chopped onion
1 clove garlic, minced
6 cooked artichoke hearts, fresh, frozen, or canned, drained and chopped (¾ c.)
⅓ lb. cream cheese
⅓ lb. ricotta cheese
1 tbsp. lemon juice

1 egg, beaten
2 tbsp. jalapeño jelly
Salt and pepper to taste

· Crust ·
1 c. all-purpose flour
2 tsp. sugar
¼ tsp. salt
8 tbsp. (1 stick) butter, chilled and diced
4 tsp. ice water
½ tsp. lemon juice

To make the filling, fry the sausage in butter for 2–5 minutes over medium heat. Add the onion and cook for 3 minutes more, stirring frequently. Put in the garlic and artichoke hearts, and cook 2 more minutes. Transfer to a mixing bowl, and stir in the cream cheese, ricotta, lemon juice, egg, and jalapeño jelly until everything is well blended. Season with salt and pepper.

To make the crust, sift the flour, sugar, and salt into a bowl. Cut in the butter with a pastry knife or fork until the dough resembles coarse meal. Mix in the liquids and form the dough into a ball. Wrap and refrigerate for at least 30 minutes. Roll out the dough and press into a 9-inch tart pan. If desired, freeze the dough up to 1 month until ready to use. Dough can be baked directly from freezer.

Preheat the oven to 425° F. Line the unbaked crust with foil and fill with dried beans. Bake for 15 minutes, remove the foil and beans, and finish baking an additional 5 minutes. The crust should be light brown.

Fill the precooked crust with the cheese mixture and lower the oven to 350° F. Bake the cheesecake in the middle of the oven until the filling sets and a toothpick inserted comes out clean, about 20 minutes. Let the cheesecake rest for 10 minutes before slicing. It is best served warm or at room temperature. Makes 6–8 servings as an appetizer

This tangy cheesecake combines spicy smoked sausage and artichokes with jalapeño jelly, but you can substitute for the artichokes roasted sweet peppers, zucchini, pesto sauce, or mint; for the jalapeño jelly spicy chutney, red pepper jelly, or sweet-hot mustard.

· sausages in sherry ·

Tapas are the little snacks the Spanish serve before dinner, and they have become quite popular in West Coast restaurants. During the summer months, dinner out west can get started quite late, as it does in Spain. These hearty hors d'oeuvres tend to be substantial enough to keep you going until you finally get to the dinner table.

If you don't have Spanish chorizo, use linguiça, Portuguese chouriço, or a high-quality pepperoni.

1 lb. Spanish chorizo or linguiça,
   sliced into rounds
2 c. thinly sliced red onions

2 cloves garlic, minced
¼ c. dry Spanish sherry

Sauté the sausages over high heat for about 5 minutes until brown, and pour off the excess fat. Add the onions, garlic, and wine, and reduce the liquid over high heat for about 2 minutes. Makes 4–6 servings as an appetizer

This quick and simple sauté is a typical tapa dish and takes only a few minutes to prepare. Eat it hot or let it cool a bit and eat it lukewarm the way they do in the tapas bars. Serve with thick slices of fresh French bread for dipping into the sauce and a glass of cool dry Spanish sherry.

· Loni Kuhn's crusty rolls with chard and sausage ·

The cottage cheese pastry used to make this flaky dough is very buttery and simple to put together. Store some in your freezer so you can use it to make savory turnovers with leftovers or when unexpected guests show up hungry.

Just about any high-quality sausage can be used to make this filling. We used a spicy Italian sausage in one test and smoked andouille in another. Both tasted just fine. Remove fresh sausages from their casings and crumble the meat as you fry it. Chop smoked sausages before browning. You can substitute spinach or other greens for the chard.

· **Cottage cheese pastry** ·
2½ c. all-purpose flour
Pinch salt
1 tbsp. chile powder blend
1 tbsp. ground cumin
½ lb. (2 sticks) cold butter, diced
1 c. small curd cottage cheese

· **Filling** ·
1 lb. fresh sausage such as hot
  Italian, removed from casings, or
  1 lb. smoked sausage such as
  andouille, chopped

1 large bunch chard, stems removed,
  blanched, squeezed dry, and finely
  chopped (about 2 c.)
1 tsp. dried oregano
3 cloves garlic, minced
3 tbsp. chopped fresh parsley
2 eggs, beaten
1 c. freshly grated Parmesan cheese
  or California dried Jack
1 c. grated Jack cheese
1 egg beaten with 2 tsp. water for egg
  wash

In a food processor or by hand, mix the flour with the salt, chile powder, and cumin. Using the pulse switch or a fork, cut the butter into the flour until it looks like coarse crumbs. Add the cottage cheese and process or stir until a dough is formed. Briefly knead the dough on a floured surface to form a ball. Divide into 2 balls, wrap in plastic wrap, and refrigerate at least 30 minutes.

To make the filling, fry the fresh sausage meat in a large skillet over medium heat, crumbling it as it cooks, for 5 minutes, or brown the chopped smoked sausage for 3 minutes. Add the chard, oregano, garlic, and parsley and stir until everything is well blended. Transfer the sausage/chard mixture to a bowl, and stir in the eggs and cheeses. Let the filling cool for at least 30 minutes in the refrigerator or overnight.

To make the rolls, roll out each dough ball ⅛ inch thick and cut each into 6 equal squares. Divide the filling into 12 equal amounts and place a row down the middle of each square. Roll each up to make a tube and seal the ends by pinching the dough. Place the rolls on a buttered baking sheet. You can refrigerate them at this point or bake immediately.

Just before baking, brush each roll generously with the egg wash and bake for 25 minutes in a preheated 350° F oven, until they are golden brown. Cool briefly and slice into 1-inch rounds before serving. Serve warm. These savory rolls can easily be rewarmed by baking for 7–10 minutes at 350° F. Makes 12 6-inch rolls or 72 individual rounds, 12 cocktail servings

· sheepherder's omelette of wild greens, potatoes, and chorizo ·

This type of thick omelette made with potatoes, sausages, and other ingredients is called a tortilla in Spain. It is enjoyed hot or cold, and is perfect for hors d'oeuvres when cut into small wedges or squares. Basque sheepherders typically prepare omelettes like this with a few eggs, a piece of cherished smoked chorizo, and some wild greens gathered from the hillsides of Northern California or Nevada. A tortilla makes a satisfying one-dish meal, and is delicious leftover, eaten cold for lunch, or as a tapa.

1 medium onion, thinly sliced
6 tbsp. olive oil
½ lb. Basque or Spanish-style
   chorizo, cut into ½-inch rounds
3 c. thinly sliced red potatoes
4 cloves garlic, chopped
4 c. chopped wild greens such as
   dandelion, milkweed, or lamb's
   quarter, or store-bought bitter
   greens such as arugula, curly
   endive, escarole, or watercress

Salt and pepper to taste
8 eggs, lightly beaten

Sauté the onions in 3 tablespoons of the olive oil in a large frying pan for 3 minutes over medium-high heat. Add the sausage rounds and cook for 2 minutes, turning them once. Put in the potatoes and cook for 10–15 minutes, shaking the pan and turning the potatoes frequently until they are tender. Stir in the garlic and greens and season with salt and pepper. Mix the potatoes, greens, and sausages with the eggs in a large bowl.

Tortillas or Spanish omelettes are a great way to use whatever's on hand in the refrigerator or garden. Artichokes, pimientos, bell peppers, spinach, and leftover ham or chicken are all delicious in omelettes but always include a little chorizo or other spicy sausage (linguiça, andouille, pepperoni) to liven things up.

Heat the remaining 3 tablespoons of olive oil in a clean 12-inch omelette pan or nonstick frying pan. Pour in the egg and potato mixture and cook over low heat until the eggs have almost set, about 5 minutes. Invert the omelette onto a plate or pan lid, slide back into the pan, and cook the other side until done, about 5 minutes more. Transfer to a platter. Let the tortilla rest for 5 minutes and then slice into wedges and serve.

Makes 6–8 servings as an appetizer, 4 as lunch

· Salinas Valley braised stuffed lettuce ·

The Salinas Valley near Monterey is often called the lettuce bowl of America. Although we are used to eating lettuce raw in salads, it can also make a delicious cooked vegetable. Many of the Italian immigrants who settled and farmed the Salinas Valley use cooked lettuce in family dishes, and the recipe below is inspired by this tradition.

Several varieties of lettuce and greens work well in this dish, including iceberg, escarole, romaine, green leafy lettuce, Swiss chard. You can vary the sausage according to your taste; any mild-flavored fresh sausage will contribute its own flavor. Try one of the fresh Asian-style sausages from this chapter, or mild Italian or California White Wine and Herb Sausage.

15 large outer leaves from romaine, iceberg, escarole, or Swiss chard
¾ lb. Chinese Pork and Shrimp Sausage (see page 248) or other mild-flavored fresh sausage such as mild Italian, in bulk or removed from casings
¾ c. fresh bread crumbs
½ c. chopped watercress
1 egg, beaten
½ tsp. salt, or more to taste
2 c. chicken stock
½ c. dry white wine
1 tsp. minced garlic
1 tbsp. olive oil
1 tbsp. lemon juice, or more to taste
2 tsp. cornstarch
Pepper to taste
Lemon wedges

Blanch the lettuce or chard leaves briefly in boiling water to make them soft and pliable. Drain and set aside.

In a bowl knead together the sausage, bread crumbs, watercress, egg, and ½ teaspoon salt. Mound 2–3 tablespoons of the mixture on the edge of each leaf. Fold in the sides like an envelope, and roll to form a package. Place the rolls, seam side down, in a nonaluminum Dutch oven or heavy casserole. Pour in the stock and wine, along with the garlic, olive oil, and 1 tablespoon lemon juice. Bring to a simmer and cook 35 minutes, until the rolls are quite tender and the filling cooked. Add more liquid if necessary. Remove the rolls to a warm platter.

Stir in the cornstarch, dissolved in 1 tablespoon water, and season to taste with salt, pepper, and lemon juice. Heat sauce to thicken. Pour the sauce over the rolls and serve, garnished with lemon wedges. Makes 4 servings as a main dish, more as an appetizer

Since the sausage meat doesn't have to be stuffed into casings, you can easily make up a batch in the food processor for this recipe. Depending on the size of the braised lettuce rolls, they can be used as an appetizer or main dish. Lettuce rolls have a subtler and milder flavor than cabbage rolls, but can be used in similar ways.

· mushroom, provolone, and smoked sausage salad ·

This tangy salad is delicious eaten as a first course or with a meal. It also combines nicely with ziti or other large pasta for a main course or hearty lunch.

½ lb. diced Oakland Hot Links
 (see page 255) or other spicy
 smoked sausage

· **Dressing** ·
1 tbsp. Dijon mustard
2 tbsp. wine vinegar
Pinch of sugar
1 clove garlic, minced
2 tbsp. chopped fresh herbs such as
 basil or oregano

6 tbsp. olive oil
¼ c. crème fraîche or sour cream
....
½ lb. mushrooms, thinly sliced
1 bunch of radishes, thinly sliced
 (about ½ c.)
¼ lb. Provolone cheese, cut into
 strips
2 tbsp. chopped fresh flat-leaf parsley
¾ lb. cold cooked pasta (optional)

Use any lean, spicy smoked sausage here such as Oakland Hot Links, andouille, or linguiça.

Fry the sausage in a heavy pan for 5 minutes over medium-high heat to render some of the fat. Remove with a slotted spoon and reserve. Discard fat.

Blend all the dressing ingredients together in a food processor or whisk in a bowl. In a large bowl or deep platter mix the browned sausage with the mushrooms, radishes, cheese, and parsley. Toss thoroughly with the dressing. Serve as is or over cold cooked pasta. Makes 4–6 servings.

· Priscilla's wilted salad of savoy cabbage, pears, and sausage ·

Priscilla Yee is a grand-champion recipe-contest winner who lives in California. Much of her spare time is spent developing delicious recipes for the cooking contests that she wins with great frequency. From this recipe you can see why. This wilted salad typifies Priscilla's cooking style: quick, easy, with fresh ingredients and ethnic touches from her Asian heritage.

8 oz. Japantown Pork and Shiitake
   Mushroom Sausage (see page 249)
   or mild Italian sausage

· **Ginger-mustard dressing** ·
¼ c. salad oil, preferably peanut
3 tbsp. lemon juice
2 tsp. light soy sauce
1 tbsp. minced fresh ginger
1 tsp. sugar
2 tsp. Dijon mustard

2 oz. snow peas, trimmed (about 24)
1 large red bell pepper, cut into
   julienne strips
4 c. savoy cabbage, cut into ½-inch
   strips
1 cucumber, peeled, seeded, and
   sliced
1 firm ripe pear, cored and sliced
2 tbsp. chopped fresh cilantro

· **Garnish** ·
Cilantro sprigs (optional)

Sauté the sausages whole in a large skillet over medium heat until browned and cooked through, about 10 minutes. Set aside to cool while you prepare the dressing by whisking all the ingredients together in a small bowl. Slice the sausage into ¼-inch rounds. Drain off all but 2 tablespoons of the drippings from the skillet, and heat over medium-high heat. Add the snow peas, bell pepper, cabbage, cucumber, and the Ginger-Mustard Dressing. Stir just until the cabbage starts to wilt, 1–2 minutes. Stir in the pear, cilantro, and sliced sausage. Spoon the salad onto 4 plates and garnish with cilantro sprigs, if desired. Makes 4 servings.

If you don't have some of our Japantown Pork and Shiitake Mushroom Sausage on hand, just substitute mild Italian sausage in this savory and easy-to-make salad. It's wonderful for lunch or a light summer supper.

· cold Chinese noodles and sausage with sesame dressing ·

Cold noodle salad with sesame dressing and savory tidbits is a favorite snack in Chinese and Japanese restaurants all along the West Coast. In fact, it is so popular that you are sure to find some type of cold noodle dish in just about every gourmet deli in California.

10 dried shiitake mushrooms

¼ lb. snow peas or Sugar Snap peas, with stems removed

2 bunches green onions or scallions, cut on the diagonal into 2-inch lengths

1 lb. Japantown Pork and Shiitake Mushroom Sausage (see page 249), or ½ pound julienned smoked ham or *cha shao*

1 tbsp. peanut oil (optional)

2 eggs, beaten (optional)

Pinch salt

2 tbsp. sesame seeds

½ lb. thin fresh Chinese egg noodles, or ¼ lb. dried vermicelli

· **Sesame dressing** ·

2 tbsp. Chinese black vinegar or Japanese rice wine vinegar

1 tbsp. soy sauce

2 tsp. sugar

6 tbsp. Oriental sesame oil

....

1 c. coarsely chopped cilantro

We used our Japantown Pork and Shiitake Mushroom Sausage here, but you could also use mild Italian sausage or julienned strips of smoked ham or Chinese cha shao (barbecued pork).

Pour boiling water over the shiitake mushrooms. Cover and soak for at least 30 minutes or up to several hours. Remove the tough stems and slice the mushrooms into thin shreds.

Bring a large pot of lightly salted water to a boil. Add the snow peas and green onions and blanch for 30 seconds. Drain under cold running water in a colander and set aside.

Fry the sausages whole in a heavy covered frying pan over medium heat until they are lightly browned and firm to the touch, about 10 minutes. Remove them from the pan, and when they are cool enough to handle, cut the sausages into thin rounds.

If desired, heat the peanut oil in a medium omelette pan. Add the eggs, beaten with a pinch of salt, to make a thin omelette. Fry until set, turn over, and fry 1 minute more. Transfer the omelette to a plate and when it is completely cool, cut it into thin shreds about 2–3 inches long.

In a small dry frying pan, roast the sesame seeds over low heat, shaking the pan continuously until they are light brown and aromatic. Transfer them to a small bowl.

Bring a 3–4-quart pot of lightly salted water to a boil, add the noodles, and cook for 1 minute, or just until they are tender. Cook dried vermicelli according to directions on the package. Taste one to see if they are cooked to your taste. Drain and cool them under running water in a colander. Run your hand through the noodles as they rinse to make sure they are cool and to help wash off the starch.

To make the Sesame Dressing, mix all the ingredients except the sesame oil together in a small bowl, and then gradually whisk in the oil.

To assemble the salad, place the noodles in a large bowl with the mushrooms, snow peas, green onions, sausage, and all but ¼ cup each of the omelette and the cilantro. Mix in the dressing until everything is well coated. Transfer the salad to a shallow bowl or platter. Scatter the remaining cilantro and egg over the surface and sprinkle the sesame seeds over all. Makes 4–6 servings

· quick and easy salads ·

With its varied flavors and textures, sausage combines beautifully with many different vegetables, greens, or pasta to make easy yet dramatic and delicious salads. They are very versatile and can serve as appetizers or first courses, lunch or buffet dishes.

It's critical to use high-quality, lean sausages in salads. Homemade are best, but good commercial sausages will also work well. Serve these salads warm, cold, or at room temperature. The variations possible are endless. A few of ours are: Tom Blower's Nopalito and Bell Pepper Salad (see page 222); Karl's Tex-Mex Rice Salad (see page 223); Mushroom, Provolone, and Smoked Sausage Salad (see page 264); Priscilla's Wilted Salad of Savoy Cabbage, Pears, and Sausage (see page 265); Cold Chinese Noodles and Sausage with Sesame Dressing (see page 266); and Phyllis's Wilted Spinach Salad with

Crispy Chorizo (see page 225).

Combine cooked sausages with seasonal vegetables: asparagus and young lettuce in spring, sweet corn and red peppers in summer, cauliflower and broccoli in fall, and cabbage and potatoes in winter. Use leftovers as your inspiration: cold pasta, leftover roast chicken, meat, or fish, assorted cheeses, yesterday's cooked vegetables, all combine well with sausages to make delightful salads.

For dressings try a Mustard Vinaigrette (see page 353), a delicious Sesame Dressing (see opposite page), a Tangy Vinaigrette (see page 353), or Lee Coleman's Rémoulade Dressing (see page 353).

· winter vegetable, sausage, and chestnut soup ·

This satisfying soup/stew combines the hearty flavors of winter vegetables like celery root and squash with the exotic taste of black mushrooms and chestnuts and the smoky tang of ham hocks and sausages. Dried chestnuts are just as good as fresh, and for this soup they are a whole lot less work to prepare. They can be purchased in Chinese groceries or Italian delis in most large cities. If you can't find them, use 1½ pounds of fresh chestnuts, peeled and prepared as described on page 346.

1 c. dried chestnuts or 1½ lbs. fresh chestnuts, peeled and with the inner skin removed

2 qts. beef or chicken stock

1 lb. ham hock, sawed into 2-inch pieces

1 lb. spicy smoked sausage such as Oakland Hot Links or andouille, sliced into ¼-inch rounds

6 Chinese black mushrooms or Japanese shiitakes, soaked in hot water to cover

1 leek, well washed and chopped

1 medium parsnip, peeled and cut into 1-inch cubes

1 medium celery root, peeled and cut into 1-inch cubes

¾ lb. white turnip or rutabaga, peeled and cut into 1-inch cubes

½ tsp. cayenne

1 bay leaf

1½ lbs. butternut squash, peeled and cut into 1-inch cubes

1 tbsp. soy sauce

3 tbsp. white or cider vinegar

2 tbsp. cornstarch

Salt, pepper, and Tabasco to taste

Soak the dried chestnuts in water overnight and drain. Bring the stock to a boil in a large pot or Dutch oven. Put in the ham hocks, and about ¼ pound of the sausage, and reduce heat. Simmer for 1 hour, uncovered. Add the chestnuts and continue to cook until the ham hocks and chestnuts are tender, about ½ to 1 hour more. Remove the tough stems from the soaked mushrooms and cut the caps into ¼-inch slices. Add the mushrooms and their strained soaking liquid to the pot, along with the leek, parsnip, celery root, turnip or rutabaga, cayenne, and bay leaf. Cook for 15 more minutes, and then add the butternut squash and the remaining sausage and cook 10–15 minutes more, or until the squash is just tender. Stir together the soy sauce, vinegar, and corn-starch, then add to the pot to give the soup a little more body. Season with salt, pepper, and Tabasco.

Makes 6–8 servings

Similar to the popular Chinese hot and sour soup, this is a bit richer, with a subtle, smoky flavor. If you prefer it spicier, stir in some Tabasco or hot chile oil. Like most of the hearty stews and soups in this book, it tastes even better the next day.

· won ton soup ·

Now that won ton wrappers are widely available in many supermarkets across the country, it is embarrassingly easy to make tasty won tons for frying or using in soup. For a filling you can utilize any of the Asian sausage recipes from this chapter (see pages 246, 248, 249, 270). Just whip up a batch in your food processor.

· Won tons ·
½ lb. Chinatown Crépinettes or other Asian sausage from this chapter, in bulk or removed from casings
½ c. chopped fresh cilantro (optional)
48 square won ton wrappers

· Won ton soup ·
1½ qts. rich chicken stock
¼ lb. snow peas, strings and tips removed
¼ c. green onions or scallions, cut into 1-inch pieces
¼ c. coarsely chopped fresh cilantro (optional)
Salt and pepper to taste

Mix the sausage and optional ½ cup cilantro together. To make the won tons, place ½ to 1 teaspoon of filling just below the center of each wrapper. Fold one side over the filling, and tuck its edge under the sausage meat. Moisten the exposed sides of the wrapper with a finger dipped in water and roll up to form a log, leaving ½ inch of wrapper unrolled at the top. Take the two ends of the roll and pull them beneath the roll until the ends meet and overlap. Squeeze the ends firmly together. Place on a platter when you have made them. If you are not cooking the won tons within 30 minutes, cover them with plastic wrap and refrigerate.

Quick and delicious — use our Chinatown Crépinettes, our quick Asian sausage, our Japantown Pork and Shiitake Mushroom Sausage, or Chinese Pork and Shrimp Sausage.

In a 3–4-quart pot, bring the stock to a boil. Add all the won tons, snow peas, and green onions. Cook 5 minutes, or until the won tons are cooked through; cut one open to test. Serve 6 wontons per guest as an appetizer or 1 dozen each as a main course. Makes 8 servings as an appetizer, 4 as a main course

· fried won tons ·
Wonderful cocktail hors d'oeuvres or party snacks!
48 won tons
Oil for frying (preferably peanut)
· Accompaniments ·
Hot Chinese mustard
Soy sauce
Chile oil

Heat 2–3 inches of oil to 375° F. Fry 6–8 won tons per batch until crisp and golden. Drain on paper towels as they cook. Serve immediately on a heated platter with hot Chinese mustard, soy sauce, and chile oil. Makes 8–10 servings as an appetizer

·Japantown miso soup with pork and shiitake sausage·

Miso is a Japanese paste made from fermented soybeans. It is a traditional thickener and flavoring in Japanese-style soups. There are two kinds — a mild white miso and a more pungent red one. For this recipe use the white miso, which can be purchased at Asian specialty shops.

½ lb. Japantown Pork and Shiitake Mushroom Sausage or other mild fresh sausage, removed from casings

6 c. chicken stock

6 dried shiitake mushrooms, stems removed, soaked for at least 30 minutes

2 c. shredded Napa cabbage or white cabbage

⅓ c. white miso

2 tbsp. sweet sherry

Salt and pepper to taste

½ c. thinly sliced green onions or scallions

Fry the sausage in a large pot over medium-high heat for 5 minutes. Pour off all the fat and add the stock. Strain the mushrooms, reserving the soaking liquid, and cut them into thin slices. Add the mushrooms, the soaking liquid, and the cabbage to the pot. Bring to a boil and then reduce heat to simmer. Add miso and sherry and cook 5 minutes, or until the cabbage is tender. Taste for salt and pepper. Ladle into individual serving bowls and garnish with green onions. Makes 6–8 servings

· quick and easy Asian-flavored sausage ·

¾ lb. ground pork

2 tsp. soy sauce

1 tsp. minced fresh ginger

1 tsp. minced garlic

1 tsp. ground Szechuan or white pepper

½ c. chopped cilantro

Mix together all the ingredients. Use in bulk or stuff into casings. This sausage freezes well.

· Chinese braised stuffed fish ·

Chinese cooks have long known that pork and seafood make an excellent combination. The savory aromas and rich flavors of sausage add succulence and texture to fish, whether whole, sliced, or in chunks. Out on the West Coast, rock cod is a favorite in Chinese restaurants, but you can use any whole freshwater or saltwater firm-fleshed fish in this recipe.

The pork-sausage stuffing here adds flavor and creates more portions from a single fish. With the addition of rice and stir-fried vegetables such as snow peas and black mushrooms or green beans, you have a very satisfying Chinese meal.

¾ lb. Asian-style sausage such as Quick and Easy Asian-flavored Sausage, Chinatown Crépinettes, Chinese Pork and Shrimp Sausage, or Japantown Pork and Shiitake Mushroom Sausage (see pages 246, 248, and 249) removed from casings or in bulk

6 fresh or 4 canned water chestnuts, chopped

2 –3 lb. whole fish, head and tail still on (use rock cod, red snapper, sea bass, pike, perch, or other firm-fleshed fish)

Salt and pepper to taste

Flour to coat fish

Peanut oil for frying

½ c. dry sherry or Chinese rice wine

1 c. chicken or fish stock

1 tsp. sugar

⅓ c. Chinese soy sauce

1 tsp. red pepper flakes

8 thin slices fresh ginger

2 cloves garlic, chopped

6 dried shiitake mushrooms, soaked in hot water for 30 minutes or more, stems removed, chopped

6 green onions or scallions, cut into ½-inch pieces

2 tbsp. Oriental sesame oil

¼ c. chopped fresh cilantro

Mix together the sausage meat and the chopped water chestnuts. Wash the fish and pat dry. Lightly sprinkle with salt and pepper and score the skin crosswise with diagonal cuts about an inch apart. Dust the fish completely with flour and stuff with the sausage mixture, which should just fill the cavity. It is not necessary to seal the cavity.

Heat about ¼-inch of peanut oil in a heavy frying pan or wok large enough to hold the fish. When the oil is almost smoking, carefully lay the fish into the pan, taking care not to splatter the oil. Fry the fish for 5 minutes until the skin is light brown. Gently turn over the fish, using a couple of spoons and spatulas, and brown the other side for 3 more minutes. Pour off any excess oil, and add the sherry, stock, sugar, soy sauce, pepper flakes, ginger, garlic, and chopped mushrooms. Scatter half the green onions over the fish. Cover the pan and reduce the heat to a simmer. Cook for 15 minutes and then baste the fish with the braising liquid. Put the cover back on, and cook for 10–15 minutes more, until the fish is just cooked and tender. Transfer the whole fish carefully to a serving platter. Sprinkle the sesame oil over the fish and pour on the sauce. Garnish with the remaining green onions and the cilantro. Makes 4–6 servings as a main course

· West Coast Cooking ·

· grilled or steamed fish
with smoky black bean sauce ·

On the West Coast fresh fish steaks are often grilled quickly over mesquite charcoal or steamed Chinese style, and accompanied by a spicy sauce. Use any firm-fleshed fish cut 1½ inches thick, about 6–8 ounces per serving. We used tuna, which is wonderful if grilled on the rare side.

· Grilled fish steaks ·

4 6–8 oz. fish steaks from any firm-
   fleshed fish such as salmon,
   halibut, swordfish, tuna, or shark
2 tbsp. peanut or olive oil

1 recipe Smoky Black Bean Sauce
   (see page 274)
10–12 sprigs cilantro
¼ c. chopped green onions or
   scallions

Brush the fish steaks with oil and grill directly over hot coals for 3–5 minutes per side, or until the fish is firm to the touch. Transfer to a platter or pan and pour Smoky Black Bean Sauce over the fish. Garnish with sprigs of cilantro and chopped green onions. Makes 4 servings

· Steamed fish steaks ·

4 firm-fleshed fish steaks or
   fillets, 6–8 oz. each
8 thin slices fresh ginger
1 recipe Smoky Black Bean
   Sauce (see page 274)

10–12 sprigs cilantro
¼ c. chopped green onions or scallions

Place the fish in a closed steamer with 2 slices of ginger on each steak or fillet. Steam for 10 minutes or until the fish is just cooked through. Transfer to a heated platter and discard the ginger. Pour the Smoky Black Bean Sauce over the fish. Garnish with sprigs of cilantro and chopped green onions. Makes 4 servings

Tangy, quick sauces for fish: herbs and chiles are often blended into compound butters, fresh salsas lend exciting notes (see page 216), and Oriental sauces add piquancy and flavor. Try our Smoky Black Bean Sauce on green beans or tofu.

· crab and Italian sausage cioppino ·

The Italian fishermen of San Francisco Bay and the surrounding waters created this hearty seafood stew. It is similar to other Mediterranean fishermen's stews like cacciucco, zuppa di mare and bouillabaisse. All these tasty stews and soups are ways to use up bits of the catch left over at the end of the day. Most make liberal use of typical Mediterranean ingredients like garlic, tomatoes, basil, and oregano. Cioppino made with the delicious Dungeness crab of West Coast waters is a true San Francisco dish, and is a favorite in Italian restaurants and homes in the Bay Area.

Although Italian sausage is not a traditional ingredient in cioppino, it adds spice and flavors that raise this wonderful peasant dish to new heights. We use hot Italian sausage, but you could add mild Italian or another flavorful sausage. If crab is unavailable, use more shrimp.

1 tbsp. fruity olive oil
1½ lbs. hot or mild Italian sausages
⅓ c. diced celery
1 c. chopped onions
3 tbsp. minced garlic
1 c. thinly sliced green onions or
    scallions
½ c. diced green bell pepper
1 lb. fresh Italian plum tomatoes,
    peeled, seeded, and coarsely
    chopped, or 2 c. coarsely chopped
    canned Italian-style tomatoes
¼ c. tomato paste
½ c. dry red wine like Chianti or
    California Zinfandel
4 bay leaves
½ tsp. dried basil

½ tsp. dried thyme
2 c. fish or chicken stock
1 c. bottled clam juice
¼ c. lemon juice, or more to taste
1 2–3 lb. Dungeness crab, cleaned
    and cut into 8 pieces
2 dozen clams or mussels, scrubbed
1 lb. thresher or other shark, cut into
    1½-inch cubes
1 lb. halibut, cut into 1½-inch cubes
1 lb. large shrimp, peeled and
    deveined
Salt and pepper to taste
· **Garnishes** ·
8–10 lemon slices
¼ c. chopped fresh parsley

In a large pot or Dutch oven (6–8 quarts), heat the olive oil over medium heat. Add the whole sausages and fry them gently for about 10 minutes, turning often until they are firm and lightly browned. Set them aside to cool and leave about 3–4 tablespoons of fat in the pan. Put in the celery and onions, and fry for 5 minutes, stirring occasionally. Add the garlic, green onions, and bell pepper, and cook 2 more minutes. Slice the sausage into 1-inch rounds and put them back into the pot along with the tomatoes, tomato paste, wine, herbs, stock, clam juice, and lemon juice. Bring everything to a boil, reduce to a simmer, and cook for 10 minutes. Add the crab and clams or mussels, and cook for 5 minutes, or until shells open. Discard any clams or mussels that have not opened. Put in

If you can't find shark or halibut, substitute other firm-fleshed fish such as swordfish or sea bass. Pay careful attention to timing and don't overcook — cooking times are just guidelines, and can vary depending on the type of fish or seafood. Taste fish while cooking, and serve the cioppino when done.

the fish and shrimp, and cook for 5 minutes more, or until the shrimp are pink and firm and the fish is cooked through. Taste for salt, pepper, and more lemon juice. Serve at once in large shallow bowls. Garnish each serving with a slice of lemon and a little chopped fresh parsley. Makes 8–10 servings

· smoky black bean sauce ·

Exotic, easy to make, and delicious. Whip up this smoky sauce in your food processor and use over fish, vegetables, grilled chicken or turkey, tofu, or noodles. Fermented black beans are found in most Asian markets.

¼ lb. spicy smoked sausage, cut into chunks

2 cloves garlic

2 tbsp. Chinese fermented black beans, rinsed

4 thin slices fresh ginger

2 tbsp. peanut oil

2 tbsp. lime juice

½ c. beer

½ c. chicken stock

1 tsp. cornstarch dissolved in 2 tbsp. water

Process sausage, garlic, black beans, and ginger in a food processor fitted with a metal blade. Fry in peanut oil for 2 minutes over medium-high heat, stirring continuously. Add lime juice, beer, and stock and bring to a boil. Cook 3 minutes over medium heat. Add cornstarch and water, bring to a boil, stirring well. Use immediately or reheat. Add more liquid if sauce is too thick. Store in refrigerator for 5 days or freeze for up to 2 months. Makes 1½ cups

braised squid stuffed with Basque chorizo and prosciutto ·

These calamari (or squid) are so delicious that it's really hard to stop eating them, so even if you serve them as tapas, they always seem to end up as the main course. Either make just a few and cut your guests off in the middle of the squid binge, or give up and make enough for everybody to munch on long into the night.

Stuffed squid also make a substantial meal served over thin spaghetti or vermicelli with a salad of mixed lettuce and tangy greens. Any leftovers can be rewarmed the next day for tapas. They are also very tasty cold. Serve with a light red wine like Gamay Beaujolais.

½ lb. Basque chorizo, Portuguese chouriço, linguiça, or other spicy sausage, finely chopped
¼ c. olive oil
¼ lb. prosciutto or smoked ham, finely chopped
½ c. finely chopped onion
2 tbsp. minced garlic
24 medium squid, cleaned, with tentacles finely chopped
¼ c. chopped fresh Italian flat-leaf parsley
1 c. fresh bread crumbs
1 egg, beaten
Salt and pepper to taste

· Sauce ·
¼ c. finely chopped onion
2 shallots, finely chopped
3 cloves garlic, finely chopped
1 tbsp. sweet Hungarian paprika
3 large ripe tomatoes or 4 canned tomatoes, peeled, seeded, and chopped
1 tbsp. tomato paste
½ c. dry red wine
½ c. clam juice, fish stock, or chicken stock
1 tsp. chopped fresh oregano or ½ tsp. dried
Salt and pepper to taste

· Garnish ·
Lemon wedges

Brown the sausage in 2 tablespoons of the olive oil in a heavy frying pan over medium heat for 2–3 minutes. Add the chopped onion and prosciutto, and cook for 5 minutes. Put in the minced garlic and the chopped squid tentacles, and cook for another minute. Transfer the contents of the pan to a large bowl, and stir in the parsley, bread crumbs, and egg. Taste for salt and pepper. Fill each squid with the stuffing and seal with a wooden toothpick. Don't pack the stuffing too tightly or the squid could burst during cooking.

Brown the squid in the remaining 2 tablespoons olive oil for 1 or 2 minutes, shaking the pan as they cook. Transfer them to a large platter as they brown. In the same pan put the ¼ cup chopped onion along with the chopped shallots and finely chopped garlic. Cook over medium heat for 5 minutes until they are soft. Stir in the paprika, and add the tomatoes, tomato paste, wine, clam juice or stock, and oregano along with the reserved squid. Bring to a boil, cover, and reduce

Most squid eaten in the United States is caught in Monterey Bay. Italians and Basques from Monterey and the Salinas Valley have a number of delicious ways of preparing calamari. To give this Basque stuffing an Italian flavor, use mild Italian sausage instead of chorizo and add 2 tablespoons of grated Parmesan.

the heat to a simmer. Cook for about 45 minutes, or until the squid are tender. If the sauce becomes too thick, add more wine or stock. Taste for salt and pepper. If you plan to serve the squid as an appetizer, let them cool a bit. Otherwise, serve them hot over pasta. Garnish with lemon wedges. Makes 8 servings as tapas, 4–6 as a main course

· Asian sausage and shark kebabs ·

You can make these delicious kebabs using any Asian-style sausage like our Chinatown Crépinettes stuffed in casings, our Japantown Pork and Shiitake Mushroom Sausage, or Chinese Pork and Shrimp Sausage, or substitute mild Italian sausage or whatever other aromatic sausage suits your fancy.

½ lb. Asian-style sausage, or other
    aromatic sausage
· **Ginger-soy marinade** ·
1 tbsp. minced fresh ginger
2 tsp. minced garlic
¼ c. mirin or sweet sherry
Juice of 1 lime
2 tbsp. soy sauce
1 tbsp. Oriental sesame oil
¼ c. chopped fresh cilantro

1½ lbs. shark cut into 2-inch cubes
12 medium-sized fresh or dried
    shiitake mushrooms (if dry, soak
    in hot water to cover for at least
    30 minutes)
1 red onion, cut into 1-inch chunks
· **Garnish** ·
Lime wedges

Many varieties of shark abound in the waters off the West Coast, and its mild flavor and firm flesh make it very popular for grilling. If shark is unavailable, use any firm-fleshed fish such as swordfish or tuna.

Poach the sausages briefly (about 10 minutes), cool, and cut into 1-inch pieces. Mix the marinade ingredients together, and marinate the sausage, fish, shiitake mushrooms, and onion at room temperature for 1–2 hours. Don't marinate much longer because the lime juice will begin to cook the fish.

To make the kebabs, alternate pieces of onion, mushrooms, sausage, and fish on bamboo skewers. Grill over charcoal, turning 2 or 3 times and basting with the marinade. The kebabs are done when the fish is no longer translucent and its flesh is tender, about 5–6 minutes. Transfer to a warm platter and serve at once garnished with lime wedges. Makes 4 servings

· salmon sausage in champagne sauce ·

This rich and elegant dish makes a lovely first course for a special dinner party, and is also wonderful for a formal lunch. You don't have to use a top-line French champagne here. A good, mid-range California or Spanish sparkling wine will be just fine.

4 oz. (1 stick) plus 1 tbsp. butter
2 tbsp. chopped shallots
¼ c. chopped fresh parsley
¼ lb. chopped mushrooms
1 c. good-quality sparkling wine
2 c. chicken stock

2 c. whipping cream
Salt and pepper to taste
8 salmon sausages (see page 247),
   Crawfish Boudin, or other seafood
   sausages

Melt 2 tablespoons of the butter in a heavy saucepan. Put in the shallots, and cook for 2 minutes, until soft. Add the parsley and mushrooms and cook for 5 minutes over medium-high heat. Pour in the sparkling wine, and boil until it is almost evaporated. Stir in the stock and cream, and cook until the liquid is reduced by half. Whisk in the rest of the stick of butter piece by piece to thicken the sauce. Taste for salt and pepper.

Fry the sausages in the remaining tablespoon of butter over medium heat, turning occasionally until they are lightly browned. Pour off excess fat and transfer to a platter. Pour the sauce over the browned sausages and serve.

Makes 4 servings

Serve a French rosé champagne or a premium California Blanc de Noir sparkling wine with this opulent dish.

· California quail and artichokes in lemon sauce ·

California grows most of the country's artichokes, and Castroville near Monterey is the state's self-proclaimed Artichoke Capital. Artichokes are very popular in California and are used in a wide range of dishes. They are tasty by themselves, but go beautifully with seafood and poultry. We've paired them with quail here, abundant and inexpensive in San Francisco's Chinese poultry shops, but you could also use game hens, chicken, or rabbit if you prefer.

    If you can't find the tender young artichokes that are ideal for this dish, use medium-sized artichokes, peel off the outer leaves, and cut them into quarters. Remove the choke before cooking, and they will work just fine. Use our California White Wine and Herb Sausage or any other mild-flavored fresh sausage such as mild Italian.

1 tbsp. olive oil
½ lb. California White Wine and Herb
   Sausage (see page 254) or other
   mild fresh sausage
Salt and pepper to taste
8 quail, or 8 chicken thighs, or
   1 rabbit, cut up
2 cloves garlic, chopped
4 shallots, chopped
1 c. chicken stock
1 tsp. chopped fresh thyme or
   ¼ tsp. dried

1 tbsp. chopped fresh basil or
   1 tsp. dried
8 small artichokes, halved, or
   3 medium artichokes, quartered,
   tough outer leaves and choke
   removed, or use equivalent frozen
   artichoke hearts
1 tsp. grated lemon zest
½ lb. small button mushrooms
2 egg yolks
2 tbsp. lemon juice, or to taste

    Heat the olive oil in a large Dutch oven or casserole and brown the sausages whole for about 5 minutes. Remove and cool. Cut the sausages into 1-inch rounds.

    Sprinkle salt and pepper lightly on the birds, and brown them on all sides in the fat remaining in the pan for about 10 minutes. Remove and reserve.

    Pour off all but about 2 tablespoons of the fat, add the garlic and shallots and cook them over medium heat for 5 minutes. Pour in the stock and scrape up any browned bits adhering to the bottom of the pot. Put in the thyme, basil, artichokes, and lemon zest along with the browned quails. Cover the pot and cook for 20 minutes or until the quail are tender. (Chicken or rabbit will take longer, about 30 minutes.) Put in the sausages and mushrooms and cook for 10 minutes more, uncovered. Transfer the quails, artichokes, and mushrooms to a warm platter or shallow serving bowl. Reduce the sauce by boiling, uncovered, until it has the consistency of heavy cream. Beat together the egg yolks and lemon juice in a small bowl. Stir 1 cup of the sauce into the egg and lemon mixture. Stir this back into the rest of the sauce off the heat. Taste for salt, pepper, and lemon juice. Pour the sauce over everything, and serve at once. Makes 4 servings

· grilled turkey paupiettes ·

This dish is inspired by the French *paupiettes de veau*, veal scallops pounded thin and stuffed with savory forcemeat. Turkey makes an inexpensive and low-calorie replacement for veal, and this wonderful stuffing is West Coast eclectic with pine nuts, shiitake sausage, and ricotta cheese. It is so flavorful and juicy that you don't need any sauce with this dish, other than a squeeze or two of lemon juice. Use any mild sausage such as the Japantown Pork and Shiitake Mushroom Sausage from this chapter or mild Italian sausage.

Grilled Turkey Paupiettes make a lovely lunch or light patio dinner with a salad of bitter greens and sliced mushrooms in a lemony dressing, some hot sourdough bread, and a glass of fruity California Chardonnay.

4 slices of turkey breast measuring about 4 x 8 inches, sliced ¼ inch thick
Salt and pepper

· **Stuffing** ·
¼ c. pine nuts
¾ lb. mild sausage such as Japantown Pork and Shiitake Mushroom Sausage (see page 249) or mild Italian, removed from casings
½ c. finely chopped onions
2 tsp. minced garlic

½ c. chopped cooked spinach or chard
½ c. chopped fresh cilantro (optional)
⅓ c. ricotta
2 tbsp. grated Parmesan cheese
⅓ c. day-old bread crumbs
1 egg, beaten
Salt and pepper to taste

....

Melted butter
Lemon wedges

Place each slice of turkey breast between 2 sheets of wax paper or plastic wrap and pound with a meat mallet or the flat of a cleaver until they are quite thin, about ⅛ inch. Lightly sprinkle with salt and pepper and set aside.

To make the stuffing, toast the pine nuts over low heat in a dry heavy frying pan, shaking continuously until the nuts are light brown. Transfer them to a bowl. Fry the sausage over medium-high heat for 5 minutes, breaking the meat up with a fork. Pour off all but about 1 tablespoon of the fat, and add the onions and garlic. Sauté for 5 more minutes until they are soft. Add this mixture to the nuts, along with the spinach or chard, cilantro (if using), ricotta, Parmesan, bread crumbs, and egg, and mix well. Taste for salt and pepper.

Spread each turkey slice on a flat surface and place ⅓–½ cup of filling in the center of each. Fold the sides over and roll up to form a rectangular packet. Tie the paupiette in 3 places with string. Brush the paupiettes with melted butter and grill over a medium fire, turning the packets a few times. They should cook for about 15 minutes, or until the interior reaches 140° F.
Serve at once, accompanied with lemon wedges.
Makes 4 servings

The versatile stuffing is also delicious in chicken breasts or veal chops.
Leftover paupiettes are great sliced in rounds and served cold as an appetizer or on sandwiches with a spicy mayonnaise.

· Anzonini's chicken livers and chorizo ·

When the great flamenco singer Anzonini del Puerto came to California from Spain, he brought with him his gypsy gusto for food, music, and life. The dishes he cooked for friends at parties and fiestas — rich with garlic, olive oil, and his spicy homemade sausages — quickly made him a patron saint of the garlic revolution in Berkeley. Filmmaker Les Blanc captured the spirit and the flavor of Anzonini's food and music in his wonderful documentary film *Garlic Is as Good as Ten Mothers*, before Anzonini died a few years ago.

¼ c. olive oil
¾ lb. Basque chorizo or other spicy
  sausage such as linguiça, paprika
  sausage, or pepperoni, sliced into
  ¼-inch rounds
1½ lbs. chicken livers, divided into
  individual lobes
Salt and pepper to taste
¼ c. dry red wine
3 small zucchini, cut into ¼-inch
  rounds

2 red or green bell peppers, seeded
  and sliced
½ c. thinly sliced red onion
6 cloves garlic, minced
8 plum tomatoes, peeled, seeded,
  and quartered
½ tsp. dried rosemary or 1 tsp. fresh
½ tsp. dried sage or 1 tsp. fresh
½ c. chopped fresh parsley
Lemon juice to taste

In a large, heavy skillet, heat 2 tablespoons of the olive oil over medium-high heat. Fry the chorizo for 3 minutes to render some of the fat and lightly brown the sausages. Transfer to a bowl and cook the chicken livers in the fat for 5 minutes, shaking the pan occasionally. Sprinkle the livers lightly with salt and pepper, and turn them over. Sauté them 3–5 minutes more, until firm. Add to the sausages. Pour the wine into the pan and deglaze, stirring up any brown bits stuck to the bottom, then pour into the bowl.

Add the remaining 2 tablespoons of olive oil to the pan. Turn up the heat to high, and put in the zucchini, peppers, onion, and garlic. Sauté for 5 minutes, stirring the pan continuously until the vegetables just become soft. Stir in the sausages, livers and any juices, along with the tomatoes, rosemary, sage, and parsley. Cover and cook over medium heat for 2–3 minutes to heat everything through. Taste for salt and pepper, and add lemon juice to taste. To serve as tapas, let the dish cool a bit; otherwise serve it hot as an entree. Makes 10–12 servings as an appetizer, 4–6 as an entree

Anzonini often served these spicy chicken livers with chorizo at his night-long celebrations of flamenco and food. They are delicious as tapas or as a main course served with saffron rice or diced potatoes fried in olive oil and garlic.

sausage, red pepper, and eggplant stir-fry ·

The Chinese were the original inventors of fast food, with their stir-fry cooking. Stir-frying takes advantage of high heat, and the wok, a bowl-shaped pan, enables the cook to stir bits of food up and around the sloping sides, cooking them quickly and evenly. This dish uses the Chinese technique with sausages, eggplant, and sweet red peppers. You can cook it Chinese-style in a wok or use a large frying pan.

½ lb. California White Wine and Herb Sausage (see page 254) or other mild sausage, cut into ¾-inch rounds

½ lb. Oakland Hot Links (see page 255) or other spicy sausage, cut into ½-inch rounds

2 tbsp. olive oil

1 medium unpeeled eggplant, cubed

2 medium red bell peppers, cut into thin strips

1 medium red onion, thinly sliced

3 cloves garlic, minced

¼ c. white wine, dry sherry, or dry vermouth

Salt and pepper to taste

· **Garnish** ·

¼ c. finely chopped green onions or scallions

Stir-fry the sausages in a wok or large skillet for about 5 minutes, until lightly browned, remove with a slotted spoon, and reserve. Add the olive oil and stir-fry the eggplant for 5 minutes, until soft. Put in the peppers and onion and stir-fry for 5 more minutes. Add the garlic and wine and cook an additional 5 minutes, until the liquid begins to reduce. Put the sausages back in and cook for 2 more minutes to heat through. Taste for salt and pepper. Serve the dish by itself or over pasta or rice, garnished with the green onions. Makes 4 servings

It's fun to combine different types of sausages in this dish, since each sausage adds its own particular flavor. We used our California White Wine and Herb Sausage and Oakland Hot Links, but come up with your own delicious combinations.

· Chinatown crépinettes braised with Napa cabbage ·

One of the most fragrant and delicious Chinese dishes is greens braised with aromatic sausage. Almost any leafy vegetable is delicious cooked this way, from bitter mustard or turnip greens to the milder-flavored bok choy, savoy or Napa cabbage. Serve this succulent dish over steamed rice with a malty Chinese beer such as Tsingtao.

2 lbs. Chinatown Crépinettes (8–10) or equivalent	½ c. Chinese rice wine or medium dry sherry
2 c. thinly sliced onions	1 c. rich chicken stock
2 tsp. minced fresh ginger	1 c. sliced green onions or scallions
1 tsp. minced garlic	2 c. coarsely chopped fresh cilantro
1½ lbs. Napa cabbage, cut crosswise into ½-inch slices	2 whole star anise
	Salt and pepper to taste

Brown the crépinettes or other sausage cut in chunks or in small patties in a heavy frying pan or Dutch oven for 5 minutes per side, turning once. Remove the sausages and add the onions, ginger, and garlic. Cook for 10 minutes over medium heat until they are soft. Add the cabbage, and cook for 2–3 minutes, stirring to coat with the pan juices. Add the wine, chicken stock, ¼ cup of the green onions, 1 cup of the cilantro, and the star anise. Return the crépinettes or other sausages to the pan, lower the heat to a simmer, and cook for 30 minutes.

Using a slotted spoon, remove the sausages and vegetables to a serving platter, and keep warm. Turn the heat to high, and reduce the liquid remaining in the skillet until it just begins to turn syrupy. Taste for salt and pepper, degrease, and pour over the sausages and cabbage. Garnish with the remaining green onions and cilantro. Serve with steamed rice. Makes 6 servings

We use our Chinatown Crépinettes wrapped in caul fat (see page 246), but you could easily substitute the same sausage meat stuffed into casings or in bulk.

artichoke and sausage ragù ·

This hearty winter dish is inspired by the Mediterranean style of cooking brought to California by the immigrants who first planted artichokes in the cool coastal valleys near Monterey Bay.

4 medium artichokes, tough outer leaves and chokes removed, quartered

½ lb. California White Wine and Herb Sausage (see page 254) or other mild fresh sausage

2 tbsp. olive oil

2–3 lbs. boneless pork butt, trimmed and cut into 2-inch chunks

Salt and pepper to taste

1 onion, thinly sliced

6 whole garlic cloves, peeled

1 tsp. crushed fennel seed

½ tsp. dried thyme or 1½ tsp. chopped fresh thyme

2 bay leaves

1 c. chicken stock

1 c. dry white wine

1 c. imported black and green olives such as Niçoise

4 fresh ripe tomatoes, peeled, seeded, and coarsely chopped

Bring 2–3 quarts of lightly salted water to a boil. Put in the artichokes and cook for 15 minutes. Cool under running water, drain, and set aside.

In a large Dutch oven or casserole, brown the whole sausages on all sides in the olive oil for about 5–7 minutes. Remove and cool. Cut into 1-inch rounds. Season the pork with salt and pepper, and add it to the fat in the pan. Continue to cook over medium high heat, turning the meat to brown evenly, about 10 minutes. Remove and reserve. Pour off all but 3 tablespoons of the fat, and add the onion and garlic. Cover and cook for 10 minutes, until the onion is soft, stirring the pot occasionally. Add the fennel seed, thyme, bay leaves, stock, and wine. Bring the pot to a boil and return the pork to it. Cook, covered, for 45 minutes until the pork is almost tender. Put in the sausages, artichokes, and olives, and cook 10–15 minutes more until the pork and artichokes are tender. Remove all the solids from the pot and transfer to a warm platter or shallow bowl. Degrease the sauce and boil it down until it just begins to thicken. Add the tomatoes and cook for 1 more minute. Taste for salt and pepper, and pour the sauce over the food. Serve at once. Makes 6 servings

Use our California White Wine and Herb Sausage or any other full-flavored mild sausage such as mild Italian or fresh bratwurst.

· Basque sheepherder's lamb stew ·

When I traveled across the United States by car fairly frequently in days past, I would carefully plan my trip to spend at least one night in Elko, Nevada, because of its two great attractions: the Basque Hotel and the Star Hotel. Both of these restaurant-boardinghouses cater to the Basque sheepherders who tend their flocks throughout western Nevada and Northern California. And when sheepherders come to town after months out there in the barren scrub with nobody but sheep for company, they put away substantial amounts of food and drink. So dinners at the Basque boardinghouses in Elko, and at similar restaurant-hotels in Winnemucca, Reno, Los Baños, and San Francisco, tend toward the gargantuan.

Everything's family-style here: you just pick a table filled with friendly Basques, sit down, and start drinking the rough young red wine they pour you from unlabeled wine bottles.

Dinner starts out with a tray of salami, olives, peppers, strong dry sheep cheese, chunks of chorizo, with red beans and sliced raw onions in vinegar and oil on the side. Salad usually follows, big bowls of chopped lettuce, tomatoes, and pimientos in a garlicky, creamy dressing (the Star in Elko has the best). Then come cauldrons of soup, usually lamb or mutton, with barley, garlic, chopped greens, beans, tomatoes — whatever is plentiful and in season. After a plate or two of pasta or paella, you are ready for the main course. This will depend on the time of year and the boardinghouse, but you're likely to tuck into a platter of lamb chops, a veal sirloin steak, roast beef, or a savory lamb stew with chorizo and peppers.

If you can't find or make Spanish-style chorizo, use linguiça, pepperoni, andouille, or another spicy sausage.

6 whole dried red chiles such as ancho or New Mexico
2 tbsp. red wine vinegar
½ tsp. salt
1 tsp. coarsely ground black pepper
½ tsp. dried thyme
½ tsp. dried oregano
1 tbsp. sweet Hungarian paprika
4 lbs. lamb stew, preferably neck or shoulder, cut into 2-inch pieces, with or without the bones
1 tbsp. olive oil

½ lb. Basque or Spanish chorizo, sliced into ¼-inch rounds
1 medium onion, chopped
6 cloves garlic, chopped
1 large fresh Anaheim chile, seeded and chopped
2 bay leaves
2 c. full-bodied dry red wine
1 c. beef, lamb, or chicken stock
4 c. diced potatoes
Salt and pepper to taste

Cover the dried chiles in water and bring to a boil. Reduce to a simmer and cook for 15 minutes. Remove the chiles from the pot and discard the stems and seeds. Process the chiles in a food processor with the vinegar and enough of the cooking liquid to make a puree. Set aside.

In a bowl, mix together the salt, pepper, thyme, oregano, and paprika. Rub the herbs and spices all over the lamb pieces. Heat the olive oil in a large Dutch oven or casserole. Add the chorizo, and fry over medium-high heat for 2–3 minutes, stirring frequently to render some of the fat. Remove the chorizo with a slotted spoon; set aside. Brown the lamb chunks in batches on all sides for a total of 10 minutes. Remove the lamb. Pour off all but about 3 tablespoons of the fat. Add the onion and garlic to the pot and cook over medium heat for 5 minutes, stirring occasionally. Put in the fresh chile, bay leaves, and chile puree, along with the wine and stock and the reserved lamb and sausage. Bring everything to a boil and then reduce to a simmer.

Cook the stew, uncovered, for 1½ hours until the lamb is tender. Add the potatoes and cook for 15–20 minutes until they are tender. If there isn't enough liquid to cover the potatoes, add more wine or stock. Taste for salt and pepper. Degrease the sauce and serve over rice. Makes 8 servings

Hearty and spicy, Basque cooking reflects the hunger of hardworking men and women who live in a rough landscape. In the West, Basques have adapted their dishes to local ingredients. This stew is typical Basque campfire cooking with lamb the only ingredient that might need refrigeration. No problem, of course, for a herder surrounded by hundreds of sheep. Serve this substantial stew with steamed rice and a gutsy California Petite Sirah or Spanish Rioja.

From Helen Evan Brown's *West Coast Cookbook* to innumerable issues of *Sunset* magazine's "Chefs of the West" to the latest trendy disquisitions on California cuisine, one constant remains: West Coast folks (especially Californians) like to cook outdoors. A mild climate, laid-back life-style, and plenty of space for backyards and decks have made Californians dedicated outdoor chefs. In the South barbecuing means long, slow cooking over hickory coals. On the West Coast these days it's more often hot mesquite charcoal and a quick sear in a hibachi.

In traditional southern barbecue the ingredients are fixed: pigmeat in most of the Old South, beef wherever the cowboys congregate. On the West Coast, however, just about anything goes. Hamburgers, steaks, and hot dogs, smothered in sweet barbecue sauce — the staples of our California childhoods — are still around, but today you're more likely to see fish and vegetable kebabs, grilled chicken or sausages, whole fish or butterflied legs of lamb, broiled polenta, and tofu. And instead of using bland commercial barbecue sauce, many talented backyard chefs have come up with their own recipes for tangy marinades and original basting sauces. In the recipes that follow we present two approaches to the new West Coast barbecuing: John King's Asian-inspired marinade and sauce and Franco Dunn's fiery sauces, which lend heat and flavor to pork, chicken, and sausages.

· Oakland barbecue with Franco's sauce ·

This spicy barbecue is based on a tangy tomato-based sauce contributed by chef Franco Dunn, who lives in Sonoma's wine country. Oakland Hot Links are the preferred sausage, but you could use any spicy smoked sausage such as andouille or smoked country sausage. Along with the sausage, cook up some chicken or pork, brush on the sauce toward the end of cooking, and save plenty of sauce in a separate bowl for guests to pour on the food.

The sauce is delicious on just about any type of grilled meat, but it is especially good with spareribs.

· Franco's barbecue sauce ·

¼ c. bacon or sausage drippings
2 c. finely chopped onions
1 c. chopped green onions or scallions
½ green bell pepper, finely chopped
4 garlic cloves, minced
14 oz. bottled chili sauce
¼ c. Worcestershire sauce
3 tbsp. cider vinegar
½ c. beer

1 c. bourbon whiskey
2 tbsp. dry mustard
2 tbsp. molasses
½ tsp. cayenne
1–2 tbsp. chile powder blend
1 tbsp. sweet Hungarian paprika
¼ tsp. ground coriander
1–2 tsp. liquid smoke, to taste
Salt, pepper, and Tabasco to taste

Melt the bacon fat in a large nonaluminum pot over medium heat. Put in the onions, green onions, bell pepper, and garlic, and cook, covered, for 10 minutes, stirring frequently, until the vegetables are soft. Stir in the remaining ingredients. Bring everything to a boil and reduce to a simmer. Cook 15–20 minutes. The sauce should be thick but easily pourable. If it is too thick, stir in some water. Add salt, pepper, and, if you like the sauce hotter, Tabasco. Makes 3–4 cups

· Oakland barbecue ·

1 lb. Oakland Hot Links (see page 255) or other spicy smoked sausages

4 pork chops or 2 lbs. country spareribs
Salt and pepper to taste
2 c. Franco's Barbecue Sauce

Heat charcoal in a covered barbecue kettle. When the coals are covered with gray ash, salt and pepper the meat and sear for 2–3 minutes on each side. Add the sausages. Cover the barbecue and cook for 10–12 minutes, turning the food once or twice. Brush the meat and sausages with the barbecue sauce and turn to cook the brushed side. After 1 minute, brush barbecue sauce on the other side, and turn them over. Cook for another minute. Pork and sausages are done when they reach an internal temperature of 155–160° F. Serve the food with additional reserved barbecue sauce. Makes 4–6 servings

· John King's Asian barbecue ·

Besides sausage, chicken, and duck, Berkeley artist (and our book illustrator) John King says his Asian-style barbecue sauce is also delicious on lamb, pork ribs, and beef (especially flank steak).

· **Sauce** ·

¼ c. Japanese-style soy sauce, such as Kikkoman

¼ c. medium dry sherry or mirin

1 c. hoisin sauce

2 tbsp. red wine vinegar

2 tbsp. Dijon mustard

2 cloves garlic, minced

1 tbsp. coarsely ground black pepper

1 tsp. ground cumin

3 tbsp. Oriental sesame oil

1 tsp. crushed fennel seed or 1 tsp. Herbes de Provence

....

4 boned duck breasts or 4 boned chicken breasts

4 Chinatown Crépinettes (see page 246) or other mild fresh sausages

Make the sauce by mixing all the ingredients together in a small bowl. It can be stored for 2–3 weeks covered in the refrigerator.

Put the duck or chicken breasts (you may remove the skin if you want) in a nonaluminum bowl or baking dish. Pour in 1 cup of the barbecue sauce and massage into the meat. Cover with plastic wrap, and marinate for 2 hours at room temperature or overnight in the refrigerator.

Fire up a covered charcoal or gas grill. Since the sauce contains a fair amount of sugar from the hoisin sauce and wine, it's best to grill over medium heat so as not to blacken the food. Remove the poultry from the marinade, and let any excess sauce drain off. Place the breasts on the grill, skin side down if it is still attached. Put the crépinettes or other fresh sausages on the grill. Cover the grill and sear the food for 3–4 minutes. Baste all the food with the remaining cup of barbecue sauce. Turn the food every 3 or 4 minutes until the poultry and sausage are firm to the touch. The poultry will take about 12–15 minutes, while the sausages will need about 15 minutes. Put out any flare-ups with squirts of water.

Transfer the food to a heated platter and serve at once, accompanied with 2 or 3 different salads. Makes 4 servings and 2 cups sauce

NEW AMERICAN CUISINE

Spinach, pork, and game
crépinettes

Atlantic seafood sausage

Baguette stuffed with
sausage and chard

Phyllis Steiber's sausage and
prawn brochette

Duck sausage with pasta
and wild mushrooms

Sausage with fettuccine,
sun-dried tomatoes, and
American chèvre

Sweetbread and chicken
sausage in a sweet red
pepper puree

Spicy lamb sausage with
Oriental eggplant and feta
cheese dressing

Wild rice and pecan salad
with grilled venison sausage

Quick and easy grills

Turkey sausage braised with
whole garlic heads

Duck or turkey sausage with
prune and red wine sauce

Duck or turkey sausage with
apples and onions

Grilled spinach, pork, and
game crépinettes with escarole
and horseradish sauce

Sausage and bitter greens
with soy, honey, and sherry
vinegar dressing

Puff pastry pie filled with
pheasant sausage

Roasted lamb sausage with
mustard-rosemary glaze

Rabbit boudin *en papillote*
with mustard and tarragon butter

Sweetbread and chicken
sausage *en papillote* with watercress and spinach butter

Wild boar sausage baked with
honey-orange glaze

Creative chefs in restaurants (and increasingly in home kitchens) all over America are revolutionizing American cooking. America's finest cooks exhibit a healthy eclecticism these days, creating dishes with new ingredients that combine elements of widely varied cuisines and traditions — French regional, Japanese, Thai, Southwest American, New England, and Cajun.

Sausages are at the forefront of this food revolution and have dramatically extended the range of American restaurant and home cooking. One of the most interesting aspects of the new American cooking is the widespread use of sausages as flavorings and condiments. Red meat and heavy dishes are out of fashion these days for both health and aesthetic reasons. A spicy sausage used to flavor a dish of fettuccine with sun-dried tomatoes and American chèvre (see page 311) provides flavor and zest without excess cholesterol and calories. Slices of grilled venison sausage (see page 297) enliven the nutty flavors of wild rice and pecan salad and a Wilted Cabbage and Roasted Walnut Salad becomes a main course along with Wild Boar Sausage Baked with Honey-Orange Glaze (see pages 351, 325). New American chefs are rediscovering what European cooks have known for eons, that sausages used as seasonings for grains, greens, and other vegetables are more appealing than dinners centered on large amounts of meat. Sausages provide a healthier and cheaper alternative, and an endless variety of tastes and flavors.

Game, increasingly available from farms in the United States and abroad, is often made into exciting new sausages that are used in a startling variety of ways. Our Pheasant and Wild Mushroom Sausage (see page 293), Buffalo Sausage (see page 294), Duck Sausage (see page 296), Wild Boar Sausage (see page 298), Rabbit Boudin (see page 302), and Spinach, Pork, and Game Crépinettes (see page 306) show how the intense flavors of game add spice and excitement in salads, on pastas, or braised with vegetables.

The new cuisine emphasizes lightness, and many chefs are experimenting with sausages made from untraditional ingredients like poultry, seafood, and vegetables. Our Zucchini and Rice "Sausage" (see page 299), Sweetbread and Chicken Sausage (see page 300), and Atlantic Seafood Sausage (see page 307) provide light textures and delicate flavors for health-conscious diners. Lamb is a very popular meat on American menus, and it is often found in

sausages with Middle Eastern or Mediterranean flavors. We've included two lamb sausages — Lamb, Rosemary, and Mustard Sausage (see page 304) and Spicy Lamb, Pine Nut, and Sun-dried Tomato Sausage (see page 305) — that combine the flavors of Provence and the Near East. Our recipe for Spicy Lamb Sausage with Oriental Eggplant and Feta Cheese Dressing (see page 313) shows lamb's particular affinity for eggplant, herbs, and spices.

Wonderfully fresh produce and vegetables of every type are now available in all seasons of the year and in almost every region of the country. Greens of all sorts are very popular, both traditional varieties such as cabbage, chard, spinach, escarole, and watercress, and more exotic types such as arugula, endive, radicchio, and mâche. They are often used with sausages in salads, stuffings, or braised dishes, like our Baguette Stuffed with Sausage and Chard (see page 308), Grilled Spinach, Pork, and Game Crépinettes with Escarole and Horseradish Sauce (see page 319), Sausage and Bitter Greens with Soy, Honey, and Sherry Vinegar Dressing (see page 320), and Sweetbread and Chicken Sausage *en Papillote* with Watercress and Spinach Butter (see page 324).

Garlic has become one of the badges of the new cookery. From being the embarrassment it often was for ethnic Americans in WASP schools a few years back, garlic's rich and pungent aromas now serve to identify the new American cook. A garlic cult seems to be growing among Americans of every ethnic persuasion. Festivals draw thousands of garlic fanciers every year, there are garlic societies and garlic banquets, and everybody loves the once scorned "stinking lily." One of the favorite dishes of today's cooks is whole baked heads of garlic, usually served with a soft white cheese and chewy bread. Our Turkey Sausage Braised with Whole Garlic Heads (see page 316) has enough of the fragrant bulb to satisfy even the most ardent garlic fanatic.

The new cuisine, eclectic and lively, is transforming America's kitchens, in restaurants and in homes. Central to the exciting new combinations American chefs are constantly coming up with is the creative use of sausage, as a condiment or an added spice in the dish. Whether you make your own or buy them from the many new artisan producers, you too can use sausages to lighten up your menu with new creations and add spice and life to traditional favorites.

HOT LINKS & COUNTRY FLAVORS

· pheasant and wild mushroom sausage ·

Colorful wild pheasants are still plentiful in many regions in America, and some of the tastiest birds feed on the grain left behind at the harvest in the Midwest. These days, farm-raised pheasants are widely available for non-hunters from specialty butchers or mail order houses. The light and elegant flavors of pheasant are very popular with American chefs, and these delicious and adaptable game birds are served in a variety of ways in new American restaurants. Home cooks can take a tip from professional chefs and use pheasant in many different types of dishes. If you have several pheasants, you can use the breasts for elegant entrees, the thighs to make tasty sausage, and the wings, back, neck, and legs in a flavorful stock. You should consign the pheasant legs to the stockpot, in any case. Don't try to make sausage from them: they have tough sinews running from the claw to the joint and very little meat. In general, try to use mature pheasants for sausages; young farm-raised pheasants can be a bit bland.

Pheasant is delicious with the many varieties of wild mushrooms that are coming into the market these days, particularly morels. If you can't find dried morels in a specialty store, use dried porcini or shiitake mushrooms.

Serve this luscious Pheasant and Wild Mushroom Sausage by itself or sautéed with apples and onions, or dress it up in puff pastry or serve it over flaky biscuits.

1 lb. boned pheasant meat with skin attached
¼ lb. pork back fat
¼ lb. pheasant fat, if available (if not, use additional pork back fat)
2 tsp. kosher salt
1 tsp. chopped fresh thyme or ¼ tsp. dried
⅓ c. (about ½ oz.) dried morels, porcini, or shiitake mushrooms, soaked in hot water for at least 30 minutes, drained, and chopped

2 tbsp. apple brandy, Calvados, or other brandy
Pinch *each* freshly grated nutmeg and ground cloves
¼ tsp. dried sage
2 tsp. chopped shallots
1 tsp. coarsely ground black pepper
1 tbsp. chopped fresh herbs such as chervil, chives, or parsley (optional)
Lamb or small hog casings

For directions on sausage making, see page 332.

Grind the pheasant, pork fat, and pheasant fat through a ¼-inch plate. Mix the ground meat and fat with the other ingredients, except the casings, until well blended together. Stuff into lamb casings or small hog casings and tie into 4–5-inch links. The sausage will keep for 3 days refrigerated or 2 months frozen.

Makes about 2 pounds

When you dress the pheasant, try to save the fat and skin, both of which add plenty of flavor to the sausage. If you can't find pheasant, you can make this sausage with chicken thighs or with other types of game birds.

· buffalo (or beef) sausage ·

Buffalo meat is much leaner than beef, but has the same rich flavors. This versatile meat is delicious grilled, baked, or in a stew. And don't worry about its being an endangered species. Commercial herds of buffalo are now raised in states such as Montana and Wyoming, and the meat is sold in specialty butcher shops. The sausage can be air-dried at room temperature and/or cold smoked, in which case be sure to add the curing salts (see page 343). Otherwise, eat buffalo sausage fresh or hot smoked.

2 lbs. buffalo meat, beefalo, or beef	1 tsp. dry mustard
1 lb. pork back fat	3 tbsp. red wine vinegar
1 shallot, finely chopped	½ tsp. dried thyme
2 tsp. Dijon mustard	4 tsp. kosher salt
1 tbsp. minced garlic	½ c. water
1 tbsp. coarsely ground black pepper	1 tsp. curing salts (optional)
2 tsp. crushed juniper berries	Medium hog casings
¼ c. chopped shelled pistachio nuts	

For directions on sausage making, see page 332.

Grind the meat through a ⅜-inch plate, and the pork fat through a ¼-inch plate. Mix the meat and fat together with the remaining ingredients, except the casings, and knead until everything is well blended. Don't forget to include the curing salts if you wish to air-dry or cold smoke the sausage. Stuff into medium hog casings and tie into 6-inch links. If you choose to air-dry the sausage, hang it overnight at room temperature, and cold smoke for 6–8 hours (see page 340 for details). Otherwise, mature the sausage, uncovered, in the refrigerator overnight. The next day you can hot smoke the sausage (see page 341 for details) or use it as is. Uncured sausage will keep 3 days in the refrigerator, cured 7–10 days. Frozen, all sausage will keep for 2 months. Makes 3½ pounds

For this hearty sausage, buy the cheaper cuts such as chuck or stew meat. If buffalo (or beefalo — a new hybrid) is unavailable, beef chuck works just fine.

turkey sausage with Drambuie ·

Wild turkeys were common in colonial America, and they still run wild in southeastern forests. If you are fortunate enough to have a wild turkey, then roast or braise the breast, and use the thighs to make this sausage. But don't fret if you don't have the wild bird. Domesticated turkey is delicious too. It's generally not a good idea to use turkey legs, because their bony sinews make them undesirable for sausage, but if you want to take the time to pull the sinews out, legs will also do.

2¼ lbs. turkey thigh meat with skin attached
¾ lb. pork back fat
½ tsp. ground sage
1 tsp. dried thyme
1 tsp. fennel seed
1 tsp. sweet Hungarian paprika
⅛ tsp. ground allspice

1 tsp. minced garlic
2 tsp. coarsely ground black pepper
1 tbsp. kosher salt
¼ c. Drambuie, or orange-flavored liqueur such as Grand Marnier
2 tsp. honey
¼ c. water
Medium hog casings

For directions on sausage making, see page 332.

Grind the meat and fat through a ¼-inch plate. Add herbs, spices, Drambuie, honey, and water and mix with your hands until all ingredients are thoroughly combined. Stuff the mixture into hog casings and tie off in 6-inch lengths. Keeps 3 days refrigerated, 2 months frozen. Makes 3½ pounds

Try these sausages with our Honey-Orange Glaze (see page 325), which complements the Drambuie in the blend very nicely. An aromatic and slightly sweet California Gewürztraminer would make a great match.

· duck sausage ·

Creative American chefs have popularized duck sausage by putting it on pizza, or serving it with sautéed fruits or with grilled radicchio. At the Aidells Sausage Company, we have two varieties: a poached duck sausage with orange and green peppercorns, and a smoked duck sausage, which we never seem to have enough of.

Duck sausages are excellent grilled or eaten with sweet sauces such as our Honey-Orange Glaze (see page 325). Try them with apples and onions (see page 318), or with prunes and red wine (see page 317).

1 lb. (approximately) meat only from the duck breasts
1 lb. (approximately) meat and skin from 2 deboned duck legs and thighs
¼ lb. smoky bacon, chilled in freezer for 30 minutes
1 tsp. finely chopped garlic
2 tsp. kosher salt
2 tsp. coarsely ground black pepper
1 tsp. sweet Hungarian paprika

½ tsp. cayenne
Pinch ground allspice
¼ tsp. ground sage
½ tsp. dried thyme
¼ tsp. dried savory
1 tsp. sugar
¼ c. orange-flavored liqueur such as Grand Marnier or Curaçao
¼ c. water
Medium hog casings

For directions on sausage making, see page 332.

In a meat grinder fitted with a ¼-inch plate, grind the meat, skin, and bacon. In a bowl, mix together the chopped meat, skin, bacon, garlic, salt, spices, herbs, sugar, orange liqueur, and water. Blend well with your hands, kneading and squeezing the meat as you mix it. Do not overmix, however, because the fat will begin to melt and make the sausage appear white. Stuff into medium hog casings and tie into 5-inch lengths. Keeps 3 days refrigerated, 2 months frozen. Makes 2½ pounds

To make these delicious sausages, use duck legs and thighs, skin and all, along with some boned and skinned lean meat from the breasts. Use the carcass and scraps to make a flavorful duck stock, perfect for cooking lentils or white beans.

· venison sausage ·

Venison sausage often suffers from lack of fat, which makes it too dry, and from too many overpowering ingredients, which can mask the rich flavor of the meat. In this recipe we use herbs that complement the flavor of venison, and we allow the meat to marinate and mellow with these herbs overnight. The sausages are delicious grilled and served with a Cumberland Sauce for Game Sausages (see page 356) along with Oven-Roasted Garlic-Rosemary Potatoes (see page 352). A good hearty red wine from the Côtes du Rhône is the best match.

1½ lbs. venison shoulder	4 tsp. kosher salt
1 lb. pork butt	2 tsp. coarsely ground black pepper
¾ lb. pork back fat	1 tsp. fresh rosemary or ½ tsp. dried
½ lb. slab bacon, rind removed	2 tbsp. brandy
1 tsp. minced garlic	3 tbsp. dry red wine
1 tsp. minced shallots	Medium hog casings
2 tsp. minced juniper berries	

For directions on sausage making, see page 332.

Cut the meat, fat, and bacon into 2-inch strips. In a large bowl, mix the meat, fat, and bacon with all the ingredients except casings. Cover and place in the refrigerator to marinate overnight.

The next day, grind the mixture through a ¼-inch plate. Add any juices remaining in the bowl. Knead to blend all the ingredients thoroughly. Stuff into hog casings and tie into 6-inch links. Dry the sausage, uncovered, in the refrigerator overnight before grilling or pan-frying. Will keep for 3 days refrigerated, 2 months frozen. Makes 4 pounds

To bring out the earthy flavors of these tangy sausages, serve them with other wild ingredients such as wild rice, morels or other wild mushrooms, and steamed wild greens (young dandelions, mâche, fiddleheads).

· wild boar sausage ·

In Northern California, the Russians introduced the European wild boar around Fort Ross in the 1800s, and it mated with feral domestic pigs to create a populous and troublesome game animal. These wild boar are found today all over Mendocino and Sonoma counties and are a real problem for farmers and grape growers. They are even spreading into Marin County just north of San Francisco, and the thought of these tusked and hairy pigs uprooting the rhododendrons next to the hot tub has many a Marinite worried. So no one is particularly outraged when grape growers, farmers, and sportsmen hunt this abundant species. As an added plus, the meat is very tasty. If you know someone who hunts in Northern California, boar meat is easier to come by than venison. If not, European wild boar is available from specialty shops, or you can substitute domestic pork in this recipe.

Boar meat is leaner, redder, and gamier than domestic pork and is usually flavored with strong herbs such as juniper or caraway that blend well with its pronounced flavor. So if you use domestic pork, you might want to lower the amounts of these ingredients in the following recipe.

Use meat from the shoulders or legs. Let the sausage mellow for a minimum of one day, preferably two, in the refrigerator before using. Particularly good with a Cumberland Sauce, Oven-Roasted Garlic-Rosemary Potatoes, or Wilted Cabbage and Roasted Walnut Salad (see pages 356, 352, and 351).

3 lbs. boar meat or pork butt	½ tsp. ground ginger
1¼ lbs. pork back fat	¼ c. dry red wine
1 tbsp. minced garlic	1 tsp. whole caraway seed
1 tbsp. coarsely ground black pepper	4 tsp. salt
¼ c. gin	Pinch ground allspice
1 tsp. ground caraway seeds	1 tsp. chopped fresh sage or
1 tsp. chopped fresh marjoram or	½ tsp. ground sage
½ tsp. dried	Medium hog casings

For directions on sausage making, see page 332.

Grind the meat and fat through a ¼-inch plate. Mix with the remaining ingredients, except the casings. Stuff into medium hog casings and tie into 5-inch links. Refrigerate the sausages uncovered a day or two before using. Keeps 5 days refrigerated, or 2 months frozen. Makes about 4 pounds

We use gin in this recipe since its major flavor is juniper, but you could replace it with a teaspoon or more of crushed dried juniper berries for a gamier character.

· zucchini and rice "sausage" ·

This sausage is almost vegetarian except for the pancetta and, of course, the hog casings. If you want to make a completely vegetarian version, leave out the pancetta, substitute sun-dried tomatoes packed in oil, and double the amount of fresh herbs. And you don't have to put the mixture into casings — just shape into "footballs," roll in bread crumbs, and deep-fry or panfry them.

2 lbs. zucchini, trimmed and washed
2 tbsp. kosher salt
Salt to taste
¾ c. arborio rice
1⅛ c. water
3 tbsp. olive oil
¼ lb. sliced pancetta (Italian bacon), cut into ¼-inch dice, or ¼ c. chopped sun-dried tomatoes packed in oil
¼ c. olive or other oil for deep-frying

1 tbsp. minced garlic
1 tbsp. lemon juice
1 tbsp. chopped fresh basil or 1 tsp. dried
1 tsp. chopped fresh marjoram or ½ tsp. dried
3 eggs, beaten
Pepper to taste
Medium hog casings (optional)
1 c. milk
1 c. bread crumbs

For directions on sausage making, see page 332.

Shred the zucchini using a mandoline, a food processor fitted with a shredding disk, or a hand grater. Transfer to a colander and sprinkle with the kosher salt until all the pieces are well coated. Set the colander in a bowl or over the sink to drain for at least 30 minutes or up to 2 hours.

While the zucchini is draining, cook the rice. In a 2-quart saucepan bring the water to a boil, add a pinch of salt and the rice. Bring back to a boil, reduce heat to a simmer, cover the pot and cook slowly for 20 minutes until all the water has been absorbed. Transfer the rice to a large bowl. Wash the zucchini very well by running cold water through the colander. Taste to see if the zucchini is sufficiently washed; it should only have the slightest taste of salt. Dry the shredded zucchini by spinning in a salad spinner or by squeezing between the colander and your hands.

In a 12-inch skillet over medium heat, fry the pancetta in 1 tablespoon olive oil until translucent and lightly brown, about 5 minutes, or fry tomatoes for 1 minute. Put in the garlic, and sauté for 1 minute. Add the zucchini and sauté for 2 to 3 minutes. Remove from the heat and add the lemon juice and herbs. Add the zucchini mixture to the rice along with 2 of the eggs. Mix well and taste for salt and pepper. Cover and cool the mixture in the refrigerator for at least 1 hour or overnight.

Using a meat grinder fitted with a sausage horn, stuff the mixture loosely into medium hog casings. Do not overstuff, since the rice may expand during cooking and cause the casings to burst. Tie into 4–5-inch links.

To cook, combine the last egg with the milk. Dip each sausage into the egg wash, then roll in bread crumbs. Panfry the sausage in the remaining olive oil over

Serve these meat-free sausages as a side dish with meat or fish, or as a vegetarian entree (omitting pancetta and casings) with a Hot Tomato and Basil Sauce or Tomato and Basil Vinaigrette accompanied with lots of grated Parmesan cheese.

medium heat for about 5 minutes a side, or until golden. Serve with either or both of our tomato-basil sauces (see pages 354 and 355).

Alternatively, the mixture can be molded into 3–4-inch football-shaped patties, rolled in bread crumbs, and deep-fried. (The mixture should be moist enough already, so don't dip it in the egg wash.) Deep-fry at 375° F until golden brown on all sides. This will take 5–7 minutes. Serve at once with the same tomato sauces suggested above. Makes 6–8 servings

· sweetbread and chicken sausage ·

This elegant and delicately flavored sausage could also be called boudin blanc. Although it involves a little work to make, the results are rewarding. Grill these sausages or lightly panfry in butter. They are delicious just by themselves, but we recommend that you use them in one of our recipes, such as sausage with red pepper puree (see page 312), or sausages in foil packets with watercress and spinach butter (see page 324). You can also substitute these sausages for the pheasant sausage in the sausage-filled puff pastry pie (see page 321).

3 tbsp. butter
¼ c. finely chopped shallots
½ c. finely chopped green onions or
    scallions
2 cloves garlic, finely chopped
¾ lb. sweetbreads, membranes
    removed
1½ lbs. chicken thighs, boned and
    skinned
¾ lb. pork back fat
¾ c. heavy cream
½ c. dry bread crumbs
1 tbsp. kosher salt
1 tsp. freshly ground black pepper

Pinch *each* freshly grated nutmeg,
    ground ginger, allspice, and
    coriander
¼ tsp. cayenne
1 lb. spinach, blanched briefly in
    boiling water, squeezed dry, and
    chopped
2 tsp. sweet Hungarian paprika
¼ bunch watercress, leaves only,
    blanched briefly in boiling water,
    squeezed dry, and finely chopped
½ c. chopped fresh chives
4 egg whites
Medium hog casings

For details on sausage making, see page 332.

      Heat the butter in a small frying pan over medium heat. Put in the shallots, green onions, and garlic, cover, and cook until the vegetables are soft, about 5 minutes. Transfer to a container and set aside in the refrigerator to cool.

Grind the sweetbreads, chicken, and pork fat through a fine ⅛-inch plate. Cool the mixture in the freezer 15 minutes and grind again.

Heat the cream in a small saucepan and stir in the bread crumbs. Continue stirring until the mixture is stiff, about 1 or 2 minutes. Transfer to a container and freeze about 15 minutes to chill well.

In the bowl of an electric mixer, mix the cooked onion/garlic/shallot mixture, and the bread crumbs and cream with the ground meats and all the remaining ingredients, except for the egg whites and casings. Beat the mixture, and add the egg whites one at a time until they are completely incorporated into the mixture.

Fry a little patty to taste and adjust the salt and pepper if necessary. Stuff into medium hog casings and tie into 5-inch links.

Poach the boudins at 180° F in a large pot of lightly salted water for 20 minutes or until the sausages are firm. Cool under running water. This sausage will keep refrigerated for 3 days or frozen for 2 months.

To cook the sausages, grill or panfry in butter over medium heat until they are lightly browned, or try one of the recipes suggested in this chapter.

Makes about 3 pounds

For a simple and elegant lunch, sauté this richly flavored boudin in butter and serve with our Onion and Mustard Confit (see page 356) and a spicy, dry Gewürztraminer.

· rabbit boudin ·

Boudin is the French term for a finely textured sausage containing meat or blood bound by some type of starch, either bread crumbs, rice, barley, or flour. Mildly flavored boudin blanc is usually made with white meats like chicken, veal, or rabbit. We use rabbit here, but you can just as easily substitute chicken or veal.

This Rabbit Boudin is excellent with Champagne Sauce (see page 277), Onion and Mustard Confit (see page 356), escarole and horseradish sauce (see page 319), or cooked in foil packets with our Mustard and Tarragon Butter (see page 323).

2 –3 lbs. rabbit, including the heart and liver, all meat removed from the bones, chilled in freezer, or equivalent amount boned chicken or veal

½ lb. lean pork butt, chilled in freezer

¾ lb. pork back fat, chilled in freezer

2 tbsp. fresh tarragon or 1 tbsp. dried

3½ tsp. kosher salt

1 tsp. finely ground black pepper

½ tsp. dried thyme

½ tsp. dried sage

1 tsp. ground juniper berries

¼ c. gin

2 tbsp. butter

1 medium onion, finely chopped

1 medium leek, split, cleaned, and finely chopped

⅛ tsp. freshly grated nutmeg

½ tsp. cayenne

1 c. rabbit or chicken stock (see opposite page)

1½ oz. dried porcini mushrooms, soaked for at least 30 minutes, strained (reserving the liquid), and finely chopped

½ c. milk

1 c. dry bread crumbs

1 egg

3 egg whites

½ cup heavy cream

Sheep or medium hog casings

For directions on sausage making, see page 332.

Grind the rabbit meat, pork, and fat twice through a ⅛-inch plate into a bowl. Dice the rabbit liver and heart into ¼-inch pieces and add to the ground meat. Mix in the tarragon, 3 teaspoons of the salt, the pepper, thyme, sage, juniper, and gin. Cover and refrigerate.

Melt the butter in a heavy 2–3-quart saucepan, then add the onion, leek, nutmeg, cayenne, and the remaining ½ teaspoon salt. Cover and cook 5 minutes over low heat. Add the rabbit or chicken stock and the strained porcini soaking liquid and continue to cook until the vegetables are quite tender, stirring occasionally, about 5 minutes. Add the milk and bread crumbs. Bring to a boil, stirring constantly, until the mixture is thick enough to hold its shape in a spoon.

Spread the bread crumb and vegetable mixture on a plate or pan and chill well in the freezer for about 30 minutes. Place the ground meats and seasonings in the chilled bowl of an electric mixer along with the bread and vegetable mixture.

Beat vigorously until everything is well blended. Add the whole egg and mix in well. Put in half the egg whites and continue beating for 1 minute. Add the remaining egg whites and beat 1 minute more until everything is incorporated. Gradually beat in the cream. Stir in the finely chopped porcini. Fry a patty and correct the seasoning.

Stuff into sheep or medium hog casings. Poach in lightly salted 180° F water for 20 minutes, or until firm. Cool under cold running water. Refrigerate for up to 3 days or freeze for 2 months.

To cook the boudin, gently fry the sausages in butter, turning occasionally, for about 10 minutes. Serve with a hot-sweet mustard or with one of the sauces suggested on page 302. Makes about 4 pounds

This delicate sausage also makes a delicious and simple-to-prepare hors d'oeuvre, brushed with mustard, rolled in bread crumbs, and broiled.

· rabbit or chicken stock ·

Simmer rabbit or chicken bones and scraps, a carrot, a rib of celery, ½ an onion, a leek top, 2 whole allspice, 4 peppercorns, a bay leaf, and a sprig of fresh thyme or ½ teaspoon dried thyme in 4 cups of water for 1–2 hours to a final volume of 1 cup. Degrease and set aside to cool.

· lamb, rosemary, and mustard sausage ·

I learned my favorite way of roasting leg of lamb from Julia Child: the lamb is brushed with a mixture of mustard, fresh rosemary, and garlic. There is never enough of this delicious glaze since it is only on the outside of each slice when you serve the lamb. So I decided to incorporate this flavoring throughout the meat by using it in a lamb sausage. Leave the sausage unlinked, brush it with a mustard glaze, and bake it in a coil in a 350° F oven for about ½ hour, or until the internal temperature reaches 155° F.

Serve this savory sausage with Oven-Roasted Garlic Potatoes (leave out the rosemary in the recipe for this dish—see page 352) and a rich and complex Pinot Noir from the Santa Cruz mountains or Oregon's Willamette Valley.

3 lbs. lamb shoulder, trimmed of
   excess fat
1 lb. pork back fat
2 tsp. kosher salt
2 tsp. soy sauce
1 tsp. chopped fresh rosemary or
   ½ tsp. dried

1 tbsp. minced garlic
3 tbsp. coarse-grain mustard
2 tbsp. fruity olive oil
Medium hog casings

For directions on sausage making, see page 332.

In a meat grinder fitted with a ⅜-inch plate, grind together the meat and fat. Put in a large bowl along with the salt, soy sauce, rosemary, garlic, mustard, and olive oil. Mix well with your hands, squeezing and kneading the mixture. Do not overmix, or the fat will begin to melt. Stuff into medium hog casings. Leave as a coil. Refrigerated, sausage keeps 3 days; frozen, 2 months. Makes 4 pounds

We recommend using pork or beef fat in this and other lamb sausage recipes since lamb fat is grainy, congeals easily, and has too strong a flavor.

· spicy lamb, pine nut, and sun-dried tomato sausage ·

Lamb sausages, often with Middle Eastern and Mediterranean flavors, are increasingly finding their way onto the menus of New American restaurants. You can grill these sausages and serve them with sautéed eggplant and feta cheese dressing (page 313), or roll them in hot flour tortillas accompanied with Yogurt and Cilantro Sauce (see page 355).

2¼ lbs. lean lamb from the shoulder or leg
¾ lb. pork back fat or beef fat
⅓ c. finely chopped sun-dried tomatoes packed in oil
2 tbsp. olive oil from the sun-dried tomatoes
¼ c. finely chopped onion
¼ c. finely chopped red bell pepper
1 tbsp. tomato paste
2 tsp. minced garlic
¼ c. toasted pine nuts

½ c. chopped fresh cilantro
1 tbsp. chopped fresh mint
½ tsp. ground allspice
1 tsp. cayenne
1 tsp. ground cumin
1 tsp. ground coriander
4 tsp. kosher salt
1 tsp. coarsely ground black pepper
¼ c. fresh lemon juice
1 egg, beaten
Medium hog or lamb casings

For details on sausage making, see page 332.

Grind the meat and fat through a ¼-inch plate. In a large bowl, mix with all the remaining ingredients, except the casings, until well blended. Stuff into medium hog casings or lamb casings, and tie into 5–6-inch links. Keeps 3 days refrigerated, 2 months frozen. Makes about 4 pounds

Lamb takes well to aromatic herbs and spices such as mint, coriander, cumin, and allspice; these spicy lamb sausages are delicious for lunch, as first courses or entrees.

· spinach, pork, and game crépinettes ·

Crépinettes are sausage patties wrapped in caul fat (usually available at pork butchers or specialty shops). The caul fat holds the moisture in the meat and makes a tight, neat package. If caul fat is unavailable, simply form the sausage meat into patties and grill or fry. Delicious grilled and served as is, as part of a mixed grill, or with a salad of bitter greens (see page 320).

2½ lbs. meat, at least half pork and the rest from furred or feathered game, including the liver, or lean lamb

½ lb. pork back fat, or more fat if mixture seems too lean

2 bunches (2 lbs.) spinach, blanched, drained, and chopped

2 tbsp. chopped shallots

½ tsp. dried tarragon

¼ tsp. dried sage

¼ tsp. dried thyme

2 tsp. coarsely ground black pepper

½ tsp. ground allspice

¼ c. port or applejack

2 tbsp. chopped fresh herbs, such as basil, tarragon, chervil, thyme, oregano, or marjoram

½ tsp. cayenne

1 tsp. ground fennel seed or star anise

1 tbsp. kosher salt

Caul fat

For directions on sausage making, see page 332.

Grind the meat and pork fat through a grinder fitted with a ⅜-inch plate. Mix with the remaining ingredients, except caul fat, in a large bowl. Knead until well blended. Shape into ¼-pound oval patties, and wrap in 6-inch squares of caul fat or leave unwrapped. Place on a platter and refrigerate. The crépinettes will keep up to 3 days refrigerated or 2 months frozen. Makes 3½ pounds

Crépinettes are a good way to use up bits and pieces of game; the amount or type doesn't matter much. Simply mix the game (up to 50 percent of the total meat) with the pork. You can use meat or livers from game birds such as pheasant or quail or red meat from venison, boar, or other game animals. Use lean lamb if you have no game.

· Atlantic seafood sausage ·

The ingredients that inspired these fish sausages are part of the bounty of the North Atlantic: cod, clams, scallops, and lobster.

1½ lbs. cod fillets
2 egg whites
1½ c. heavy cream
2 tsp. kosher salt
½ tsp. finely ground black pepper
2 tsp. tomato paste
1 tsp. chopped fresh thyme or ½ tsp.
   dried

¼ lb. diced cooked clams
¼ lb. small bay scallops, cut in half, or
   diced sea scallops
1 c. diced cooked lobster or shrimp
3 tbsp. sweet sherry
Sheep casings

For directions on sausage making, see page 332.

Put the food processor bowl and metal blade into the freezer for at least 30 minutes before starting this recipe. Cut the cod into ¾-inch chunks and freeze for 15 minutes. Using the metal blade, process the cod until it is smooth. With the motor running, gradually add the egg whites until they are fully incorporated. Pour in the cream in a steady stream until it is thoroughly blended in. Add the salt, pepper, tomato paste, and thyme and process 10 seconds.

Any firm, white-fleshed fish such as red snapper or Pacific rock cod can be used here instead of cod, and shrimp can replace the lobster.

Transfer the fish mixture to a bowl and fold in the remaining ingredients, except the casings, until everything is well mixed. Make a small ball of the mixture, poach in simmering water for 5 minutes, and taste to correct seasonings if necessary. Stuff the seafood-fish mixture into sheep casings, and tie into 6-inch links.

Bring a large pot of lightly salted water to a boil. Put in the sausages, and adjust the heat to below a simmer, about 180° F. Poach the sausages for about 15 minutes, or until they are firm. Drain and serve immediately, or cool under running water and refrigerate. To rewarm the sausages, gently fry them in butter. They are also good eaten cold with a mayonnaise enhanced with cooked minced clams, lemon, and parsley. This sausage will keep 3 days in the refrigerator, but does not freeze well. Makes 2½ pounds

· baguette stuffed with sausage and chard ·

Serve these appetizing stuffed baguettes as cocktail hors d'oeuvres at dinner parties, or cut the baguettes into sandwich-sized pieces and have them for lunch or as a simple dinner with a green salad.

2 baguettes or other French bread
½ lb. andouille or other lean smoked
   sausage
2–3 garlic cloves, minced
3 green onions or scallions, finely
   chopped

1 c. ricotta
Grated Parmesan cheese to taste,
   about ½ c.
½ bunch chard without stems,
   chopped, steamed, and squeezed
   dry

We prefer to use andouille in this easy-to-make appetizer because it is lean, spicy, and deliciously smoky, but any good-quality smoked sausage will work.

Cut a thin slice off the top of each baguette and hollow out the center. Save the top to use for bread crumbs. Chop the sausage finely in a food processor fitted with the metal blade, along with the garlic and onions. Pour into a bowl and mix with the cheeses and cooked chopped chard. Save a little Parmesan to sprinkle over the top. Stuff the loaves and place them on a baking pan. Sprinkle with the remaining Parmesan cheese and bake in a 375° F oven for 15–20 minutes, or until the tops have begun to brown and the cheese has melted. Cool a couple of minutes and cut into 1½-inch slices for hors d'oeuvres or into 6-inch pieces for sandwiches. Makes 32 hors d'oeuvre slices or 8 6-inch pieces, enough for 4–6 servings

· Phyllis Steiber's sausage and prawn brochette ·

Phyllis Steiber is an excellent impromptu cook who is always coming up with imaginative dishes like this delectable brochette, often put together from whatever ingredients happen to be at hand.

· **Marinade** ·
½ c. Japanese soy sauce
2 tbsp. brown sugar
2 tsp. minced garlic
2 tsp. Oriental sesame oil
2 tsp. finely chopped ginger
....

½ lb. large shrimp, in their shells
1 medium red onion, cut into 1-inch chunks
3 Japanese eggplants, cut into ¾-inch rounds
½ lb. Duck Sausage (see page 296)
¼ c. sweet mango chutney

In a bowl combine the soy sauce, brown sugar, garlic, sesame oil, and ginger. Add the shrimp, onion, and eggplants, and toss to cover with the marinade. Marinate for 15 minutes to 1 hour in the refrigerator.

Meanwhile, poach the sausages for 15 minutes in lightly salted water. Cool under running water, and slice into 1-inch rounds.

Alternate pieces of sausage, shrimp, eggplant, and onion on skewers. Grill over medium-hot coals for 2 minutes. Brush the top side of the skewers with the chutney. Turn the skewers over and brush again with the chutney. Cook 2 minutes on the other side, and then 2 more minutes on each side, or until the eggplant is soft, the shrimp pink and firm, and the sausage heated all the way through. Altogether, it may take 8–10 minutes. Delicious with bulgur or wild rice.

Makes 4 servings

Try this quick and tasty brochette with other sausages such as Turkey Sausage with Drambuie or some of the Asian sausages from the West Coast chapter.

· duck sausage
with pasta and wild mushrooms ·

This tasty pasta dish was created by Tom Blower, a San Francisco Bay Area chef.

1 oz. dried morels, porcini, or shiitake mushrooms

6 tbsp. butter

1 lb. Duck Sausage (see page 296), poached for 15 min., cooled, and cut into ½-inch rounds

1 c. julienned red and yellow bell peppers

2 tsp. minced garlic

¾ lb. fresh fettuccine

Pour 1½ cups boiling water over the mushrooms, and soak for at least 30 minutes or up to several hours. Melt 2 tablespoons of the butter in a 10–12-inch sauté pan over medium heat. Put in the sausages, and sauté for 5 minutes, until they begin to brown. Add the bell peppers and garlic, and sauté for 1–2 minutes. Add the mushrooms, with their strained soaking liquid, turn the heat to high, and reduce the liquid by half. Remove the pan from the heat and whisk in the remaining butter until it is incorporated and the sauce is smooth. Toss with cooked fresh fettuccine and serve. Makes 4–6 servings

Use morels if you can find them. Their earthy, slightly smoky flavor is wonderful. If not, dried porcini or shiitakes add their own rich nuances.

HOT LINKS & COUNTRY FLAVORS

sausage with fettuccine, sun-dried tomatoes, and American chèvre ·

This recipe, also from chef Tom Blower, makes use of two ingredients that have become quite popular in New American restaurants these days, sun-dried tomatoes and fresh goat cheese.

For the sausage, try our Spinach, Pork, and Game Crépinettes, California White Wine and Herb Sausage (see pages 306, 254), or a mild Italian sausage.

This light and tangy dish makes a great summer lunch or dinner accompanied by a salad of marinated onions and greens, some crusty French bread, and a chilled bottle of crisp California Fumé Blanc or French Sancerre.

20 sun-dried tomatoes, plain or
   packed in oil
3 tbsp. butter
4 whole sausages such as Spinach,
   Pork, and Game Crépinettes,
   California White Wine and Herb
   Sausage, or mild Italian sausage

1 tbsp. minced garlic
1 tbsp. minced shallot
3 c. chicken stock
¾ lb. fresh fettuccine
4 oz. mild fresh chèvre
¼ c. chopped fresh basil, or finely
   chopped green onions or scallions

If you are using sun-dried tomatoes that are not packed in oil, cover them with boiling water and let them soak for at least 30 minutes. Drain and cut them into thin strips. If you use oil-packed tomatoes, just cut them into thin strips and set aside.

In a heavy skillet, heat 1 tablespoon of the butter over medium heat and fry the sausages for 10 minutes, or until firm and lightly browned, turning them at least once. Transfer them to a platter. Cool and cut into ⅜-inch slices.

Leave about 1 tablespoon of fat in the pan. Add the garlic and shallot and cook them 1–2 minutes. Add the tomatoes and stock. Bring to a boil and return the sausages to the pan. Continue boiling until the liquid is reduced by half. Remove the pan from the heat and stir in the remaining 2 tablespoons of butter. The sauce should be smooth and slightly thickened.

Toss freshly cooked fettuccine in the sauce and transfer to a shallow bowl or serving platter. Crumble the goat's cheese over the dish and sprinkle with the chopped basil or green onions. Serve at once. Makes 4 servings

Use a fresh creamy goat's cheese, preferably one of the excellent American versions handmade by cheesemakers like Laura Chenel or Sadie Kendell. A fresh French chèvre such as Montrachet would also work well.

· sweetbread and chicken sausage in a sweet red pepper puree ·

Sauces made by pureeing sweet red bell peppers are widely used in New American restaurants with delicate foods such as swordfish or chicken, as well as more intensely flavored meats like lamb. This sweet red pepper puree is particularly delicious and colorful with our Sweetbread and Chicken Sausage. The tangy sauce works equally well with Rabbit Boudin or Seattle's Pike Place Salmon Sausage (see pages 302 and 247).

1 large red bell pepper, fire-roasted, peeled, and seeded (see page 208)
1 c. heavy cream
1 lb. Sweetbread and Chicken Sausage (see page 300)
2 tbsp. butter
2 cloves garlic, minced

2 shallots, thinly sliced
2 tsp. sweet Hungarian paprika
¼ c. chicken stock
¼ c. dry white wine
½ tsp. dried marjoram
Salt and pepper to taste
1 tbsp. chopped fresh parsley

Cut the fire-roasted bell pepper in quarters, julienne one of the quarters, and reserve. Place the other 3 quarters in a food processor and puree with ¼ cup of the heavy cream. Set aside.

Slice the sausages into 1-inch rounds, and sauté over medium heat in the butter for 2–3 minutes, or until lightly browned and cooked through. Remove the sausage and add the garlic and shallots. Cook for 2 minutes, or until the shallots are soft but not colored. Remove from the heat and stir in the paprika so that the shallot/garlic mixture is well coated. Return to medium heat, and cook for approximately 1 minute, then add the stock, wine, and marjoram. Cook until reduced by half. Pour in the remaining ¾ cup of cream and cook for 5 minutes, or until the sauce begins to thicken. Stir in the red pepper puree and sausage and cook for 1 or 2 minutes. Season with salt and pepper. Garnish with the julienned red pepper and parsley, and serve immediately. Makes 4 servings

For a truly elegant presentation, serve the dish spooned into puff pastry cases (bouchées à la reine). Otherwise, it tastes great over fresh egg noodles, homemade spaetzle, or buttered rice.

spicy lamb sausage with oriental eggplant and feta cheese dressing·

Eggplant is featured in many delectable Middle Eastern dishes; it seems to have a special affinity for lamb. This eggplant preparation goes particularly well with our Spicy Lamb, Pine Nut, and Sun-dried Tomato Sausage, Spinach, Pork, and Game Crépinettes, or the Venison or Wild Boar Sausages in this chapter (see pages 305, 306, 297, and 298). If the smaller Oriental eggplants are unavailable, use regular-sized eggplants.

½–1 c. olive oil
2 medium onions, thinly sliced
6 unpeeled Japanese or Chinese
   eggplants or 1 medium regular
   eggplant, sliced lengthwise in
   ¼-inch slices
4 very ripe tomatoes, diced
1 tbsp. lemon juice
Pinch ground cinnamon
1 tsp. ground turmeric
Salt and pepper to taste

· **Dressing** ·
¼ c. feta cheese
¼ c. buttermilk
....
8 Spicy Lamb, Pine Nut, and Sun-
   dried Tomato Sausages (see
   page 305)

Heat ¼ cup of the olive oil in a large skillet. Add the onions and adjust heat to a moderate temperature, so that the onions cook without burning and need only to be stirred every so often. This way you can devote your attention to finishing the rest of the dish. Continue frying the onions until they are deep brown and crispy. This will take about 45 minutes. Transfer the onions to a plate and set aside.

While the onions are cooking, heat ¼ cup of the olive oil over medium-high heat in another large skillet. Fry the eggplant slices in batches, 3–5 minutes on one side, 2–3 minutes on the other, until lightly browned and soft. As they are done, transfer the eggplant slices to your serving platter and arrange them in decorative rows. Continue frying the remaining eggplants, adding more olive oil as needed.

When the eggplant is finished, pour off any excess oil. You can use the same frying pan to finish the sauce, if the bottom is not burnt. Otherwise, use a fresh pan. Add the tomatoes, lemon juice, cinnamon, and turmeric. Cook over medium heat about 5 minutes, or until the tomatoes begin to release some of their juice. Taste for salt and pepper. Spoon the tomato mixture over the eggplant.

In a food processor or blender, combine the feta and buttermilk to make a thick but pourable dressing. Scatter spoonfuls of the dressing around the platter. Finally, sprinkle all the crispy onions over the platter. Grill the sausages according to the directions on page 315, and arrange on the platter with the eggplant. Makes 4–6 servings

You can prepare the eggplant ahead of time and serve it Middle Eastern–style at room temperature, or cold. Grill the sausages just before serving.

· wild rice and pecan salad with grilled venison sausage ·

Wild rice and roasted nuts make a splendid combination that complements the flavor of venison beautifully. The salad also works well with our Wild Boar, Buffalo, or Duck Sausages (see pages 298, 294, and 296).

1 c. raw wild rice, or 3–4 c. cooked
½ tsp. salt
½ c. shelled pecans
1 tbsp. peanut oil
1 lb. Venison Sausage (see page 297)
2 green onions or scallions, thinly sliced
1 c. chopped fresh Italian flat-leaf parsley
¼ c. sherry wine vinegar or red wine vinegar
½ c. walnut oil
Salt and pepper to taste

To prepare wild rice, carefully wash the rice and remove any dirt or foreign material. Bring 3 cups of water to a boil in a heavy 2–3-quart saucepan. Add the rice and salt. When the water returns to a boil, reduce the heat, cover the pot, and simmer for about 40 minutes or longer, until the rice is tender.

While the rice is cooking, roast the pecans in the peanut oil in a medium skillet over medium-low heat for 5 minutes, shaking the pan constantly. When they begin to brown, become crispy, and develop a nutty aroma, immediately remove the nuts, along with any oil remaining, to a large bowl.

Grill or panfry the sausages, following the directions on page 315. Transfer to a platter and let them sit for 5 minutes while you finish the salad.

Add the cooked rice, green onions, parsley, vinegar, and walnut oil to the roasted pecans in the bowl. Toss well to combine the ingredients. The rice should be evenly coated with the oil and vinegar. Season to taste with salt and pepper. Mound the salad on a platter or in a shallow bowl. Slice warm Venison Sausage on an angle, arrange over rice, and serve at once. Makes 4 servings

Serve as a luncheon or light dinner with a hearty red wine like California Syrah or French Rhône.

· quick and easy grills ·

Just about every sausage discussed in this book is delicious grilled. What could be simpler or more satisfying for lunch or supper than a couple of browned and juicy grilled sausages on a plate with roasted potatoes and a green salad?

Whether you cook over charcoal or on a gas grill, you should try to keep the flames to a minimum when grilling sausages. A covered kettle-type barbecue with medium-hot charcoal is best, but a spray bottle filled with water can control most flare-ups. If you grill sausages under a broiler, use the maximum heat and turn the sausages frequently. Make sure to use a broiler pan with a rack so the juices drip through and don't catch fire.

The secret to grilling sausages is to turn them frequently as they cook to ensure even browning. Keep the heat as even as possible and put out any flare-ups as soon as they occur. And don't overcook the sausages. Raw fresh sausages such as Italian sausages will take about 12–15 minutes to cook. Cooked sausages such as Rabbit Boudin, hot dogs, or smoked kielbasa will take 7–10 minutes to get hot all the way through. Your best bet to get the sausages exactly right is to use an instant-read thermometer. Simply slip the tip into the end of the sausage about 2 inches in so it penetrates to the center. When it registers 155–160° F, the sausage is done.

· turkey sausage braised with whole garlic heads ·

We take our garlic pretty seriously here in Berkeley. Some years back Chez Panisse started holding garlic orgies to celebrate Bastille Day, with the odoriferous bulb served in every course, even dessert — chocolate-covered garlic and garlic ice cream, for example. The idea caught on and eventually many restaurants in the Bay Area were hosting their own special garlic celebrations. During the four years I cooked at Poulet in Berkeley, we also held garlic dinners, which had special significance, since I was also the recipe writer for the *Garlic Times*, a monthly newsletter for "Lovers of the Stinking Rose," an organization for garlic crazies. So they all expected a lot from me when it came to the heavy garlic. And they got it! Because you will have plenty of delicious sauce, serve this dish with lots of buttered rice.

2 tbsp. butter
2 tbsp. olive oil
8 heads garlic, with ½ inch of stem
   end cut off
12 whole Turkey Sausages with
   Drambuie or other full-flavored
   fresh sausages such as mild Italian
   (about 3 lbs.)

3 c. chicken stock
2 c. dry white wine
1 tsp. dried thyme
Salt and pepper to taste
1 c. crème fraîche or sour cream

You'll need to use a full-flavored sausage here to stand up to the garlic. We braised our Turkey Sausage with Drambuie (see page 295), but any substantial fresh sausage will do. Try our California White Wine and Herb Sausage, Spinach, Pork, and Game Crépinettes, or a good-quality mild Italian sausage.

In a large, high-sided skillet or a Dutch oven, heat the butter and olive oil over medium heat. Add the garlic heads with the cut side down. Fry until the cut side of the garlic becomes golden brown, about 7 minutes. Adjust the heat so you do not burn the garlic. Transfer the whole garlic heads to a platter and reserve.

Add the sausages to the fat remaining in the pot and brown them on all sides. This will take 5 or 6 minutes. Remove and reserve, and pour off most of the fat. Pour in the stock and wine and scrape up any browned bits that adhere to the bottom of the pot. Add the thyme and arrange the sausages and garlic in the pot. Cover and cook over low heat for 25 minutes, or until the sausages are firm and the garlic tender (test with a skewer). Transfer the sausages and garlic heads, cut side up, to a heated serving platter while you finish the sauce.

Reduce the sauce over high heat until it begins to thicken. Degrease the surface, and taste for salt and pepper. Remove from the heat, and stir in the crème fraîche or sour cream. Pour the sauce over the garlic and sausages and serve at once, 2 sausages and 1 garlic head per person. Guests should peel the garlic cloves and eat the creamy insides. The extra garlic heads are for the real garlic fanatics. Makes 6 servings

duck or turkey sausage with prune and red wine sauce ·

Aromatic and satisfying duck or turkey sausages take well to sweet, fruity accompaniments. This rich prune and red wine sauce is delicious with these fresh sausages, smoked sausages like our Smoked Country Sausage, and other full-flavored pork sausages such as California White Wine and Herb Sausage.

1 c. rich chicken or duck stock
2 c. dry red wine
½ c. raspberry or red wine vinegar
2 tbsp. minced shallots
¼ c. sugar
1 4-inch strip orange zest
1 4-inch strip lemon zest
2 medium cloves garlic, whole

1 sprig fresh thyme or ½ tsp. dried thyme
¼ tsp. ground sage
½ lb. pitted prunes
8 Duck Sausages or Turkey Sausages with Drambuie (see pages 296 and 295)

Combine all ingredients except the prunes and sausages in a heavy 4-quart saucepan and boil for 5 minutes. Put in the prunes and reduce the heat. Simmer until the prunes are tender, about 10 minutes. Remove the prunes, transfer 6 of them to a food processor, and puree until smooth; reserve the others. Strain the sauce, return it to the pot, and stir in the pureed prunes. Boil the sauce down until it becomes syrupy, then add the reserved whole prunes. Keep the sauce warm while you cook the sausage.

You could serve any mild sausage with this savory sauce or try it with sautéed duck livers or as an accompaniment to smoked ham or pork chops.

Heat a heavy 12-inch skillet over medium heat. Add duck or turkey sausages, whole, and brown on one side, about 5 minutes. Turn and brown another 3 minutes. Pour off any fat. Add the sauce. Simmer the sausages in the sauce for 10 minutes. Serve with wild rice, brown rice, or bulgur pilaf. Makes 4–6 servings

· duck or turkey sausage with apples and onions ·

Many European countries have dishes that combine sausages with apples. This savory mix works particularly well for fresh pork sausages, but is even better with duck or turkey sausages. The addition of red onion to the apples adds a piquant note, but you can leave the onions out if you want more apple flavor.

2 tbsp. unsalted butter
6 Duck Sausages or Turkey
 Sausages with Drambuie (see
 pages 296 and 295)
1 large red onion, thinly sliced
2 small green apples, cored and
 sliced

¼ c. sweet white wine such as
 Riesling or Chenin Blanc, or apple
 cider
1 c. heavy cream (optional)
1 lb. fresh pasta (optional)

Melt 1 tablespoon of the butter in a large frying pan. Over medium heat, brown the sausages, whole, for 5 minutes on each side. Remove and add the remaining butter and the onions to the pan. Fry over medium-high heat for 5–7 minutes, or until the onions are soft. Add the apples and sauté for 2 or 3 more minutes. They should be cooked but still firm. Pour in the wine or cider and reduce over high heat for 3 or 4 minutes, until the sauce is syrupy. Lower the heat to medium and return the sausages to the pan. Cover and cook for an additional minute and serve. *Or* add the optional cream, reduce by half, then return the sausage. Cook, covered, 1 more minute. Serve over fresh pasta if you wish. Makes 4–6 servings

To give richness to the sauce, add cream and serve over pasta. This simple dish is also delicious without the cream and served with panfried potatoes.

grilled spinach, pork, and game crépinettes with escarole and horseradish sauce ·

This sauce was inspired by a sausage dish served at MacArthur Park, a highly successful New American restaurant in San Francisco. Chef Ed Kasky presents spicy seafood sausages on a bed of braised escarole flavored with lemon and horseradish. In experimenting, we found that this mixture could be pureed into a sauce that makes an excellent accompaniment to the crépinettes from this chapter.

· Escarole and horseradish sauce ·
3 tbsp. butter
2 cloves garlic, minced
1 medium head escarole, leaves
  separated and washed well
1 tbsp. prepared horseradish

2 tbsp. lemon juice, or more to taste
Salt and pepper to taste
....
8 Spinach, Pork, and Game
  Crépinettes (see page 306)

In a high-sided frying pan or a Dutch oven with a lid, melt the butter over medium heat. Add the garlic and cook 1 minute. Put in the escarole, cover the pot, and cook until the leaves are completely wilted and soft. Transfer the escarole and the juices from the pot to a food processor. Add the horseradish, lemon juice, and pinches of salt and pepper to the food processor and process to yield a coarse puree. Taste for additional salt, pepper, and lemon juice. Return to the pot and keep warm.

Meanwhile, grill the crépinettes over medium coals 12–15 minutes, turning occasionally, in a covered kettle-type barbecue, following the directions on page 338. The sausages are done when they are firm to the touch and completely cooked through — at 155–160° F.

Serve 2 crépinettes per person with the escarole sauce to the side of the plate. Accompany with Oven-Roasted Garlic-Rosemary Potatoes (see page 352), fresh corn on the cob, or a flavorful rice pilaf. Makes 4 servings

This tangy and versatile sauce is delicious with any game sausages as well as our Rabbit Boudin (see page 302) or Sweetbread and Chicken Sausage (see page 300). It keeps well refrigerated and can be gently rewarmed.

· sausage and bitter greens with soy, honey, and sherry vinegar dressing ·

In response to the trend toward lighter eating, many restaurants are serving hot grilled meats, sausages, and fish over salad greens. These composed salads are very popular for lunch or as a light dinner entree.

For this zesty salad, use two or three types of greens, mixing bitter and sweet together. We particularly like curly endive, red leaf lettuce, and escarole, but use any combination that suits your fancy. If you have access to such exotic greens as mâche or arugula, give them a try.

Sausages that work well here are Duck, Turkey, Boar, Venison, Spinach, Pork, and Game Crépinettes; any of the Asian sausages from the West Coast chapter; or a good-quality mild Italian sausage.

½ c. walnuts
1 tbsp. peanut oil

· **Soy, honey, and sherry**
vinegar dressing ·
1 tbsp. sherry wine vinegar or white
  wine vinegar
2 tsp. honey
1 tsp. semidry or sweet sherry
1 tsp. soy sauce

2 tbsp. walnut oil + 1 tbsp. peanut oil
  or 3 tbsp. peanut oil

8 whole sausages, as described above
  (2 lbs.)
¼ head *each* curly endive, escarole,
  and red leaf lettuce, washed, dried,
  and torn into small pieces

In a small pan, fry the walnuts in the peanut oil until they are brown and have a toasty, nutty aroma. Transfer to a small bowl immediately and reserve. To make the dressing, whisk all the ingredients together in a small bowl.

Grill the sausages until done in a covered kettle-style barbecue following the directions on page 338, or panfry. Toss the greens and dressing together in a large bowl. Distribute the salad equally on 4 dinner plates. Cut the grilled sausages into ¼-inch diagonal slices and arrange slices from 2 sausages over the greens on each plate. Garnish with the walnuts and serve. Makes 4 servings

Another delicious and simple preparation: Serve the sausages on a bed of peeled, seeded, and thinly sliced cucumbers. Use about ½ cucumber per serving.

· puff pastry pie filled with pheasant sausage ·

This rich and elegant dish makes a wonderful first course for a special dinner party. Its beautiful appearance and buttery aromas make for a very dramatic presentation that will impress your guests, and whet their appetites for more gustatory delights to come.

You can substitute any other mild fresh sausage such as our Rabbbit Boudin, bockwurst, Sweetbread and Chicken Sausage, or Michigan Dutch Farmer's Sausage.

Be sure that the filling is completely cold before you put it into the pastry so that the pastry shell is not warmed. Brush egg wash over the pastries just before baking to produce a handsome golden crust.

½ oz. dried porcini, morel, or shiitake mushrooms
1¼ lb. Pheasant and Wild Mushroom Sausage (see page 293) or other mild fresh sausage
2 tbsp. butter
¼ c. finely chopped carrots
⅓ c. finely chopped celery
3 tbsp. finely chopped shallots
1 c. fincly choppcd onions
1 tsp. minced garlic

2 oz. dried coppa or prosciutto, finely chopped (optional)
½ tsp. dried thyme
½ c. chicken stock
1 c. heavy cream
2 egg yolks
1 lb. commercial puff pastry, or use your own recipe
1 egg beaten with 2 tbsp. water for egg wash

Pour 1½ cups boiling water over the mushrooms, and soak them at least 30 minutes or up to several hours. Chop them coarsely, and strain and save the soaking liquid.

Lightly brown the whole sausages on all sides in the butter for 10 minutes in a skillet over medium heat. Transfer them to a platter, cool, and cut into ½-inch rounds. Leave about 3 tablespoons of fat in the pan, and add the carrots, celery, shallots, onions, and garlic along with the optional coppa or prosciutto and the thyme. Cover and cook over medium heat, stirring occasionally, until the vegetables are soft but have not begun to color, about 5 minutes. Stir in 1 cup of the mushroom soaking liquid, leaving any grit behind, along with the stock and cream. Bring to a boil and cook until the liquid is reduced to one-third and the sauce thickens. Whisk some of the sauce into a bowl containing the egg yolks. Stir the sausage and the rest of the sauce into the bowl, cover, and cool in the refrigerator while you prepare the pastry. This may be done a day ahead.

Commercial puff pastry comes frozen, already rolled out in 2 sheets. Cut one of the sheets into a rectangle measuring 5 x 10 inches. This will form the bottom of the pastry. Cut the other sheet into a rectangle measuring 6 x 11 inches for the top. Place the bottom piece on a baking pan covered with a sheet of parchment paper. Spoon the cold filling into the center of the pastry, leaving about a 1-inch border of pastry all around. Brush the border gently with water and lay

Once you've assembled the pie, it can be frozen on a baking sheet and wrapped. The pie and pan together can then go directly from the freezer to the oven. Increase baking time by 10 minutes.

the top pastry sheet over the bottom sheet and the filling. Gently seal the dough to form a plump rectangle, trimming off the edges with a pastry wheel or knife to yield a neat package. The pastry can be frozen at this point. Otherwise, refrigerate it for 30 minutes to let it rest. If any filling and dough remain, make a smaller pie with them.

Preheat the oven to 425° F. Brush the egg wash generously over the pastry. Bake in the middle of the oven for 20 minutes at 425° F. Turn the oven down to 350° F, and continue baking for 25–30 minutes, or until the pastry is golden. The pastry should puff up all around to about 3 inches high when done. After you take the pastry out of the oven, let it rest 5–10 minutes before serving. Using a serrated knife, cut the pastry into 1½-inch slices and serve. Makes 4–6 servings as a first course, 4 as an entree

·roasted lamb sausage with mustard-rosemary glaze·

This is a beautiful centerpiece for a dinner party, and one that will wow your guests. The Lamb, Rosemary, and Mustard Sausage described on page 304 makes a great presentation for a dinner or party buffet. Once the sausage is roasted, present it whole on a platter for your guests to admire, and then cut it into chunks at the table.

· Mustard-rosemary glaze ·
½ c. smooth Dijon mustard
1 tbsp. soy sauce
2 tsp. minced garlic
2 tsp. chopped fresh rosemary

2 tbsp. fruity olive oil
....
1 4-lb. Lamb, Rosemary, and
    Mustard Sausage in one piece,
    coiled

Mix together the mustard, soy sauce, garlic, and rosemary. Gradually whisk in the olive oil until it is absorbed into the sauce. Preheat the oven to 375° F. Place the sausage coil in a roasting pan. Brush generously with all the glaze and roast for 30 minutes, or until the glaze begins to brown and the sausage is firm and cooked through.
Makes 8 servings

This mustard-rosemary glaze is also excellent on leg of lamb, rack of lamb, or roast beef. You can also brush it on venison, buffalo, or boar sausages from this chapter, or any full-flavored fresh sausages, and either grill or roast them.

· rabbit boudin *en papillote* with mustard and tarragon butter ·

Cooking and serving delicate fish or fowl with aromatic herbs and vegetables in a parchment envelope is a classic technique in European kitchens. The food steams in its own juices and absorbs the flavors of the seasonings and spices. Cooking *en papillote* also provides a very dramatic presentation when you cut open the envelope and the glorious aromas steam out in a fragrant cloud at the table.

Besides the sausages suggested below, you can use this with any delicately flavored precooked sausage such as bockwurst, weisswurst, boudin blanc, or veal sausage.

· **Mustard and tarragon butter** ·
4 tbsp. (½ stick) softened butter
2 tsp. chopped fresh tarragon or 1 tsp. dried
1 tbsp. coarse-grained mustard

....

½ medium leek, white part only, cut into fine shreds 2 inches long
1 medium carrot, cut into fine shreds 2 inches long

4 Rabbit Boudins (see page 302) or other delicate precooked sausages, cut into ¼-inch-thick diagonal slices
2 fresh or presoaked dried shiitake mushrooms, cut into thin shreds
4 12-inch-square sheets of aluminum foil or parchment

In a small bowl, combine the butter, tarragon, and mustard. Set aside.

Bring 2–3 inches of water to a boil in a small saucepan. Blanch the leek and carrot together for 30 seconds. Drain in a sieve and cool under running water.

To assemble the packets, place the slices from 1 sausage in the center of each foil or parchment sheet. Sprinkle each with one quarter of the leek and carrot mixture and one quarter of the shiitake mushrooms. Spread one quarter of the mustard and tarragon butter over the top of each. Fold the foil or parchment over the food to form a 6 x 12-inch rectangle. Seal all the edges by making several thin folds and crimping tightly with your fingers.

Preheat the oven to 450° F. Place the packets on a baking sheet, and bake for 10–12 minutes. Open a packet to check. The sausage should be completely heated through and the butter melted. If not, reseal the packet and bake another 5 minutes. Place 1 envelope on each plate. Cut open with a knife or scissors and eat at once.

Makes 4 servings

These days many cooks simplify the parchment technique by using aluminum foil. The visual effect is not as elegant, perhaps, but it is a lot easier, and just as fragrant and delicious.

· sweetbread and chicken sausage *en papillote* with watercress and spinach butter ·

This flavorful compound butter goes particularly well with Sweetbread and Chicken Sausages, but is also delicious with grilled fish or poultry.

· **Watercress and spinach butter** ·
4 tbsp. butter
¼ c. chopped watercress leaves
¼ c. chopped spinach leaves
Pinch *each* salt and pepper
1 tbsp. finely chopped chives, or
   green onions or scallions
2 tsp. lemon juice
....
½ leek, white part only, cut into fine
   shreds 2 inches long

½ medium carrot, cut into fine shreds
   2 inches long
4 fresh or presoaked dried shiitake
   mushrooms, cut into fine shreds
4 Sweetbread and Chicken Sausages
   (see page 300) or other delicate,
   precooked sausages, cut into ¼-
   inch-thick diagonal slices
4 12-inch-square sheets of aluminum
   foil or parchment

Soften the butter. Combine the watercress, spinach, butter, salt, pepper, chives, and lemon juice in a food processor or mixing bowl. Make the sweetbread and chicken sausage papillotes as in the preceding recipe, using the Watercress and Spinach Butter instead of the Mustard Butter. Bake in the same way.
Makes 4 servings

· wild boar sausage baked with honey-orange glaze ·

Baking sausages in a Honey-Orange Glaze sounds a bit unusual, but the results are delicious. The sweet, tangy sauce complements the gamey flavors of the boar sausage perfectly. It is also good with our Spinach, Pork, and Game Crépinettes, or turkey or duck sausages from this chapter. Serve with Wilted Cabbage and Roasted Walnut Salad (page 351).

· **Honey-orange glaze** ·
1 medium onion, finely chopped
1 tbsp. olive oil
½ c. orange juice
¼ c. honey, preferably orange
   blossom
2 tbsp. red wine vinegar
1 tbsp. grated orange zest
¼ tsp. dried sage
½ tsp. dried thyme
Pinch ground cloves

Pinch ground allspice
¼ tsp. ground ginger
2 bay leaves
¼ tsp. finely ground pepper
2 tbsp. orange-flavored liqueur
   such as Grand Marnier or Curaçao,
   or brandy

....

1½ lbs. Wild Boar Sausage (see page
   298) or other full-flavored fresh
   or smoked sausage

To make the glaze, fry the onion in the olive oil in a heavy saucepan over medium heat for 5 minutes, stirring occasionally. Stir in all the remaining glaze ingredients. Bring to a boil and reduce to a simmer. Cook, uncovered, for 5 minutes, or until the sauce becomes syrupy. Set aside to cool, or store in a covered jar in the refrigerator. The glaze will keep for several weeks.

To roast the sausages, first poach them in 180° F water for 10 minutes. If you are using already cooked or smoked sausage, leave this step out.

Preheat the oven to 350° F. Spread the sausages out on a baking sheet and brush generously with the Honey-Orange Glaze. Bake for 20–25 minutes, basting the sausages at least three times with the glaze. Serve at once. Makes 4 servings about 1½ cups glaze

Make a double batch of the glaze — it keeps for several weeks refrigerated. This allows you to whip up a very palatable meal with little or no effort. All you have to do is roast some sausages, baste with the sauce, and serve them with home fried potatoes and a salad. The glaze is also delicious on ham or pork.

APPENDIX 1

· making sausage in the home kitchen ·

Making sausage at home is not difficult or overly complicated, and it can be a lot of fun. There's something about chopping the meat and mixing in the spices, stuffing the sausage into casings, and tying off the plump links that is, in a word, satisfying. When you panfry your own linguiça or andouille, chorizo or boudin, and the rich smells drift through the house, the effort seems like nothing. You join those uncounted generations of sausage makers who have made the world, and its food, a bit more lively and interesting.

Home sausage making can also provide you with sausages that have real advantages over most commercial products. First and foremost, you know exactly what goes into the sausages that you and your family eat. There are no additives, extenders, or other ingredients to cause worry or concern. If you choose to cold smoke or air-dry your homemade sausages, you need to add curing salts for safety's sake (see page 343, "Note on Nitrites"), but it is your choice. As you will see, you certainly don't have to cold smoke or air-dry sausages (you can hot smoke them or leave them fresh), and the amount of curing salts you might use will be at the absolute minimum to retard bacterial growth if you follow our directions.

An added plus is the lower amount of fat used in sausages made in the home kitchen. Some fat is necessary for flavor and juiciness in all sausages, but you can keep it to a minimum, and well below most store-bought sausage. Amounts vary for each type, but in general the fat content of homemade sausage is significantly lower than most commercial products (see page 329).

Even though we've designed this book to let you cook many of our recipes without making your own sausages, there are plenty of easy-to-make sausages that should tempt you to try your hand. We think you'll be surprised at how easy it all is and how tasty and delightful homemade sausages can be.

When you do make sausage, invite some friends over to pitch in and help. Sausage making has always been a communal activity, and making sausages together, frying up samples, and tasting, can double the fun and halve the work.

· equipment ·

No special equipment is necessary — a sharp knife or food processor will do — although if you really get into sausage making you might want to acquire some specialized tools of the trade such as a meat grinder and/or sausage stuffer. For a simple sausage, all you have to do is mince the meat and fat to the desired texture, mix in the spices, form the meat into patties, and fry — as easy as making hamburgers. Or you can go a step further and use a long funnel to stuff the sausage meat into casings and tie off links. You just slip the casing over the end of the funnel and push the chopped meat in by hand or with the end of a wooden spoon. It can be a bit slow for large quantities, but you'll be making sausage the same way Italian or Polish grandmothers have over the centuries, and they get very few complaints.

A meat grinder, however, will make your sausage making a lot easier, especially if you want to make up any quantity. If you add a sausage horn attachment for the grinder and a small kitchen scale, you'll be well on your way to becoming a bona fide sausage maker.

We prefer to use a meat grinder, hand operated or electric, equipped with plates of different hole sizes (⅛ inch, ¼ inch, and ⅜ inch) to allow for varied textures, along with a sausage stuffing attachment or horn. With the various-sized plates you can grind the meat as fine or as coarse as you like. Then, after the meat is mixed and seasoned, just attach the horn to the grinder, slip the sausage casing over the tip, and use the grinder to feed the meat into the casing simply by turning the handle. Hand grinders and some electric models are relatively inexpensive; an electric grinder makes sense if you are going to put up large batches of sausage. Keep the blade and plates clean and dry, and lubricate the moving parts of the grinder with vegetable oil each time you use it. The meat grinder attachment and sausage horn available for the KitchenAid mixer work well and are easy to use. Incidentally, food processors are all right occasionally to grind meat, but they don't always produce pieces of consistent size and texture.

If you make sausage on a regular basis or in large lots, you might want to get a sausage stuffer—a long cylinder with a piston that pushes the ground meat into the casings (see illustration). For sausage-making equipment, visit a hardware store or butcher-supply house in an Italian, German, or Polish neighborhood, or consult our listing of mail order sources (page 357).

Any good kitchen scale should work fine for measuring ingredients. If you don't have a scale, remember that 2 cups of ground meat weighs about 1 pound. If you are fortunate enough to have a friendly butcher, you might be able to buy the meat and fat, and have him grind it for you. Tell the butcher to use the "chili" blade, so the meat is not too finely ground. Be sure to have the meat ground fresh and use it the same day you buy it.

ingredients

meat

Meat for sausage making should be as fresh as possible and kept refrigerated right up to the time you use it. It is all right to use the tougher and cheaper cuts because the meat is going to be ground or chopped. Shoulder cuts are best, as they are cheap, flavorful, and easy to bone. Pork is preferred for most types of sausage, and the shoulder, sometimes called Boston butt, provides juicy, tasty meat. Beef chuck and lamb shoulder are also popular. If you are using venison or other large game, the shoulder is the best cut for sausage, although loin or leg can be used.

When boning and cutting up meat for sausage making, be sure to remove and discard any gristle or connective tissue. Meat trimmings are sometimes used to make sausage, but sufficient amounts of trimmings are usually available only in a butcher shop or large restaurant kitchen.

· fat ·

Sausage needs fat for juiciness and flavor. Commercial products can contain from 30 to 50 percent fat, while sausages made in the home from our recipes and by artisan producers use between 15 and 25 percent. (For comparison, lean hamburger contains 15–22 percent fat, regular up to 30 percent.) The amount of fat you consume will be significantly less if you follow our usual practice and drain off the excess after browning the sausages.

Pork fat is preferred for its mild flavor and high melting point. Lamb has too strong a flavor, while poultry fats are too soft and melt too easily. Beef is acceptable, although a bit too grainy for some sausages. Pork back fat with the skin removed has the best texture, and is favored for most sausages. Belly or bacon fat is too soft, and kidney fat too hard. Most butchers will be more than willing to sell or give you the type of fat you need for virtually any sausage.

If the meat is coarsely ground on a ⅜-inch plate and the fat on a finer plate, ⅛-inch or ¼-inch, much less fat can be used. Our recipes generally follow this procedure. Finer-ground sausages tend to need more fat because they have a mealier texture, while chunky meat stays juicier with less fat added.

Since you will be using less fat than commercial sausages, you should be careful not to overcook the sausages. An internal temperature of 155–160° F when you insert an instant-read thermometer into the end of the sausage is more than adequate to produce a safe and juicy result. Commercial sausage makers are only required to cook pork sausage to an internal temperature of 144° F, so you will be well beyond the minimum.

· seasonings ·

The spice blend is what gives each sausage its unique taste, and fresh spices are essential to fine sausage making. Throw out spices that are on the shelf more than three months, and buy fresh ones. We prefer to grind our own black pepper, usually coarsely, although we do call for a fine grind in some smoother sausages. In general, it is best to grind most other spices, such as nutmeg, coriander, cloves, etc., just before using. When you make your next batch of sausages, you'll taste the difference.

Fresh herbs can be used in place of dried (in the proportion of two fresh to one dried) and amounts of cayenne and other hot peppers depend on the heat levels you prefer. Herbs and spices vary widely in flavor and potency, so you should always fry up a small portion of the sausage meat and taste it, then let your taste buds be your guide.

As mentioned earlier, salt is an important element for preservation and flavor. It discourages the growth of unwanted bacteria and other organisms, and enhances the tastes of the other spices. We use less salt in our recipes than most commercial sausage makers, and prefer kosher salt for its purity and milder flavor. If you don't have kosher salt, use 20 percent less pure table salt than the recipe calls for. To test salt for additives, dissolve a couple of teaspoons in a glass of water. If the solution remains cloudy after stirring, the salt has too many impurities and should not be used.

· other ingredients ·

The average commercial sausage is often loaded with extenders, MSG, binders, preservatives, sugar, and water. We think they provide a pretty good argument for making your own sausages or for seeking out the small artisan producers of authentic sausages. We will occasionally add a little bit of sweet wine or sugar if a recipe calls for it and use small amounts of water or wine to moisten the meat and help blend together the ingredients. In our recipes we do recommend adding curing salts if you are going to cold smoke or air-dry sausages, for safety's sake (see page 340, "Note on Nitrites.") They are not necessary for fresh sausage or if you choose to hot smoke sausages (see page 341, "Smoking Sausages").

· casings ·

Casings are not necessary for home sausage making, and most of our sausages are delicious if the mixture is just formed into patties and fried. Many of our recipes call for bulk sausage, and you can wrap and freeze meal-sized portions of any sausage for future use.

But a juicy link hot from the grill is so toothsome and delicious that you'll most likely want to stuff at least some of your homemade sausages into casings. Most authentic sausages are stuffed into natural casings of hog, lamb, or beef intestines, thoroughly cleaned with the soft tissues removed. These thin membranes are dried and packed in salt for storage. Many commercial sausages use artificial casings made of collagen or are sold "skinless."

Casings are usually sold in bundles called "hanks." Depending on the type and size of the casing, a hank will take care of 50 to 150 pounds of meat, but don't worry if that sounds like a lot. Packed in salt, casings can last several years in the refrigerator. They can be purchased from custom butchers, butcher-supply houses, or by mail order (see page 357).

Hog casings are the most versatile and popular, and range in size from 1¼ to 2½ inches in diameter. They are relatively tender, not very expensive, and easy to work with. If you were to pick one casing to buy, we would recommend a medium hog casing (32–35 mm or 1¼ inches). This is the size, for example, of the standard Italian sausage, and almost all of our sausage recipes can be made using this size casing. One hank will hold 100–125 pounds of sausage meat.

Lamb or sheep casings are the narrowest and most delicate; they are also the most expensive. Typically used in breakfast links and old-fashioned hot dogs, they range from ½ inch to a little over 1 inch in diameter. One hank should hold about 50–60 pounds of sausage meat.

There are two popular types of beef casings: beef middles and beef rounds. The rounds, which are used for sausages such as ring bologna or ring kielbasa, range in diameter from 2–3 inches, and will hold between 75–100 pounds of product per hank. Beef middles are often sold sewed and are used to make large, semidry sausages such as summer sausage, as well as liverwurst and braunschweiger. An individual sewed middle will range in diameter from 2–4½ inches and will hold 2–3 pounds of meat. Beef casings can be tough and are most often peeled away before eating the sausage.

Caul fat is a membranous fat that can be used to wrap patties of meat called crépinettes (see Chinatown Crépinettes, page 282). This membrane helps to keep the juices in and gives the patty a nice appearance. Caul fat can be stored frozen, and unused caul fat can be refrozen. It can be difficult to find, although specialty butchers and wholesale meat distributors often carry it.

handling and storage ·

We cannot stress enough how important fresh meat and proper storage and handling are to quality sausage making. Meat should be purchased from a reputable butcher and used the same day. You can use frozen meat, but it should be frozen at its peak of freshness. For best results, meat should be thawed as slowly as possible, for 1 or 2 days in the refrigerator, depending on how big the pieces are. Frozen meat should not be kept for more than 3 months; otherwise it can develop a rancid taste. You may use frozen fat, as this is often the only way to find it. As long as you don't let the fat warm up to above 45° F, you can refreeze it.

Ground meat will spoil sooner than whole cuts, so keep sausage meat cold and use it as quickly as possible. We suggest you cut the meat up in pieces and put it into the freezer for 30 minutes before grinding. After you've ground the meat and fat, put the mixture back into the refrigerator until you are ready to stuff the casings. If you are making more than one type of sausage at one time, grind and season all the mixtures, refrigerate, and then stuff them into the casings all at once. When making sausage, the temperature of the meat should not get above 50° F for any extended period of time.

· sanitation ·

1. After washing the grinder and stuffer with hot water, cool them in the refrigerator or freezer before use. Have all your cutting boards, tables, equipment, and knives scrupulously clean. Sterilize wooden cutting boards with bleach and water periodically and rinse with clean water. Wash hands frequently with plenty of soap and hot water during sausage making.

2. When making several varieties of sausage, preweigh the meats and fat, and store them in labeled bowls in the refrigerator until you are ready to grind them. Work on only one batch at a time, and keep the other batches refrigerated. After the meat has been ground and the spices mixed in, store it in the refrigerator until ready to stuff into the casings.

3. Make your sausages during the cooler times of the day, morning or evening. If possible, the room temperature should not be above 70° F.

4. Have all the ingredients ready to go, spice mix made in advance.

5. Don't let the grinder or stuffer sit with meat in it. If you are going to take a break or move on to something else, take the grinder apart, and remove and discard any residual meat or fat. Wash and dry the grinder and reassemble it when you are ready to use it again. Meat should not sit in a grinder or stuffer for more than 15–20 minutes at 70° F room temperature, less time if the room is hotter.

6. When smoking or drying sausage, do not dry them in too warm a place. Always hang sausage on clean sticks.

· step-by-step method for making sausage at home ·

· using a meat grinder ·

1. If you have a meat grinder, hand operated or electric, attach the size plate (with holes of ⅛ inch, ¼ inch, or ⅜ inch) that the recipe calls for. Cut the meat and fat into ¾ x ¾-inch-wide strips (no larger than the mouth of the grinder), 1 to 6 inches long. While cutting up the meat, take care to remove any gristle and connective tissue. The mixture should come off the grinder plate in "worms." If the meat looks mushy, it means the grinder knife is not making good contact with the plate or the knife is dull. Remove the plate and knife, clean away any gristle, and reassemble, making sure the plate is reasonably tight against the knife. If you continue to have this problem, you might have to buy a new knife.

2. Grind the meat and the fat together into a large bowl. Add salt and spices, and mix in any liquid and optional curing salts. Knead the sausage meat with your hands, squeezing and turning the mixture. Do not overmix, as this could cause the fat to melt and might give the sausage a white, fatty appearance.

3. Make a small patty of the sausage meat and fry it. Taste and adjust the salt or other seasonings. Cover and refrigerate the meat mixture until you are ready to stuff it into the casings or use in a recipe. You should try to stuff the sausage meat into the casings on the same day it was ground, since it gets quite stiff and difficult to handle if refrigerated too long.

· using a food processor ·

1. Cut the meat and fat into ¾-inch cubes to get reasonably consistent chopping. Process in very small batches of 1 pound or less by using the pulse switch or turning on and off until the desired consistency is reached. Do not overprocess the meat. For 3–4 pounds of sausage you will probably need to process 3 or 4 batches, depending on the size of your food processor. Mini food processors or blenders should not be used to make sausage.

2. In a large bowl, mix the meat and fat together with the salt, spices, any liquid, and optional curing salts. Knead by hand as described above until well blended. Refrigerate until ready to use.

· preparing and stuffing the casings ·

1. You will need about 2 feet of medium hog casings or 4 feet of sheep casings for each pound of sausage mixture.

2. For salt-packed casings, remove a length of casing from the salt and place it in a bowl of warm water. Put the bowl in the sink and attach one end of the casing to the kitchen faucet. Gently run warm water through the casing to wash out the salt. Continue to soak the casing in warm water for 1–2 hours, or until it is soft and pliable. If you are using preflushed, liquid-packed casings, you have to soak them in clean warm water for only 15–30 minutes, and flush them briefly as above.

3. Attach a sausage-stuffing horn to the front of the grinder or stuffer. Don't forget to remove the plate and knife. Spread open one end of the casing and shake a drop of water into it. The water will help lubricate the casing as you gently pull it over the end of the horn. Carefully push the whole casing onto the horn, leaving 3 or 4 inches dangling.

4. Fill the grinder or stuffer with the sausage meat and feed it through the grinder until it begins to enter the casing. Tie the end of the casing into a knot, and with a skewer or hat pin prick any air bubbles that may appear as the casing fills up. A second pair of hands is very helpful when stuffing sausage. Continue to stuff the casing, using your thumb against the tip of the horn to control the rate and tightness of the filling. Do not fill the casings too full, or the sausage might burst during linking or cooking, but do pack them firmly.

5. When you have filled all but 3–4 inches of casing (still attached to the horn), remove the horn from the grinder and push any remaining sausage meat through the

horn into the casing with the handle of a wooden spoon. Slip the casing off the horn.

6. Drain any leftover casings, salt with kosher salt, and refrigerate for later use.

· linking ·

1. Depending on the type of sausages, links should be 5 to 8 inches in length. Starting from the knotted end of the casing on your right, measure the desired length and pinch the casing between your right thumb and forefinger. Move the same number of inches down the casing and pinch again to form a second link. Holding the second link in both hands, twirl it clockwise so that it twists the casing at both ends and seals both links. Measure to the left the same length again and pinch the casing, then measure and pinch off again to form link number four. Twist the fourth link to seal it and link number three. Continue to twist alternate links until you reach the end of the casing. Knot the end to seal the last link. There should be approximately ¼ to ½ inch of twisted casing between each link. Cut through the middle of the twisted casing to separate each sausage and seal the ends.

2. If the sausage bursts while linking—and this happens to even the most experienced sausage makers—cut through the casing at the break and tie off or knot both ends and continue linking. You can either restuff the left-over meat or make patties out of it.

maturing and storing sausage ·

The meats, spice, and other flavorings need time to mature in the sausage mixture. This maturation will contribute to a mellow flavor and better texture. Place the sausages, uncovered, on a rack in the refrigerator overnight or suspend them by a hook from a rack in the refrigerator. We don't recommend maturing sausages that do not contain curing salts unrefrigerated unless you have a very cold garage or basement that does not get above 40° F. Use a thermometer to be sure, since fresh sausages are basically raw ground meat, and can spoil easily. Unsmoked raw sausages should be kept no more than 3 days in the refrigerator. If you want to keep fresh sausages longer, wrap them well in freezer paper or foil, and freeze them for up to 2 months. Smoked sausage will keep refrigerated for a week; frozen, it will keep for 2 months.

cooking sausage ·

We like to panfry raw sausage in a dry heavy skillet over medium heat. Put the sausages into a cold pan, cover, and cook them in their own juices, turning them until they are browned on all sides. This should take 10–15 minutes, depending on the thickness of the sausages. When panfrying smoked sausages, add about ¼ inch of water to the skillet to help soften the casings. Cover and cook until the liquid evaporates. Continue to cook until the sausages are evenly browned, about 10 minutes.

Grilling is a wonderful way to cook sausages. You can grill them raw or precook them by poaching in hot (180° F) water for 15–20 minutes for sausages in medium hog casings. If you intend to grill sausages directly over a charcoal fire, it's a good idea to prepoach them to reduce the amount of fat that will drip onto the fire and flare up. We prefer to cook poached sausages in a covered kettle-style barbecue, turning them frequently until they are evenly browned, which takes 7–12 minutes, depending on the diameter of the sausages and how hot your coals are. The internal temperature of the sausages should reach 155–160° F when measured by inserting an instant-read thermometer 2–3 inches into the end of a sausage. Don't use extremely hot coals, which can cause excessive flaming and will burn the outside of the sausages before the insides have cooked. (See "Quick and Easy Grills," page 315.)

The trick to poaching sausages is to cook them very gradually so that the moisture stays in the sausage and they don't become too dry. (This is why we don't suggest you prick sausages beforehand.) To poach 3 pounds of sausage stuffed into medium hog casings, bring 2—3 gallons of lightly salted water to a temperature of 180—200° F. An accurate instant-read thermometer is useful here. The water should not be boiling. Put the sausages in the hot water and poach them over very low heat. The water should stay between 160 and 180° F. Depending on the thickness of the sausages, they will take 15—40 minutes to cook to an internal temperature of 155—160° F. Sausages stuffed in medium hog casings should take about 20 minutes, thicker or thinner sausages will take more or less time. Remove the sausages and eat at once, or cool in a colander under cold running water and refrigerate or freeze. Reheat them later by panfrying, grilling, or poaching.

smoking sausages

Country people have long known that meat hung in the smoke of hearths and chimneys lasts longer and often tastes better than fresh meat. Smoking, drying, and salting were the main means of preserving meats in the days before refrigeration.

In early America, salted and smoked meat and fish were the mainstays of rural householders. Farmhouses and plantations, from the poorest prairie sod huts to the rich estates of the Tidewater, all had their smokehouses to preserve the summer's harvest of flesh through the cold, hard winter. Virginia ham or smoked hog jowl, Nova Scotia lox or kippered herring, andouille or kielbasa—the products of the smokehouse became an integral part of the flavor of American cooking.

converted refrigerator smoker

Today, with modern refrigeration, we are not so concerned with smoking as a means of preserving meat, poultry, and fish. We don't need to hang hams or sausages for days or even weeks to keep them from spoiling over the winter. Rather, we are looking for the fragrant smoky flavors of hickory or oak, applewood or mesquite.

With very little equipment or effort, the home cook and sausage maker can achieve the taste and aroma of traditionally smoked foods. Whether it's done in a kettle-style barbecue, a water smoker, a semi-professional commercial smoker, or a converted old refrigerator, home smoking can give a flavor of the past and that special tang of hearth or campfire that brings back a hint of an ancient, savory feast.

water smoker

· cold smoking ·

The type of smoking most common on plantations and farms in
America over the last two centuries is called cold smoking.
The term "cold," however, is misleading since it's not very cool
in country smokehouses. In general, cold smoking takes place
at temperatures that range between 90° and 120° F, not
enough to cook most foods, whereas hot smoking uses higher temperatures to
cook the food as it smokes. Cold smoking is used to produce country or Virginia hams, most commercial smoked sausages, and bacon, all of which are
then cooked before eating. Since uncooked food absorbs flavors more
quickly, cold-smoked sausages are generally smokier in flavor than hot-
smoked. Cold smoking can be done successfully at home using a homemade
smoker, water smoker, or small electric smoker, following the instructions
(page 340). Cold-smoked sausages must include sodium nitrite curing salts for
safety (see page 343).

· hot smoking ·

covered kettle barbecue

If you have ever eaten Texas-style barbecued
meat, then you've eaten food that has been
hot smoked. This type of smoking is done at temperatures high enough to cook the food while
imparting a mild and pleasantly smoky flavor.
Hot smoking is really a type of smoke-cooking.
Again, as with cold smoking, the word "hot" is
a relative term. Usually hot smoking takes
place at temperatures that range between 150° and 250° F, the aim being to
slowly roast the meat or sausage while it absorbs a smoky flavor. Because it is
cooked slowly and evenly, the meat or sausage comes out tender and juicy.
With the advent of the covered kettle barbecue and the water smoker, hot
smoking has become quite popular with home cooks, and most sausage recipes in this book can be hot smoked that way. Hot-smoked sausages do not
require the addition of sodium nitrite or curing salts, as at the hotter temperatures the food cooks before unwanted bacteria and other organisms can multiply. Hot-smoked food has the same perishability as any roasted meat. It will
keep about 5–7 days in the refrigerator.

· smoking: art or science? ·

Smoking is not an exact science, and no recipe can be absolutely precise. The
many variables make exact instructions impossible. The temperature, density,
and thickness of the meat or sausage, the outside air temperature and humid-
ity, the type of smoke, the amount of food in the smoker, and the smoking

temperature all make a difference. Don't worry, though; you will get good results if you pay attention to temperatures by using an instant-read thermometer to monitor the food as it is smoking. To use an instant-read thermometer, insert it into the meat or sausage from time to time to determine when the proper temperature is reached—for hot smoking, 155°–160° F. For cold-smoked meats, follow the directions on page 341. If your model does not have a built-in thermometer, a second instant-read thermometer can be set into the top vent of a smoker to keep track of the smoking temperatures. Do not use a traditional meat thermometer that is left in the meat while cooking, as they are often unreliable.

Some home smoking enthusiasts keep a smoking journal to record information like temperature, type of wood, length of smoke, etc., for future reference.

· woods ·

Hardwoods are best for smoking. Softwoods such as pine, fir, cedar, and spruce are not suitable because they produce smoke so full of pitch and resin that it gives food a turpentine flavor and coats everything with a black, sticky film. If you can't positively identify the wood, don't use it for smoking. Never use backyard clippings, which may contain noxious insecticides, or poisonous plants such as oleander or poison oak. The most popular woods for smoking sausages are hickory, alder, mesquite, oak, and fruitwoods such as apple or cherry. Dried corncobs also make a good smoking fuel. Different woods impart different flavors; some work better with fish or poultry, while others are more compatible with beef or pork. Try experimenting with your own combinations of wood and sausage to see what suits your taste. For hot smoking you should use chunks of wood, soaked first so that they'll smolder and not burn. You can use wood chips, but you'll have to replenish them more often. For cold smoking, use hardwood sawdust or wood chips.

· equipment ·

· **gas or electric smokers** · These are small versions of commercial smokers, usually consisting of a metal box with a gas or electric heating element on the bottom. Wood chips or hardwood sawdust are placed in a pan over the heat. Sausages or meat are put on a rack or suspended on hooks over the fragrant smoke. If you pay careful attention to the temperature and heat source, these smokers can be used successfully for both cold and hot smoking. (See directions pages 340 and 341 and follow the manufacturer's instructions.) They can be purchased from camping, hardware or sporting goods stores, and are also available by mail order (see page 357).

· **homemade smokers** · These may be as simple as a converted 55-gallon drum, a metal garbage can, or an old refrigerator, or as elaborate as a custom-built brick smokehouse. Designs abound in do-it-yourself journals and books on country living. Like commercial smokers, they usually consist of a heat source such as a hot plate, a pan to hold the wood chips or sawdust, and racks or poles to hold the meat or sausages. Depending on the design, they tend to work well for cold smoking, but are often inadequate for hot smoking because consistent high temperatures are hard to maintain. Generally, with most homemade smokers it's a good idea to smoke the food first, and then finish it by cooking in a slow oven at 200° to 250° F. We built our own smoker out of an old refrigerator, and have used it successfully over the years to smoke sausages and other meats. We followed the basic design set forth in Jacques Pepin's *The Art of Cooking,* Volume II (Knopf, 1988).

· **water smokers and kettle barbecues** · In recent years these versatile barbecue-smokers have become quite popular, and are now widely available. Most use charcoal as the heat source, but there are also gas or electric models. Most water smokers have a domed top and look like an elongated kettle barbecue. At the bottom there is a fire pan for charcoal and aromatic wood. Above the heat source is a water pan, and one or two grills to hold the food. Water smokers are quite versatile, and can serve as a covered barbecue, steamer, open braiser, dry roaster, and hot or cold smoker. Kettle barbecues can also be used to grill, roast, or smoke-cook meats, poultry, and fish.

· step-by-step method for air-drying and cold smoking (for sausages with curing salts only) ·

1. When the sausages have been filled, hang them from a stick in a cool place (under 70° F). Have a fan going on slow speed about 5 feet away. Air-dry overnight to create a dry surface, which will help the sausage absorb the smoke better.

2. Set up your smoker *outside*. Place 6 cups of hardwood sawdust in a pan or cast-iron pot on the bottom of the smoker or on the heat source.

3. Put 1 cup of hardwood sawdust in a 6–8-inch frying pan over high heat on a portable hot plate or burner set up outside. *This must be done outside; never indoors.* After a minute the sawdust will begin to smolder and smoke.

4. When all the sawdust in the pan has turned black, with tiny glowing embers and areas of gray ash, remove the pan from the heat, and dump the burning sawdust on top of the sawdust inside the smoker.

5. Arrange the sausages in a single layer on a rack or suspend the sausages from a smoke stick.

6. Partially open the vents of the smoker and insert an instant-read thermometer into one vent. The temperature should stay between 90° and 120° F throughout the smoking process.

7. About every 3—4 hours gently stir the sawdust in the pan. Be sure that smoke is gently rising out of the vents of the smoker. Throughout the smoking period, add more sawdust as necessary, making sure to stir the old ashes over the new sawdust.

8. Consult the individual recipe to see how long to smoke the sausage. Most recipes recommend smoking overnight. You don't have to get up in the middle of the night to add more sawdust, though. Make sure the pan is full of sawdust and just give the sawdust in the smoker a good stir before you go to bed, and another as soon as you wake up. If the fire has burned out, restart as described above.

9. As long as the temperature inside the smoker does not exceed 130° F, it won't be necessary to check the internal temperature of the sausage. Cold-smoked sausage will require further cooking before eating, however.

· hot smoking or smoke-cooking ·

· in a water smoker ·

The Fire: Set up the smoker outside. Put a layer of charcoal briquettes in the bottom of the smoker. Remove the top and center rings. Open all vents. Start the fire with a fire chimney or electric starter. Don't use liquid charcoal starters, which can impart an unpleasant taste to the smoke. The coals are ready when they are coated with a light gray ash, usually after about 30 minutes. Spread the coals evenly and set up the smoker. Put the water pan in position and fill with hot water or other liquid. Carefully put the middle ring in place on top of the bottom section.

The Food: Set the cooking racks in place and arrange the sausages on them in a single layer. Leave an inch or two between sausages so the smoke can circulate.

The Wood: Open the side door of the smoker, and add three or four 2 x 3-inch chunks of wood that have been soaking in water for at least an hour. Shake off any excess water before placing them on top of the coals, using tongs to keep from burning your hands. Using mittens or hot pads, partially close all the vents while hot smoking. Insert an instant-read thermometer in the top vent. After 30 minutes it should read at least 170° F; the ideal range for hot smoking is between 170° and 250° F. The water smoker functions best when not opened frequently. After 3½—4 hours you'll probably need to add more hot water to the water pan, which should always be at least half full of liquid. For long periods of smoking you'll have to add more charcoal, and possibly more wood. Add a dozen or so charcoal briquettes every 1½ hours. If the smoker is not maintaining sufficient heat (more than 170° F), open the vents. If the fire is dying out, open the side door, and the additional oxygen will get the fire going again. If the smoker is still too cool, add more charcoal. If the temperature gets too hot (above 250° F), try closing the vents. If this doesn't work, add some cold water to the water pan, or remove some of the briquettes.

When Food Is Done: It should take roughly from 1½ to 4 hours to hot smoke sausages, depending on the diameter and type of sausage. Remember to rely on your instant-read thermometer—155° to 160° F is the desired internal temperature. Insert the thermometer 2–3 inches into the end of a sausage. Hot-smoked meat is often bright pink just below the surface, so don't rely on the appearance in determining whether sausages are done or not.

· in a kettle barbecue ·

Soak 3–4 cups of hickory chips or 4–6 chunks of hardwood in water for at least 30 minutes. Mound 10–15 charcoal briquettes to one side of a covered barbecue. Once the coals are hot, allow them to burn down to the medium-low point. This takes about 30 minutes, and they should be covered with gray ash. Spread the coals in a single layer on one side of the barbecue. Sprinkle 2 cups of hickory chips or 2–3 chunks of soaked hardwood over the coals. Place a drip pan with a little water in it on the opposite side from the charcoal. Replace the grill and spread the sausages on it over the pan. Cover the barbecue, making sure the vent in the lid is directly above the sausages. Open the top and bottom vents about ¼ inch. Smoke the sausages at 170°–250° F. You can measure the temperature by inserting an instant-read thermometer into the partially opened top vent. Add more chips and charcoal as needed. After 30 minutes, turn the sausages over and continue to smoke for another 30 or more minutes, or until an instant-read thermometer inserted through the end measures 155°–160° F. Sausages in medium hog casings will take about 1½ hours to smoke-cook; in wide beef casings they may take as long as 4 hours. You should turn the sausages occasionally as they cook.

· safety tips and helpful hints ·

W A R N I N G: SMOKING SHOULD BE DONE OUTSIDE ONLY. NEVER SMOKE ANYTHING INDOORS AS THE FUMES PRODUCED CAN BE *LETHAL*. DO NOT USE GASOLINE, ALCOHOL, OR ANY OTHER HIGHLY FLAMMABLE LIQUID TO IGNITE CHARCOAL. READ ALL MANUFACTURER'S INSTRUCTIONS PROVIDED WITH YOUR SMOKER FOR ANY SAFETY INFORMATION.

▶ Don't use commercial fire starters.

▶ Never pour water directly onto hot coals. Dust and soot could coat the food.

▶ Because of the variables in smoking, always allow extra cooking time. Use an instant-read thermometer to test for doneness.

▶ The smoker can become very hot during use, so set it up away from the house, and out of the way of general traffic.

- ► Always smoke with the cover on.
- ► Use mittens or hot pads when handling the hot smoker.
- ► Turn food with tongs to prevent piercing the sausages and losing juices.
- ► Look at the food only when absolutely necessary. Every time you lift the lid, you add 15 minutes to the cooking time.
- ► Close all vents when finished to allow the fire to burn out. Do not use water to extinguish the coals, because it can damage the finish of the smoker.

· note on nitrites: curing salts ·

Sodium nitrite, long used in curing meats and sausages, became a bad word in the 1970s because it was thought to produce cancer-causing compounds called nitrosamines. The National Science Foundation investigated and found that nitrites did not cause problems in most cured meats and sausages (bacon was the exception). Current scientific opinion holds that the use of sodium nitrite within legal limits causes no significant health problems and prevents the growth of botulinums and other noxious organisms.

On the other hand, we'd just as soon not use sodium nitrite or any other additive unless we need to. Raw sausages and hot-smoked sausages do not require the addition of curing salts, because they are kept refrigerated or frozen and are cooked at high enough temperatures to arrest bacterial activity. If you decide to air-dry or cold smoke sausages, however, curing salts must be used to prevent any possibility of botulism. During cold smoking and air-drying the temperatures are ideal for the growth of bacteria, so the protection offered by curing salts is necessary for safety.

The United States Department of Agriculture (USDA) requires 6.1 grams of sodium nitrite to cure 100 pounds of meat. Since these are very small quantities to measure accurately, home sausage makers rely on professionally mixed curing salts that contain nitrite mixed with other substances such as salt or sugar. Instead of 6.1 grams, 4 ounces by weight of one of these premixed curing salts is used for 100 pounds of meat. Purchase various brand-name curing salts such as Prague Powder, Ham Cure, or Morton Quick Cure from butcher-supply houses or by mail order (see page 357).

IN OUR RECIPES WE SPECIFY AMOUNTS FOR THE COMMERCIAL CURING SALTS, AND NOT FOR PURE SODIUM NITRITE. DO NOT USE SALTPETER (POTASSIUM NITRATE) AS A CURING SALT, SINCE IT IS NO LONGER RECOMMENDED BY THE USDA.

· brines and pickles ·

The brining of meat before smoking provides the salty flavor and pink color characteristic of many smoked foods. Brine, also called wet cure or pickle, is a solution of salt, water, sugar, and often curing salts. Meat placed in a brine is preserved by reducing the moisture content and replacing the moisture by salt. Spices and other seasonings can be added to the brine for more flavor.

Just as with smoking, there are many variables that will affect the curing time. The most important are the strength of the cure (how salty it is), the temperature during curing, and the thickness of the piece of meat to be cured. In commercial operations, brine is injected into hams and other meats in order to speed up the curing time. In the home, however, we rely on soaking the meat in the brine, which works fine for smaller cuts of meat. Curing hams or other large pieces of meat is beyond the scope of this book. Recipes are guidelines only and curing times may vary. If the meat is too salty, decrease the curing time next time. If not salty enough, increase it. Remember to do any curing that takes longer than 2 hours in the refrigerator to prevent spoilage.

· basic brine recipe ·

Good for pickled pork, bacon, and pork loins.

1½ c. kosher salt
1 c. white or brown sugar
1 gal. water
½ c. curing salts

In a 2-gallon nonreactive container dissolve the salt and sugar in the water, stirring until completely absorbed. Add the curing salts and stir until dissolved. Put in the meat and make sure it is completely submerged in the brine, weighting it down with a heavy plate if necessary. If the meat is to be cured for more than 3 days, remove the meat, stirring the brine to make sure any undissolved particles are reabsorbed, then replace the meat in the brine.

· stuffings and extras ·

Sausage is used in many of America's favorite stuffings for turkey, chicken, or pork, and often it is paired with oysters, mushrooms, or chestnuts. Most recipes use the traditional black-pepper-and-sage sausage made all over the South and Midwest, but you can open up a whole spectrum of new flavors if you experiment with other styles of sausages in your stuffings.

And while you're experimenting with different types of sausages, why not try stuffing something other than just turkey, chicken, or pork chops — whole baked fish, for example, boned shoulder or leg of lamb, game birds, and many vegetables. Stuffings can also be delicious simply baked in a casserole and served as a savory side dish.

In any of the following recipes, however, be sure to use a high-quality homemade or store-bought sausage. Too much fat can ruin a stuffing, and the extenders and additives of some of the commercial products can result in unpleasant flavors and textures. Make the sausage yourself or buy the best you can find.

· wild rice, dried mushroom, and sausage stuffing ·

1 oz. dried porcini mushrooms
½ lb. aromatic fresh sausage, removed from casings
1 tbsp. butter
½ small onion, chopped
1 rib celery, chopped

2 garlic cloves, chopped
2 shallots, chopped (optional)
½ tsp. dried thyme or 1 tsp. chopped fresh thyme
2 c. cooked wild rice
Salt and pepper to taste

Pour 1 cup boiling water over the porcini, and soak for at least 30 minutes. Strain and save the soaking water, and coarsely chop the mushrooms. Fry the sausage meat in butter for 3 minutes to render the fat. Add the onion, celery, garlic, optional shallots, and thyme, and cover and cook for 3 more minutes. Add 2 tablespoons of the porcini liquid and cook another 2 minutes, until the vegetables are soft. Place in a bowl to cool. Mix in the cooked wild rice and chopped porcini. Season with salt and pepper to taste. Stuff into birds, pork, or lamb roast, or bake in a buttered, covered casserole at 350° F for 30 minutes.
Makes enough for 4 servings

Use any full-flavored fresh pork sausage such as mild Italian (page 104), Pheasant and Wild Mushroom Sausage (page 283) or California White Wine and Herb Sausage (page 254). This is excellent as a stuffing or as a side dish with chicken and game birds or with roast pork, venison, or lamb.

· sausage, spinach, and mushroom stuffing ·

1 tbsp. unsalted butter
½ lb. California White Wine and Herb
   Sausage (see page 254), Spinach,
   Pork, and Game Crépinettes (see
   page 249), or other mild, flavorful
   fresh sausage
½ c. chopped onion
¼ c. chopped celery

¼ lb. mushrooms, sliced
1 bunch spinach, coarsely chopped
   (2 c.)
½ tsp. dried thyme
4 c. dried bread cubes
¼ c. grated Parmesan cheese
½ c. chicken stock, as needed
Salt and pepper to taste

Melt the butter in a heavy 12-inch frying pan or Dutch oven. Remove the
sausage from the casings and fry over medium heat until no longer pink, about 5
minutes. Add the onion and celery, and sauté for 10 minutes, or until soft. Add
the mushrooms, spinach, and thyme and cook for 1–2 minutes, until the spinach
is wilted. In a large bowl, mix together the bread cubes, vegetable-sausage mixture, and Parmesan cheese. The stuffing should be moist but not wet. If needed,
add some of the chicken stock. Taste for salt and pepper. Stuff into birds or bake
in a buttered, covered casserole at 350° F for 45 minutes. Makes enough stuffing
for 6 squab, 4 game hens, 2 chickens, or 8 quail. For a medium-sized turkey,
multiply ingredients by 4

· sausage and chestnut stuffing ·

**Four times this recipe will make more than can be stuffed into a medium-
sized turkey, so you should have plenty left over for hungry guests. It will
stuff 2 large roasting chickens.**

1 c. fresh chestnuts (about ¾ lb.)
1 c. chicken or turkey stock
1 tbsp. unsalted butter
½ lb. White Wine and Herb Sausage
   (see page 254) or Spinach, Pork,
   and Game Crépinettes (see
   page 249), mild Italian, or other
   fresh sausage

½ c. chopped onion
¼ c. chopped celery
½ tsp. dried oregano
¼ c. dry white wine
2 c. dried bread cubes
Salt and pepper to taste

To prepare fresh chestnuts preheat the oven to 450° F. Cut a deep cross
on one side of each chestnut. Roast for 15 minutes, or until the shells begin to
open. Remove the shells and inner skin. Bring the stock to a boil in a medium pot.
Add the chestnuts, reduce heat to low, and simmer until tender, about 20 minutes.
Drain chestnuts and reserve stock.

Chop the cooked chestnuts coarsely. Place a 12-inch frying pan over medium heat and melt the butter. Remove the sausage meat from the casings and fry for 5 minutes. Put in the onion, celery, and oregano. Cook until the onion is soft, about 10 minutes. Pour in the white wine and cook 5 minutes more. In a large bowl, mix together the chestnuts, sausage-vegetable mixture, and bread cubes. Mix well and add some of the reserved stock to moisten. The dressing should be moist but not wet. Taste for salt and pepper. Loosely stuff the birds and roast at 350° F until done, about 1½–2 hours for a 5–6-pound roasting chicken (meat thermometer should read 170° F).

To bake stuffing outside the birds, preheat the oven to 350° F. Butter a 4–6-quart casserole, fill with stuffing, dot with butter, cover, and bake for 45 minutes. Makes 5–6 cups

· chorizo, rice, and chile stuffing ·

This rich and spicy stuffing might be a bit too potent for the Thanksgiving turkey, but it will certainly enliven chicken, game hens, or other small poultry. There is enough here (8 cups) for 8 game birds, two 3-pound chickens, or a 6–8-pound capon or roaster. We used El Paso Beef, Pork, and Chile Sausage, but any lean, spicy chorizo would do as well.

2 c. finely diced onion
2 tbsp. olive oil
2 tsp. finely chopped garlic
2½ lbs. El Paso Beef, Pork, and Chile
  Sausage or other sausage, removed
  from casings
4 Anaheim chiles, fire-roasted,
  peeled, seeded, and coarsely
  chopped (see page 239)

4 c. cooked rice
Salt and pepper to taste
2 eggs, beaten lightly
1 bunch cilantro, coarsely chopped
  (1 c.) (optional)

Fry the onion in the olive oil over medium heat until soft. Add the garlic, sausage, and chiles, and cook for 10 minutes. Remove from the heat and add the rice. Taste for salt and pepper, then add the eggs and optional cilantro. Mix well. Stuff birds loosely or bake in a buttered covered casserole at 350° F for 40 minutes. Makes 8 cups

· sausage and cornbread stuffing ·

Use any premium fresh bulk sausage combined with a good-quality smoked sausage in this recipe, such as our Kentucky-Style Pork Sausage and Smoked Country Sausage. The recipe below will make enough stuffing for a 14–16-pound turkey, so scale down as necessary (or up, if you are thinking of stuffing a wild boar or great bustard). This stuffing is not only good with turkey and chicken, but also delicious with roast pork or ham.

1 lb. bulk Kentucky-Style Pork
   Sausage (see page 9) or other
   sage-flavored fresh sausage
4 tbsp. (½ stick) butter
1 lb. Smoked Country Sausage (see
   page 11) or other smoked
   sausage, cut into ¼-inch dice
4 ribs celery, chopped
3 c. chopped onion
1 medium green bell pepper,
   chopped

1 medium red bell pepper, chopped
2 bags dried cornbread stuffing such
   as Pepperidge Farm, or 8–10 c.
   homemade cornbread cut into
   coarse crumbs and dried
1 tsp. dried thyme
1 tsp. ground sage
2–3 c. turkey or chicken stock
Salt and pepper to taste

Brown the bulk sausage in the butter for 5 minutes in a heavy skillet over medium heat, breaking the meat apart with a fork as it cooks. Put in the chopped smoked sausage and fry for an additional 3 minutes. Add the celery and onion, cover the pan, and cook for about 10 minutes, until the vegetables are soft. Add the peppers and cook, covered, for 5 minutes. In a large bowl, mix the cornbread and the sausage and vegetables (including pan juices) with the thyme and sage. Add 2 cups of stock and mix well. The stuffing should be just moist enough to stick together when mounded on a spoon. You can add more stock, if necessary. Correct the seasoning and stuff bird lightly.

If you cook the dressing separately in a casserole it should be a little more moist than if you plan to stuff a turkey. Add an extra ½ cup of stock, put the dressing in a large buttered casserole, cover with foil, and bake at 350° F for 45 minutes. Makes 6–8 cups

· oyster stuffing with fresh and smoked country sausage ·

Oyster stuffing is not only an excellent complement to turkey, but it goes well with roast chicken or pork as well. The recipe below calls for baking the dressing by itself in a casserole next to the bird. If you are going to stuff a turkey or chicken, use a little less liquid, since the dressing will absorb liquid as the bird cooks. We've given amounts for a 5–6-pound roasting chicken or small turkey. Use any good-quality country-style smoked sausage and fresh bulk country sausage.

½ lb. Smoked Country Sausage (see page 11) or other smoked sausage, finely chopped
½ lb. Spicy Fresh Country Sausage (see page 7) or other sage-flavored fresh bulk sausage
2 tbsp. butter
1 c. finely chopped onion
¼ c. finely chopped celery
¼ c. finely chopped green bell pepper
½ c. finely chopped red bell pepper
½ c. finely chopped green onions or scallions

1 tsp. minced garlic
1 12-oz. jar oysters, or 18 medium shucked oysters
½ tsp. dried thyme
½ tsp. ground sage
¼ tsp. dried savory
½ tsp. cayenne
½ tsp. black pepper
3–4 c. dried bread cubes, preferably homemade from French bread
1–2 c. chicken stock blended with oyster liquid
Salt and Tabasco to taste

Preheat the oven to 350° F. Over medium-high heat, brown the sausage in the butter in a large heavy skillet for 5 minutes. Lower the heat to medium and add the onion and celery. Cover the pan and cook for about 10 minutes, or until the vegetables begin to color. Add the green and red bell peppers, the green onions, and the garlic, and cook for 5 minutes more.

Meanwhile drain the oysters, saving the liquid. If they are large, coarsely chop them into ¾-inch pieces; otherwise leave them whole. Add the oysters to the vegetable and sausage mixture and cook for another 2 minutes. Remove the pan from the heat and mix in the herbs, spices, and bread cubes. Add the reserved oyster liquid and enough chicken stock to make the stuffing moist but not soggy. Add salt and Tabasco to taste. Place the dressing in a buttered casserole and smooth the surface lightly with a spatula. Bake, uncovered, for 35–40 minutes, until the stuffing is hot. Makes 6–8 cups

For hard-core stuffing addicts: Try stuffing a turkey with this oyster stuffing in the neck cavity and the preceding cornbread dressing in the body of the bird.

· Italian sausage and fresh fennel stuffing ·

Fresh fennel or finocchio is a delicious and unusual vegetable that is available during the winter months. It adds a subtle anise flavor and a delightful crunchy texture to this flavorful dressing. Use it to stuff a turkey, or scale the recipe down for chicken, veal or pork roasts, or extra-thick pork chops.

4 tbsp. (½ stick) butter
1½ lbs. mild or spicy Italian sausage,
  removed from casings
1 large bulb fresh fennel, coarsely
  chopped
2 ribs celery, coarsely chopped
1 medium onion, coarsely chopped

1 tbsp. minced garlic
1 tsp. ground sage
2 bags packaged stuffing, or 8–10 c.
  dried bread cubes
2–3 c. turkey or chicken stock
Salt and pepper to taste

Melt the butter in a 12-inch skillet over medium heat. Add the sausage and fry for about 5 minutes, breaking the meat up into small pieces. Add the fennel, celery, onion, garlic, and sage to the sausage and cook for about 10–12 minutes, or until the vegetables are soft. Put the sausage and vegetable mixture in a large bowl along with the stuffing mix or bread cubes. Add 2 cups of the stock and mix well. The stuffing should be moist enough to hold together when mounded on a spoon. Add more stock if necessary. Taste for salt and pepper. When you stuff the bird, do not pack too tightly. You can also cook this stuffing outside the bird in a buttered covered casserole at 350° F for 45 minutes. Dot the surface of the stuffing with butter and add a little more stock to make up for the lack of extra juices the stuffing would absorb if inside the bird. Makes enough for a 14–16-pound turkey

· wilted cabbage and roasted walnut salad ·

The earthy, faintly bitter flavors of cabbage underline the spice and liveliness of sausage beautifully, which is why the two are so often paired in traditional dishes. The roasted walnuts in this recipe lend new interest to the combination, especially when you serve this satisfying salad with a game sausage baked with Honey-Orange Glaze (see page 322). It is also delicious with grilled sausages, fresh or smoked, mild or spicy.

½ c. shelled walnuts
4 tbsp. (½ stick) butter
½ head cabbage, cored and shredded
¼ tsp. salt

½ tsp. pepper
1 tbsp. soy sauce
3 tbsp. cider vinegar

Spread the walnuts on a cookie sheet and roast in a 350° F oven for 10 minutes, until the nuts are lightly browned and have a rich, nutty aroma. Set the walnuts aside while you finish the salad.

In a large, high-sided frying pan, melt the butter over medium heat. Put in the cabbage, salt, and pepper. Toss the cabbage as it cooks so it is well coated with the butter. Cover the frying pan and cook for 7 minutes, stirring occasionally, until the cabbage is completely wilted but still crisp. Pour in the soy and vinegar, and cook for 2 minutes, uncovered. Arrange the salad on a plate and put grilled or baked sausage on top. Garnish with roasted walnuts. Makes 4 servings

For an elegant presentation of this hearty dish, cut cooked sausage in four large diagonal slices, arrange them over the salad, and garnish with roasted walnuts.

· oven-roasted garlic-rosemary potatoes ·

Simple to prepare and filled with hearty flavors, these crisp-skinned, golden potatoes are always a hit, and go well with grilled, baked, or fried sausages of every kind imaginable. Rosemary's piny aroma ties in beautifully with the garlic, but you could also use other herbs such as oregano, marjoram, thyme, or savory in the same amounts as the rosemary.

2 lbs. unpeeled red or white boiling
   potatoes, cut into wedges or
   quartered
½ c. olive oil
1 tbsp. chopped fresh rosemary or
   2 tsp. dried

½ tsp. salt
1 tsp. pepper
2 heads garlic, separated into
   individual cloves but not peeled

Preheat the oven to 400° F. Put the potatoes, olive oil, rosemary, salt, and pepper in a bowl and toss until the potatoes are completely coated. Spread the potatoes in a baking pan and spread them out so that they are not touching. Dump any leftover oil and herbs over the potatoes. Roast for 15 minutes, then turn the potatoes over with a spatula, and scatter the whole unpeeled garlic cloves all around the pan. Continue baking for 20–30 minutes, until the potatoes are golden brown. You can serve them immediately, or make the potatoes up an hour or two ahead and rewarm them at 350° F for 10 minutes when you are ready to eat. At my house people fight over the garlic, savoring the nutty cloves.
Makes 4–5 servings

Sausages are so adaptable and full of flavor that often all you need is a bit of grilled sausage, some greens or pasta, and a piquant sauce to make a simple, delicious meal. Many of the salad dressings and sauces included here are referred to throughout the book, and they can be used wherever appropriate on salads, seafood, grilled sausages, or pasta.

Lee Coleman's rémoulade dressing ·

Lee is a talented chef and teacher in the San Francisco Bay Area.

2 green onions or scallions, coarsely chopped
½ c. coarsely chopped fresh parsley
2 ribs celery, coarsely chopped
1 clove garlic, chopped
¼ c. prepared horseradish
2 tbsp. Creole or other coarse-grain mustard
3 tsp. Worcestershire sauce

3 tbsp. tomato paste
1 tbsp. white vinegar
2 tbsp. lemon juice
2 tsp. grated lemon zest
2 tsp. Tabasco
1 tbsp. paprika
2 egg yolks
1½–2 c. light olive oil
Salt and pepper to taste

Put the vegetables in a food processor and process until they are finely chopped. Shut off the machine and add the remaining ingredients except the oil, salt, and pepper. Process for 15 seconds. Then in a slow, steady stream pour in the olive oil with the processor on. Add enough oil to achieve a loose mayonnaise. Correct for salt and pepper. Refrigerated, the dressing will keep for about 5 days. Makes 2–3 cups

mustard vinaigrette ·

1 tbsp. Dijon mustard
2 tbsp. red wine vinegar
½ tsp. minced garlic

Pinch salt and pepper
6 tbsp. olive oil

In a food processor or bowl, blend together the mustard, vinegar, garlic, salt, and pepper. Gradually add oil to produce a creamy dressing. Makes ½ cup

· tangy vinaigrette dressing ·

1 tbsp. Dijon mustard
¼ c. red wine vinegar
2 cloves garlic, minced
3 tbsp. fresh herbs, such as chives,
    oregano, or basil (optional)

¼ tsp. Tabasco
½ tsp. Worcestershire sauce
¼ tsp. salt
¾ c. olive oil

    In a food processor or bowl, blend together all the ingredients except the oil. Gradually process or whisk in the oil to produce a creamy dressing. Makes 1½ cups

· hot tomato and basil sauce ·

Both this simple tomato sauce and the one that follows are wonderful accompaniments to the Zucchini and Rice "Sausage," as well as the Spicy Lamb, Pine Nut, and Sun-dried Tomato Sausage, Spinach, Pork, and Game Crépinettes, and the Buffalo Sausage (see pages 299, 305, 319, and 294) or Italian sausage. The sauce is best made with very ripe Italian-style tomatoes and fresh basil and should be eaten fresh, although it can be rewarmed. It will keep for 2 or 3 days in the refrigerator.

¼ c. finely chopped onion
2 tbsp. fruity olive oil
2 tsp. minced garlic
6 fresh ripe Italian plum tomatoes or
    6 canned Italian-style tomatoes,
    peeled, seeded, and chopped

2 tbsp. chopped fresh parsley
¼ c. chopped fresh basil
Salt and pepper to taste

    In a small nonreactive saucepan, sauté the onion for 5 minutes in the olive oil over medium heat. Add the garlic and cook an additional minute. Add the tomatoes and cook 5 minutes more. Put in the parsley and basil and cook 1 minute. Season with salt and pepper, and serve. Makes about 1½ cups, enough for 4–6 servings

·tomato and basil vinaigrette·

Use the ripest, freshest tomatoes you can find to make this simple but flavorful sauce. Use immediately — the sauce loses its fine, fresh flavor when kept even overnight in the refrigerator.

¾ c. very ripe fresh tomatoes, finely chopped
3 tbsp. balsamic or raspberry vinegar
⅓ c. virgin olive oil

¼ c. chopped fresh basil
2 anchovy fillets, finely chopped
Salt and pepper to taste

Mix together all the ingredients in a bowl, or briefly pulse in a food processor. Season with salt and pepper and serve immediately.
Makes 1½ cups, enough for 4–6 servings

·yogurt and cilantro sauce·

This sauce can be served either cold or warm with the Spicy Lamb, Pine Nut, and Sun-dried Tomato Sausages. It is also good with our Wild Boar, Venison, and Buffalo Sausages, and makes a good accompaniment to the fresh sausages in the Southwest chapter.

¼ c. finely chopped leeks
4 tbsp. (½ stick) butter *or* 3 tbsp. olive oil
1 c. chopped fresh cilantro (1 bunch)

2 tbsp. chopped fresh mint
1 c. yogurt
Salt and pepper to taste
Lemon juice (optional)

Cook the chopped leek in the butter or oil for 5 minutes over medium heat. Add the cilantro and mint, and cook 1 minute more. Remove the pan from the heat and whisk in the yogurt. Season with salt and pepper, and add lemon juice if desired. Serve warm at once or refrigerate and serve cold. The sauce will keep 2 days refrigerated. Makes 1½ cups, enough for 4–6 servings

· Cumberland sauce for game sausages ·

This recipe was adapted from Harriet Jarvis Barnett's *Game and Fish Cook-book*.

Zest from 2 oranges, cut into thin
  strips
Zest from 2 lemons, cut into thin
  strips
Juice from same 2 oranges
Juice from same 2 lemons
10-oz. jar red currant jelly

1 c. port
2 tbsp. Worcestershire sauce
2 tsp. finely chopped fresh ginger
½ tsp. ground dried ginger
¼ tsp. cinnamon
1 sprig fresh thyme or ½ tsp. dried
1 tsp. dry mustard

Parboil the rinds in water 2–3 minutes. Drain and set aside. Mix all the remaining ingredients together in a small saucepan. Bring to a boil and continue to cook until the liquid is syrupy. Add the rinds and cook 1–2 minutes more. Serve hot with grilled Wild Boar or Duck Sausage or any game. The sauce can be reheated. Refrigerated in a sealed jar, it keeps 3 weeks. Makes 2–3 cups

· onion and mustard confit ·

This sauce is delicious with mild sausages such as bockwurst, Rabbit Boudin, or Sweetbread and Chicken Sausage.

1 lb. sweet onions, halved and very
  thinly sliced
4 tbsp. (½ stick) butter
¼ c. Creole or other spicy coarse-
  grain mustard

1 c. heavy cream
Salt and pepper to taste

In a heavy pot, cook the onions, covered, slowly in the butter until quite soft and almost disintegrating, 35–40 minutes. Add the mustard and cream, and simmer 10 minutes more. If the sauce becomes too thick, add more cream. Season with salt and pepper. The sauce keeps well and can be gently rewarmed before serving. Makes 1½ cups, enough for 4–6 servings

mail order sources ·

· sausages, game, smoked meats ·

· Aidells Sausage Company ·
1575 Minnesota Street
San Francisco, CA 94107
(415) 285-6660

*Andouille, tasso, duck, Italian, New
Mexican, chicken, and chorizo
sausages, and many others*

· Balducci's ·
424 Avenue of the Americas
New York, NY 10011
(212) 673-2600

Italian and French sausages

· Corralitos Sausage Co. ·
569 Corralitos Road
Watsonville, CA 95076
(408) 722-2633

*Mexican, Portuguese, Polish, and
German sausages*

· Cravings by Mail ·
P.O. Box 4430
Portland, OR 97208
(800) 272-8466

Assorted sausages, smoked meats

· Czimer Foods, Inc. ·
13136 West 159th Street
Lockport, IL 60441
(708) 301-7152

Game, smoked products

· Harrington's ·
Main Street
Richmond, VT 05477
(802) 434-4444

Smoked meats, summer sausages

· Heid Meat Service ·
427 Edgewood Drive
Kaukauna, WI 54130
(414) 788-4888

German sausages

· Jugtown Mountain Smokehouse ·
77 Park Avenue
Flemington, NJ 08822
(201) 782-2421

*Portuguese and venison sausages,
smoked poultry, smoked ham and
bacon*

· New Braunfels Smokehouse ·
P.O. Box 311159
New Braunfels, TX 78131
(512) 625-7316

*German and Texas-style smoked
sausages, smoked turkey, bratwurst,
jerky*

· North Country Smokehouse ·
P.O. Box 1415
Claremont, NH 03743
(603) 542-8323

*Kielbasa, summer sausages, smoked
meat and poultry*

· Polarica ·
P.O. Box 880204
San Francisco, CA 94188-0204
(800) 426-3872

Game, birds, some sausage

· E. M. Todd Company ·
P.O. Box 5167
Richmond, VA 23220
(800) 368-5026

*Virginia ham, country-style smoked
sausages*

· Fred Usinger, Inc. ·
1030 N. Old World Third Street
Milwaukee, WI 53203
(800) 558-9998

*German, brats, and Eastern
European sausages*

· Weaver's ·
P.O. Box 525
Lebanon, PA 17042
(717) 274-6100

Lebanon bologna

· Zingerman's ·
422 Detroit Street
Ann Arbor, MI 48104
(313) 663-3354

*Andouille, duck, and chicken
sausages, tasso*

· sausage casings, curing salts, equipme

· Aidells Sausage Company ·
1575 Minnesota Street
San Francisco, CA 94107
(415) 285-6660

· Carlson Butcher Supply ·
50 Mendell Street, #12
San Francisco, CA 94124
(415) 648-2601

· The Sausage Maker ·
177 Military Road
Buffalo, NY 14207
(716) 876-5521

· smoking equipment ·

· Cook'n Cajun Water Smokers ·
P.O. Box 3726
Shreveport, LA 71133
(318) 925-6933

· MECO Water Smokers ·
P.O. Box 1000
1500 Industrial Road
Greeneville, TN 37744
(800) 251-7558

· Weber-Stephen Products Company ·
200 East Daniels Road
Palatine, IL 60067
(312) 934-5700

· Williams-Sonoma ·
P.O. Box 7456
San Francisco, CA 94120-7456
(415) 421-4242

· Asian and Middle Eastern ingredients ·

· Ginn Wall Co. ·
1016 Grant Ave.
San Francisco, CA 94133
(415) 982-6307

· Haig's ·
642 Clement Street
San Francisco, CA 94118
(415) 752-6283

· Cajun seafood ·

· Bon Creole Seafood ·
Route 3, Box 518-D
New Iberia, LA 70560
(318) 229-8397

Crawfish, crawfish fat, crabs

· Catfish Wholesale ·
P.O. Box 759
Abbeville, LA 70510
(318) 643-6700

Catfish, drum, flounder, gar, gasper goo, buffalo fish, crawfish tails, crabmeat, alligator meat

· C.J.'s Seafood ·
Route 1, Box 1416
Breaux Bridge, LA 70517
(318) 845-4413

Crawfish

· Eastern European specialty items ·

· Paprikas Weiss ·
1546 Second Avenue
New York, NY 10028
(212) 288-6117

· Italian ingredients ·

· Balducci's ·
424 Avenue of the Americas
New York, NY 10011
(212) 673-2600

Pasta, beans, oils, herbs, vinegars, etc.

· G. B. Ratto & Co. ·
International Grocers
821 Washington
Oakland, CA 94607
(800) 228-3515 (within Calif.)
(800) 325-3483 (outside Calif.)

Pastas, dried beans, olive oils, balsamic vinegars, herbs, etc.

· Mexican ingredients ·

· El Nopalito #1 ·
560 Santa Fe Drive
Encinitas, CA 92024
(619) 436-5775

· specialty produce ·

· Frieda's Finest Produce Specialties ·
P.O. Box 58488
Los Angeles, CA 90058
(213) 627-2981

index ·

· photographic acknowledgments ·

Photographs reproduced in this book were provided with the cooperation and kind permission of the following:

p. 13, country picnic: Courtesy of the Atlanta Historical Society

p. 51, "Hot Boudin": © 1989 Tom Jimison

p. 102, Feast of San Gennaro: UPI/Bettmann Newsphotos

p. 147, "Pork Sausage" sign: The Historic New Orleans Collection, 533 Royal Street, New Orleans

p. 163, Polish-American wedding: Polish-American Folkdance Company, Brooklyn, New York

p. 212, Rancho de Las Golondrinas Living Museum: Mark Nohl, New Mexico Economic Development and Tourism Department

p. 251, Chinese-American grocery store: UPI/Bettmann Newsphotos

Bruce Aidells was born and raised in California. He graduated from the University of California at Berkeley and holds a Ph.D. from the University of California at Santa Cruz. He is the chef and owner of the nationally known Aidells Sausage Company, and he teaches cooking. A founder of and formerly the chef at Poulet Restaurant and Charcuterie in Berkeley, he has also served as a restaurant consultant in the Bay Area. His articles have appeared in *Food & Wine* and *Bon Appétit*.

Denis Kelly was born in Brooklyn, New York, graduated from St. Mary's College in Moraga, California, and did graduate work at the Sorbonne in Paris and at Indiana University. Now living in Oakland, he teaches wine classes at the University of California Extension and throughout the Bay Area. He has written many articles on food and wine for such publications as *Wines & Spirits* and the Oakland *Tribune*.

· **a note on the type** ·

The text of this book was set in Century Old Style, a type designed in 1894 by Linn Boyd Benton (1844–1932). Benton cut Century in response to a request by Theodore L. DeVinne for an attractive, easy-to-read type face to fit the narrow columns of his *Century Magazine*. Early in the 1900s Benton's son, Morris Fuller Benton, updated and improved Century in several versions for his father's American Type Founders Company. Century remains the only American type face cut before 1910 that is still widely in use today.

Composed by Dix Type Inc., Syracuse, New York
Printed and bound by Kingsport Press, Kingsport, Tennessee
Designed by Stephanie Tevonian